HONOUR KILLINGS IN INDIA
A CRIME AGAINST HUMANITY

HONOUR KILLINGS IN INDIA

A CRIME AGAINST HUMANITY

MANPREET KAUR
MANDEEP KAUR

ANAMIKA PUBLISHERS & DISTRIBUTORS (P) LTD.
4697/3, 21A, Ansari Road, Daryaganj, New Delhi 110 002
Phones: 011-2328 1655, 011-2327 0239
E-mail: anamikapublishers@yahoo.co.in

First Published 2015

ISBN 978-81-7975-578-5

PRINTED IN INDIA

Published by Anamika Publishers & Distributors (P) Ltd., 4697/3, 21A, Ansari Road, Daryaganj, New Delhi 110 002. Typeset by VGA, Delhi 110034 and Printed at Vikas Computer & Printers, Tronica City, Ghaziabad.

Contents

Preface

Crimes in the name of 'honour' has become a serious problem now a days. The number of cases of honour killings, in India and the world, has increased manifold since 2001. Recently, the National Commission for Women (NCW) in India has reported the registration of 333 complaints on honour crime in financial year of 2013 apart from *suo motu* cognizance in 11 cases of honour killings.

All the right thinking persons, Governmental and Non-governmental organizations, are worried about the continuing barbarity of honour crimes. The 242nd report of the Law Commission of India has also stressed upon the need for a stand alone legislation to stop caste councils, known as *Khap Panchayats* in north India and *Katta Panchayats* in Tamil Nadu, from issuing diktats to young persons for marrying partners belonging to the same *gotra* or a different caste/religion.

In rural India the law and the law enforcers are no protection against the writ and the might of village elders and community heads who owe their position to feudal custom and traditional authority and believe that they are above the law of the land. They not only constitute kangaroo courts but also order social boycott or expulsion from village and use coercion and force to enforce their diktats. Moreover, political parties, *khaps* and politically influential castes and community groups are interdependent. Political parties need these for mobilization of electoral and public support. They got fear going against them. Astonishingly, some prominent politicians of Haryana are defending the *Khap* Panchayats saying that these are not caste panchayats and are in fact group of villages that work like NGOs. They even deny that *Khaps* are based on dominant castes and have ever passed a diktat to kill any couple.

The Supreme Court of India has initiated a fair process of examining the alleged role of these *Khaps* and police officials by inviting them to present their views on their alleged role in incidents of honour killings. The representatives of these *khaps* had, however, denied having any direct or indirect role in honour crimes. They had expressed their anguish over same *gotra* marriages and also demanded amendment in the Hindu Marriage Act.

Some of the *Khaps* are trying to change with time. They have realized that it has become difficult to arrange marriages outside the *gotra*. The *Chahal Khap* in Kaithal district of Haryana recently adopted a resolution and decided to ease some *gotra* restrictions for marriages. It announced that it would not object to a marriage in which the grandmothers of the couple have the same *gotra*. However, the condition that the couple's *gotra* and their mothers' *gotra* should not match will continue to exist.

This book, "Honour Killings in India : A Crime Against Humanity" mainly deals with honour crimes, their definitions, origin and history in the world in general and in India in particular. It studies this problem more deeply and explores different aspects of such crimes with special reference to social system and legal remedies available. Role of *Khap/Katta panchayats* and efforts of Indian Judiciary to minimize such crimes are discussed in details. The Law Commission of India in its 242nd report and the model bill proposed by it is appended for easy reference. Some suggestions are also given to stamp out this menace along with conclusion in the last.

Though sincere efforts have been made by us to cover all aspects of 'honour killings' but we also have certain limitations. Despite of that we hope the book will help the law students, lawyers, social workers as well as laymen in understanding the problem.

Acknowledgements

We gratefully acknowledge our deep sense of gratitude to Dr. Vimal Joshi, Head of Department of Law, B.P.S. Mahila Vishwavidyalya, Khanpur Kalan, Sonepat, Haryana and his noble crew, particularly, Dr. Ashok Kumar, Astt. Professor, for the help, moral support and inspiration extended by them during the process of working on the topic.

We also appreciate S. Man Singh Deora, former Librarian of the Indian Council of World Affairs, New Delhi for helping in locating various important UN Documents and other material available in ICWA Library. The views of prominent authors incorporated in the book are also acknowledged with thanks.

We cannot skip our thanks to S. Gurminder Singh, who supported both of us and helped us in updating the information on the subject and Sukhvinder Singh Deora, Asst. Professor, N.C. Institute of Computer Science, Israna, Panipat for editing the manuscript and Mr. Rakesh Sharma, a scholar of repute for giving final touch. Finally, we express our thanks to Shri Pankaj Sharma, Anamika Publishers & Distributors (P) Ltd. for taking personal interest in bringing out this book in a very short time.

Manpreet Kaur
Mandeep Kaur

1. Introduction

In India, crimes against women are increasing drastically. According to National Crime Records Bureau 2011, annual growth rate of crimes against women between 2001 and 2011 was 4.7%. In the year 2011 alone 2,28,650 crimes were reported against women.

The honour killings, which basically deal with crimes against women, has become burning topic now a days as the cases of honour killings has increased manifold since 2001. Killings in the name of honour had become a problem not only for India but also for the world. Its number is rising day by day. If we study the incidents of honour killings, we will find that more than 20,000 women become victim of honour killings in the world each year.[1] So far as India is concerned honour killings are rising in northern region, mainly in states like Punjab, Rajasthan, Haryana and Uttar Pradesh. Some cases of honour crimes have also been reported in Tamil Nadu. In the year 2010, roughly 900 cases of honour killings were noticed in the northern Indian states alone while 100-300 additional honour killings took place in the rest of the country. Punjab had a large number of honour killings. According to Punjab Police, 34 honour killings were reported in the state between 2008 and 2010: 10 in 2008, 20 in 2009, and 4 in 2010.[2] Recent report tabled in the State Assembly of Haryana on 26 March 2013 disclosed that the number of runaway couples, who sought police security during the past two years has increased 400 per cent. In 2010 the number of such couples were 366 only that went up to 1345 in 2012.[3]

Other major countries facing this problem are Egypt, Jordan, Lebanon, Morocco, Pakistan, the Syrian Arab Republic, Turkey, Yemen, and Mediterranean and Persian Gulf countries. Even Western countries like France, Germany and United Kingdom are not remained untouched where migrant communities are residing.[4] Honour killings in Bangladesh, Brazil, Ecuador, Israel, Italy, Sweden, Turkey, and Uganda are also common.[5] USA claims that honour killings have been brought by the migrants of Asian countries.[6] Although there are not many cases of honour killings within the United States, the overwhelming majority of honour killings are perpetrated by Muslims against Muslims '(90 per cent of honour killings known to have taken place in Europe and the United States from 1998 to 2008)'.[7] Even in Latin America honour killings are sometimes referred to as dowry deaths and bride burnings.

In Peru 70 per cent of the murders of women per year are committed by husband, boyfriend or lover, and most often jealousy or suspicions of infidelity are cited as the reasons for the murders.[8] If we go in details we will find that about 40 cases of honour killings were reported in Germany by *Papatya*, a Turkish women's organization since 1996. Mr. Nazir Afzal, Director of Britain's Crown Prosecution Service West London, disclosed that the United Kingdom has seen "at least a dozen honour killings" between 2004 and 2005. Most of the attacks were made in cities that had high immigrant populations'.[9]

In the Middle East the cases of honour killings are reported in Turkey, Iraq, Saudi Arabia, Palestine etc. In Istanbul, the largest Turkish city, averagely one honour killing every week was reported by Turkish Prime Ministry's Human Rights Directorate Report of 2008. It has reported over 1,000 honour killings during the previous five years. In Lebanon 2 or 3 honour killings are reported per month on an average.[10] This enforced Lebanese Parliament on 4 August 2011 to abolish Article 562 relating to honour killings from its penal, which for years had worked as an excuse for honour killings. Executive Director of the UNICEF while speaking about crimes against women on 7 March 2000 disclosed that two-thirds of all killings in the Palestinian territories were honour killings. It was reported that 29 women were killed between 2007 and 2010, whereas 13 women were killed in 2011 and 12 in the first seven months of 2012.[11]

In Jordan, which is considered as one of the most liberal countries in the Middle East, according to UNICEF, averagely 23 honour killings per year are committed. In Basra alone, the city of Iraq, as many as 47 women were killed in 2006 in the name of honour.[12] The honour killings had also spread in Canada beside United States of America. A study conducted by Dr. Amin Muhammad and Dr. Sujay Patel of Memorial University Canadian 2007 reported that the practice of honour killings was brought to Canada by Asian migrants.

Honour killings have a high level of support in Pakistan's rural society.[13] From 1999 to 2004, more than 4,000 women have died as victims of honour killings in Pakistan.[14] In 2002 alone over 382 honour killings were noticed in Pakistan and out of these 245 women and 137 men were from the Sind province alone. In 2005 the average annual number of honour killings for the whole nation was stated to be more than 10,000 per year.[15]

If we trace the history of its origin we will find that honour killing is not a new phenomenon. It has its roots in the pre-history of man. The evolution of civilization brought not only the positive changes in the way of life of man but also certain limitations on the relationship of persons in general and male-female in particular. The origin and development of family system bound people related by blood or marriage or a strong common bond, in such a way that family became an important unit of society with a universal and basic role. Families that have common bonds and interests later on formed different groups and clans to protect the life, property and honour of their fellow members. With the passage of time these clans/groups developed certain rituals or beliefs of their own and start practising them in their day to day life. The rituals, beliefs, norms, routines and rules bound them together in such a way that a wrath of family or clan became inevitable if any member of the family or clan violated any of these rules. The regular practice of these beliefs or norms later on became traditions and customs. Traditions and customs persist and evolve for thousands of years.

Honour killings and punishments have been documented over centuries among a wide variety of ethnic and religious groups throughout the world. For example, the Code of Hammurabi of Babylon which was issued in 1790 BC penalized adulterous couples by drowning. The 1075 BC Assyrian law of the civilization of Mesopotamia stated that the father of a defiled virgin shall punish his daughter however he saw it fit.

In the *Bible*, the Book of Genesis, Judah demanded for the burning of his daughter-in-law Tamar, whom he was told to be pregnant via harlotry; this view is then supported in Book of Leviticus. Matthew Goldstein also noted that honour killings were encouraged in ancient Rome, where male family members who did not take actions against the female adulterers in their family were "actively persecuted".

Dr. Amin A. Muhammad traces origin of honour killings dates back to pre-Islamic era when Arab settlers occupied Baluchistan, a region adjacent to *Sindh*. Settlers had strong patriarchal traditions with such practices as the live burial of unwanted newborn daughters.

In medieval India the practice of killing girls—female infanticide—was prevailing in *Rajput* kings who believed that the girls would bring dishonour to their family. The fear of dishonour was the main reason of *Sati* system and the system of *Johar*. Even the inter-religion marriages were not acceptable. Akbar's marriage with Jodhabai, the daughter of Raja Man Singh, was decried by many *Rajput* kings. The love stories of *Heer-Ranjha, Sohni-Mahiwal, Mirja-Sahiba, Sassi-Punnu* of old Punjab were tragically ended. In short, the practice of killing in the name of honour continued. The honour crimes were sometimes incorrectly classified as death due to "fate and destiny." Such crimes often went unreported or were disguised and classified as accidents or suicides.[16]

'Honour killing' is not defined in any dictionary of law. In fact the National Commission for Women has recommended removal of the word 'honour' from honour killings while describing crimes when a person is killed to save a family's 'honour'.[17] It is the homicide of a member of a family or social group by other members, due to the belief of the perpetrators that the victim has brought dishonour upon the family or community. Accused of these crimes think that they are morally right and the act of killings have brought honour back to their families.

Honour killings have wider scope. There is no special law against 'honour killings' in most of the countries, including India. In India, 'Honour killings' are being treated as culpable homicide amount to murder prescribed under Section 300 to 302. Section 120B and Section 34 of the IPC deals with criminal conspiracy and act committed by more than one person. Therefore "honour killing" is considered as a murder committed against a woman/man for actual or perceived "immoral" behaviour that is deemed to have breached the 'honour code' of a household or community. Dishonour brought to the family may be because of adultery, rape, bearing a child without marriage, love affairs or any other immoral act.

There is a difference of opinion on declaring honour killing cases as "rarest of the rare". According to Justice V.S. Sirpurkar and Justice Deepak Verma of the Supreme Court of India such killings do not fall in the category of rarest of the rare as the family of the girl has to face lot of taunts and humiliation in the society for the acts of the girl. However, the Supreme Court in its recent judgement in Bhagwan Das vs. State (NCT of Delhi) [(2011) 6 SCC 396][18] laid down the proposition that the so-called honour killing comes within the category of 'rarest of the rare' cases deserving death punishment.

The root cause of honour killings in India is caste system. According to a survey 75 per cent honour killings in Hindu families are caste-based.[19] The caste system during *Vedic* period was based on *varna* and not on birth. In the ancient period, Hindu society was divided into religiously mandated castes by Hindu law giver Manu. Manu gave women right to select her husband in certain conditions. The rules of marriage within the caste were established during the post Aryan period. Later on castes became hereditary and effectively permanent. At the higher rung of ladder were the *Brahmanas*. The lowest rung of the ladder were *Dalits* (the oppressed). *Dalits* were also called as untouchables. Under this ridden caste system that still continues, Hindu religious customs and traditions strictly forbid marrying or having sexual relations with a member of a different caste. Romantic involvement with someone from the same sub-caste (*gotra*) was also forbidden.[20] The vast majority of Hindu honour killings target the young suspected of violating any one of these two commandments. Other reasons of honour killings are refusing to enter into an arranged marriage or marriage against family's approval, being the victim of a sexual assault, seeking a divorce—even from an abusive husband—or (allegedly) committing adultery, pre-marital sex or having a child out of wedlock etc. The mere perception that a woman has behaved in a way that "dishonours" her family is sufficient to trigger an attack on her life.[21]

In northern part of India, particularly Haryana, Rajasthan, Uttar Pradesh and Punjab, where honour killings are common, *Khap Panchayats* are dominating the rural life. They define their own laws based on age old customs and traditions. There are incidents when these *Panchayats* declared *sagotra* marriages null and void. In some other cases it is alleged that they have abetted death as a punishment for socially unapproved marriages. It is said that they use these methods to restore faith in the orthodox approaches of the rural people. The Law Commission of India in its 242nd report criticized the high-handed and unwarranted interference by the caste assemblies or *panchayats* with *sagotra*, inter-caste or inter-religious marriages, which are otherwise lawful and will prevent the acts endangering the liberty of the couple married or intending to marry. The Law Commission also proposed a bill that recommends that members gathering for such purpose, i.e., for condemning the marriage with a view to take necessary consequential action, are to be treated as members of unlawful assembly for which a mandatory minimum punishment was prescribed.

A bench of Justice Aftab Alam and Ranjana Prakash Desai of Supreme Court, while hearing a Public Interest Litigation seeking protection of young couples who married inter-caste or within the same *gotra* from the wrath of *Khaps*, expressed its concern about increasing role of *Khap panchayats* in honour killings and described their *diktats* as against fundamental rights. The Union Government also fervently pleaded with the apex court to put in place a mechanism to monitor the crime against women by *Khap panchayats*, the caste based councils, as the police had not been able to protect the women facing ordeal at their hands. The Supreme Court has invited the *Khap panchayats* to hear their views before issuing any order to stop them from allegedly harassing and abeting killing couples, particularly women in the name of family honour for entering into same village, inter-caste or *inter-gotra* marriages.[22] On the other hand the *Khap panchayats* are insisting upon the amendment in the Hindu Marriage Act 1955 that no marriage should be made legal in blood relations and brotherhood set up in *gotras*.[23] A 17 member committee formed by the *Khaps* is to appear before the Supreme Court to demand *Lok Adalat* status to the *Khaps* beside amendment in the Hindu Marriage Act.[24]

To get rid of honour killings there is a need to liberate and emancipate women from the shackles of ancient law, traditions and customs for better promotion and readjustment of their rights on the lines of equality, dignity and non-exploitation. The United Nations and other international organizations like European Union, Amnesty International and Human Rights Watch and in India National Commission for Women and other NGOs are working to tame this problem. *The Shakti Vahini*, a NGO headed by advocate Ravi Kant had filed a PIL, in June 2010 in the apex court demanding guidelines to rein in *Khaps* for their alleged involvement in honour crimes. The Law Commission of India, on the recommendations of Commission headed by Justice (Retired) P.V. Reddi, proposed a legislation 'The Prohibition of Interference with the Freedom of Matrimonial Alliances Bill' to combat the honour crimes in 2012. The proposed Bill is yet to be considered by the Parliament.

The book is divided into ten chapters. The **introductory Chapter** of this book deals with description of honour killings, historical development of families, formation of groups, clans and development of caste system to protect the life, property and honour of their fellow members. It highlights the rigidity of caste system and prohibition of inter-caste, inter-religion and same *gotra* marriages. The chapter also draws attention to honour killings in the northern part of India particularly in Uttar Pradesh, Rajasthan, Panjab and Haryana and Indian government's efforts to curb this problem by referring this matter to the Law Commission of India the recommendations of which were published in its report of 2012.

The first part of the **Second Chapter,** elaborates definitions of honour killing as defined in *Oxford Dictionaries, Human Right Watch* and *Free Dictionary*. Since all acts of killings are not honour killings so to clarifying it more precisely comparison has been made with other types of killings like culpable homicide, suicide, dowry death, *Sati* and death due to domestic violence etc. and gender disparity under the heading **Scope of Honour Killings** in the second part of the Chapter. The third part of the chapter highlights in details the **Origin of Honour Killings** with special references to marriage rules and the concept of purity of blood. The present World **scenario** of honour killings is also described in details in this part.

In the **Third Chapter** attempt is made to trace the reasons of honour killings. Status of women, unequal power relations between men and women, subordinate position of women compared with men and they are being viewed as property is discussed. Other important reasons of honour killings discussed are marriage without family's acceptance, refusal of girls to marry persons selected by their parents, rigidity of caste system, difference in religion between the husband and wife, broken marital relationship, love affairs, sex before marriage, adultery, cultural gaps and biased role of police and lack of governance.

Though majority of honour killing cases are believed go unreported, Position of honour killings in India particularly in regions dominated by *Khap panchayats*, role of media and Non-Governmental Organizations and the steps taken by the Central government to eradicate honour killings are discussed in the first part of the **Fourth Chapter**.

The **Second Part** of Fourth Chapter highlights certain important incidents of honour killings in India. **Manoj and Babli case** of Karnal and some recent cases of honour killings, collected from the press clippings, are incorporated in this section. These cases are classified under different heads i.e. love/inter-caste and same *gotra* marriage cases; kidnapping and rape cases; inter-religion marriage cases and same village marriage cases.

The **Fifth Chapter** of the book describes in depth **Khaps and their role** in honour killings. Beside the definitions of Khap and people represented by it, its social recognition, constitutional validity, powers, nature of functionality, difference between panchayati raj system and Khap panchayat and legality of Khaps is discussed in details.

Efforts of Union Government to curb the honour killings and the recommendations of Law Commission of India report

2012 and the proposed draft Bill prepared by the Commission for legislation is discussed in **Chapter Sixth**.

The present laws against Honour Killings—both International and National—are discussed in **Seventh Chapter** of this study. This chapter is divided into two parts. The first part deals with **International laws** that obligate member states to protect women from gender-based violence, including violence by family members, and to disqualify "honour" as a legal defence for acts of violence against women. The Resolution passed by the European Parliament Assembly in 2009; Declaration of International Convention on Human Rights (1948); the International Covenant on Civil and Political Rights (ICCPR) and the Convention on the Elimination of All Forms of Discrimination against Women (1979) are discussed.

The second part of the Chapter presents certain **Indian laws** relating to marriages. The Hindu Marriage Disabilities Removal Act, 1946; the Indian Civil Marriage Act, 1954 ; Hindu Marriage Act (1955) that permit inter-caste, inter-religion and same gotra and same village marriages are discussed in details.

There is no separate law for honour killings in India. The Indian laws that take cognizance of killing a person make no distinction between honour killing or murdering a person. It is a punishable offence in the IPC u/s 300-302 (murder), Sections 120B (criminal conspiracy) and 34 (acts done by several persons in furtherance of common intention). Moreover, the perpetrators in 'honour killing' can also be punished under articles 14, 15 (1) and (3), and 21 of the Constitution of India granting women right to live, right to move freely, right to equality and right to security.

The **Eighth Chapter** of the book discusses in details the **Role of Judiciary** in putting curb on the rising cases of honour killings. The judgments of Supreme Court in Sushma Prabhu vs. State of Maharashtra case of 2004, *Lata Singh vs. State of U.P.* (2006), *Arumugam Servai vs. State of Tamil Nadu* and *Bhagwan Das vs. State (NCT of Delhi)* related to honour killings are critically evaluated. The details of the proposition of Supreme Court that the so-called honour killing comes within the category of ***rarest of the rare cases*** deserving death punishment and the directions issued to the administration and police departments to ensure that couples in such relationships are not harassed or subjected to violence, adding that inter-caste marriages are in the national interest and would help dismantle India's age-old caste system are also highlighted. A Public Interest Litigation against rampant honour killings in Panjab, U.P., West Bengal and Haryana filed by *Shakti Vahini*, a NGO, in Supreme Court in 2010 the hearing of which is still going on is also mentioned.

Certain **preventive measures** are suggested against the honour crimes in **Ninth Chapter.** The fundamental rights like choice of marriage partner, Right to life and Constitutional provisions of harmony and brotherhood, encouragement of Inter-caste marriages, *Sagotra* marriages, fast-track courts, total abolition of caste system, implementation of the recommendations of the Law Commission of India Report 2012, curtailment of powers of *Khap* panchayats, need of a separate law for honour killings, joint responsibility of the *Khap* panchayats that order the killings in the name of honour and those executing the order, shifting the 'Burden of proof' on the accused family members against whom the charges of 'Honour Killing' are framed, the need for setting up the State are some of the important suggestions. Commission for Scheduled Castes with adequate representation to women as a mechanism for the redress of grievances to restore dignity and morale of the Scheduled Castes are some of the suggestions given in this study.

The **Concluded Chapter** sums up the problem of honour killings as a whole recalling all aspects of honour killings and suggested measures to curb this menace. A select bibliography of books, articles, UN documents, judicial cases and the list of newspapers consulted is attached for further study of the subject. In an annex Draft model bill proposed by the Law

Commission of India is also attached as annex for ready references. *Endnotes* are also provided in all chapters for reference, record and further study.

REFERENCES

1. Fisk, Robert, "The Crime-Wave that Shames the World", *Independent*, London, 7 September 2010.
2. *Hindu*, Chennai, Madras, 11 July 2010.
3. *Times of India*, 29 March 2013, p. 5.
4. The UN Commission on Human Rights Report (E/CN.4/2002/83).
5. *Ibid.*
6. *Telegraph*, 02-09-2008.
7. Chesler, Phyllis, "Are Honour Killings Simply Domestic Violence?", *Middle East Quarterly*, Spring 2009, pp. 61-69.
8. International Press Service, 6 June 2006.
9. Ray, Ashis "Honour Killing Cases Among South Asians in the UK Rising", *The Indian Times*, 4 December 2011.
10. Amnesty International Report 2007.
11. Palestinian Independent Commission for Human Rights Report 2012.
12. U.N.'s Office for the Coordination of Humanitarian Affairs, IRIN News, 2006.
13. *Taipei Times*, September 2011.
14. "Pakistan Rejects Pro-Women Bill", BBC News, 2 March 2005.
15. Warraich Sohail, "'Honour Killings' and the Law in Pakistan" in Sara Hossain and Lynn Welchman, *Honour, Crimes, Paradigms and Violence against Women*, Zed Books, 10 November 2005.
16. Warrick, C., "The Vanishing Victim: Criminal Law and Gender in Jordan", *Law and Society Review*, 39(2): 2005, 315-348.
17. *Times of India*, 23 August 2012.
18. Bhagwan Das vs. State (NCT of Delhi) [(2011), 6 SCC 396].
19. Chesler, Phyllis, *Worldwide Trends in Honour Killings, Middle East Quarterly*, Vol. 17, No. 2, Spring, 2010, pp. 3-11.
20. *The Australian* (Sydney), 3 April 2010.
21. "Violence against Women and Honour Crimes", *Human Rights Watch* (2006).
22. *Times of India*, 5 January 2013.
23. *Hindustan Times*,10 January 2013.
24. *Times of India*, 15 January 2013.

2. Definition, Scope and Origin

The issue of women rights often causes uneasy discussions. Though women have made great advances in the academic and professional fields, they still face social discrimination. They do not have social autonomy. The UN Convention on the Elimination of All Forms of Discrimination against Women (CEDAW) resolution which was adopted more than thirty years before has failed to provide equal opportunities to women. They are still treated in a traditional manner, with negligence to their basic rights. In many countries, women are not entitled to own property or inherit land. Social exclusion, female genital mutilation, trafficking, restricted mobility, early marriage and killing women on the background of honour of the family etc. are some of the major problems women and girls are still facing.

Honour crimes are often understood as a product of a fundamentalist culture that stresses honour and purity of women inside the family unit. Honour, is a concept that defines one's self worth through behaviours and actions, and whether those behaviours are in-line with modesty and cultural traditions of the community. The mere perception that a woman has behaved in a way that "dishonours" her family is sufficient to trigger an attack on her life.

The term 'honour killings' is often interchangeably used with terms such as honour crimes, femicide, crimes of tradition or crimes of honour. Although these concepts often overlap, there is not yet a standard definition or agreement of the best term to use.[1]

Honour killing is a crime that has not only threatened the unity and harmony of the community but also acted as a barrier preventing women from progressing in their lives. Gender based violence against women is defined as violence that is directed against a woman because she is a woman and affects her disproportionately.[2] By invoking the twin notions of honour and dishonour, the families try to regulate the inappropriate behaviour of the woman. What is sacred and inviolable is *izzat* or *ghairat* i.e., honour and it is always presumed to be justified to kill and die for honour.[3] An action to uphold honour or *izzat* is always a male prerogative while women may only incite action.

2.1. DEFINITION

'Honour killing' is not specifically defined in any dictionary of law. Therefore there is no precise definition of 'Honour killing' available in any law dictionary. In plain words, it is the homicide of a member of a family or social group by other members, due to the belief of the perpetrators that the victim has brought dishonour upon the family or community. Accused of these crimes think that they are morally right and the acts of killings have brought back the last honour to the family.

2.1.1. Oxford Dictionaries

The word honour killing is a combination of two words, 'honour' and 'killing'. The term Honour is derived from the Latin word *'honos'* which is an abstract concept of a perceived quality of worthiness, respectability and moreover the perceived standing of an individual in large social bodies such as schools, neighbourhoods, cities or nations. The word 'honour' in the Oxford Dictionary Thesaurus is described as 'high respect'; 'something that is a privilege or pleasure'; 'a clear sense of what is morally right'.[4]

Honour, as concept defines one's self worth through their behaviours and actions, and whether those behaviours and actions are in-line with modesty and cultural traditions of the family or community. The word 'killing' means 'causing the death'.[5] The *Oxford Dictionary* defines honour killing as "the killing of a relative, especially a girl or woman, who is perceived to have brought dishonour on the family."

Thus dictionary meaning of the honour killing may be defined as an act of causing death of any person specially women bringing disrespect to family and such type of killing is 'morally right'. It means when a family member, or clan member, takes the life of another family member (who has shamed the family) in order to restore honour to the family or clan. Both men and women are victims of honour killings, however, women tend to be the victim more often.

2.1.2. Human Rights Watch

Human Rights Watch has given more precise definition of honour killing. According to it "Honour killings are acts of vengeance, usually death, committed by male family members against female family members, who are held to have brought dishonour upon the family".[6] Honour killing is originally the product of a particular social interaction amongst members of the society which believes in a strong patriarchal structure. These killings are qualitatively different from other types of killings.[7]

2.1.3. Free Dictionary

Free Dictionary describes honour killing as—an ancient tradition still sometimes observed; a male member of the family kills a female relative for tarnishing the family image.[8]

Abu Odeh while elaborating the meaning of honour killing said "honour crime is the killing of a woman by her father or brother for engaging in or being suspected of engaging in sexual practices before or outside marriage[9] and includes different types of manifest violent behaviour against her like assault, confinement, imprisonment, interference with choice in marriage, declaring her to be minor and insane including her brutal murder.[10]

To sum up we can say that honour killing is the traditional practice of killing a family member who is believed to have brought "shame" to the family. The apparent "shame" could be caused by a victim refusing to enter into an arranged marriage or for having a relationship that the family considers to be inappropriate, for examples, having extramarital and premarital relationships, marrying within the same *gotra* or outside one's caste or marrying a cousin from a different caste. Some victims are driven to suicide from the pressure of their families. Accused of these crimes think that they are morally right and the act of killings have brought honour to the family. In the eyes of law it is a homicide—the killing of a human being by another human being. Men can also be the victims of honour killings by members of the families of women with whom they are perceived to have an inappropriate relationship. The loose term of "honour killing" applies to killing of both men and women in cultures that practice it.

2.2. SCOPE OF HONOUR KILLINGS

Honour killing is different from other kinds of killings. Let us discuss the scope of honour killings and identify the areas in which one see the acts of killings carried out.

2.2.1. Honour Killing and Culpable Homicide

The term 'honour killing' was introduced by a Dutch scholar from Turkish background in 1978 to separate such killings from other kind of killings in the families and communities.

Therefore, there is no special law against 'honour killings.' In most of the countries, including India, honour killings are being treated as culpable homicide amount to murder. The word so-called "honour" of the family, in the name of which the heinous crime is committed, is being used by the courts. But such types of crimes are rarely declared as 'rarest of the rare' cases. Justice V.S. Sirpurkar and Justice Deepak Verma of the Supreme Court of India, in a case where the brother of the girl, who belonged to Uttar Pradesh, had killed five members, including his brother-in-law who was a Scheduled Caste, said such types of "murders were the outcome of a social issue like a marriage with a person of so-called lower caste. Such killings do not fall in the category of the rarest of the rare as the family of the girl has to face a lot of taunts and humiliation in the society for the acts of the girl.These cases are not fit for considering death sentence in such circumstances".

In other words, the court classified the shameful caste based 'honour killings' as different from other homicides in which the maximum punishment of death can be awarded. Therefore an "honour killing" is a murder committed against a woman/man for actual or perceived "immoral" behaviour that is deemed to have breached the 'honour code' of a household or community.

We may highlight some of the important distinctions between 'honour killings' and homicides.

While honour killing shares many of the elements of the criminal offence of homicide, it is established that there are important distinctions between the two offences and the prosecutions of the two should not be treated the same. Homicide on the other hand is a crime which is well understood and has had a well-established jurisprudence. Honour killing is a relatively newer concept of crime.

The main difference between the two lies in the motivation of the crime. Murders/homicides are usually motivated by monetary gains or some other strategic benefits or revenges, whereas honour killings are purely motivated by the desire to eliminate the person and somehow restoring the 'honour' back to the family. Secondly, honour killings are the fact of shared relation between the perpetrators and the victims. The perpetrators unlike the crimes of homicide are not stranger or third persons. The perpetrators are usually family members of the victims. Thirdly, so long as the honour of the family or group or community is not affected by the shameful and dishonourable conduct, the community or group does not necessarily retaliate or kill in return. The final distinct feature which separates honour killing from homicide is the fact that the perpetrator does not act on his sole motivation. Rather, he is either fuelled by desires and directions of his family relatives or by the desire of the local village in rural settings. Therefore, the guilt burden should not be solely on the trigger puller but rather on every person that was responsible for the abetment and incitement of the crime.

2.2.2. Honour Killing and Suicide

Suicide means the action of killing oneself intentionally or deliberately. It is often committed out of despair. Depression, bipolar disorder, alcoholism, or drug abuse, financial problem etc. are some of the frequent causes attributed to suicides. Attempted suicide, is criminally punishable in India. Abetment to commit suicide is a murder. Honour killing on the other hand is killing by family members though intentionally but to restore the 'lost honour of family.' It is not self killing but killing by others. Therefore, suicide is different from honour killing.

Many countries have failed to undertake initiatives to ascertain the rate of violence against women.[11] Thus, such crimes often go unreported or are disguised and classified as accidents or suicides. While reporting the cases honour killings were not reported as murders but as "deaths resulting from suspicious circumstances and criminal acts." The honour crimes were incorrectly classified as death due to "fate and destiny".[12]

2.2.3. Rape Victim and Honour Killing

Rape and adultery are different because they usually bring shame not only on the performer but also their kin as well as on the victim and the victim's kin. Therefore, they stain the collective honour of the group, which in return is responsible for the extreme reaction of violence or killing in retaliation of the lost honour.

2.2.4. Dowry Death and Honour Killing

Dowry is still the primary cause of perpetration of violence on women. In the year 2011, 6,619 cases were filed in India under the Dowry Prohibition Act of 1961.[13] Most common dowry related incidents are killings by pouring kerosene on women, stabbing the woman with knife or any other dangerous weapon, beating her up with tube lights and thrusting glass into her vitals, throwing her into a well or trying to run her over with a vehicle and attempting to push her off the roof. In Latin America, honour killings are sometimes referred to as dowry deaths and bride burnings.

Honour killings are different from the dowry deaths. In the case of dowry death, the perpetrators of that action claim that they have not been given enough material rewards for accepting the woman into the family. There is a lot of harassment from the in-laws and more times than one, it has been noted that the wife commits suicide rather than being killed by the in-laws, though it has to be said that she has been mentally killed, if not physically. In rare cases, some parents who cannot afford dowry kill their daughters in the name of honour.

2.2.5. Domestic Violence and Honour Killing

Honour killing is different from the domestic violence. These killings are frequently performed out in the open, and the perpetrators rarely act alone. The Protection against Domestic Violence Act 2005, which have cultural acceptance, recognises crimes against women like wife-beating, threat to throw her out of the marital home, emotional and psychological stress on her for various reasons. But it is a civil law that gives aggrieved women their rights and practical remedies in terms of protection order, a home, monetary relief, temporary custody and compensation, among other benefits. In the year 2011 total applications filed by women under DVA in India were 42,148.[14] But the purpose of DVA is to safeguard the family and also to provide relief to female victims of domestic violence or abuse.[15] In other words the DVA does not recognises honour killings. Honour killings are not extremism of domestic violence as suggested by some lawyers because domestic violence is not due to morality or cultural traditions. Planning in advance is missing. Moreover honour killings are planned in advance and to comply it multiple family members involved. Perpetrators of honour killings often do not face negative stigma in their families or communities.

2.2.6. *SATI* SYSTEM AND HONOUR KILLING

The honour killing differs from the ancient Indian practice of *Sati*. The term *Sati* was initially a feminine participle derived from the verb—to be. The term was frequently used in a number of ways to reflect the devotion of a woman to her husband. In *Sati* system a widowed woman have to immolate herself on the burning funeral pyre of her husband to reflect the devotion to her husband. In a subsidiary sense, *Sati* denoted a woman who—is burned on the pyre along with the dead body of her husband.[16]

The act of *Sati* and walk into funeral pyres may be out of a sense of pure devotion or the feelings of effectiveness of self-sacrifice simply because this is one way of asserting their freedom and sense of self-worth in making a decision that is made independently. It is also possible that some elements of sudden grief and bereavement may lead to de-personalization during which social and cultural pressures may lead to acts being carried out. It is not likely that these women are suffering from either severe depression or psychosis that leads to the acts of self-immolation.[17] But we should not overrule that social pressure created by surrounding kinship and other villagers is what causes the widow to take such an extreme measure. Therefore, social pressure is one of the most important causal links of *Sati*. The third parties play an important role in such crimes. Though the practice of *Sati* was initially banned in 1829 by the British in India but it continued even in 20th century. After independence the Indian Government took various measures to curb the practice of *Sati*. In 1987 the Commission of *Sati* (prevention) Act was passed to eliminate this practice. The legislation made no distinction between any passive observer or the active promoters of the event of *Sati* and all were held to be equally guilty. Measures were also taken to stop the promotion of 'glorification' of the dead women by setting up temples at the place of death or by creating shrines to the dead. The act of glorifying is now punishable with 1-7 years in prison.

Both, the crimes of *Sati* and honour killing are based on different ideologies. In both the crimes social and cultural pressures play a great role rather than individual mental illness. Without pressure it would be impossible in many cases for the perpetrators to commit such crimes. In honour killing the element of restoration of family respect which was lost by the girl by not agreeing to the parents wish becomes the major cause of killing instead of sense of pure devotion or the feelings of effectiveness of self-sacrifice of the *Sati*. Honour killing is a homicide whereas *Sati* may be the act of suicide or abetment to commit suicide due to social pressure.

2.2.7. Gender and Honour Killing

Honour crimes although are targeting more often towards women, they are in no way restricted to women alone. Men can also be the victims of honour killing by the family members of the woman with whom they are perceived to have an inappropriate relationship.[18] Amnesty International in its annual report of 1999 disclosed that the Human Rights Commission of Pakistan has analysed the deaths of 97 men as well as 158 women in *Karo-Kari* 'Honour Killings' in the province of Sindh, Pakistan.[19]

2.3. ORIGIN OF HONOUR KILLINGS

Honour killings has its deep rooted origin in the Indian society. It was observed that it relates to the family system bound by marriage, beliefs, routines related to certain rules that persist in societies. Not only in India, these have been practised in China, Jordan, Leban, Morocco, Pakistan, the Syrian Arab Republic, Turkey, Yemen, and other Mediterranean and Persian Gulf countries too along with western countries like France, Germany and United Kingdom.

2.3.1. History

History does not give definitive explanation about the origin of honour killings. Its origin may be traced in the evolution of civilizations that brought not only the positive changes in the way of life of man but also put certain limitations on the relationship of persons in general and male-female in particular. The origin and development of family system bound people related by blood or marriage or a strong common bond, in such a way that family became an important unit of society with a universal and basic role. Families with common bonds and interests formed different groups/clans to protect the life, property and honour of their fellow members. With the passage of time these clans/groups developed certain rituals or beliefs of their own and start practising them in their day to day life. These rituals, beliefs, norms, routines and rules bound them in such a way that a wrath of family or clan become inevitable if any member of the family or clan violates any of these rules. The regular practices of these beliefs or norms later on become traditions and customs. Traditions and customs persist and evolve for thousands of years. Efforts have been done to trace its origin by many scholars. Dr. Amin A. Muhammad traced its origin dates back to pre-Islamic period when Arab settlers occupied a region adjacent to Sindh, which was known as Baluchistan. Settlers had strong patriarchal traditions with such practices as the live burial of unwanted newborn daughters.[20]

A Christian Arab writer Norma Khouri (2011) states that this "cultural norm" was started under the rule of Hammarabi and other Assyrian tribes dating back to 1200 B.C. whereas Goldstein traces its origin in Roman period. According to him in Ancient Rome the honour killings were accepted as a noble act. Killing woman for bringing dishonour to the family was considered to be a "merciful act." Such killings were treated as rationalized and justified.[21] For long time in Greece, the laws provided powers to husbands over wives as women were believed to be socially below the men. In many ancient cultures including Babylonian, Egypt, Native American and Persian cultures, women convicted of infidelity were given harsh sentences. Chinese husbands would cut off the hair of wives accused of illicit relationships and crush them to death by elephants. *Karo-kari* tradition was used as a camouflage for men who murder other men in personal disputes. This tradition was manipulated by tribes to settle rivalries in Pakistan the typical example was that of "Mukhtara Mai? Women who demand divorces from their husbands. In Sindh area of Pakistan the *Karo-Kari* practice was followed by the poor communities for easily acquiring the women's share of inheritance of their household by declaring her as *Kari*. To stop transfer of women's share of wealth to another family widow or divorced mothers were not allowed to remarry. Although the origin might be disputed, one can clearly see the plausibility of the occurrence of honour killing since the status of women was already very low in such patriarchal societies.

2.3.2. World Scenario

Duelling was a practice in Western societies. In Britain-the fifth wife of Henry VIII was killed on the bases of allegation of adultery. In British literature, Shakespeare's Desdemona was killed over allegations of infidelity. In the early times of Peru, the laws on such cases permitted husbands to starve their wives to death as punishment for committing an adulterous act. Aztec laws resulted in death by stoning or strangulation for female adultery during the early times of Mexico.[22]

The honour killing has spread its wings world over now. Robert Fisk (2010) said that more than 20,000 women become victim of honour killings each year.[23] The Rapporteur of the United Nations concerning cultural practices in the family that are violent towards women disclosed that honour killings were also reported in Egypt, Jordan, Leban, Morocco, Pakistan, the Syrian Arab Republic, Turkey, Yemen, and other Mediterranean and Persian Gulf countries. Western countries like France, Germany and United Kingdom, also not remained untouched where migrant communities are residing.[24]

Since 1996 about 40 honour killings were reported in Germany by *Papatya*, a Turkish women's organization. United Kingdom (UK) officials also estimated that within Asian and Middle East families at least a dozen women became victims of honour killings every year. According to Mr. Nazir Afzal, Director of Britain's Crown Prosecution Service West London, the United Kingdom has seen "at least a dozen honour killings" between 2004 and 2005. 'There was 47 per cent rise of honour-related crimes in Britain in 2010. In this year the UK police agencies reported 2283 cases of honour killings. Most of the attacks were conducted in cities that had high immigrant populations'.[25]

In the Middle East the cases of honour killings were reported in Turkey, Iraq, Saudi Arabia, Palestine etc. In Istanbul, the largest Turkish city, averagely one honour killing every week was reported by Turkish Prime Ministry's Human Rights Directorate report of 2008. It reported over 1,000 honour killings during the previous five years.

The Amnesty International has also reported the practice of Fake Honour Killings. According to 2007 report of Amnesty International in Lebanon 2 or 3 honour killings reported per month on an average. This enforced Lebanese Parliament on 4 August 2011 to abolish Article 562 relating to honour killings from its penal, which for years had worked as an excuse for honour killers. Executive Director of the UNICEF, while speaking about crimes against women on 7 March 2000, disclosed that two-thirds of all killings in Palestinian territories were honour killings. It was reported by the Palestinian Independent Commission for Human Rights that 29 women were killed between 2007-2010, whereas 13 women were killed in 2011 and 12 in the first seven months of 2012.

In Jordan, which was considered one of the most liberal countries in the Middle East, according to UNICEF, averagely 23 honour killings per year are committed. There men killing receive reduced sentences for killing their wives or female family members if they are deemed to have brought dishonour to their family. Rana Husseini, a leading journalist on the topic of honour killings, states that "under the existing law, people found guilty of committing honour killings often receive sentences as light as six months in prison". In Basra, the city of Iraq, as many as 47 women were killed in 2006 for honour killings.[26]

A study conducted by Dr. Amin Muhammad and Dr. Sujay Patel of Memorial University Canada in 2007 reported that the practice of honour killings was brought to Canada and United States of America by the migrants from Asian countries.[27] Although there are not many cases of honour killings within the United States, the overwhelming majority of honour killings are perpetrated by Muslims against Muslims (90 per cent of honour killings known to have taken place in Europe and the United States from 1998 to 2008) disclosed Phyllis Chesler in 2009.

Despite widespread condemnation by human rights groups, honour killings have a high level of support in Pakistan's rural society.[28] From 1999 to 2004, more than 4,000 women have died as victims of honour killings in Pakistan.[29] In 2002 alone over 382 people, about 245 women and 137 men, became victims of honour killings in the Sind province of Pakistan. In 2005 the average annual number of honour killings for the whole nation was stated to be more than 10,000 per year.[30]

Similarly, the cases of "honour killing" are rising in north India, mainly in Punjab, Rajasthan, Haryana and Uttar Pradesh. Haryana and Punjab has a large number of honour killings. According to data compiled by the Punjab Police, 34 honour killings were reported in the state between 2008 and 2010: 10 in 2008, 20 in 2009, and 4 in 2010. In 2010, there were roughly 900 reported honour killings in the northern Indian states of Haryana, Punjab, and Uttar Pradesh alone while 100-300 additional honour killings took place in the rest of the country.[31]

REFERENCES

1. Kogacioglu, D., "The Tradition Effect: Framing Honour Crimes in Turkey", *Journal of Feminist Cultural Studies*, 2004, 15(2), p. 118.
2. Welchman, L., and Hossain, S. (Eds.). *Honour. Victoria*, 2005, Spinifex Press and London, Zed Books, p. 24.
3. Omvedt, G., *Violence Against Women: New Movements and New Theories in India*, 1990, New Delhi, Kali for Women, pp. 5-6.
4. *Oxford Dictionary Thesaurus*, 2001, p. 429.
5. *Ibid.*, p. 495.

6. "Human Rights Watch" (2001), "Violence Against Women and "Honour Crimes".
7. *Ibid.*
8. TheFreeDictionary.com.
9. Welchman, L., and Hossain, S. (Eds.). *Honour. Victoria*, 2005, Spinifex Press and London, Zed Books, p. 5.
10. *Ibid.*
11. Human Rights Watch Report, 2006.
12. Warrick, C., "The Vanishing Victim: Criminal Law and Gender in Jordan", *Law and Society Review*, 2005, 39(2): 315-348.
13. *Tribune*, 22 January 2013.
14. *Ibid.*
15. "Domestic Violence", *Tribune*, 30 January 2013.
16. Courtright, P.B., "The Iconographies of Sati", in J.S. Hawley (Ed.), *Sati: The Blessing and the Curse*, pp. 27-43, 1994, NY, OUP.
17. Bhurga, D., "Sati: A Type of Non-Psychiatric Suicide", *Journal of Crisis Intervention and Suicide Prevention*, July 2005, 26(2), pp. 73-77.
18. "Afghan Couple Stoned to Death—Central and South Asia", Al Jazeera English, 16 August 2010.
19. Amnesty International, 1999a:6.
20. Muhammad, Dr. Amin A., "Magnitude and Dynamics of "Honour Killing: The Local Perspective", Memorial University of Newfoundland.
21. Goldstein, Matthew A., "The Biological Roots of Heat-of-Passion Crimes and Honour Killings", *Politics and the Life Sciences*, September 2002, 21(2), p. 29.
22. *Ibid.*, 20.
23. Fisk, Robert, "The Crime-wave that Shames the World", *Independent*, London, 7 September 2010.
24. UN Document E/CN.4/2002/83.
25. Ray, Ashis, "Honour Killing Cases Among South Asians in the UK Rising", *The Indian Times*, 4 December 2011.
26. U.N.'s Office for the Coordination of Humanitarian Affairs, IRIN News 2006.
27. *Telegram*, 2 September 2008.
28. *Taipei Times*, 24 September 2011.
29. "Pakistan Rejects Pro-Women Bill", BBC News, 2 March 2005.
30. Warraich, Sohail, "'Honour Killings' and the Law in Pakistan", in Sara Hossain and Lynn Welchman, *Honour, Crimes, Paradigms, and Violence Against Women*, Zed Books, 10 November 2005.
31. *The Hindu*, Chennai, Madras, 11 July 2010.

3. Responsible Factors

Women are targeted by her family for a variety of reasons, for example: refusing to enter into an arranged marriage or marriage against family's approval, being the victim of a sexual assault, seeking a divorce—even from an abusive husband—or (allegedly) committing adultery, pre-marital sex and having a child out of wedlock. The mere perception that a woman has behaved in a way that "dishonours" her family is sufficient to trigger an attack on her life.[1] Some of the important possible factors responsible for honour killings are discussed below:

3.1. STATUS OF WOMEN

Honour crimes, are mostly 'crimes against women'. To trace the factors responsible for this crime it is essential to study the position of women in society. Historically, crimes against women are manifestation of unequal power relations between men and women. Women have subordinate position compared with men. They are being viewed as property. This dominant position of men encouraged discrimination against the women. Women are treated as inferior to men since ancient period. *Manusmriti, Yajnavalkya, Satpatha Brahmana, Mahabharata* and *Buddha's opinions* highlight their position in ancient India. According to *Manusmriti,* in childhood a female remains subject to her father, in youth to her husband, when her husband is dead to her sons. A women is never be independent. Though women are being given equal rights and opportunities in the modern period but practically they are still dependent. They are not liberated from the yoke of patriarchal form of society. Social Milieu tends to predominate in societies where individual rights are circumscribed by communal solidarities, patriarchal authority structures, and intolerant religious and tribal beliefs. Under such conditions, control over marriage and reproduction is critical to the socio-economic status of kinship groups and the regulation of female behaviour is integral to perceptions of honour. The violation of such rules is seen as revolt not only against the family but also against community as a whole. A woman who refuses to enter into an arranged marriage, seeks a divorce, or fails to avoid suspicion of immoral behaviour is viewed by her family as having dishonoured them and killing her is seem to be the only way for the family to restore its lost honour.

3.2. ARRANGE MARRIAGES

Marriage according to Hindu scriptures is considered a 'sacrament' rather than a 'contract.' Women, since ancient time, are treated as property of family heads. Even during *Ramayana* and *Mahabharata* era, women were not free to choose their husbands. Matrimony entailing love making (*Gandharva Vivah*), marriage by force, by purchasing the spouse and other demonical behaviour were described as *Raksasi, Asuri* and *Pisaci* scandalisation. They have all been decried to save the alliances solemnised according to scriptures.[2]

Honour crimes generally occur as a result of people marrying without their families' acceptance. The refusal of girl to marry person selected by their parents may also become a reason of honour killing. A family which want to decide the future of their daughter and daughter challenge their decision brings humiliation to the family members. The family members feel insulted and kill their daughter.

3.3. RIGIDITY OF CASTE SYSTEM

Vedic culture was the main driving force behind the philosophic principles of Hindus. The society was divided according to the vacations and duties of persons. Such classification was referred to as *Varna Vyavastha*. According to vedic culture human is born as a *Sudra* (known as first birth). Knowledge earned through education and self-discipline makes him fit for the second birth. He is classified into caste according to his deeds and character. He may become *Brahmin* or other caste in his manner. Some sages were from mixed heritage and were adored by the *Brahmins*. According to Dr. S. Radhakrishnan, *Vyas* had fishermen as his parents. *Vasistha* was a son of a courtesan. *Parasar* was a son of a *Candal* woman (she who helps in performing the last rites at the cremation). The king of *Agroha, Agarsen*, who was a *Ksatriya*, from the warrior class later becomes *Vaisya* (from trading classification) due to his thoughts and deeds. His descendants are known as *Agrawals* today.[3] Lord Krishna also said in *Gita*: "I have created *Varna* (vocational classification) according to the professions and qualities of individuals".[4]

However, some thinkers believe that an individual is born in a particular caste as per his or her deeds in the previous life. Caste system became vitiated over the time and is now considered to be by birth. The idea of considering caste by birth created caste-wise discrimination, untouchability, and other disorders of the society.

The caste system by birth continues to be at its rigid best. The Indian constitution outlaws discrimination on the basis of caste, but it does not outlaw the caste system itself. As the basis for discrimination is still in place, it is little surprise that discrimination persists despite the law.

Caste and kinship plays great role in marriage. "As marriage provides the structural link-up between kinship and caste, a closer surveillance is accorded to the marital alliances. Kinship linkages provided by marriage, give a caste group its strength, recognition and leverage in wider society and polity." Again, "the familial ties are extended through ties of blood to the clan and then the caste/community. The blood tie makes them co-shares of this honour. They must all join to safeguard and preserve it. If family members fails to uphold this honour, the community steps in. The imagery of blood kinship or brotherhood ensures it enabling a collective enforcement."[5]

This ideological scheme of caste system was theoretically composed of about 3000 sub-castes, which in turn was claimed to be composed of about 90,000 local sub-groups, with people marrying only within their sub-group. If any daughter dares to disobey her parents on the issue of marriage and decides to marry a man of her wishes but from another *gotra* or outside her caste, it would bring disrepute to the family honour and hence they decide to give the ultimate sentence, which is death, to the daughter. The fear of losing their caste status through which they gain many benefits makes them commit this heinous crime. The mentality of people has not changed. They just cannot accept that marriages can take place in the same *gotra* or outside one's caste.

Moreover, if a lower-caste man is involved with a higher caste woman, he is invariably killed. And the girl, whether belonging to the higher caste or the lower caste, is also certainly eliminated. According to a survey 75 per cent honour killings in Hindu families are caste-based.[6]

3.4. INTER RELIGION MARRIAGE

The other popular reason of honour killing is difference in religion between the husband and wife. Even though the law of the land provides special laws making such marriages legal, the society in India still continues to reject these marriages on various levels. The main reason behind passing the Special Marriage Act, 1954 was to provide a special form of marriage for

marriage, or even due to a non-sex relationship perceived as inappropriate, may invite killing by family members or husband feeling humiliation in the society. "Immoral character" victims were considered rebellious or licentious but were not suspected of being romantically involved with a specific individual. Even chatting by women with strangers on facebook is being considered good enough a reason to kill them. Some people accuse facebook for destroying the moral fabric of society. Saudi Arabia is an example of it. However, it is noteworthy that husband had the right to kill wife in Brazil, until 1991. In Colombia, until 1980, a husband could legally kill his wife for committing adultery."

3.9. HOMOSEXUALITY

Homosexuality refers to "an enduring pattern of or disposition to experience sexual, affectionate, or romantic attractions" primarily or exclusively to people of the same sex." Not only women, homosexual men too have fallen prey to honour killings. Engaging in heterosexual acts outside marriage and engaging in homosexual acts may become the reason of dishonour brought by the victim to the family or the community. Hundreds of gay Iraqi men have been murdered since 2004. In 2008, a 26-year-old Turkish student Ahmet Yildiz was reportedly gunned down by his father for tarnishing the family honour.

3.10. INFLUENCE OF WESTERN CULTURE

India is fastly moving from developing country towards developed nation. The influence of globalization and western culture is slowly and gradually wiping out the Indian culture. It had already made its presence in Metro's & now slowly heading towards other parts of the country. The Western culture has greatly affected our traditions, customs, our family and our respect and love for others. Today's generation has very little knowledge about their culture, traditions and roots. The influence of western culture on young generation discarding Indian traditions, customs and family values has contributed in the rise of honour killings.

3.11. CULTURAL CHANGE

Change in cultural and economic status of women may also invite the occurrences of honour killings. Women in largely patriarchal cultures who have gained economic independence from their families go against male-dominated culture. The shift towards greater responsibility for women and less for their fathers may cause their male family members to act in oppressive and sometimes violent manners in order to regain authority. Dressing in a manner that is unacceptable to the family or community, talking, meeting or dating men may also be treated as bringing dishonour to the family or community. The life and relationships of women were controlled by their families and every step towards independence was perceived as a threat to family honour. Women were pressurised and intimidated to become obedient.and passive to surrender their will.

3.12. HAILING OF KILLERS

Prem Chowdhry, a prominent research scholar of *Haryanvi* culture, disclosed that the killings in the name of honour have 'complete sanction and legitimacy' because killers are being treated as 'moral guardians of the community'. They hailed themselves for the act of violence and are being hailed by other members of the community.[12] Therefore, it is generally the moral booster for someone who indulges in the crime of killing for 'honour' since the executioner feels 'righted' in his own right and action. Such types of sanction may become one of the reasons for encourging the honour killings.

3.13. DUBIOUS ROLE OF POLICE

While studying the subject of honour killings we found that the perpetrators' thinking of honour killings is limited not only to the village elders or the village mob, but is embedded so deep into every institution of society that it is difficult for the victim's to seek shelter. This support spreads from police agencies to the judicial officers entrusted with upholding the rule of law. The enforcement agencies, particularly, the Haryana, Panjab and Uttar Pradesh police, knowingly or unknowingly, conspire with the killers and community in the upholding of family honour and norms. It is because, they also 'subscribe to the same norms and believe in the same over-arching ideology.'

Manoj and Babli murder case highlights the dubious role of police in honour cases. Manoj and Babli ran away from home on 5th April 2007 and got married on 7 April 2007 in Chandigarh against the wishes of their parents. On 26 April, Babli's family filed a FIR against Manoj and his family for kidnapping Babli. On 15 June, Manoj went to court with Babli, testifying that they had married in conformity with the law and that he did not kidnap Babli. The judge ordered police protection for the two. After the trial, Manoj and Babli, accompanied by a team of five police officers assigned to them for protection, left for Chandigarh. The police left them at Pipli and slipped away. Suspecting foul play, Manoj and Babli did not continue toward Chandigarh, instead boarded a bus for Karnal. Babli's relatives stopped the bus and kidnapped the couple and killed them.

A senior police officer of Narela while investigating a harassment following an inter-caste marriage between a Jat girl and *Dalit* boy in Narela admitted biased role of police in such cases. The Station House Officer/Superintendent of Police, a Jat (higher caste) himself, made clear statements in an interview claiming that the police is also a part of the society and as such police is not above it. Police officers from Uttar Pradesh and Haryana, the most honour killings prone area, are of the view that 'they did not come across any incident of *Khaps* directing any honour killing'.[13] ASI Ravinder Singh, a relative of a minor girl. Minakshi who was killed for honour at Bapoli village of Panipat district in Haryana on 22 September 2013, assisted the family members in tracing her without lodging a complaint.[14] However, Mr. Rajbir Deswal, a Commissioner of Police in Haryana, denied this notion and said 'the police is worried and serious in pursuing such cases'.[15]

3.14. LACK OF GOVERNANCE

Another reason for honour killings is that the formal governance has not been able to reach the rural as well as urban areas. The shortage of infrastructure to help women, the lack of protection officers accessible to women right up to the village level to create awareness about the help available to women as their right and nonavailability of women police in PCR vans helps increase in the killings of girls.

3.15. LACK OF SOCIAL AUTONOMY

Education is widely regarded as one of the key tools of women empowerment. It enhances their agency and autonomy. Since 1983 the female participation in attending schools has increased tremendously. The central and the state governments have initiated various education programmes such as National Programme for Education of Girls at an Elementary Level, Kasturbha Gandhi Balika Vidyalaya, Mahila Samakhya Programme and Sarv Shiksha Abhiyan etc. These programmes might have given women economic independency but education on the whole has failed to increase social autonomy for women in substantive ways. They are not free to take social decisions or decisions affecting thier life independently in a patriarchal society like India. The girl who tries to take decisions affect her life herself and deviates the customs invites troubles.

3.16. ECONOMIC FACTOR

The girls right to have share of property given under the Hindu Succession Act, 1956 which was passed to amend and codify the law relating to intestate or unwilled succession among Hindus further promoted the caste base honour killings.

The Act lays down a uniform and comprehensive system of inheritance. It is hailed for its consolidation of Hindu laws on succession into one act. The Hindu women's limited estate was abolished by this Act. According to the Act any property possessed by a Hindu female is to be held by her absolute property and she is given full power to deal with it and dispose it of by will as she likes. The Act was amended in 2005. Prior to that pressure was made by rural societies and the landowners of Haryana-Panjab to get this clause abolished. Haryana assembly tried three times, in 1967, 1979 and 1989, to amend this Act without success.

A bench of justices R. M. Lodha and Jagdish Singh Khehar of the Supreme Court in *Ganduri Koteshwaramma case* (2011) ruled that under the Hindu Succession (Amendment) Act, 2005, the daughters are entitled to equal inheritance rights along with other male siblings, which was not available to them prior to the amendment. The apex court further clarified that the female inheritors would not only have the succession rights but also the same liabilities fastened on the property along with the male members.

The girl's right to have share in family property is seen as a 'slur on the family name'. This closed the doors of marrying men of girls' choice. The villagers think that a 'girl who defies society to choose her own husband is more likely to have the confidence to claim her share of inheritance too.'[16] For them the loss of ancestral land equals a loss of pride and is unacceptable to the community having landed property. The leader of Dhankar Khap, Mr. Om Prakash Dhankar, criticised this clause of the Hindu Succession Act and described it as unfair as it is upsetting the social balance of our society. He said, "It is blind to the fact that the girl also gets a share from husband's side. It is not fair that she gets two shares."[17]

Thus the amended Act "aroused and continues to arouse tremendous anxieties in rural society. The rural people thinks that marrying outside the caste or within the village is dangerous as the intorduction of a rank outsider into the family, who can and may claim the property on behalf of his wife."[18] The Khaps want to stop this effectively.

3.17. CONCLUSION

To conclude we can say that the reasons for honour killings may be various, but the common elements in the killings are womens' sexuality, loss of control of womens sexuality and the shame brought by it to the family and community.

Other important reasons of honour crimes are people marrying without their family's acceptance. Marrying outside their caste or religion. Same *Gotra* marriage often led to violent reaction from the family members or the community members. Contentious and mixed marriages violating the rule of caste endogamy, territorial exogamy, religious exogamy, widow remarriage, *gotra* exogamy are treated as an attack upon *izzat* and have mainly led to honour crimes. The Caste Councils popularly known as *'Khap Panchayats'* try to adopt the chosen course of 'moral vigilantism' and enforce their diktats by assuming to themselves the role of social or community guardians.

REFERENCES

1. Human Rights Watch, 2006, "Violence Against Women and Honour

Crimes".

2. Garg, Pyar L., *The Ultimate Quest*, New Delhi, Northern Book Centre, 2013, p. 4.
3. Radhakrishnan, S., *The Hindu View of Life*, pp. 86, 87.
4. *Ibid.*, 2, pp. 3-4.
5. Chowdhry, Prem, "Concept of Honour in Honour Crimes," *Tribune*, 13 Oct. 2013, p. 9.
6. Chesler, Phyllis, *Worldwide Trends in Honour Killings*, *Middle East Quarterly*, Vol. 17, No. 2, Spring 2010, pp. 3-11.
7. Byatnal, Amruta, "Hindutva Vigilantes Target Hindu-Muslim couples," *Hindu*, 14 Oct. 2013, p.1.
8. International Press Service, 6 June 2006.
9. *The Australian* (Sydney), 3 April 2010.
10. Choudhary, Rohit, "Enabling Police to Handle Rape Cases", *Tribune*, 1 February 2013, p. 11.
11. *Tribune*, 25 February 2013, p. 3.
12. Chowdhry, Prem, "Concept of Honour in Honour Crimes," *Tribune*, 13 Oct. 2013, p. 9.
13. *Hindustan Times*, 15 January 2013.
14. *Tribune*, 25 September 2013.
15. Deswal, Rajbir, "When Family Kills its Own for Honour," *Tribune*, 11 Oct. 2013, p., 11.
16. Dogra, Chander Suta, "Women's Right to Inheritance Still a struggle," *Hindu*, 22 Oct. 2013, p.1, 10.
17. Dogra, Chander Suta, "Women's Right to Inheritance Still a Struggle," *Hindu*, 22 Oct. 2013, p.1,10
18. Chowdhry, Prem, "Concept of Honour in Honour Crimes," *Tribune*, 13 Oct. 2013, p. 9.

4. Important Incidents

We have seen that honour killings are perpetuated by socio-cultural factors and are product of clash between traditional and modern values, intensified by high economic growth and increasing social mobility. Like Pakistan Indian society is also misogynistic and hates women. Boys are preferred and girls are seen as a burden. An estimated four to twelve million selective abortions of girls have taken place in India in the past three decades. The 2011 Indian Census found 914 girls for every 1,000 boys among children of six or younger.[1] This is linked with dowry burnings in which man and/or his mother douses his wife with cooking oil and burns her alive so that a new bride and dowry can be obtained, are as big a problem as honour killings in India.

Media has very carefully and accurately documented, a marked increase in the number of reported honour killings in India in recent years. It is believed that Majority of the honour cases go unreported. In 2010, there were roughly 900 reported honour killings in the northern Indian states of Haryana, Punjab, and Uttar Pradesh alone while 100-300 additional honour killings were reported in the rest of the country.[2] A government-funded study on the prevalence of honour crimes in India found in 2010 that honour crimes are most common in regions dominated by *Khap Panchayats* and increasingly involve inter-caste, rather than intra-sub-caste marriages[3] in these regions. Local politicians turn a blind eye to the murders and resist efforts by the central government and parliament to deal with the problem while local police collude in honour killings or help cover them up, often mischaracterizing the murders as suicides.[4] In 2011, theatres in Haryana refused to screen an Indian film on honour killings because of threats by *Khap Panchayats*.[5] Therefore, overwhelming majority of killings are caste-related, generally targeting young men and women shortly after they eloped and before they could have children.

Media have done aggressive investigative reporting on the issue. In 2010, an undercover reporter working for the Indian television channel *Headlines Today* found two policemen from Haryana who boasted about their willingness to hand over a young woman to be honour murder. "Cut her into pieces and then throw her in some river," one said.[6] Besides media, a number of Indian non-governmental organizations are working to save women from honour killings. *The Love Commandos*, a NGO with 2,000 volunteers and a 24-hour national hotline, is devoted to protect newly-weds who defy their families.[7]

The government of India has taken important steps to combat the practice of honour killing. In 2010, Prime Minister Manmohan Singh ordered a cabinet-level commission to draft national legislation designed to cap honour killings.[8] The proposals included an amendment to the Indian Penal Code allowing *Khap Panchayats* leaders to be prosecuted for sanctioning murders as well as the revocation of the 30-day notice period required by the Special Marriage Act, which has enabled families to track down and pre-emptively kill the couples.

The Law Commission of India, under the Ministry of Law and Justice, recently drafted a new bill—The Endangerment of Life and Liberty (Protection, Prosecution and Other Measures) Act—designed to prevent *Khap Panchayats* from denouncing couples who violate caste restrictions. According to the proposed bill: "It shall be unlawful for any group of persons to gather, assemble or congregate with the ... intention to deliberate, declare on, or condemn any marriage or relationship such as marriage between two persons of majority age in the locality concerned on the basis that such conduct or relationship has dishonoured the caste or community or religion of all or some of the persons forming part of the assembly or the family or the people of the locality concerned".[9] The fate of this legislation seems to be uncertain; as the *Khap Panchayats'* control over local voting blocs has enabled them to blunt legislative reforms in the past.

The government has made more progress on the judicial front also. The Supreme Court of India, in 2010, instructed the governments in Haryana and six other states to take steps to protect potential honour killing victims.[10] In 2011, it decried honour killing as a "barbaric and shameful" practice that must be "ruthlessly stamped out." The apex court also declared honour killings ordered by *Khap Panchayats* to be illegal and warned that government officials who fail to act against honour crime offenders will be prosecuted.[11]

Although fear of caste ostracism makes it difficult to find cooperative witnesses, Indian courts have begun aggressively prosecuting honour killers and their accomplices. In 2010, a Haryana court sentenced five men to death for the honour murder of a young couple who had married despite being members of the same sub-caste while giving a life sentence to the head of the *Khap Panchayat members* that ordered their deaths.[12] In November 2011, an Indian court sentenced eight men to death and twenty others to life imprisonment for involvement in three honour killings.[13] Increasingly, local police officials have been suspended and even arrested for collusion in honour killings.[14]

India still has a long way to go for stamping out honour killings. While the Indian government continues to face resistance and evasion of responsibility on the part of local officials, it has not encountered the same kind of virulent, often violent, opposition to women's rights typical of Pakistani Islamists. There is little doubt that India is determined to win what promises to be a long battle against honour killings.

4.1. IMPORTANT RECENT INCIDENTS

It is very difficult to ascertain the number of honour killing incidents in India, the accused involved and the specific reasons etc. Though the Government authorities of the States where incidents often occur were addressed to furnish the necessary information about honour killings to the Director (SR) in the Ministry of Home Affairs in 2010 but no state has responded. Following are some of the important incidents of honour killings cases collected from the newspaper reports and reports from various other sources.

4.1.1. LOVE/INTER CASTE/SAME *GOTRA* MARRIAGES

- *Manoj and Babli*, both residents of Karora village, in Haryana belong to the same caste of Banwala, a Jat community, began to show interest in each other since 2005. They run away from home on 5th April 2007. They married on 7 April 2007, at Durga temple, Chandigarh against the wishes of their parents. On 26 April, Babli's family filed a First Information Report (FIR) against Manoj and his family for kidnapping Babli. On 15 June, Manoj went to court with Babli, testifying that they had married in conformity with the law and that he did not kidnap Babli. The judge ordered police protection for the two. After the trial, Manoj and Babli, accompanied by a team of five police officers assigned to them for protection, left for Chandigarh. The police left them at Pipli and slipped away. Suspecting foul play, Manoj and Babli did not continue their journey towards Chandigarh, instead boarded a bus for Karnal. Babli's relatives stopped the bus near Raipur Jatan village, about 20 kilometres from Pipli. They kidnapped the couple and beated them up. Babli's brother Suresh forced her to consume pesticide, while four other family members pushed Manoj to the ground, her uncle Rajinder pulling a noose around

Manoj's neck and strangled him in front of Babli. They wrapped the bodies in gunny sacks and dumped them in Barwala Link Canal in Hisar district. On 23 June, nine days later, their mutilated bodies, hands and feet tied were fished out of the canal by Kheri Chowki police. On 29 March 2010, after 33 months of 50 hearings with 41 witnesses, the Karnal district court found the accused guilty of murder, kidnapping, conspiracy and destroying evidence under respective sections in the IPC.

- The next day, 30 March, for the first time in the history of Haryana, a death penalty verdict was announced in the double murder case for the five accused. They were relatives of Babli; brother Suresh, cousins Gurdev and Satish, paternal uncle Rajender, and maternal uncle Baru Ram. The leader of the *Khap Panchayat* Ganga Raj (52), was given a life sentence for conspiracy, while the driver, Mandeep Singh, held guilty of kidnapping and was given a jail term of seven years. Reacting to the verdict a *Maha Khap Panchayat* (grand caste council) representing 20 *Khap Panchayats* of Haryana, Uttar Pradesh, and Rajasthan hold a meeting on April 13, 2010, in Kurukshetra and decided to challenge the court verdict and support those sentenced to death in the case. They blocked the Kurukshetra-Kaithal highway in protest and demanded that the Hindu Marriage Act be amended to ban same-*gotra* marriages. The *Khaps* also threatened to boycott any MP and assembly member from Haryana who did not back the *Khap's* request.
- The wife, Sunita Devi, 22 and the husband, Jasbir Singh, 27, both Jats and of legal age for marriage, fell in love against the wishes of the parents. As a result both were killed by Sunitas father and other relatives on May 9, 2008 in Balah village of Haryana.
- In an Andhra village, a lower caste boy entered into marital relations with an upper caste Reddy girl. The two were stoned to death by angry villagers led by the girl's father.[15]

- In another case of honour killing, a 30-year-old woman was allegedly murdered by her brother-in-law for eloping with her neighbour in Jaffarpur Kalan, southwest Delhi.[16]
- Ved Pal Mor, 23, married same *gotra* girl Sonia of Banwala village in Haryana against the wishes of villagers in 2008. He went to get his wife back from her parent's custody accompanied by court orders from the High Court of Punjab and Haryana state along with a warrant officer and few policemen. When they arrived at the girls parents house the mob scared away the warrant officer who was able to escape with few injuries, leaving Ved Pal to the mercy of the mob. He was then lynched to death by the mob in the name of honour and his body was left at a crossing at the village for the entire village to witness his state.[17]
- A young girl was hacked to death by her father and other family members over a love affair with a boy of the same caste in *Khalidabad* village in district Kaushambi, UP.[18]
- In Koderma (Jharkhand) Delhi-based journalist Nirupama Pathak was strangulated to death by her mother as Nirupama wanted to marry her Kayastha boyfriend Priyabhanshu Ranjan.[19]
- In a Haryana village near Sonipat two girls were killed by the family members for allegedly having affairs with their cousins.[20] In an inter-caste marriage case Reuben Joseph and the girl's father, Edward, killed the duo on the spur of the moment after they found them in a compromising position at the girl's residence in Friends' Colony, New Delhi. The paramour Hari Lal was from Punjab and Bimal, a Christian from Bihar.[21]
- In a suspected case of honour killing in village *Ghari Madhiya* in Ghaziabad district of Uttar Pradesh, a Muslim girl and a Muslim boy were allegedly murdered by the girl's family members who were opposed to their alliance.[22]
- A 20-year-old *Gujjar* girl was allegedly cut into pieces by family members after she married her Dalit Software Engineer

colleague.[23]

- A 14-year-old Indian girl, S. Rajinilatha, was murdered by her father not because she was involved with any particular man but merely because she wrote love poetry.
- Meena, an 18-year-old Hindu girl, was shot to death because she left her village for three days, and her family was not satisfied with her explanation of where she had been.[24,25]
- A 17-year-old Anup Kumar of Haryana was electrocuted in 2011 for being in a relationship with a girl from the same sub-caste.[26]
- Barjinder, the son of a Congress worker, Teja Singh Gill, adviser in the District Congress Committee, allegedly killed his 25-year-old sister Navdeep Kaur and her 'lover', Harpreet Singh Johal, alias Happy (25), from *Thrike* village by shooting them. The incident took place at Hambran village, around near Ludhiana, on 1 February 2012. The accused, identified as Barjinder Singh, allegedly sprayed bullets on the 'couple' after "spotting them in a compromising position in his house".[27]
- In Haryana, Kusum, 20, a Scheduled caste girl of *Sadarpur* village of Karnal district and Karambir, an upper caste youth from *Chudi Jatan* village in Kurukshetra district, had eloped and got married in July 2012, against the wishes of their families. Kusum, who was three-month pregnant was killed by her father and maternal uncle. Girl's father Rajbir buried her body in his house after strangulating her with a wire. He dug up the corpse and threw it into a canal on November 3, 2012. The killing came to light when Karambir filed a complaint with the police that his wife Kusum had gone missing after her father took her away.[28]
- Deepti Chikara, 26, a resident of *Kanjhawala* in New Delhi was strangled to death by her brother Mohit (22), her mother Veermati (50) and uncle on the night of April 19, 2012 for marrying a man from a so-called lower caste much to the dislike of her family. Her body was carried to Roorkee where

it was tossed into a canal.[29]

- A 24-year-old youth Sanni Sharma was allegedly shot dead in Indira Colony of Muzaffarnagar, UP on 12 February 2013 by Menpal with whose sister Sharma was reportedly having an affair. According to police, the girl's family was against the relationship as the two were from different castes.
- Abdul Hakim and Mehwish were neighbours at Adoli village of *Bulandshahr* in Uttar Pradesh. They got married against the wishes of Mehwish's family. After their marriage, the local *Panchayat* allegedly announced an award of ₹ 50,000 for killing. the couple and banished Hakim's family from the village. The family moved to Bhargardi village. In 2011, Mehwish gave birth to a girl. She got pregnant in August 2012 and came to stay with Hakim's family till the delivery of her baby. On November 22, 2012 when Hakim had come to visit Mehwish, he was shot dead.
- Sachin Dharu and two of his friends were murdered on 1 January 2013 in Ahmednagar of Maharashtra state. Sachin Dharu, a dalit, has alleged to have had a relationship with an upper-caste girl, which was opposed by her family. "Members of the girl's family summoned Sachin and two of his friends from the school where they were working, and hacked them to death." Killers were arrested under the Prevention of Atrocities against *Dalits* Act.
- Mahroon, a 20-year-old girl of Tejpur village in Rabipur area of the Bahraich District of Uttar Pradesh, was killed by her brother Nanke by chopping off her head on 9th March 2013. It was alleged that she wanted to marry a 50-year-old person.[30]
- Shashi Dhankar, a 21-year woman of Serla village, under Behal block of Bhiwani town in Haryana, was strangled to death by her father in the third week of March 2013 for marrying against her parents' wishes on 28 February 2013 with a boy Gautam, a resident of *Khap* and was with whom she had reportedly fallen in love. Both belonged to the Jat

community, but their parents were against love marriage. Confirming the honour killing, *Loharu* deputy superintendent of police Suresh Kumar Hooda said, "The victim's father was unhappy over her decision to marry against the family's wishes. He believed that love marriage would bring disrepute to the family."[31]

- A 19-year-old Dalit youth, E. Ilavarasan of Naikkankottal village in Dharamapuri district of Tamil Nadu, whose marriage to a Vanniyar girl Divya of upper caste led to caste tensions in Tamil Nadu last year, was found dead near a railway track in Dharmapur on 4th July 2013.[32]
- Twenty year old Nidhi Barak and twenty-three year old Dharmender Barak who were of same village of Garnaathi in district Rohtak, Haryana and of same gotra were killed in the village allegedly by girl's parents on 18 September 2013. It is said that both Nidhi and Dharmender, who were studing at institutes in Rohtak town, had been in a relationship for almost three years. The father of the boy who was beheaded did not report to the police fearing social bycott.[33]
- Minakshi a minor girl of Bapoli village at Panipat district of Haryana was killed for honour allegedly by her father and brothers on 22 September 2013. The girl was reportedly gone missing from her house a fortnight back and was recovered and brought back by family members about ten days ago. The family members suspected that she had eloped with a boy of Bahadurgarh village who belonged to a different caste while the girl was from barber community.[34]

4.1.2. Same-Village Marriage

- In the case of Sonia Devi and Rampal Dahiya of Asandha village in Jhajjar district of Haryana. The couple was married for over one year. Sonia was three month pregnant. The Rathi caste *Panchayat* of Asandha declared that the couple could only be brother and sister. The judgment was based on the rule that the husbands caste, inhibit the same village as Sonia's parents. At the *Panchayat* hearing Rampal was warned that he would be physically attacked if he would not tied a *rakhi*.

- The bodies of a young couple, Tejpal (24) belonged to the Swarn Samaj, his wife Sushila (20) a *Dalit*, who got married against the wishes of their parents in August 2012, were found hanging from a tree at Khera village in Bhiwani district of Haryana. Both were the residents of the same village. They got married at an Arya Samaj temple at Ghaziabad in Uttar Pradesh and got their marriage registered on August 14. Following this, they started living at Pilani in Rajasthan.[35]
- Meenakshi, 21, was shot dead by her father Surajmal in Nasirpur village, near Muzaffarnagar on 17 March 2013 as she was in a relationship with a boy of the same village and wanted to marry him.[36]

4.1.3. Kidnapping and Rape

- A 19-year-old Rohit Kumar, a resident of Sampla in Rohtak district of Haryana, who was facing a case in a juvenile court for allegedly kidnapping and raping a girl, was shot dead in a busy market in Sampla town of Rohtak on 20 February 2013. The girl, who was also a resident of Sampla, was minor at the time of the alleged kidnapping and rape in 2011.[37]

4.1.4. Inter-Religion Marriage

- Uma Chakravarti reported in a book that in India —a Hindu woman who had a relationship with a Muslim man, was dragged out of her house, stripped and killed, and then left on the street as an example to all other women of the punishment to be inflicted on women who transgressed the boundaries of communities.[38]

- In Nainital, Reshma Pravin, a Hindu girl, married Shahbuddin, a Muslim, against the wishes of her family in 2007. One year later her brothers killed their pregnant sister and her husband for marrying against their wishes. The court awarded life imprisonment to the culprits.[39]
- Rizwanur Rahman, a computer trainer, secretly married Priyanka. The Todi family took their daughter home for a few days. Rizwan was found dead near the railway tracks in Kolkata.[40]

REFERENCES

1. *The New York Times*, 24 May 2011.
2. *The Hindu*, 11 July 2010.
3. *Tribune*, 14 May 2010.
4. Human Rights Watch, "India: Prosecute Rampant 'Honour' Killings: Amend and Enforce Laws to End Barbaric Practice", 18 July 2010.
5. *Indian Express*, 30 July 2011.
6. *India Today*, 17 September 2010.
7. *The Guardian* (London), 10 October 2010.
8. *Times of India*, 9 July 2010.
9. *The Hindu*, 8 June 2011.
10. *Times of India*, 21 June 2010.
11. *Times of India*, "Crime and Punishment", 27 April 2011.
12. *The Australian*, 3 April 2010.
13. *International Business Times* (New York), 16 November 201 .
14. *Ibid.*, 12.
15. *Indian Express*, 27 May 2009.
16. *Indian Express*, 28 June 2009.
17. *Tribune*, "He Died for Her, but She Takes a U-turn", 25 July 2009.
18. *Indian Express*, 29 March 2010.
19. *Hindustan Times*, 4 May 2010.
20. *Times of India*, 28 June 2010.
21. *Times of India*, 13 July 2010.
22. *Times of India*, 14 July 2010.
23. *Times of India*, 20 July 2010.
24. *Times of India*, 16 February 2011.

25. *Mid-Day*, 15 February 2011.
26. *Times of India*, 28 January 2011.
27. *Tribune*, 2 February 2012.
28. *Times of India*, 15 January 2013.
29. *Times of India*. 29 June 2012.
30. *Hindu*, 11 March 2013, p. 3.
31. *Hindustan Times*, 30 March 2013, pp. 1, 4.
32. *Hindu*, 5 July 2013, p. 1.
33. *Tribune*, 19 September 2013
34. *Tribune*, 25 September 2013
35. *Indian Express*, 24 December 2012.
36. *Hindustan Times*, 17 April 2013.
37. *Times of India*, 21 February 2013.
38. Chakravarti, Uma, "Honour Crimes", Lynn Welchman and Sara Hossain (Eds.), pp. 308-331.
39. *Hindustan Times*, 19 May 2009.
40. *Times of India*, 9 May 2010.

5. Role of *Khaps*

Khaps are said to be playing a vital role in honour killings. They are against inter-caste or *gotra* marriages. The marriages within the same village are also banned by these caste panchayats. *Khaps* are also responsible for other actions such as issuing diktats, prescribing dress code for women and restricting their movement after sunset, beside preventing them using mobile phones. They are demanding amendment in the Hindu Marriage Act 1955 making same *gotra* marriages as invalid. To understand the role of khaps in honour killings, let us first understand the village exogamy and caste endogamy.

5.1. VILLAGE EXOGAMY

Exo means 'external' or 'outside' and the word gamy, which has its origin from Greek word *gamos,* means marriage. Simple meaning of exogamy is 'marriage outside' of a specific group especially as required by custom or law. The village for this purpose is treated as a specific group and the village exogamy, therefore, means marrying outside the village. Customary, village exogamy also means that all men and women of the same clan, the same localized clan and the same village are bound by the morality of brother-sister and, therefore, that both sex and marriage are prohibited between members of any of these units.[1]

5.2. CASTE ENDOGAMY

Let us define first the meaning of the word endogamy. Endogamy is the combination of two words i.e endo meaning–'internal' or 'within' + Greek word *gamos* meaning 'marriage'. *Oxford dictionary* defines endogamy as the custom of marrying only within the limits of a local community, clan, or tribe. Caste endogamy therefore means a custom of marrying only within caste.

Caste system has two important distinct features difference and hierarchy. These features are widely acknowledged and accepted. To maintain these features, the principle of strict caste endogamy has to be followed. Inter-caste marriages create differences between different caste groups and disturb the recognized caste hierarchies. Therefore, anyone daring to transgress this law is out-casted, expelled or worse killed as a result.[2]

Let us now define *Khap*, population represented by it, its social recognition, constitutional validity, powers, nature of functionality and difference between *panchayati raj* system and *Khap panchayat*.

5.3. MEANING OF *KHAP*

The origin of the word *Khap* is disputable. Some scholars believe that *Khap* in *Sanskrit* is short form of the word *Khapur* meaning sky kingdom. Some traces its origin in *Hindi* words *Khappar* and *Chappar* meaning roof. But the meaning of these words do not reflect the functioning of present day *Khaps*. The word *Khap* is probably originated from a word *Khap* means deep thinking or discussion and the word *Khap* may be a broader word of *Khap* means an assembly of peoples of praticular caste or community or area resolvign disputes amicably by discussions. *Khap* is, therefore, an endogamous institution of clan. It is a *gotra* centric *panchayat* and covers a cluster of villages dominated by a particular gotra. *Khaps* mostly exist around Delhi, Haryana, Western Uttar Pradesh, Punjab and adjoining areas.

5.4. REPRESENTATION AND POWERS OF *KHAP*

Khap is represented by community or caste. Community, which is also known as *biradari*, refers to not just one concrete structural unit at the village level but rather to patrilineal connection, real, putative or fictional and includes the agnates and cognates. It sometimes refers to the entire village, irrespective of the differences in caste, class or creed.[3] Each caste has its own *biradari* to enforce its rules but when the matter cannot be settled by the caste *Panchayat* of a particular caste group due to few households of that caste in a village, it is usually referred to the dominant caste of region which then assumes the power of enforcing the internal behaviour of the endogamous group.[4] Observing the norms of the *biradari* is must for the *izzat* honour of the caste, group or village.

Khap (caste) Panchayats define their own rules and regulations by running their own parallel judicial institution to the courts. They declare socially unaccepted marriages null and void. It is alleged that in some cases they announce death penalty for those violating the socially accepted traditions of *gotra* marriages to restore faith in the orthodox approaches of the rural people.

Lt. Gen. (Retd.) D. P. Vats traces the history of *Khap panchayats* with King Harsha Vardhan Bains who, according to him, consolidated the Sarva khap panchayats in 643 A.D.

5.5. SOCIAL RECOGNITION OF *KHAP*

The *Khap Panchayats* have no statutory social recognition. The 73rd and 74th Constitutional amendments of 1993 had devolved a significant amount of power over social sector and development planning to local level governments or *panchayats*. Even after that their voices continue to be heard. The Legislation doesn't dare to pass any laws for the enforcement of these amendments due to the support the local MLA's and MP's receive during election campaigns from the *Khap Panchayats*. Lt. Gen. (Retd.) D.P. Vats considers *Khaps* as the most effective mass-based custodians of social customs and traditions in rural India.

5.6. PANCHAYATI RAJ AND *KHAP*

Panchayati Raj, a decentralized form of Government where each village is responsible for its own affairs, is the foundation of Indian political system. The word "*panchayat*" literally means "assembly" (*ayat*) of five (*panch*) wise and respected elders chosen and accepted by the local community. Mahatma Gandhi advocated it as Gram Swaraj ("village self-governance"). Balwant Rai Mehta Committee, appointed by the Government of India in January 1957, recommended the launching of *Panchayati Raj* Institutions throughout the country to establish 'democratic decentralisation.'

The 3-tier *Panchayati Raj* system—*Gram Panchayat* at the village level, *Panchayat Samiti* at the block level, and *Zila Parishad* at the district level was adopted by state governments during the 1950s and 60s, as laws were passed to establish *panchayats* in various states.

It also found backing in the Indian Constitution with the 73rd amendment in 1992 to accommodate the idea. The Amendment Act of 1992 contains provision for devolution of powers and responsibilities to the *panchayats* both for the preparation of economic development plans and social justice, as well as for implementation in relation to 29 subjects listed in the eleventh schedule of the Constitution.

But what the leaders could not have envisaged was the mental freeze of culture and the problems the system would create with coping up to the fast growing and modernizing India. These values of local governance seemed to have been frozen in times of orthodox practices like, untouchability, rigidity of caste system and *gotra* marriage system, inter religion orthodoxy, *sati* system and so on. With the passage of time these traditional *Panchayats* became so powerful that to go against them became electorally suicidal. It is perhaps because of this that the Chief Minister of Haryana, Bhupinder Singh Hooda has declared *Khaps* as a part of the social structure and preservers of age old traditions in rural Haryana.

Caste *Panchayat* usually enforces conduct appropriate to the caste. The caste and village councils exercise complete control on an individual's conduct. Being part of the socio-political life of village communities, they are informal, decision-making, caste based bodies consisting of the elderly and wise men drawn from their respective castes. They are mostly dominated by the land-owning class and the upper caste members who are not elected or self-appointed but are the members by consensus of the community and sometimes hold the post by heredity.[5] Since caste perpetuates through the institution of marriage, the dominant caste in the region arrogates to itself the power of regulating the marriage behaviour of the endogamous groups. The size and composition of the *panchayat* vary with the gravity of the problem.[6]

It is a fact that *Panchayati raj* (rule) is increasingly becoming a training ground for leadership at higher levels, and it is widely felt that the state leaderships may emerge from these institutions.[7] Therefore, it receives plenty leverage from the higher state authorities when it comes to *ultra vires* decisions made by the *Panchayats*.

5.7. LEGAL AND CONSTITUTIONAL POSITION OF *KHAP*

Khap panchayats are neither legal nor constitutional entities. Only the *Panchayats* constituted under the provisions of Constitution of India have legal powers. In *Manoj and Babli murder case* the Karnal sessions court judge had said that the

Khap had no say at any stage except that it condemned incestuous marital relationship. The judge 'criticised the *Khap Panchayats* for functioning contrary to the Constitution and said they had become a law unto themselves'. No gathering of individuals can take the place of judicial courts and run their own parallel judicial institution. They are *ultra vires* to the spirit of the Constitution of India. The session court, in this case, convicted the *Khap Panchayat* leader along with six others.

On the other hand, the Chief Minister of Haryana, Bhupinder SIngh Hooda, while denying "*Khaps* have any legal sanctity, said that *Khaps* are a part of the social structure and are preserving age old traditons."[8] Similarly, Mr. Yashpal Malik, president of the All-India Jat Arakshan Sangharsh Samiti, also was of the view that *khaps* have a social responsibility regarding protecting the customs.[9]

5.8. MARRIAGES AND *KHAPS*

Khaps neither recognize the basic human rights or liberty of an individual nor the ideological changes that are taking place in spheres of gender equality and the struggle against discrimination. *Khaps* have been hitting back, often mercilessly those youngsters defying the family control over the institution of marriage.[10] Marriages within the neighbouring villages belonging to other *Khaps* are also banned. Any marriage in violation of these rules is met with stringent punishments and barbaric edicts by the *Khap Panchayat*s like annulling the marriage, declaring the married couple as siblings and dissolving their marital tie, ostracizing the families and ordering killings,[11] temporary or permanent ex-communication, corporal punishment, religious expiation and forcing the girl to divorce her husband. Death executed by the caste *Panchayats* is one of the worst articulations of violence. Usually, violence and death are considered preferable to condoning or accepting a mixed marriage.[12] The sanctions also include nominal or substantial fining, ritual expiation, public humiliation which means blackening the face or rubbing the nose in the dust before the aggrieved party or the entire gathering, touching other's feet, shaving the head or drinking or dipping the nose in the urine of one or more persons, beating, giving feast to the caste members, out-casting, expelling from the village or requiring the offender to repent by seeking forgiveness of the village elderly. Out-casting being serious punishment requires an inter-village *Panchayat* of the caste members.[13]

Thus, the much disapproved inter-caste marriages are usually resolved by the family members in a confidential way by forceful elimination of the couple or the girl. But, when the news spreads in the wider community, it is tackled by the community acting through the traditional caste *Panchayat* wielding wide dictatorial power as extra-judicial authorities, with almost no legal knowledge and imposing justice according to its notions.

Applying and enforcing repressive gender and caste codes, they attempt to operate as parallel legal systems in the country. The intervention of these traditional bodies has been at the cost of individual rights, more particularly woman's rights.[14] In many cases, even if a family approves an inter-caste marriage or itself arranges such marriage, the caste *Panchayat*s have objected to such marriages and have penalized the families by expelling them from the *biradari* or by socially boycotting them.[15]

As we know that difference and hierarchy are the two most widely acknowledged and characteristic features of the caste system. To maintain these characteristics, the principle of strict caste endogamy has to be maintained. Inter-caste marriages lead to a blurring of the differences between different caste groups and disturb the recognized caste hierarchies.[16] *Khaps* are totally against *gotra* marriages and declare these marriages as immoral. *Khap* Maha-*Panchayat*, in its recent statement told that honour killings cannot be avoided in same *gotra* marriages since they are immoral in the Hindu society and should be banned and the guilty should be punished.[17] The *Sarv Khap Panchayat*, in an affidavit filed before the Supreme Court hearing a PIL by NGO *Shakti Vahini* denied allegations of promoting honour killings while expressing its reservations against same *gotra* marriage. Lt. Gen.(Retd.) D. P. Vats, while explaining the reasons against same-gotra and same village marriage in an affidavit in the Supreme Court said, "Established by ancient sages, intra-gotra marriages are not customary, hence objected to. These are based on established findings of medical science and genetics. In-breeding results in and accentuates genetically transmitted diseases while cross-breeding dilutes and diminishes these diseases effectively." According to him, by avoiding same-gotra marriages and tying of nuptial knot among blood relations, dangers and adverse effects of consanguinity and in-breeding are checked." The *khap* also demanded amendment in the Hindu Marriage Act 1955 to debar marriages in the same *gotra*.[18] Same kind of views were expressed by the Gathwala (Malik) *Khap* of Jats in northern India. It claimed that no *Khap Panchayat* had given decision of killings. However, the *Khap* also demanded an amendment in the Hindu Marriage Act, saying that the government should ban same *gotra* marriages.[19]

Sarva Khap Mahapanchayat, in a meeting held on 22 September 2013 in the backdrop of recent honour killing of a runaway couple at Garnawathi village of Rohtak district in Haryana asked the Central government to immediately amend sections of the Hindu Marriage Act 1955 to restrain couples from same gotra and same village from entering into wedlock. The Mahapanchayat also demanded the reintroduction of moral education subject at the school and college level. It also asked the Central government to take appropriate measures to curb pornography on mobile phones. The meeting was presided over by Dada Baljit Singh Malik, presedent of the Malik Gathwala Khap and was attended by repersentatives of various Khaps, including Khaps of Jhakkar, Hoods, Kadian, Dahiya and Rohrai-Panchgama. Jasbir Singh Malik, the convenor of the

Mahapanchayat, while expressing concern and grief over the Garnawathi killings said, "as soon as the change in the Hindu Marriage Act is promulgated, the couples would themselves refrain from such alliances and this would curb the honour killings, which have become a blot on society."[20]

Meanwhile, Barha Khap panchayat of Jhajjar district in Haryana issued a diktat on 22 September 2013 barring girls of 12 villages from wearing jeans and using mobile phones to curb honour killings. Barah Birohar *Khap* and Sarv Khap Haryana, defended these restrictions on girls in the name of upholding societal morals. They said that wearing of a pair of jeans, going for a drive with a male friend or even talking on a mobile phone is the "unconventional behaviour of the girls and young women. These *Khaps* believe that 'a woman should be covered from head to the toe in loose fitting clothes that do not attract the male eye.'[21] The village surpanch Rajesh Kumar, who was of the view that "often girls, especially college-going, wear provocative cloths, inviting attention of boys. It results into crimes against women," he said.[22] The Khap panchayats in the region are said to have set up secret units to tail college girls violating the rule.[23]

*Khap Panchayat*s may be notorious for issuing diktats in cases of honour killings but not a single case has been registered against them anywhere in Haryana since 2001. Though, according to Jagmati Sangwan a woman activist, the involvement of *Khap Panchayat*s in honour killings had been quite clear and "the *Khap* leaders are accused in many cases like Kaithal's *Manoj Babli* case and *Sonia Rampal* honour killing case in Jind district, the police had booked the *Khap* leaders as individuals and not as representatives of the *Khap*".[24]

In Jondhi and Asanda villages of Jhajjar district *Khap panchayats* declared married couples as siblings. In Paintawas and Samaspur in Bhiwani district *khaps* declared the marriages as viod. However, in both the cases later on they retracted because of High Court guidelines and public outcry. Not only this, *Khaps* were helping families of victims moneytary also. The appeal of Gathwala khap head at its conclave held at Kurukshetra on April 13, 2010 for contributing ten Rupees each to help the killers of *manoj-babli* is an evidence of financial help by *khaps*.

It is also alleged that *Khaps* are indirectly promoting honour killings. They persuade the family members of the deviant girl indirectly by making their life in the village unbearable by taunts and sneers. It was this psyche that drove the father of the girl in Girnawati, near Raohtak, to murder the couple. However, Dr. Prem Singh Dahiya said the *Khaps*' role is hyped by the media and the so-called modernists. Khaps do not mould the psyche of the people when they themselves are deeply rooted in thier traditions and customs which are handed down to them over the centuries.[25]

5.9. DECISION-MAKING METHODS

For deciding a matter, the traditional *Panchayat* mobilizes a large number of people on the basis of family, kin, *gotra*, caste, community and village, even from outside the local area, making the *Panchayat* all the more powerful. The dominant caste leaders settle the dispute of the castes below them only by the unanimous consensus of the presiding leaders. If they do not agree, the *Panchayat* meeting is dissolved without any decision being taken. Later, either a similar *Panchayat* or a larger *Panchayat* involving many more villages is reconvened. Any decision to which the powerful elements in the village strongly oppose cannot be taken. But a powerful person can ignore the wishes of the majority, if he had not participated in the decision or disagrees with it. Once the decision is taken, its enforcement is the responsibility of the leaders of the village in which the penalized party lives.[26] If anyone venturing to transgress this law, is out-casted, expelled or worse killed as a result. For the execution of punishment, the *Khap Panchayats* do not afford the luxury of having a standby executing police force, instead they count on irrational of mob thinking. This mob then makes believe to each member that their actions are a justified reaction. Khaps consider such cleansing as mere settling of the disturbed balance. The Indian social set up operates as the major catalyzing factor behind the increasing rate of the honour crimes committed against women in India.

At the time of newly gained independence of India, it was felt that the land was difficult to administer due to its wide spread geographic area. The leaders of new independent India believed that people are best left to govern themselves and this was the ideology behind the freedom struggle. Implementing these principles they believed that due to the lack of infrastructure and administrative set up, it would be best to set up local governance structure which would deal with local village level affairs directly. This led to the growth of *Panchayati Raj*. However, *Khap* (caste) *Panchayat*s in some parts of India define their own laws by running their own parallel judicial institution to the courts. Not only do these *Khap* (caste) *Panchayat*s declare marriages null and void, but also go beyond by awarding death as a punishment in many cases. These killings are used to restore faith in the orthodox approaches of the rural people. They believe that these socially unapproved marriages must be punished by extreme measures, including death. Legally speaking, under the Hindu Marriage Act (1955) which is the governing law of the land on marriage in India, except for the observation of certain prohibited degrees of relationship, legal restrictions on the choice of marriage partner are almost non-existent. This implies that under the law, both *agora* (kin in the patrilineal line of descent whose members claim descent from the same *gotra* ancestor) and inter-caste marriages are permitted. Thus the Act makes the functioning of the *Khap Panchayat*s not only obsolete but *ultra vires* the law Despite of that the Khaps still seem to flourish in north India due to the political support that they hold or enjoy.

To conclude we can say that though village *Panchayats* formed under the *Panchayati Raj* system are the elected and constitutional bodies of local self government with economic and social powers but caste or community *Panchayats* dominate them. Caste *Panchayats* are *ultra vires* to the Constitution of India and are illegal even then their dictations are being obeyed by the community fearing out-caste. The need of the hour is to strengthen the *Panchayati Raj* system and defy the illegal orders of *Khaps*.

REFERENCES

1. Hershman, P., *Punjabi Kinship and Marriage,* Delhi, Hindustan Publishing Corporation, 1981.
2. Chowdhry, Prem, "Caste *Panchayats* and the Policing of Marriage in Haryana: Enforcing Kinship and Territorial Exogamy", *Contribution to Indian Sociology* (January 2004), 38(1-2), pp. 1-42.
3. Chowdhary, P., *Contentious Marriages, Eloping Couples: Caste and Patriarchy in Northern India*, New Delhi, Oxford University Press, 2007, pp. 95-96.
4. *Ibid.*, p. 150.
5. Chowdhary, P., *Contentious Marriages, Eloping Couples: Caste and Patriarchy in Northern India*, New Delhi, Oxford University Press, 2007, pp. 33-35, 96.
6. *Ibid.*, pp. 97-98.
7. Bathla, Har Bhagwan, *Panchayati Raj and Political Parties: An Empirical Study at Grass-Root Level in Haryana,* Kurukshetra: Nirmal Book Agency, 1994.
8. *Tribune*, 6 Oct. 2013, p. 1.
9. *Tribune*, 11 Oct. 2013, p. 4.
10. *Telegraph*, "Calcutta, India—Court Comes to Sibling Couples Rescue." 16 October 2004.
11. Chaudhry, D.R., "Feudal Mindset: In the Heart of Darkness," *Deccan Herald*, 1 August 2010.
12. Chowdhary, P., *Contentious Marriages, Eloping Couples: Caste and Patriarchy in Northern India*, New Delhi, Oxford University Press, 2007, p. 163.
13. *Ibid.*, pp. 98-100.

14. *Ibid.*, pp. 12-14, 139.
15. *Ibid.*, pp. 168-72.
16. Chowdhry, Prem, "Caste *Panchayats* and the Policing of Marriage in Haryana: Enforcing Kinship and Territorial Exogamy", *Contribution to Indian Sociology* (January 2004), 38(1-2), pp. 1-42.
17. Pandey, S., "Talking Tough : *Khap Panchayats* Refuse to Mend Medieval Way", *Deccan Herald*, 15 November 2010.
18. *Hindustan Times*, 20 February 2013, p. 2.
19. *Tribune*, 20 February 2013, p. 7.
20. *Tribune*, 23 September 2013.
21. Dogra, Chander Suta, "Women should be Covered from Head to Toe," *Hindu*, 19 Oct. 2013, p.1
22. *Hindustan Times*, 24 September 2013.
23. *Hindustan Times*, 26 September 2013.
24. *Times of India*, 15 January 2013.
25. Dahiya, Prem Singh, "Khaps subscibe to Indian Philosophy," *Tribune*, 15 Oct. 2013, p. 8.
26. Chowdhary, P., *Contentious Marriages, Eloping Couples: Caste and Patriarchy in Northern India*, New Delhi, Oxford University Press, 2007, pp. 98-100.

6. Law Commission Recomendations

The continuing barbarity, retrograde practice of caste discrimination, strong patriarchal structure of society and role of *Khaps, the* caste *panchayats,* in promoting violence that ends in murder, separation or social boycott necessitated a strong legislation to deal with honour crimes. Various organizations—both governmental and non-governmental—suggested different measures to deal with this growing problem. The All India Democratic Women's Association (AIDWA), a voluntary body looking after the welfare of women, prepared a draft legislation to combat honour killings and submitted that to the Central Government which in turn made this reference to the Law Commission of India in 2009 asking it to examine various aspects relating to honour killings. The Commission was headed by Justice (Retd.) P. V. Reddi. Its other members were Justice (Retd.) Shiv Kumar Sharma and Amarjit Singh.

The Commission, in its report '*Prevention of Interference with the Freedom of Matrimonial Alliances (in the name of Honour and Tradition): A Suggested Legal Framework*' traced the trend of honour killings in the world, including India and highlighted reasons for increase of such crimes. It also recommended certain measures to cap the honour crimes.

6.1. FINDINGS

Following were some the major findings of the Law Commission.

6.1.1. Marriage and Gotra System

While tracing the causes of honour killings the Commission disclosed that "the honour crimes mostly occur as a result of people marrying without their family's acceptance and for marrying outside their caste or religion. Marriages between the couple belonging to same *Gotra* (family name) have also often led to violent reaction from the family members or the community members. The Caste councils or *Panchayat*s popularly known as '*Khap Panchayat*s' try to adopt the chosen course of 'moral vigilantism' and enforce their diktats by assuming to themselves the role of social or community guardians."

The Commission also discussed the dimensions of problem and stressed upon the need for a separate law for honour killings. Expressing grave concern on the matters of rising cases of honour killings, the Commission criticised the role played by the caste or community *Panchayat*s in this regard and suggested that "if they exceed their limits, as it is often happening, impose their decisions in matters relating to matrimony and interfere with the legitimate choices of youngsters and indulge in acts of endangering their life and liberty, the law cannot remain a silent spectator in our progressive democratic polity wedded to cherished constitutional values."

6.1.2. Khap Panchayats

The Commission noticed frequent intervention of '*Khap Panchayat*s' and '*Katta Panchayat*s' in the occurrence of offences relating to honour crimes and was of the view that the penal law lacks direct application to the illegal acts of such caste assemblies. It further said that the practice of *Khap Panchayats* taking law into their own hands and pronouncing on the invalidity and impropriety of *Sagotra* and inter-caste marriages and handing over punishment to the couple and pressurizing the family members to execute their verdict by any means amounts to flagrant violation of rule of law and invasion of personal liberty of the persons affected. The Commission said "that the views of village elders or family elders cannot be forced on the willing couple and no one has a right to use force or impose far-reaching sanctions in the name of community or family honour. The Commission took strong exception to the drastic actions, including wrongful confinement, persistent harassment, mental torture, bodily harm infliction of or threats of severe taken by close relations or some third parties against the so-called erring couple either on the exhortations of some or all the *Panchayatdars* or with their connivance.

In order to effectively check the existing social malady the Law Commission proposed a Bill to be known as the 'Prohibition of Interference with the Freedom of Matrimonial Alliances Bill'. Following were some of the salient features of the Commission's report.

6.2.1. Salient Features

Treating the honour killings as threat to social order and peace, the Commission noted that, "the powerful influence of the caste or community *Panchayats* and the aggressive role played by them in controlling the freedom of choice of marrying couple is the root cause of honour related crimes. There must be a check on such unwarranted interference by the members of *Panchayats*. The couple marrying against the wishes of members of the bodies like *Khap Panchayats* ought not to be driven to a state of insecurity and misery. Their life and liberty is 'endangered' because they are exposed to threats and socio-economic deprivations. The close family members of the couple are also brought into the picture to enforce the diktats of such informal body of *Panchayats*/councils. This is directly affecting the community and the family life in the villages, thereby posing a threat to social order and peace."

The Commission further felt that there is a need to divest the *Panchayatdars* or caste 'elders' of their self assumed hegemony and controlling influence in these matters. It was of the opinion that there should be a threshold bar against the congregation or assembly for the purpose of disapproving an intended marriage or the conduct of the young couple and this objectionable conduct of the *Panchayatdars* should be brought within the purview of penal law.

To render the convening and conduct of such assemblies unlawful and punishable two sections proposed in the bill were Section 3, which made the acts endangering liberty punishable, and Section 4 with criminal intimidation by the members of unlawful assembly or others to secure compliance with the illegal decision of the assembly. Such acts of criminal intimidations which are punishable in the Indian Penal Codes were specifically introduced for the purpose of meting out higher punishment to those members of unlawful assembly. The criminal acts other than those falling under the three penal provisions of the Act can still be dealt with under the provisions of the Penal Code including the provisions relating to abetment and conspiracy. Section 5 was introduced to make it clear that the provisions of Sections 2, 3, and 4 of the proposed Bill are without prejudice to the provisions of IPC.

For sufficient deterrent effect, a mandatory minimum punishment was prescribed while taking care to see that such punishment has an element of proportionality. The District Magistrate or the SDM were given powers to take preventive measures and to take note of the information laid before them by the marrying couple or their family members and to extend necessary protection to them.

The officials were made accountable for the failure or

omission on their part to take necessary steps to prevent unlawful assembly (caste *Panchayat*s, etc.) or to give protection to the targeted couple. It was provided that the offences shall be tried by a Court of Sessions in the District presided over by the Sessions Judge or Additional Sessions Judge as notified by the High Court.

The unlawful assembly under the Indian Penal Code and the unlawful assembly contemplated by Section 2 of the proposed Bill were not the same. Moreover, a punishment higher than that prescribed for unlawful assembly under IPC has been prescribed under Section 2. As regards Section 4 dealing with criminal intimidation was introduced with a view to provide for higher punishment in the case of acts of criminal intimidation by the members of unlawful assembly within the meaning of this proposed Bill.

6.2.2. Autonomy of Choices and Liberty

The autonomy of every person in matters concerning oneself—a free and willing creator of one's own choices and decisions—is now central to all thinking on community order and organization. Such autonomy with its manifold dimensions is a constitutionally protected value and is central to an open society and civilized order. Duly secured individual autonomy, exercised on informed understanding of the values integral to one's well being is deeply connected to a free social order. Coercion against individual autonomy will then become least necessary.

In moments and periods of social transition, the tensions between individual freedom and past social practices become focal points of the community's ability to contemplate and provide for least hurting or painful solutions. The wisdom or wrongness of certain community perspectives and practices, their intrinsic impact on liberty, autonomy and self-worth, as well as the parents' concern over impulsive and unreflective choices—all these factors come to the forefront of consideration.

The problem, however, is the menacing phenomena of repressive social practices in the name of honour triggering violent reaction from the influential members of community who are blind to individual autonomy.

The proposed bill focused on the conduct which endangers life and liberty and highlighted the civilizing perceptions on liberty and autonomy. Social protection has consistently been the paramount goal of modern criminal law. Criminal punishment typically achieves such protection through its capacity to motivate people to conform to socially acceptable rules of behaviour with threats of serious penalties for non-conformity. "Punishment serves as a weapon which society uses to prevent conduct which harms or threatens to harm its interests" the largest social interests or community values cannot be judged by a handful of influential persons whose beliefs are grounded in superstition and dogmas totally opposed to constitution and the laws.

The self-styled *Panchayats* or assembly of people constitute a close knit section of people bonded by certain common perspectives and values. Caste plays a pivotal role in this bondage. While these assembly of people may be playing some role in protecting certain basic cultural mores, their deviant role in subjecting to peril the life and liberty of persons who do not conform to their views and values cannot be condoned and it needs to be directly tackled and necessarily subjected to the disciplines of law. The law should aim at counter and domineering position of the caste/Community *Panchayats* in so far as they act as centres of coercion and intimidation Regard and respect for life, liberty and autonomy of persons need to be the larger focus and the perceived strength of such assemblies or combinations will have to be appropriately dealt with by law.

6.2.3. Honour Killing and Section 300 of IPC

The Commission refused to introduce a provision in Section 300 IPC in order to bring the so-called 'honour killings' within the ambit of this provision. The existing provisions in IPC are adequate enough to deal with such situations leading to overt acts of killing or causing bodily harm to the targeted person who allegedly undermined the honour of the caste or community. The Commission was of the view that motive behind killing a person does not furnish real justification to introduce a separate provision in section 300. The provision if introduced may create confusion and interpretational difficulties.

6.2.4. Burden of Proof

Further, the commission opined that "shifting the burden of proof on the basis of mere accusations of involvement in the serious offence of murder etc. or abetment is not desirable. It will be against the cardinal principles of jurisprudence accepted and absorbed into our criminal justice system. It is neither logic nor rationale in treating the accused in the so-called honour killing cases as a separate class in the matter of application of doctrine of burden of proof. Moreover, the difficulties in proof before a court of law may not by itself be a legitimate ground to deviate from the well established canons of criminal jurisprudence. Any attempt to drastically expand the rigour of criminal procedure to cope up with ad hoc situations may be counter-productive.

So far as presumptions are concerned the commission expressed that Penal law handles proof of facts by direct and circumstantial evidence. Principles of inference and logic are involved in both modes of proof. Statutes relating to evidence have engaged themselves in grappling with problems of natural non-availability or paucity of evidence in certain offence situations. Presumptions have usually emerged as a tool of logic to fill these gaps. Presumptions state cause-effect relationships in such circumstances. Care must, however, be taken to ensure that the causal link is not too remote or too thin. Presumptions generally do not affect the position of burden of proof but only shift the burden of evidence or the burden of persuasion. The presumption which is eminently suitable in the context of the present problem is the one incorporated in Section 6 of the proposed Bill. It raises a presumption to the effect that the participants in unlawful assembly intended to commit and abet the offences punishable under Section 3 and 4 of the Bill in order to carry out the illegal decision taken by them. Such presumption will supply an important link in the chain of evidence. The presumption proposed to be introduced is as follows: Every person participating in an unlawful assembly, shall be presumed to have also intended to commit or abet the commission of offences under Section 3 and 4 of the Act.

Thus, in respect of the overt acts under Sections 3 and 4, this presumption would be attracted. On a fair balance of various conflicting considerations, we feel that the presumption as above would be appropriate and effective.

In the matter of burden of proof, the Commission felt that the analogy sought to be drawn from the provisions of the Commission of Sati (Prevention) Act, 1987 is not appropriate for more than one reason. 'Sati' is a barbaric, deeply entrenched social evil which was prevalent in certain parts of the country. The magnitude and seriousness of that evil cannot be compared to the problem on hand. More important, the offence of 'Sati' always remained an open affair with all the rituals and ceremonies attached to it and the persons actively participating therein could be identified without difficulty. The accusations in such cases are based on solid evidence.

6.2.5. Registration of Marriage

The Commission also suggested that to avoid unnecessary hassles and harassment from external sources directed against the couple who are intending to marry and even their family members who would like to go according to their wishes, the Special Marriage Act should be simplified.

The time gap between the date of giving notice of marriage and the registration should be removed and the entire process of registration of marriage should be expedited. The domicile restriction should also be removed.

REFERENCES

1. http//lawcommissionofindia.nic.in.

7. Laws Relating to Honour Killings

Honour killings, as we have seen, is a world problem. To stamp-out this problem many international organizations have come forward. The United Nations, European Union, Human Rights Watch, Amnesty International and others have passed various resolutions, declarations, conventions to protect the rights of women. International law obligates member states to protect women from gender-based violence, including by family members, and to disqualify "honour" as a legal defence for acts of violence against women.

7.1. INTERNATIONAL LAWS

There have been various international laws that deal with cases relating to honour and crimes thereof. Organizations like the United Nations, European Union, Human Rights Commission etc. have taken various initiatives to restore the honour and dignity of women in different environments. Important of them are:

7.1.1. European Union Resolution

In 2009 European Parliamentary Assembly passed a Resolution No. 1681 which noted the dire need to address honour crimes. The resolution stated that: "On so-called 'honour crimes,' the Parliamentary Assembly notes that the problem, far from diminishing, has worsened, including in Europe. It mainly affects women, who are its most frequent victims, both in Europe and the rest of the world, especially in patriarchal and fundamentalist communities and societies. For this reason, it asked the Council of Europe member states to 'draw up and put into effect national action plans to combat violence against women, including violence committed in the name of so-called 'honour,' if they have not already done so".[1]

7.1.2. Human Rights Violation

'Honour killings' are an extreme and brutal abuse of human rights. It violates the most basic of human rights—the right to life—as well as every other article in the International Convention on Human Rights (1948). The presence of laws that treat 'honour killings' leniently is also a brazen disregard of the International Convention of Civil and Political Rights (1966), protecting individuals against the use of the death penalty except for the most serious of crimes.

7.1.3. Right to Marry

Right to marry with a person of his/her own choice was recognized in Article 1651 of the Universal Declaration of Human Rights, 1948. Article 16 and 23 of the United Nations International Covenant on Civil and Political Rights 1976, also recognizes the right of men and women of marriageable age to marry and have a family.

Article 16 of the convention says:—

1. Men and women of full age, without any limitation due to race, nationality or religion, have the right to marry and to found a family. They are entitled to equal rights as to marriage, during marriage and at its dissolution.
2. Marriage shall be entered into only with the free and full consent of the intending spouses.
3. The family is the natural and fundamental group unit of society and is entitled to protection by society and the State.

Article 23 of the convention says:—

1. The family is the natural and fundamental group unit of society and is entitled to protection by society and the State.
2. The right of men and women of marriageable age to marry and to found a family shall be recognized.
3. No marriage shall be entered into without the free and full consent of the intending spouses.
4. States Parties to the present Covenant shall take appropriate steps to ensure equality.[2]

7.1.4. UN Declaration on the Elimination of Violence Against Women (1993)

Article 1 of the above Declaration proclaim that "the term 'violence against women' means "any act of gender-based violence that results in, or is likely to result in, physical, sexual or psychological harm or suffering to women, including threats of such acts, coercion or arbitrary deprivation of liberty, whether occurring in public or in private life".[3]

7.1.5. UN Fourth World Conference on Women

The Platform for Action on Women's Human Rights from the UN Fourth World Conference on Women calls upon states to "take urgent action to combat and eliminate violence against women, which is a human rights violation resulting from harmful traditional or customary practices, cultural prejudices and extremism".[4]

7.1.6. International Covenant on Civil and Political Rights (ICCPR)

The International Covenant on Civil and Political Rights (ICCPR) asserts that "every human being has the inherent right to life" in addition to "the right to liberty and security of person".

7.1.7. Convention on the Elimination of All Forms of Discrimination Against Women (1979)

'Honour killings' also violate the provisions of Convention on the Elimination of All Forms of Discrimination against Women (1979).

Article 1 of the Convention states that:

> "For the present Convention, the term 'discrimination against women' shall mean any distinction, exclusion, or restriction made on the basis of sex which has the effect or purpose of impairing or nullifying the recognition, enjoyment or exercise by women, irrespective of their marital status, on the basis of equality of men and women, of human rights and fundamental freedoms in political, economic, social, cultural, civil or any other field."

Article 2 states that "States Parties condemn discrimination against women in all its forms, agree to pursue by all appropriate means and without delay a policy of eliminating discrimination against women and, to this end, undertake:

(c) To establish legal protection of the rights of women on an equal basis with men and to ensure through competent national tribunals and other public institutions the effective protection of women against any act of discrimination;

(f) To take all appropriate measures, including legislation, to modify or abolish existing laws, regulations, customs and practices which constitute discrimination against women;

(g) To repeal all national penal provisions which constitute discrimination against women."

This UN charter has been signed by 186 countries world-wide—

over 90 per cent of the members of the United Nations—including most countries where 'honour killing' occurs. 'Honour killings' violate both the wording and the spirit of this law. India is also a part of it.[5]

7.1.8. Human Rights Council

The UN General Assembly also adopted a Resolution 55/66 that established the Human Rights Council back in 2006 stated "that the Council shall be responsible for promoting universal respect for the protection of all human rights and fundamental freedoms for all, without distinction of any kind and in a fair and equal manner".

Thus we can see that International Laws on Human Rights are against Honour killings and are in no mood to save it in the name of "cultural or traditional rights".

7.2. INDIAN LAWS

Indian laws against honour killings can be viewed in the light of status of women in ancient and present days. Though India is worried about rising crimes against women after independence its roots are lying in the mentality of society which never gave equal treatment to women even in family. Caste system and traditional rules for marriage are still being followed. The rights of women in ancient India are prescribed in various Hindu scriptures like *Manusmriti, Srimad Bhagwad Geeta and Rigveda.*

Manusmriti, the ancient source of Hindu Law, is very vocal regarding the rights of woman. It emphasized upon, by X.63, *Ahimsa Dharma*, abstention from injuring others ought to be upheld by all the four castes. *Manusmriti* III.55 prescribes highest respect, regard and protection for women by their fathers, brothers, husbands and brothers-in-law throughout their life because the welfare of all of them is possible only, if they are honoured and adorned. *Manusmriti* III.57 states that if the women folk live in grief then the whole family perishes but the house prospers if they are happy. Thus, there is the need to protect the rights of all in the society including the women for protecting *Dharma*, lest all will get destroyed. (*Manusmriti*, VIII.15).[6,7]

Rigveda, *Mandala* 5, *Sukta* 60, *Mantra* 5 emphasizes that none is superior (*ajyestasaha*) or inferior (*akanishthasha*). Since all are brothers, need is to strive collectively for the interest and progress of all.

Article 51(e) of the Indian Constitution enumerates the fundamental duty to promote harmony and the spirit of common brotherhood amongst all people of India transcending religious, linguistic and regional or sectional diversities and to renounce practices derogatory to the dignity of women.

7.2.1. Laws Relating to Marriage

Before embarking on Penal laws relating to honour killings we may first discuss laws relating to marriage.

Hindu Marriage Disabilities Removal Act, 1946

The Hindu Marriage Disabilities Removal Act, 1946 was enacted with a view to dispel any doubts in regard to *sagotra* or inter-caste marriages. The Act expressly declared the validity of marriages between the Hindus belonging to the same '*gotra*' or '*pravara*' or different sub-divisions of same caste.

Indian Civil Marriage Act, 1954

Marriages amongst the Hindus, Sikhs, Muslims, Jains and Christians are performed according to the customary ceremonies of their respective religion or communities. Under the Indian Civil Marriage Act, 1954 civil marriages are performed to avoid social taboos and ostensibly to save the heavy costs involved in traditional marriages.

The main purpose of the Special Marriage Act, 1954 was to provide a special form of marriage for the people of India and all Indian nationals in foreign countries, irrespective of the religion or faith followed by either party. The Act permits any person, irrespective of religion to perform marriage. The only condition of marriage is the bridegroom must be 21 years of age; the bride must be 18 years. Inter-religious marriages may promote national integrity and unity.

Hindu Marriage Act, 1955

Legally speaking, under the Hindu Marriage Act (1955) which is the governing law of the land on marriage in India, except for the observation of certain prohibited degrees of relationship, legal restrictions on the choice of marriage partner are almost non-existent.

This implies that under the law, both *sagotra* (kin in the patrilineal line of descent whose members claim descent from the same *gotra* ancestor) and inter-caste marriages are permitted.

Domestic Violence Act, 2005

Preventing a woman from marrying a person of her choice is an emotional abuse under the Protection of Women from Domestic Violence Act, 2005.

7.2.2. Penal Laws

There is no separate law for honour killings in India. The Indian law takes cognizance of killing a person. It makes no distinction between honour killing or murdering a person. Honour killing is a punishable offence in the IPC under Sections 120B (criminal conspiracy), 302 (murder) and 34 (acts done by several persons in furtherance of common intention).

Murder U/S 300 to 302

Indian Penal Code 1860 Chapter XVI, Sections 299 to 377

deal with Offences affecting the human body. Sections 299 to 311 relate with Offences Affecting Life including murder, culpable homicide. Honour killings are treated as murder in section 300 to section 302. Murder is defined in Section 300 of the IPC as "Except in the cases hereinafter excepted, culpable homicide is murder, if the act by which the death is caused is done with the intention of causing death." Section 301 of IPC deals with culpable homicide by causing death of person other than person whose death was intended.—" If a person, by doing anything which he intends or knows to be likely to cause death, commits culpable homicide by causing the death of any person, whose death he neither intends nor knows himself to be likely to cause, the culpable homicide committed by the offender is of the description of which it would have been if he had caused the death of the person whose death he intended or knew himself to be likely to cause. The punishment for murder is prescribed in Section 302 of the IPC that says 'Who ever commits murder shall be punished with death, or [imprisonment for life], and shall also be liable to fine.'

Common Intention

Section 34 of the IPC deals with acts done by several persons in furtherance of common intention.

Criminal Conspiracy

The participants and abettors in the honour killings can also be tried under Section 120B of the IPC dealing with criminal conspiracy. The section 120B says:

1. Whoever is a party to a criminal conspiracy to commit an offence punishable with death,
2. [imprisonment for life] or rigorous imprisonment for a term of two years or upwards, shall, where no express provision is made in this Code for the punishment of such a conspiracy, be punished in the same manner as if

he had abetted such offence.

Abetment

107 of the IPC defines abetment of a thing.--A person abets the doing of a thing, who:—

First : Instigates any person to do that thing; or

Secondly : Engages with one or more other person or persons in any conspiracy for the doing of that thing, if an act or illegal omission takes place in pursuance of that conspiracy, and in order to the oing of that thing; or

Thirdly : Intentionally aids, by any act or illegal omission, the doing of that thing.

Explanation 1. : A person who, by wilful misrepresentation, or by wilful concealment of a material fact which he is bound to disclose, voluntarily causes or procures, or attempts to cause or procure, a thing to be done, is said to instigate the doing of that thing.

Explanation 2. : Whoever, either prior to or at the time of the commission of an act, does anything in order to facilitate the commission of that act, and thereby facilitates the commission thereof, is said to aid the doing of that act.

Abettor

108 of the IPC defines. Abettor as—A person abets an offence, who abets either the commission of an offence, or the commission of an act which would be an offence, if committed by a person capable by law of committing an offence with the same intention or knowledge as that of the abettor.

Explanation 1. : The abetment of the illegal omission of an act may amount to an offence although the abettor may not himself be bound to do that act.

Explanation 2. : To constitute the offence of abetment it is not necessary that the act abetted should be committed, or that the effect requisite to constitute the offence should be caused.

Explanation 3. : It is not necessary that the person abetted should be capable by law of committing an offence, or that he should have the same guilty intention or knowledge as that of the abettor, or any guilty intention or knowledge.

Explanation 4. : The abetment of an offence being an offence, the abetment of such an abetment is also an offence.

Explanation 5. : It is not necessary to the commission of the offence of abetment by conspiracy that the abettor should concert the offence with the person who commits it. It is sufficient if he engages in the conspiracy in pursuance of which the offence is committed.

Therefore, the existing Indian laws against honour killing are sufficient. Recently, Criminal Law (amendment) Ordinance, 2013 was issued by the President of India which provides for amendment of Indian Penal Code, Indian Evidence Act, and Code of Criminal Procedure, 1973 on laws related to sexual offences. This new Ordinance has created some new offences or have expressedly created certain offences which were dealt under related laws. These new offences like, acid attack, sexual harassment, voyeurism, stalking has been incorporated into the Indian Penal Code (IPC).

Indian Constitution

The perpetrators in 'honour killing' can also be punished under articles 14, 15(1) and (3), and 21 of the Constitution of India granting women right to live, right to move freely, right to equality and right to security.

REFERENCES

1. Chesler, Phyllis, "Are Honour Killings Simply Domestic Violence?", *Middle East Quarterly*, Spring 2009, pp. 61-69.
2. United Nations International Covenant on Civil and Political Rights, 1976.
3. UN Declaration on the Elimination of Violence Against Women (1993).
4. UN Fourth World Conference on Women.
5. Convention on the Elimination of All Forms of Discrimination Against Women (1979).
6. Jois, M.R., *Ancient Indian Law—Eternal Values in Manu Smriti*, Delhi, Universal Publishing Co., 2002, pp. xii, 22, 27, 30.
7. Buhler, G., *The Laws of Manu*, New Delhi: Ahuja Book Company, 1990, pp. 5, 85, 255, 416.

8. Role of Judiciary

Judiciary had played, and is playing, an important role in reducing or preventing honour killings that have been increased since 2000. The landmark judgement of Session Court of Karnal district of Haryana state in *Manoj and Babli murder case* is an example.

Supreme Court also is playing a vital role in combating the honour killings and excessive role played by *Khaps* in marriages. A Supreme Court bench comprising of Justice Markandeya Katju and Justice Gyan Sudha Misra, who were hearing a case of caste discrimination in 2011 called for an end to customary practices which promote "honour killings", saying the brutal tradition of parents killing their children to protect their so-called reputation is "barbaric" and "shameful". The two judges said,

> "We are of the opinion that this is wholly illegal and has to be ruthlessly stamped out,"

The apex Court also directed all administrative and police departments to ensure that couples in such relationships are not harassed or subjected to violence, adding that inter-caste marriages are in the national interest and would help dismantle India's age-old caste system. "There is nothing honourable in such killings, and in fact killings they are nothing but barbaric and shameful acts of murder committed by brutal, feudal-minded persons who deserve punishment," said the judgment. "Only in this way can we stamp out such acts of barbarism the court opined."

The Supreme Court is also hearing a Public Interest Litigation filed by *Shakti Vahini*, a NGO, in 2010 against rampant honour killings in Panjab, U.P., West Bengal and Haryana. The Court, by a notice, has invited *Khap Panchayats* also to present their views on their alleged role in incidents of honour killings and has asked them not to function like kangaroo courts in villages. Though, some *Khap Panchayats* are expressing their views of toleration on inter-caste marriages but they are not seem to be compromising for *gotra* marriages for which they demand amendment in the Hindu Marriage Act of 1955. However, some of the important judgments of the Supreme Court are discussed in this chapter.

8.1. SUSHMA PRABHU vs. STATE OF MAHARASHTRA

Prabhu, Sushma's husband, was killed by her brother, Dilip Tiwari, and his associate in Mumbai in May 2004. The reason was a mismatched-caste marriage. Sushma was a Brahmin and Prabhu belonged to a low caste. The fast-track sessions court in Mumbai sentenced all the accused to death.

The Bombay High Court upheld it, but the Supreme Court in December 2009 reduced the death sentence to 25 years in prison. The Supreme Court said:

> "It is common experience that when the younger sister commits something unusual and in this case it was an inter-caste, inter-community marriage out of [a] secret love affair, then in society it is the elder brother who justifiably or otherwise is held responsible for not stopping such [an] affair."[1]

The judgment read as:

> "If he became the victim of his wrong but genuine caste considerations, it would not justify the death sentence. The vicious grip of the caste, community, religion, though totally unjustified, is a stark reality."

It appeared in this case that the Supreme Court tacitly conferred a measure of legitimacy to honour killing. The SC's views were a stark reality. After a few weeks of this judgment, a teenage girl was hacked to death in Sitapur village, near Lucknow, by the brother for eloping with her lover.[2]

8.2. LATA SINGH VS. STATE OF U.P.

The Supreme Court of India in Lata Singh vs. State of U.P.,[3] while observing the honour killing as a social evil had issued certain directions as under:

> "This is a free and democratic country, and once a person becomes a major he or she can marry whosoever he/she likes. If the parents of the boy or girl do not approve of such inter-caste or inter religious marriage the maximum they can do is that they can cut off social relations with the son or the daughter, but they cannot give threats or commit or instigate acts of violence and cannot harass the person who undergoes such inter-caste or interreligious marriage. We, therefore, direct that the administration/police authorities throughout the country will see to it that if any boy or girl who is a major undergoes inter-caste or inter-religious marriage with a woman or man who is a major, the couple are not harassed by any one nor subjected to threats or acts of violence, and anyone who gives such threats or harasses or commits acts of violence either himself or at his instigation, is taken to task by instituting criminal proceedings by the police against such persons and further stern action is taken against such persons as provided by law. We sometimes hear of 'honour' killings of such persons who undergo inter-caste or inter-religious marriage of their own free will. There is nothing honourable in such killings, and in fact they are nothing but barbaric and shameful acts of murder committed by brutal, feudal minded persons who deserve harsh punishment. Only in this way can we stamp out such acts of barbarism."

8.3. ARUMUGAM SERVAI VS. STATE OF TAMIL NADU

In a recent case—Arumugam Servai vs. State of Tamil Nadu,[4] the Supreme Court strongly depreciated the practice of *Khap/ Katta Panchayats* taking law into their own hands and indulging in offensive activities which endanger the personal lives of the persons marrying according to their choice.

8.4. BHAGWAN DAS VS. STATE (NCT OF DELHI)

In Bhagwan Das vs. State (NCT of Delhi),[5] the Supreme Court laid down the proposition that the so-called honour killing comes within the category of rarest of the rare cases deserving death punishment. It was observed:

> "this is necessary as a deterrent for such outrageous, uncivilized behaviour. All persons who are planning to perpetrate 'honour killing' should know that the gallows await them".

These decisions—in Arumugam Servai (supra) case and Bhagwan Das case—were rendered by the same Bench. A copy of the judgment was directed to be sent to all the High Courts who shall circulate the same to all the Sessions Judges.

Following the judgments and directions given by the Supreme Court in *Arumugam Servai* (supra) and *Bhagwan Das vs. State,* most of the accused in the so-called honour killing murder cases were sentenced to death by the Sessions Courts in U.P. and Delhi. Such a blanket direction given by the Supreme Court making death sentence a rule in "honour killings" cases, makes a departure from the principles firmly entrenched in our criminal jurisprudence by virtue of a series of decisions rendered by larger Benches of Supreme Court, for e.g. *Bachan Singh vs. State of Punjab* and *Machhi Singh vs. State of Punjab*. It is settled law that aggravating and mitigating circumstances should be weighed and it is only in very exceptional and rare cases, death sentence should be imposed. Death sentence, in other words, is a last resort. Further, where there is more than one accused, the degree of participation and culpability may vary. It is needless to emphasise that each case must be judged by the facts and circumstances emerging in that case. No hard and fast rule can be laid down in the light of the Supreme Court's consistent approach towards death sentence vs. life imprisonment issue. This judgment in the case of *Bhagwan Das* is bound to create uncertainty in the state of law.

To sum up we may say that judiciary has taken various measures by issuing guidelines and other orders to strengthen the legal provisions and to effectively deal with the social malice—honour killings. The court ordered the states and central government to seize the matter. The apex court on 9th July 2013 has directed the central government to file a status report within six weeks on the Law Commissions' model bill for enacting a law to deal with honour killings and the role of *Khap Panchayats* in such incidents.[6]

REFERENCES

1. Sushma Prabhu vs. State of Maharashtra, Criminal Appeal No. 1026 of Supreme Court 2008.
2. *Hindu*, 4 June 2010.
3. Lata Singh vs. State of U.P. [(2006) 5 SCC 475].
4. Arumugam Servai vs. State of Tamil Nadu [(2011) 6 SCC 405].
5. Bhagwan Das vs. State (NCT of Delhi) [(2011) 6 SCC 396].
6. *Tribune*, 10 July 2013.

9. Preventive Measures

Certain preventive measures are suggested in the following paragraphs against the honour crimes.

9.1. HARMONY AND BROTHERHOOD

Though Article 51(e) of the Indian Constitution enumerates the fundamental duty to promote harmony and the spirit of common brotherhood amongst all people of India transcending religious, linguistic and regional or sectional diversities and to renounce practices derogatory to the dignity of women, its true realization in spirit is much awaited.

9.2. MARRIAGE

'Marriage' according to Hindu scriptures, is not essentially for the sexual gratification of humans but has spiritual connotations as well. Matrimony entailing love making (*Gandharva Vivah*), marriage by force, by purchasing the spouse and other demoniacal behaviour have been described as *'Raksas'*, *'Asuri'* and *'Pisaci'* scandalisation. They have all been decried save the alliances solemnised according to scriptures. Inter-caste marriages were not debarred in ancient India.[1]

9.2.1. RIGHT TO CHOOSE LIFE PARTNER

Violence against woman clubbed with the prohibitions on marital choice is a total negation of her rights. Since, the right to choose life partner at the time of marriage constitutes an integral part of her right of self-preservation, majority of the International Conventions, Declarations and Protocols fall in line by emphasizing that her consent and choice in the matters relating to marriage should be weighed and prohibit resultant violence against her due to the difference of opinion in these matters.

The maiden attempt, specifically addressing the issue of honour crimes against women at the international level, has been the adoption of Resolution 55/66 by the General Assembly explicitly identified the crimes based on the human right issue and clearly voice the obligation of the State parties to exercise due diligence to prevent, investigate and punish the perpetrators of such crimes and provide protection to the victims.[2]

Therefore, honour should not be made as a ground of defence in cases of assault or murder of a female family member.

9.2.2 INTER-RELIGIOUS MARRIAGES

The main purpose of the Special Marriage Act, 1954 was to provide a special form of marriage for the people of India and all Indian nationals in foreign countries, irrespective of the religion or faith followed by either party. The Act permits any person, irrespective of religion to perform marriage. The only condition of marriage is the bridegroom must be 21 years of age; the bride must be 18 years. Inter-religious marriages may promote national unity and integrity.

In some of the Indian states like Karnataka, Kerala and Maharastra hate campaign against Hindu-Muslim relationship has been started by some 'vigilant groups' like *Hindu Raksha Samiti (HRS)* and *Hindu Janjagaruti Samiti (HJS)* with a purpose to 'save' Hindu women from Muslim men. These groups claim that Muslim men are luring Hindu women into marriages with the aim of increasing their own population. They call this campaign as "Love Jihad."[3] The government of these states should make some arrangements against this false propaganda.

9.2.3. Inter-Caste Marriages

In modern period Inter-caste marriages have been validated in India as early as in 1949 by the Hindu Marriages Validity Act, 1949. The Special Marriage Act, 1872 and 1954 legalize marriage between members of different castes and religions. Hindu Marriage Act, 1955, diametrically against the customary marriage rules in India, offers more freedom in marriage by doing away with identification of marital partners according to caste and permits both *sagotra* and inter-caste marriages. Preventing a woman from marrying a person of her choice is an emotional abuse under the Protection of Women from Domestic Violence Act, 2005. The European parliament, on 10 October 2013, passed a resolution recognising caste-based discrimination and discrimination based on work and descent as violation of human rights and an obstacle to development.

The need of the hour is to encourage inter-caste marriages. Various social and Non-Governmental Organizations should come forward to protect these marriages.

9.2.4. *Sagotra* Marriages

Gotras were originally merely surnames. Members of the same *gotra* have no real tie of consanguinity. Therefore, prohibition on the *sagotra* marriages makes little sense. Even in the presence of such a tie, it would be highly irrational to prohibit marriages since the members of any particular *gotra* today are removed by hundreds of generations from its original founder. Again, historically, the members of a *gotra* are not descended from a *rishi* since many *gotra* are named after territory or profession in significance. The general public ought to be made aware of this reality.

9.3. ABOLITION OF CASTE SYSTEM

Rigveda, *Mandala* 5, *Sukta* 60, *Mantra* 5 emphasize that none is superior *(ajyestasaha)* or inferior *(kanishthasha)*. Since all are brothers, need is to strive collectively for the interest and progress of all.[4] Caste system based on birth has harmed our country in the past and is doing the same today.

Anthropological Survey of India (ASI) has in 2006, identified 2,800 castes including 450 Scheduled Castes, 461 Scheduled Tribes and 766 Backward Castes in India.[5] For unity and integrity of the country there is an urgent need of abolishing the caste system. Despite all efforts, opposition and criticism, unfortunately castes still persist in India display their tremendous vitality and resilience. If their total abolition is neither possible nor desirable then there is a need to transform these castes and sub-castes into mutually endogamous groups.

The promotion of higher education, urbanization, social mobilization and sensitization can weak the grip of the caste system. To end the caste system the importance attached to purity and pollution should be withdrawn. Dr. B.R. Ambedkar was of the view that self rule without caste-less society has no importance. He also advocated inter-caste marriages for breaking caste system.

9.4. POWERS OF *KHAP PANCHAYATS* BE CURTAILED

Though the Supreme Court has invited *Khap Panchayats* to hear their views before issuing any order to stop them from allegedly harassing and killing couples, particularly women in the name of family honour for entering into inter-caste or inter-*gotra* marriages the powers of the caste *Panchayats* need to be curtailed by appropriate legislation. Strong political will is required to put cap on the *Khaps*. It is found that political parties continue to turn a blind eye to the *Khaps* despite Supreme Court strictures. They are fearing loosing their vote banks. Recent killings of Nidhi Barak and Dharmendra Barak of Garnawathi village of Rohtak district in Haryana on 18 September 2013 all the major political parties avoided commenting on the barbaric act. The Secretary of the Haryana unit of All India Democratic Women Association Ms. Savita criticised the state government for doing nothing to curb this crime.[6]

Since *Khaps* are important influencial bodies of rural areas they should be persuaded to help in sheding the culture of intolerance in villages in the name of traditions. They can help in promoting harmony and brotherhood by asking the villagers not to make the life of the family members of 'deviant girl in the village unbearable by taunts and sneers. They should also be persuaded to change their patriarchal mindset and authoritarian attitudes by gender justice and progressive laws. *Khaps* should rather start awareness campaigns against honour crimes, female foeticide, liquor consumption and other social evils. They should concentrate on larger social issues like women education, sex-ratio, eradication of poverty, social harmony and development.

9.5. RECOMMENDATIONS OF LAW COMMISSION BE ADOPTED

The model bill proposed by the Law Commission in 2012—Prohibition of Unlawful Assembly (Interference with the Freedom of Matrimonial Alliance) Bill—should immediately be passed. Law Commission has proposed upto one-year imprisonment and ₹ 10,000 fine for those who participate in *Khap* meetings convened to condemn any inter-caste marriage. The Bill also proposed punishment of upto two years of imprisonment and ₹ 20,000 fine if one was found taking steps to prevent such marriages; a three-year jail term and ₹ 30,000 penalty for anyone resorting to criminal intimidation of such couples.[7]

9.6. AMENDMENT IN IPC REQUIRED

As we are aware that there is no provision of 'honour killing' in the IPC, the honour killing should be made a separate offence by amending Section 300 of Indian Penal Code, adding a new definition of 'Murder' in the form of 'Honour Killing'. This amendment will help the judges to classify the 'honour killing' cases.

9.7. JOINT RESPONSIBILITY FOR KILLINGS

Those *Khap Panchayats* that order the killings in the name of honour and those executing their order must jointly be held responsible for such honour killings. They should be tried u/s 120B of the Indian Penal Code dealing with criminal conspiracy. The degree of participation should not be considered in such cases.

We must keep in mind the deterrence theory of crime for tackling and preventing this types of crimes. It is necessary to eliminate the peripheral enticing elements as well because the crime is possible only when all the elements of planning and enticement are met. Therefore, each person who played a role, directly or indirectly, in committing any crime must share the burden of punishment as well.

9.8. HAILING OF KILLERS BE STOPPED

It is noticed in some cases, as in the case of couple killed by the father recently in Garnawati, near Rohtak, where father who killed his daughter did not repent, that the killers of couples hail themselves and are being hailed by the community members for showing 'highest moral act of courage'. The killers are being treated 'as moral guardians of the community'. Efforts should be made to stop this type of hailing by awareness and education. Hailers should be treated as conspirators.

9.9. BURDEN OF PROOF

Amendments should be made in the relevant sections of Indian Evidence Act, 1872, shifting 'burden of proof' on the accused family members against whom the charges of 'Honour Killing' had been framed.

9.10. PUBLIC AWARENESS BE CREATED

The public in general be made to understand the importance of the female population, value of life and horror of honour crimes through public debates and discussion, media coverage etc. The family and the community attitude may be changed by having a discourse with them.

To liberate and emancipate women from the shackles of ancient law, traditions and customs for better promotion and readjustment of their rights on the lines of equality, dignity and non-exploitation general public be made aware that there exists no honour in domestic violence, honour killings and crimes against women but only shame. *Amnesty International* has started in February 2013 'One Billion Rising' campaign which aims to unite people across the globe to fight violence against women. Such type of awareness should be promoted.

Amnesty India has set up a unique phone line (09243723939) for women across India to call and express their views or to vent their ire on the issues of sexual violence or gender discrimination. This should be given wide publicity.

9.11. LEGAL AWARENESS AND EDUCATION

Women should be made aware of social changes and their legal rights and duties by starting legal awareness and social movements at large scale. They should be made to understand and accept that there exists no violation of the family or caste honour, if they educate them-self, develop their personalities, express their desires in marital choices, and have friendships with opposite sex. The organization of seminars, workshops, lectures and debates in schools, colleges and other social organizations will help in this matter.

9.12. ATTITUDE OF POLICE, LEADERS AND JUDICIAL OFFICERS

Honour killings can properly be checked only if the police, judiciary and public representatives consider these crimes as the most heinous killings and help in meeting out stringent punishment. Judicial measures to curb these killings should be strong, effective and without leniency towards the perpetrators of these crimes on the basis of any custom, tradition or religious considerations. It is necessary to impart and inculcate moral values and streamline the police. Similarly, leaders both rural and urban should show the requisite political will, courage and conviction to deal ruthlessly with crimes against women in general and honour killings in particular. They should avoid giving any statement that may promote honour killings.

9.13. FAST TRACK COURTS

Martin Luther King has said that "injustice anywhere is a threat to justice." Unusual delay in justice also means injustice. It is a well known dictum that justice delayed is justice denied.

Our criminal justice system is so slow that delivering a verdict takes years. The denial of speedy justice not only emboldens offenders but erodes the faith of victims in the judiciary. Judicial delay encourges partiality, corruption, unfairness and low quality judgement. Reasons for judicial delay may be various like corruption in society, corrupt judicial practices, shortage of judges, poverty and lack of legal awareness among the masses. Moreover, the Indian judiciary is overloaded with cases. The need of the hour is to increase the judges-cases ratio by appointing more judges. Though the Supreme Court had already issued guidelines that investigations into cases registered under ST/SC (Prevention of Atrocities) Act should be completed within a month the scope of guidelines should also be extended to the honour cases. It has become necessary that offences of honour killings should be addressed by dedicated courts on fast track basis.

So far as, heinous crimes against women like rape, murder and honour killings etc. are concerned Fast Track Courts should be set up in all the states for speedy trials. Haryana has set up 21 Fast Track Courts (FTCs) in the state for speedy trial in cases of heinous crimes against women.[8] Honour killing should also be treated as heinous crime against women.

9.14. STATE COMMISSION FOR SCHEDULED CASTES

A "Parliamentary Committee on the Welfare of Scheduled Castes and Scheduled Tribes which visited Haryana against the backdrop of rape cases against *Dalit* women in 2012 had recommended the setting up of the State Commission for Scheduled Castes with adequate representation to women as a mechanism for the redress of grievances to restore dignity and morale of the Scheduled Castes in the state that was completely eroded due to the high-handedness of the dominant caste".[9] Though the government of Haryana, after the recommendation of the Committee, had set up the Scheduled Castes Commission for the state many state governments had not yet set up the Commission in their states to investigate, examine and monitor all matters relating to the safeguards provided for the Scheduled Castes. The Commission should be set up in all the states at the earliest. It will help trace the inter-caste marriages related honour killings.

ACTION PLANS

States effected by honour killings and other crimes against women should prepare action plans to deal with such crimes. Special fund should be allocated by these states for strengthening measures to curb honour crimes.

9.15. WOMEN'S PROPERTY RIGHT

The girl right to have share of family property given under the Hindu Succession Act, 1956 amended in 2005 should be equated as human right.

9.16. SELF-DEFENCE SKILLS

Women and girls should be trained in the skill of self-defence in protecting themselves using *Judo, Tykwando, Karate* etc. These can be started as compulsory sports activity for girls in all the schools.

REFERENCES

1. Garg, Pyar L., *The Ultimate Quest*, New Delhi, Northern Book Centre, 2013, p. 4.
2. UN General Assembly Resolution 55/66.
3. Byatnal, Amruta, "Hindutva Vigilantes Target Hindu-Muslim Couples," *Hindu*, 14 Oct. 2013, p.1.
4. Rigveda, Mandala 5, Sukta 60, Mantra 5.
5. Anthropological Survey of India (ASI) Report 2006.
6. *Hindu*, 20 September 2013, p. 3.
7. Law Commission of India, Report 2012.
8. *Haryana Review*, Vol. 27, No. 4, April 2013, p. 32.
9. *Tribune*, 17 February 2013, p. 3.

10. Conclusion

To sum up we may say that the honour killings, which basically deal with crimes against women, has become burning topic now a days. The cases of honour killings have increased manifold since 2001 in the world over. Some of the major countries, other than India, facing this problem are Egypt, Jordan, Leban, Morocco, Pakistan, Syrian Arab Republic, Turkey and Yemen. Honour killings have also spread its wings in Western Countries like United Kingdom, France and Germany. This evil has been brought by Asian migrants into America and Canada. Even the small countries like, Bangladesh, Brazil, Ecuador, Israel, Sweden, Italy and Uganda are not spared by it. In India honour killings are rising in northern region mainly in states like Punjab, Rajasthan, Haryana, Uttar Pradesh. In some cases honour crimes are reported in Tamil Nadu.

Honour killing has its roots in the primitive history of man. The evolution of civilization brought not only the positive changes in the way of life of man but also certain limitations on the relationship of persons in general and male-female in particular. The origin and development of family system bound people related by blood or marriage or a strong common bond, in such a way that family has become an important unit of society with a universal and basic role. Families with common bonds and interests later on formed different groups and clans. These groups and clans framed certain norms to protect the life, property and honour of their fellow members. The regular practices of these beliefs or norms later-on became traditions and customs. Honour killing is one of those norms framed to protect family honour.

Historically, honour killings and punishments have been documented over centuries among a wide variety of ethnic and religious groups throughout the world. For example, the Code of Hammurabi of Babylon which was issued in 1790 BC penalized adulterous couples by drowning. The 1075 BC Assyrian law of the civilization of Mesopotamia stated that the father of a defiled virgin shall punish his daughter howsoever he thinks it fit.

In the *Bible*, the Book of Genesis, Judah demanded for the burning of his daughter-in-law Tamar, whom he was told to be pregnant via harlotry; this view is then supported in Book of Leviticus. Matthew Goldstein also noted that honour killings were encouraged in ancient Rome, where male family members who did not take actions against the female adulterers in their family were "actively persecuted".

Dr. Amin A. Muhammad traces origin of honour killings dates back to pre-Islamic period when Arab settlers occupied a region adjacent to *Sindh*, which was then known as Baluchistan. Settlers had strong patriarchal traditions with such practices as the live burial of unwanted newborn daughters. In medieval India the practice of killing girls-female infanticide-was common in Rajput kings who believed that the girls would bring dishonour to their family. The fear of dishonour was the main reason of *Sati* system and the system of *Johar*. Even the inter-religion marriages were not acceptable. Akbar's marriage with Jodhabai, the daughter of Raja Man Singh was decried by many Rajput kings. The love stories of *Heer-Ranja, Sohni-Mahiwal, Mirja-Sahiba, Sassi-Punnu* of old Punjab were tragically ended.

'Honour killing' is not defined in any dictionary of law. It is the homicide of a member of a family or social group by other members, due to the belief of the perpetrators that the victim has brought dishonour upon the family or community. Accused of these crimes think that they are morally right and the act of killings has brought back the lost honour to the family.

The major cause of honour killings in India is caste system.

According to a survey 75 per cent honour killings in Hindu families are caste-based. Other reasons of honour killings are entering into marriage against family's approval, adultery, sexual assault, divorce, pre-marital sex or having a child out of wedlock etc. The mere perception that a woman has behaved in a way that "dishonours" her family is sufficient to trigger an attack on her life.

Khap Panchayats are dominating in Haryana, the northern part of India. To restore the rural people's faith in customs and traditions regarding *gotra* marriages these *Khap Panchayats* define their own laws. Some times, they declare marriages violating such rules as null and void. It is also alleged that they abet death as punishment. However, *Khap Panchayats* deny these allegations. Moreover, these allegations have never proved and hence seem to be exaggerated.

The Law Commission of India in its report of 2012 has criticized the high-handed and unwarranted interference by the caste assemblies or *Panchayats* with *sagotra*, inter-caste or inter-religious marriages, which are otherwise lawful and will prevent the acts endangering the liberty of the couple married or intending to marry. The Law Commission proposed a bill which recommended that members gathering for such purpose, i.e., for condemning the marriage with a view to take necessary consequential action, are to be treated as members of unlawful assembly for which a mandatory minimum punishment was prescribed.

The *Shakti Vahini* filed a PIL, in June 2010 in the apex court demanding guidelines to rein in *Khaps* for their alleged involvement in honour crimes. A bench of Justice Aftab Alam and Ranjana Prakash Desai of Supreme Court, hearing this PIL, seeking protection of young couples who married inter-caste or within the same *gotra* from the wrath of *Khaps*, expressed concern about increasing role of *Khap Panchayats* in honour killings and described their diktats as against fundamental rights. The Supreme Court has invited the *Khap Panchayats* to hear their views before issuing any order to stop them from allegedly harassing and killing couples, particularly women in the name of family honour for entering into same village, inter-caste or inter-*gotra* marriages. On the other hand the *Khap Panchayat*s are insisting upon an amendment in the Hindu Marriage Act that no marriage should be made legal in blood relations and brotherhood set up in *gotra*s. The 17 member committee was formed by the *Khaps* to appear before the Supreme Court. They are also demanding *Lok Adalat* status to the *Khaps*.

Some of the Khaps in Haryana have started taking concrete steps to stop discrimination and atrocities against women. To rebuild their damaged image due to their alleged role in honour crimes they have started various social welfare campaigns like improvement of sex ratio, equal rights to women, anti abortion movement and others. For this purpose Kandela Khaps have formed groups in certain villages to conduct special sessions and disseminate information about the importance of these measures.

The United Nations and other international organizations like European Union, Amnesty International and Human Rights Watch and in India National Commission for Women and other NGOs like All India Democratic Women Association (AIDWA) etc. are keeping tabs on this problem. "Honour killings" are a recognized form of violence against women in international human rights laws because they violate women's rights to life and security of the person. International law obligates member states to protect women from gender-based violence, including by family members, and to disqualify "honour" as a legal defence for acts of violence against women.

Right to marry with his/her own choice was recognized in Article 1651 of the Universal Declaration of Human Rights, 1948. Article 23 of the United Nations International Covenant on Civil and Political Rights 1976 also recognizes the right of men and women of marriageable age to marry and have a family.

'Honour killings' violate Universal Declaration of Human Rights, 1948, the Convention on the Elimination of All Forms of Discrimination against Women (1979) and provisions of UN Declaration on the Elimination of Violence against Women (1993).

In India, women have been given right to choose their life partner. The Indian Constitution enumerates the fundamental duty to promote harmony and the spirit of common brotherhood amongst all people of India transcending religious, linguistic and regional or sectional diversities and to renounce practices derogatory to the dignity of women. Hindu Marriage Disabilities Removal Act, 1946; Indian Civil Marriage Act, 1954; Hindu Marriage Act (1955) and Protection of Women from Domestic Violence Act, 2005 protects their right to marry.

At present, honour killing is being treated as murder in the Indian Penal Code U/Ss 302 (murder), 120B (criminal conspiracy) and 34 (acts done by several persons in furtherance of common intention). Though this law is sufficient to deal with the honour crimes a separate law as demanded by some to punish those involved may be enacted to curb this inhuman practice.

The judiciary in general and Supreme Court in particular is playing a vital role to combat honour killings. The judgment of *Manoj and Babli* murder case by a session court of Karnal is a landmark in the history of honour killings. The Supreme Court of India in *Lata Singh vs. State of U.P.* (2006, 5 SCC 475) issued directions that the administration/police authorities throughout the country will see to it that if any boy or girl who is a major undergoes inter-caste or inter-religious marriage with a woman or man who is a major, the couple is not harassed by any one nor subjected to threats or acts of violence, and any one who gives such threats or harasses or commits acts of violence either himself or at his instigation, is taken to task by instituting criminal proceedings by the police against such persons and further stern action is taken against such persons as provided by law. "We sometimes hear of 'honour' killings of such persons who undergo inter-caste or inter-religious marriage of their own free will. There is nothing honourable in such killings, and in fact they are nothing but barbaric and shameful acts of murder committed by brutal and feudal minded persons who deserve harsh punishment. Only in this way we can stamp out such acts of barbarism", the apex court said.

In a recent case—*Arumugam Servai vs. State of Tamil Nadu* [reported in (2011) 6 SCC 405], the Supreme Court strongly deprecated the practice of *Khap/Katta Panchayat*s taking law into their own hands and indulging in offensive activities which endanger the personal lives of the persons marrying according to their choice.

In *Bhagwan Das vs. State* (NCT of Delhi) [(2011) 6 SCC 396] the Supreme Court while laying down the proposition that the so-called honour killing comes within the category of "rarest of the rare" cases deserving death punishment.

To get rid of honour killings there is a need to liberate and emancipate women from the shackles of ancient law, traditions and customs for better promotion and readjustment of their rights on the lines of equality, dignity and non-exploitation. This can be done by creating public awareness. Women should be made aware of social changes and their legal rights and duties by starting legal awareness and social movements at large scale.

All the religious scriptures have stressed upon human oneness. The *Bhagavad Gita* said that good of all and happiness of all is of utmost importance. *Rigveda* emphasizes that none is superior or inferior. Since all are brothers, need is to strive collectively for the interest and progress of all. The social reformers like, *Kabir, Ravidas, Nanak, Dayanand* stressed upon brotherhood of mankind.

To end the caste system the importance attached to purity and pollution should be withdrawn. For breaking caste system interacted-marriages should be encouraged.

Khaps have played a pivotal role in preserving the age old value system, traditions and customs prevailing in Indian culture. Even during the Delhi *Saltnate*, and British period khaps succeeded in preserving these values and helped in keeping the society bound together. They also nurtured brotherhood among all castes in the rural part of northern India. Now they are struggling against the impact of globalisation and Western culture which according to them is spoiling the Indian culture.

*Gotra*s were originally merely surnames. Members of the same *gotra* have no real tie of consanguinity. Therefore, prohibition on the *Sagotra* marriages makes little sense The caste *Panchayats* need to understand this reality and lift the prohibition on *sagotra* marriages. The Satrol khap, while keeping in mind the need of the hour and social problem of unmarried marriageable youth as brides are hard to come by, has recently allowed marriage ties among about 100 different gotras living in 42 villages falling under its jurisdiction in Narnaund block of Hisar district in Haryana. This step of Satrol khap was welcomed by many other khaps.

The recommendations of Law Commission of India Report 2012 and proposed bill should be adopted without delay to put cap on the *Khap Panchayat*s and those participating in the honour killings. 'Burden of proof' should also be shifted on the accused family members against whom the charges of 'Honour Killing' have been made. The police, judiciary and public representatives should consider honour crimes as the most heinous killings and should help in meeting out stringent punishment. Judicial measures to curb these killings should be strong, effective and without leniency towards the perpetrators of these crimes. It is necessary to impart and inculcate moral values and streamline the police for better result. Offences of honour killings should be addressed by dedicated courts on fast track basis.

Annexure-1

TEXT OF LAW COMMISSION OF INDIA REPORT NO. 242

Prevention of Interference with the Freedom of Matrimonial Alliances (in the name of Honour and Tradition): A Suggested Legal Framework, Report No. 242, August, 2012

1. INTRODUCTION

1.1 In pursuant to the discussion in the Parliament on a Calling Attention Motion and the assurance given by the then Union Home Minister that various aspects relating to "honour killings" will be got examined, a reference was made to the Law Commission of India by the Ministry of Law and Justice in September 2009. That is how the subject has been taken up for consideration.

1.2 At the outset, it may be stated that the words 'honour killings' and 'honour crimes' are being used loosely as convenient expressions to describe the incidents of violence and harassment caused to the young couple intending to marry or having married against the wishes of the community or family members. They are used more as catch phrases and not as apt and accurate expressions.

1.3 The so-called 'honour killings' or 'honour crimes' are not peculiar to our country. It is an evil which haunts many other societies also. The belief that the victim has brought dishonour upon the family or the community is the root cause of such violent crimes. Such violent crimes are directed especially against women. Men also become targets of attack by members of family of a woman with whom they are perceived to have an 'inappropriate relationship'. Changing cultural and economic status of women and the women going against their male dominated culture has been one of the causes of honour crimes. In some western cultures, honour killings often arise from women seeking greater independence and choosing their own way of life. In some cultures, honour killings are considered less serious than other murders because they arise from long standing cultural traditions and are thus deemed appropriate or justifiable. An adulterous behaviour of woman or pre-marital relationship or assertion of right to marry according to their choice, are widely known causes for honour killings in most of the countries. The report of the Special Rapporteur to U.N.1 of the year 2002 concerning cultural practices in the family that are violent towards women indicated that honour killings had been reported in Jordon, Lebanon, Morocco, Pakistan, United Arab Republic, Turkey, Yemen and other Persian Gulf countries and that they had also taken place in western countries such as France, Germany and U.K. mostly within migrant communities. The report "Working towards the elimination of crimes against women committed in the name of honour" submitted to the United Nations High Commissioner for Human Rights is quite revealing. Apart from the other countries named above, according to the UN Commission on Human Rights, there are honour killings in the nations of Bangladesh, Brazil, Ecuador, India, Israel, Italy, Morocco, Sweden, Turkey and Uganda. According to Mr. Widney Brown, Advocacy Director for Human Rights Watch, the practice of honour killing "goes across cultures and across religions". There are reports that in some communities, many are prepared to condone the killing of someone who have dishonoured their family. The 2009

European Parliamentary Assembly noted the rising incidents of honour crimes with concern. In 2010, Britain saw a 47% rise of honour-related crimes. Data from police agencies in the UK report 2283 cases in 2010 and most of the attacks were conducted in cities that had high immigrant populations. The national legal Courts in some countries viz., Haiti, Jordon, Syria, Morocco and two Latin American countries do not penalize men killing female relatives found committing adultery or the husbands killing their wives in flagrante delicto. A survey by Elen R. Sheelay revealed that 20% of Jordanites interviewed simply believe that Islam condones or even supports killing in the name of family honour which is a myth.

1.4 As far as India is concerned, "honour killings" are mostly reported from the States of Haryana, Punjab, Rajasthan and U.P. Bhagalpur in Bihar is also one of the known places for "honour killings". Even some incidents are reported from Delhi and Tamil Nadu. Marriages with members of other castes or the couple leaving the parental home to live together and marry provoke the harmful acts against the couple and immediate family members.

1.5 The Commission tried to ascertain the number of such incidents, the accused involved, the specific reasons, etc., so as to have an idea of the general crime scenario in such cases. The Government authorities of the States where incidents often occur have been addressed to furnish the information. The Director (SR) in the Ministry of Home Affairs, by her letter dated 26 May 2010, also requested the State Governments concerned to furnish the necessary information to the Commission. However, there has been no response despite reminder. But, from the newspaper reports, and reports from various other sources, it is clear that the honour crimes occur in those States as a result of people marrying without their family's acceptance and for marrying outside their caste or religion. Marriages between the couple belonging to same Gotra (family name) have also often led to violent reaction from the family members or the community members. The Caste councils or Panchayats popularly known as 'Khap Panchayats' try to adopt the chosen course of 'moral vigilantism' and enforce their diktats by assuming to themselves the role of social or community guardians.

2. THE DIMENSIONS OF PROBLEM AND THE NEED FOR A SEPARATE LAW

2.1 The rising incidence of commission of murders of persons marrying outside their caste or religion and other serious offences perpetrated or hostility generated against them and also causing harm to their close relatives or a section of the community on considerations of caste and 'gotra' are matters of grave concern. Those who may be directly involved in the actual commission of acts of violence or murder are either part of a community or section of the people and may also include members of the family concerned in the case of objected marriages. Very often such incidents and offences are not even taken cognizance at the threshold. The domineering position and strength wielded by caste combinations and assemblies, silence or stifle the investigating and prosecuting agencies. In so far as the caste or community panchayats play a constructive role in addressing the common problems concerning the society or amicably settling the disputes between the local inhabitants and families, dissuading the people from a criminal path, the mission and the work of these village elders and Panchayatdars can be commended; but, if they exceed their limits, as it is often happening, impose their decisions in matters relating to matrimony and interfere with the legitimate choices of youngsters and indulge in acts of endangering their life and liberty, the law cannot remain a silent spectator in our progressive democratic polity wedded to cherished constitutional values.

2.2 As said earlier, incidents involving grave offences

committed against persons marrying or proposing to marry sagotras or outside their castes/religions are periodically reported. It is learnt that number of cases go unreported for fear of reprisals or cascading effects. The intervention of caste/community assemblies in the name of 'Khap Panchayats', 'Katta Panchayats' etc. in the occurrence of these offences and other related incidents involving serious life and liberty consequences, are frequently noticed. Such assemblies gathered on caste/community lines assume to themselves the power and authority to declare on and deal with 'objectionable' matrimonies and exhibit least regard for life and liberty and are not deterred by the processes of administration of justice. The penal law lacks direct application to the illegal acts of such caste assemblies. Innocent youth are harassed and victimized while such assemblies continue to wield unhindered authority and also seem to resist any suggestion of being subjected to any social control.

2.3 The pernicious practice of Khap Panchayats and the like taking law into their own hands and pronouncing on the invalidity and impropriety of Sagotra and inter-caste marriages and handing over punishment to the couple and pressurizing the family members to execute their verdict by any means amounts to flagrant violation of rule of law and invasion of personal liberty of the persons affected.

2.4 Sagotra marriages are not prohibited by law, whatever may be the view in olden times. The Hindu Marriage Disabilities Removal Act, 1946 was enacted with a view to dispel any doubts in this regard. The Act expressly declared the validity of marriages between the Hindus belonging to the same 'gotra' or 'pravara' or different sub-divisions of same caste. The Hindu Marriage Act does not prohibit sagotra or inter-caste marriages.

2.5 The views of village elders or family elders cannot be forced on the willing couple and no one has a right to use force or impose far-reaching sanctions in the name of vindicating community honour or family honour. There are reports that drastic action including wrongful confinement, persistent harassment, mental torture, bodily harm infliction of or threats of severe is resorted to either by close relations or some third parties against the so-called erring couple either on the exhortations of some or all the Panchayatdars or with their connivance. Several instances of murder of one or the other couple have been in the news. Social boycotts and other illegal sanctions affecting the young couple, the families and even a section of local inhabitants are quite often resorted to. All this is done in the name of tradition and honour. The cumulative effect of all such acts have public order dimensions also.

2.6 In a recent case – *Arumugam Servai vs. State of Tamil Nadu* [reported in (2011) 6 SCC 405], the Supreme Court strongly deprecated the practice of khap/katta panchayats taking law into their own hands and indulging in offensive activities which endanger the personal lives of the persons marrying according to their choice. In another case, Lata Singh vs. State of U.P. (2006, 5 SCC 475), the Supreme Court observed and directed as under:

> "This is a free and democratic country, and once a person becomes a major he or she can marry whosoever he/she likes. If the parents of the boy or girl do not approve of such inter-caste or inter religious marriage the maximum they can do is that they can cut off social relations with the son or the daughter, but they cannot give threats or commit or instigate acts of violence and cannot harass the person who undergoes such inter-caste or inter-religious marriage. We, therefore, direct that the administration/police authorities throughout the country will see to it that if any boy or girl who is a major undergoes inter-caste or inter-religious marriage with a woman or man who is a major, the couple are not harassed by any one nor subjected to threats or acts of

violence, and any one who gives such threats or harasses or commits acts of violence either himself or at his instigation, is taken to task by instituting criminal proceedings by the police against such persons and further stern action is taken against such persons as provided by law. We sometimes hear of 'honour' killings of such persons who undergo inter-caste or inter-religious marriage of their own free will. There is nothing honourable in such killings, and in fact they are nothing but barbaric and shameful acts of murder committed by brutal, feudal minded persons who deserve harsh punishment. Only in this way can we stamp out such acts of barbarism".

2.7 Some proposals are being mooted proposing amendments to Section 300 I.P.C. by way of including what is called 'Honour Killing' as murder and shifting the burden of proof to the accused.

These proposals have been studied. The views from various quarters at an informal level have also been ascertained. After a preliminary examination of these and certain other models of law, the framework of proposed law has been prepared and annexed to the Consultation Paper. The Consultation paper together with the draft Bill prepared is at Annexure II. The views of the public were invited with reference thereto. We shall advert to the responses received and the Commission's views thereon. The draft legislation has been slightly recast by the Commission after further consideration. The draft Bill now proposed by the Law Commission is at Annexure I

2.8 The idea underlying the provisions in the draft Bill is that there must be a threshold bar against congregation or assembly for the purpose of objecting to and condemning the conduct of young persons of marriageable age marrying according to their choice, the ground of objection being that they belong to the same gotra or to different castes or communities. The Panchayatdars or caste elders have no right to interfere with the life and liberty of such young couples whose marriages are permitted by law and they cannot create a situation whereby such couples are placed in a hostile environment in the village/locality concerned and exposed to the risk of safety. Such highhanded acts have a tendency to create social tensions and disharmony too. No frame of mind or belief based on social hierarchy can claim immunity from social control and regulation, in so far as such beliefs manifest themselves as agents of enforcement of right and wrong. The very assembly for an unlawful purpose viz. disapproving the marriage which is otherwise within the bounds of law and taking consequential action should be treated as an offence as it has the potential to endanger the lives and liberties of individuals concerned. The object of such an assembly is grounded on disregard for the life and liberty of others and such conduct shall be adequately tackled by penal law. This is without prejudice to the prosecution to be launched under the general penal law for the commission of offences including abetment and conspiracy.

2.9 Given the social milieu and powerful background of caste combines which bring to bear intense pressure on parents and relatives to go to any extent to punish the 'sinning' couples so as to restore the community honour, it has become necessary to deal with this fundamental problem. Any attempt to effectively tackle this socio-cultural phenomenon, rooted in superstition and authoritarianism, must therefore address itself to various factors and dimensions, viz:, the nature and magnitude of the problem, the adequacy of existing law, and the wisdom in using penal and other measures of sanction to curb the power and conduct of caste combines. The law as it stands does not act either as a deterrence or as a sobering influence on the caste combinations and assemblies who regard themselves as being outside the pale of law. The socio-cultural outlook of the members of caste councils or Panchayats is such that they have minimal or scant regard for individual liberty and autonomy.

3. SALIENT FEATURES OF THE PROPOSED BILL

3.1 We may broadly indicate the general lay-out and the main features of the proposed legislation. Given the fact that the powerful influence of the caste or community Panchayats and the aggressive role played by them in controlling the freedom of choice of the marrying couple is the root cause of honour related crimes, there must be a check on such unwarranted interference by the members of Panchayats. The couple marrying against the wishes of members of the bodies like khap panchayats ought not to be driven to a state of insecurity and misery. Their life and liberty is 'endangered' because they are exposed to threats and socio-economic deprivations. The close family members of the couple are also brought into the picture to enforce the diktats of such informal body of panchayats/councils. This is directly affecting the community and the family life in the villages, thereby posing a threat to social order and peace. As there is a need to divest the Panchayatdars or caste 'elders' of their self assumed hegemony and controlling influence in these matters, this Bill has been thought of, on balancing various considerations. It is proposed that there should be a threshold bar against the congregation or assembly for the purpose of disapproving an intended marriage or the conduct of the young couple and this objectionable conduct of the Panchayatdars should be brought within the purview of penal law. A preventive provision prohibiting such assemblies and penalizing the participation in such assemblies has also been introduced.

3.2 Having rendered the convening and conduct of such assemblies unlawful and punishable under law, consequential penal provisions dealing with offences committed in relation thereto have been proposed. Two sections are proposed to be introduced, i.e., 'Section 3, which makes punishable the acts endangering liberty, which are also particularized in the Section.

The other Section, i.e., Section 4 would deal with criminal intimidation by the members of unlawful assembly or others to secure compliance with the illegal decision of the assembly. Such acts of criminal intimidation which are punishable under the general law, i.e., the Indian Penal Code have been specifically introduced for the purpose of meting out higher punishment to those members of unlawful assembly. The other penal provisions and the situations referred to above are not taken care of nor covered by the provisions of Penal Code. At any rate, there is a room for doubt as regards the invocation of the provisions of IPC. However, the criminal acts other than those falling under the three penal provisions of the Act can still be dealt with under the provisions of the Penal Code including the provisions relating to abetment and conspiracy. For instance, if a person who is a party to the unlawful assembly has committed or abetted the commission of an offence of grievous hurt against the targeted couple or one of them or their relatives, the IPC provisions will be attracted. That is why Section 5 has been introduced to make it clear that the provisions of Sections 2, 3, and 4 of the proposed Bill are without prejudice to the provisions of IPC. In order to have sufficient deterrent effect, mandatory minimum punishments have been prescribed while taking care to see that such punishment has an element of proportionality. Apart from these penal provisions, a specific section has been proposed to empower the District Magistrate or the SDM to take preventive measures and a further obligation is cast on them to take note of the information laid before them by the marrying couple or their family members and to extend necessary protection to them.

The officials are made accountable for the failure or omission on their part to take necessary steps to prevent unlawful assembly (caste panchayats, etc.) or to give protection to the targeted couple. It has been provided that the offences shall be tried by a Court of Sessions in the District presided over by the Sessions Judge or Additional Sessions Judge as notified by the High Court. The need for constitution of special courts can be reviewed at a later stage. The offences are cognizable, non-bailable and non-compoundable.

3.3 The overlapping with the provisions of IPC has been, as far as possible, avoided. Though, at first look, it may appear that the offence of unlawful assembly is nothing other than what we find in Section 141 of IPC, it needs to be pointed out that the unlawful assembly of the kind contemplated by the proposed Bill does not strictly fall within the scope of the said section. The ingredients of 'unlawful assembly' under the Indian Penal Code and the unlawful assembly contemplated by Section 2 of the proposed Bill are not the same. Moreover, a punishment higher than that prescribed for unlawful assembly under IPC has been prescribed under Section 2. As regards Section 4 dealing with criminal intimidation, as already clarified, this Section has been introduced with a view to provide for higher punishment in the case of acts of criminal intimidation by the members of unlawful assembly within the meaning of this Bill. Thus, the provisions of the proposed Bill coupled with those in IPC would, it is hoped, be effectively able to combat the menacing trend of dastardly actions and drastic social sanctions directed against the hapless young couple and their families.

4. AUTONOMY OF CHOICES AND LIBERTY—A VALUE TO BE PROTECTED.

4.1 The autonomy of every person in matters concerning oneself—a free and willing creator of one's own choices and decisions, is now central to all thinking on community order and organization. Needless to emphasize that such autonomy with its manifold dimensions is a constitutionally protected value and is central to an open society and civilized order. Duly secured individual autonomy, exercised on informed understanding of the values integral to one's well being is deeply connected to a free social order. Coercion against individual autonomy will then become least necessary.

4.2 In moments and periods of social transition, the tensions between individual freedom and past social practices become focal points of the community's ability to contemplate and provide for least hurting or painful solutions. The wisdom or wrongness of certain community perspectives and practices, their intrinsic impact on liberty, autonomy and self-worth, as well as the parents' concern over impulsive and unreflective choices—all these factors come to the fore-front of consideration.

4.3 The problem, however, is the menacing phenomena of repressive social practices in the name of hon or triggering violent reaction from the influential members of community who are blind to individual autonomy. How best to tackle it is the question. In this context, the instrumentalist role of law to grapple with such situations assumes importance. The thought behind the proposals in this report is to bring to greater focus on the conduct which endangers life and liberty and to highlight the civilizing perceptions on liberty and autonomy.

4.4 Social protection has consistently been the paramount goal of modern criminal law. Criminal punishment typically achieves such protection through its capacity to motivate people to conform to socially acceptable rules of behaviour with threats of serious penalties for non-conformity.

> "Punishment serves as a weapon which society uses to prevent conduct which harms or threatens to harm its interests". The largest social interests or community values cannot be judged by a handful of influential persons whose beliefs are grounded in superstition and dogmas totally opposed to constitution and the laws.

4.5 The self-styled Panchayats or assembly of people constitute a close knit section of people bonded by certain common perspectives and values. Caste plays a pivotal role in this bondage. Having regard to the hegemony and the social or political power available to these Panchayats, their dictates on questions of caste relationships, matrimony etc. are formidable. Different caste groups have their own combinations. While these assembly of people may be playing some role in protecting certain basic cultural mores, their deviant role in subjecting to peril the life and liberty of persons who do not conform to their views and values cannot be condoned and it needs to be directly tackled and necessarily subjected to the disciplines of law. It would be unwise and socially incorrect to leave life and liberty of vulnerable people, at the mercies of dominant and authoritarian caste councils and such other groups whose commands and decisions cannot be easily ignored by the family and community acting the misdirected power members. The law should aim at counter- and domineering position of the caste / Community Panchayats in so far as they act as centers of coercion and intimidation. Regard and respect for life, liberty and autonomy of persons need to be the larger focus and the perceived strength of such assemblies or combinations will have to be appropriately dealt with by law.

5. WHETHER 'HONOUR KILLING' TO BE INCLUDED IN SECTION 300 IPC

5.1 The Commission is of the view that there is no need for introducing a provision in Section 300 IPC in order to bring the so-called 'honour killings' within the ambit of this provision. The existing provisions in IPC are adequate enough to take care of the situations leading to overt acts of killing or causing bodily harm to the targeted person who allegedly undermined the honour of the caste or community. The motive behind killing a person does not furnish real justification to introduce a separate provision in section 300, as is contemplated to be done under the proposed Government's Bill (as published in the newspapers). Probably, the addition of such clause may create avoidable confusion and interpretational difficulties.

6. BURDEN OF PROOF

6.1 Further, shifting the burden of proof on the basis of mere accusations of involvement in the serious offence of murder etc. or abetment thereof is not desirable. Such a move will be against the cardinal principles of jurisprudence accepted and absorbed into our criminal justice system. If burden of proof has to be shifted in such a case, logically, it will have to be done in a large number of other heinous crimes. We find neither logic nor rationale in treating the accused in the so-called honour killing cases as a separate class in the matter of application of doctrine of burden of proof. The difficulties in proof before a court of law may not by itself be a legitimate ground to deviate from the well established canons of criminal jurisprudence. The evidence may not be forthcoming in many cases of ghastly murders and barbaric killings or the witnesses may be scared to speak against notorious criminals. A holistic approach is called for and any attempt to drastically expand the rigour of criminal procedure to cope up with ad hoc situations may be counter-productive. The introduction of such a drastic provision will be out of tune with the criminal justice system and the salutary principles we have accepted as part of it. As an alternative to this, the Commission is of the view that an appropriate presumption of intention to commit the prohibited acts in clauses 3 and 4 of the proposed Bill, can be legitimately drawn against a member of an unlawful assembly. Having regard to the natural course of human conduct and the authoritarian mindset of Panchayatdars, it is reasonable to think that they would not be content with merely taking a decision condemning the so-called objectionable marriage, but they would like to go further and give effect to the decision by acts of coercion and harassment if necessary. The offensive acts done in the aftermath of the decision cannot be dissociated from their role and hegemony. The presumption to some extent solves the problem arising from the difficulty in the identification of actual role that may be played by one or more members of the assembly and in securing evidence to implicate the guilty. In such a situation, the presumption as envisaged by clause 6 will assume a significant role.

6.2 Penal law handles proof of facts by direct and circumstantial evidence. Principles of inference and logic are involved in both modes of proof. Statutes relating to evidence have engaged themselves in grappling with problems of natural non-availability or paucity of evidence in certain offence situations. Presumptions have usually emerged as a tool of logic to fill these gaps. Presumptions state cause-effect relationships in such circumstances. Care must, however, be taken to ensure that the causal link is not too remote or too thin. Presumptions generally do not affect the position of burden of proof but only shift the burden of evidence or the burden of persuasion. The presumption which is eminently suitable in the context of the present problem is the one incorporated in Section 6 of the proposed Bill. It raises a presumption to the effect that the participants in unlawful assembly intended to commit and abet the offences punishable under Section 3 and 4 of the Bill in order to carry out the illegal decision taken by them. Such presumption will supply an important link in the chain of evidence. The presumption proposed to be introduced is as follows: Every person participating in an unlawful assembly, shall be presumed to have also intended to commit or abet the commission of offences under Section 3 and 4 of the Act.

6.3 Thus, in respect of the overt acts under Sections 3 and 4, this presumption would be attracted. On a fair balance of various conflicting considerations, we feel that the presumption as above would be appropriate and effective.

6.4 In the matter of burden of proof, the Commission feels that the analogy sought to be drawn from the provisions of the Commission of Sati (Prevention) Act, 1987 is not appropriate for more than one reason. 'Sati' is a barbaric, deeply entrenched social evil which was prevalent in certain parts of the country.

.The magnitude and seriousness of that evil cannot be compared to the problem on hand. More important, the offence of 'Sati' always remained an open affair with all the rituals and ceremonies attached to it and the persons actively participating therein could be identified without difficulty. The accusations in such cases are based on solid evidence.

7. HONOUR CRIMES BILL: RESPONSES AND SUGGESTIONS

7.1 As already stated, the Commission received responses from some State Governments, Law Universities and others. The list of persons/organizations from whom responses have been received are given in Annexure III. The Commission appreciates the effort of West Bengal National University of Juridical Sciences in presenting a critical analysis of the provisions of the proposed Bill and putting forward important suggestions. The Commission has also looked into the suggestions of Faculty of Amity Law School, Noida. None of the responses have opposed in principle, the Commission's proposed recommendations and the draft Bill. Some of those suggestions have been considered and changes to the extent considered appropriate have been made in the draft Bill.

7.2 One major suggestion is that relationships akin to marriage not prohibited by law should also be included in the meaning of the word 'marriage' occurring in clause 2 of the draft Bill. This means that live-in relationships should also be included and the protection of the law secured for persons in such relationships. While on first flush, this suggestion may deserve acceptance, it is felt that bringing such relationship within the scope of this law may unduly dilute its efficacy and is likely to meet with resistance/and disapproval from various quarters and dimensions. As of now, the marriage laws of our country do not cognize live-in relationships as a form of marriage. Unless a substantive law in the realm of marriage deals with that question comprehensively, it is not advisable at this point of time to bring in such relationships within the scope of the proposed law, whose object is to strike at the root of unwarranted interference of village assemblies even in relation to perfectly legal marriages and to generate important social perspectives on liberty rights and autonomy of individuals. Another suggestion is that forced marriages at the instance of family members should also be brought within the net of the proposed law. The problem of forced marriages has a different dimension as the members of khap panchayats and the like do not come into the picture there. They can be effectively taken care of within the ambit of general penal law and Child Marriages (Prohibition) Act. Further, it is felt that by enlarging the scope of the proposed law to include offensive conduct of individual family members/relatives, the integrity of the proposed law will be lost in so far as it aims to replace or substitute the entire corpus of existing criminal law on the subject.

7.3 Another comment that the criminalization of the acts of groups and focus on punishment by itself will not be able to abate the mischief and the prevention/protection aspects should also receive due consideration. However, it may be seen that the proposed Bill as recast deals with all these aspects. Reining in the high-handed acts of caste assemblies within the pale of penal law with emphasis on deterrent element is a desideratum that needs to be given due priority to combat the existing evil.

7.4 The National Commission for Women has crafted a Bill titled "Prevention of Crimes in the name of Honour and Tradition". The Bill is closer in thinking to the law proposed by the Law Commission. It suggests certain prohibitive and penal measures. It provides for recording of declaration of an intended marriage by the couple concerned as a means of seeking protection apart from penalizing the acts of harassment etc. caused to the woman or her partner. However it misses the necessity and desirability of the focus on directly dealing with unlawful assemblies and their vicious influences. Further, the offences under general law are also included in the said Bill. But, certain aspects contained in that Bill have been usefully incorporated in the proposed law.

7.5 The Government of National Capital Territory of Delhi through its Department of Home, has forwarded the comments of an officer of the Law Department. The main point highlighted is that since the subject of unlawful assembly stands covered by Section 141 of the Indian Penal Code and Section 506 I.P.C. provides for criminal intimidation, there is no need for the proposed law. It further says that necessary amendments to the Code of Criminal Procedure should take care of the situation.

These views have been examined. In fact, they have been considered and kept in mind while drafting the proposed law. Section 141 I.P.C. fifth clause alone has some resemblance to the subject on hand. However, the thrust of that clause is the conduct of subjecting—"any person to do what he is not legally bound to do or to omit to do what he is legally entitled to do". It is doubtful whether the unlawful assembly of the nature contemplated by the proposed Bill is covered under Section 141. That apart, the proposed law intends to deal with the conduct of local bodies or caste assemblies and to strike at the blind fury of such associations acting in disregard of liberty of persons.

A special class of unlawful assembly with a different punishment is, therefore, suggested as a measure of greater efficacy. In any event, Section 149 I.P.C. read with Section 141 (which envisages five or more persons of 'unlawful assembly' acting in furtherance of common object) is not to be affected. It would apply to situations other than those contemplated by the present law. Further, the above view failed to perceive the shift in perspectives and the need to intensify the focus, as already stated, to act in promotion of liberty and its contours. The Commission is unable to share the view that the amendments to

Cr.P.C. would be able to serve the intended purpose of the proposed law.

7.6 The other response has come from the Government of Odisha (Law Department). According to this opinion, some overlap between Section 141 and 149 I.P.C. and the proposed law is seen.

This misconception is again rooted in the conceptual misgivings. It must be seen that the provisions of this Act coupled with those in IPC can be simultaneously worked in some areas and they can be complementary to each other. Care has also been taken to see that the offence dealt with under general criminal law are not, as far as possible, brought within the purview of the proposed law. It has been made clear that the provisions of this law are not in derogation of those in IPC, but will be in addition thereof. However, the Commission would like to clarify that bringing the offence of criminal intimidation into the gamut of this law is to prescribe more severe punishment. The Commission is of the view that instead of adding the same provision in IPC, it is better that this stand alone law dealing with honour crimes should contain such provision.

7.7 One more response has come from the Law Department of Government of Madhya Pradesh. Apart from suggesting the increase of length of imprisonment, it has been suggested that the 'pardon' shall be granted to an accused who is willing to depose as prosecution witness so that there would be better scope for conviction.

8. COUNSELLING AND AWARENESS

8.1 Apart from legislation to effectively curb honour related crimes, it is equally important that the steps should be taken to organise counselling programmes for the village communities, for instance to explain to them that sagotra marriages are not opposed to law, religion 'sadachar' or medical science. In the initial stages, social workers and volunteers may not be in a position to accomplish this task as they may meet stiff resistance and they may not able to build up much needed trust. The spiritual or religious leaders or respected elderly persons like retired officials and political personalities, members of legal profession, teachers, etc., can be requested to address the village gatherings and explain to them the real position and the need to shed superstition and abominable practices. So also the services of medical practitioners of repute should be utilised by the official establishment to convince the people that the sagotra marriages do not have any adverse effects on the health and well-being of the couple or progeny. Side by side, discourses on electronic media by respected persons and scholars should be organised. Media too can play very useful role in shaping the mindset of the people concerned. So also, the District and Taluqa Legal Services bodies can undertake this task through appropriate means.

9. REGISTRATION OF MARRIAGE

9.1 In order to avoid unnecessary hassles and harassment from external sources directed against the couple who are intending to marry and even their family members who would like to go according to their wishes, it is desirable that the procedure under the Special Marriage Act is simplified. The time gap between the date of giving notice of marriage and the registration should be removed and the entire process of registration of marriage should be expedited. The domicile restriction should also be removed. We are aware, that already an amendment is proposed to the Special Marriage Act by the Government of India by introducing a Bill in the Parliament. It is, therefore, not necessary to make a detailed study and give specific recommendation on this aspect.

10. A RECENT SUPREME COURT JUDGMENT, RE: DEATH SENTENCE

10.1 Before we conclude this Report, we would like to refer to one recent decision of the Supreme Court wherein a direction of far reaching consequences has been given by the Supreme Court while laying down the proposition that the so-called honour killing comes within the category of rarest of the rare cases deserving death punishment. It was observed "this is necessary as a deterrent for such outrageous, uncivilized behaviour. All persons who are planning to perpetrate 'honour killing' should know that the gallows await them". This decision in Bhagwan Das Vs. State (NCT of Delhi) [(2011) 6 SCC 396] as well as the decision in Arumugam Servai (supra) were rendered by the same Bench. A copy of the judgment was directed to be sent to all the High Courts who shall circulate the same to all the Sessions Judges.

Following this judgment, in the recent times, as seen from the newspaper reports, almost all the accused in the so-called honour killing murder cases were sentenced to death by the Sessions Courts in U.P. and Delhi. With great respect, we are constrained to say that such a blanket direction given by the Supreme Court making death sentence a rule in "honour killings" cases, makes a departure from the principles firmly entrenched in our criminal jurisprudence by virtue of a series of decisions rendered by larger Benches of Supreme Court, for e.g. Bachan Singh Vs. State of Punjab and Machhi Singh Vs. State of Punjab. It is settled law that aggravating and mitigating circumstances should be weighed and it is only in very exceptional and rare cases, death sentence should be imposed. Death sentence, in other words, is a last resort. Further, where there is more than one accused, the degree of participation and culpability may vary. It is needless to emphasis that each case must be judged by the facts and circumstances emerging in that case. No hard and fast rule can be laid down in the light of the

Supreme Court's consistent approach towards death sentence vs. life imprisonment issue. This judgment in the case of Bhagwan Das is bound to create uncertainty in the state of law and we are sure that in the near future, the correctness of such proposition will be tested by a larger Bench of Hon'ble Supreme Court.

11. SUMMARY OF RECOMMENDATIONS

11.1 In order to keep a check on the high-handed and unwarranted interference by the caste assemblies or panchayats with sagotra, inter-caste or inter-religious marriages, which are otherwise lawful, this legislation has been proposed so as to prevent the acts endangering the liberty of the couple married or intending to marry and their family members. It is considered necessary that there should be a threshold bar against the congregation or assembly for the purpose of disapproving such marriage/intended marriage and the conduct of the young couple.

The members gathering for such purpose, i.e., for condemning the marriage with a view to take necessary consequential action, are to be treated as members of unlawful assembly for which a mandatory minimum punishment has been prescribed.

11.2 So also the acts of endangerment of liberty including social boycott, harassment, etc. of the couple or their family members are treated as offences punishable with mandatory minimum sentence. The acts of criminal intimidation by members of unlawful assembly or others acting at their instance or otherwise are also made punishable with mandatory minimum sentence.

11.3 A presumption that a person participating in an unlawful assembly shall be presumed to have also intended to commit or abet the commission of offences under the proposed Bill is provided for in Section 6.

11.4 Power to prohibit the unlawful assemblies and to take preventive measures are conferred on the Sub-Divisional/ District Magistrate. Further, a SDM/DM is enjoined to receive a request or information from any person seeking protection from the assembly of persons or members of any family who are likely to or who have been objecting to the lawful marriage.

11.5 The provisions of this proposed Bill are without prejudice to the provisions of Indian Penal Code. Care has been taken, as far as possible, to see that there is no overlapping with the provisions of the general penal law. In other words, the criminal acts other than those specifically falling under the proposed Bill are punishable under the general penal law.

11.6 The offence will be tried by a Court of Session in the district and the offences are cognizable, non-bailable and non-compoundable.

11.7 Accordingly, the Prohibition of Interference with the Freedom of Matrimonial Alliances Bill 20___ has been prepared in order to effectively check the existing social malady.

[Justice (Retd.) P. V. Reddi]
Chairman

[Justice (Retd.) Shiv Kumar Sharma]
Member

[Amarjit Singh]
Member

Annexure – I
[Refer para 2.7 of the Report]

Source: http://lawcommissionofindia.nic.in

Bibliography

BOOKS

Ahuja, R. (2006), *Social Problems in India*, Jaipur: Rawat Publications.

Altekar, A.S. (1959), *The Position of Women in Hindu Civilization: From Prehistoric Times to the Present Day*, Delhi: Motilal Banarsidass Publishers.

Banerjee-Dube, I. (Eds.), (2008), *Caste in History*, New Delhi: Oxford University Press.

Bathia, Har Bhagwan (1994), *Panchayati Raj and Political Parties: An Empirical Study at Gross-Root Level in Haryana*, Kurukshetra: Nirmal Book Agency.

Buhler, G. (1990), *The Laws of Manu*, New Delhi: Ahuja Book Company.

Chakravarti, U. (2003), *Gendering Caste: Through a Feminist Lens*, Calcutta: Stree.

Courtright, P.B. (1994), "The Iconographies of Sati" in J.S. Hawley (Ed.), *Sati: The Blessing and Curse*, New York: Oxford University Press

Devi, L. (Ed.), (1998), *Social Stratification Setup and New Approaches to Sociology*, New Delhi: Anmol Publications.

Dewan, V.K. (2000), *Law Relating to Offences against Women*, New Delhi: Orient Law House.

Gupta, D. (Ed.), (1991), *Social Stratification*, New Delhi: Oxford University Press.

Hershman, P. (1981), *Punjabi Kinship and Marriage*, Delhi, Hindustan Pub. Corporation.

Jois, M.R. (2002), *Ancient Indian Law—Eternal Values in Manu Smriti*, Delhi: Universal Pub. Company.

Liddle, J. and Joshi, R. (1986), *Daughters of Independence: Gender, Caste and Class in India*, New Delhi: Kali for Women.

Omvedt, G. (1990), *Violence Against Women: New Movements and New*

Theories in India, New Delhi: Kali for Women.

Oxford Dictionary Thesaurus, New Delhi: Oxford University Press, 2001.

Radhakrishnan, S. (2009), *Hindu View of Life*, Harper Collins Publishers.

Rajshekar, V.T. (2007), *Caste: A Nation within the Nation: A Recipe for a Bloodless Revolution*, Bangalore: Books for Change.

Rao, M. (2008), *Law Relating to Women and Children*, Lucknow: Eastern Book Company.

Roohi, S. and Samaddar, R. (2009), *Key Texts on Social Justice in India*, New Delhi: Sage Publications.

Sen, Purna (2005), *Crimes of Honour; Value and Meaning-Honour: Crimes, Paradigms, and Violence Against Women.*

Sharma, A. (2004), *Hinduism and Human Rights: A Conceptual Approach*, New Delhi: Oxford University Press.

Singh, D. (2005), *Human Rights Women and Law*, Faridabad: Allahabad Law Agency.

Srinivas, M.N. (1991), *India: Social Structure*, Delhi: Hindustan Publishing Corporation.

Thakur, U. (1962), *Suicide in India*, Delhi: Munshiram Manoharlal.

Tripathy, P.C. (2000), *Crime Against Women*, New Delhi: APH Publishing Corp.

Walker, A. (1987), *Woman Physiologically Considered as to Mind, Morals, Marriage, Slavery, Infidelity and Divorce*, Delhi: Motilal Banarsidass Publishers.

Warraich, Sohail (2005), "Honour Killings and the Law in Pakistan" in Sara Hossain and Lynn Welchman, *Honour Crimes Paradigms and Violence Against Women*, London: Zed Books

Welchman, L. and Hossain, S. (Eds.), (2005), *Honour Victoria*, London: Zed Books.

ARTICLES

"Afghan Couple Stones to Death-Culture", *Al Jazeera* (English), 16 August 2010.

Bhurga, D. (2005), "Sati: A Type of Non-psychiatric Suicide," *Journal of Crisis Intervention and Suicide Prevention*, Vol. 26, No. 2, pp. 73-77.

Byatnal, Amruta (2013), "Hindutva Vigilantes Target Hindu-Muslim Couples," *Hindu*, 14 October 2013, p.1.

Chaudhry, D.R. (2010), "Feudal Mindset in the Heart of Darkness,"

Deccan Herald, 1 August 2010.

Chesler, Phyllis (2009), "Are Honour Killings Simply Domestic Violence?", *Middle East Quarterly*, Spring 2009, pp. 61-69.

Choudhary, Rohit (2013), "Enabling Police to Handle Rape Cases", *Tribune*, 1 February 2013, p. 11.

Chowdhry, Prem (2004), "Caste *Panchayat*s and the Policing of Marriage in Haryana: Enforcing Kinship and Territorial Exogamy", *Contribution to Indian Sociology*, Vol. 38, No. 1-2, January 2004, pp. 1-42.

Chowdhry, Prem (2013), "Concept of Honour in Honour Crimes," *Tribune*, 13 October 2013, p. 9.

"Court Comes to Sibling Couples Rescue", *Telegraph* (Calcutta), 16 October 2004.

"Crime and Punishment", *Times of India* (New Delhi), 27 April 2011.

Dahiya, Prem Singh (2013), "Khaps Subscribes to Indian Philosophy," *Tribune* 15 October, 2013, p. 8.

Deswal, Rajbir (2013), "When Family Kills its Own for Honour," *Tribune*, 11 October 2013, p.11.

Dogra, Chander Suta (2013), "Women's Right to Inheritance Still a Struggle," *Hindu*, 22 October 2013, pp. 1&10.

Dogra, Chander Suta (2013), "Women Should Covered from Head to Toe," *Hindu* 19 October 2013, p.1.

"Domestic Violence", *Tribune*, 30 January 2013.

"Fast Track Courts", *Haryana Review*, Vol. 27, No. 4, April 2013, p. 32.

Fisk, Robert, " Crime-wave that Shames the World", *The Independent* (London), 7 September 2010.

Goldstein, Matthew A. (2009), "Biological Roots of Heat of-passion Crimes and Honour Killings", *Politics and the Life Sciences*, Vol. 21, No. 2, September 2002, p. 29.

"He Died for Her, But She Takes a U-Turn", *Tribune*, 25 July 2009.

"India Prosecute Rampant 'Honour' Killings", *Human Right Watch*, 18 July 2010.

Kogacioglu, D. (2004), "Tradition Effect: Framing Honour Crimes in Turkey", *Journal of Feminist Cultural Studies*, Vol. 15, No. 2, 2004, p. 118.

Pandey, S. (2004), "Talking Tough: *Khap Panchayats* Refuse to Mend Medieval Way", *Deccan Herald*, 15 November 2010.

Ray, Ashis (2011), "Honour Killing Cases Among South Asians in the U.K. Rising", *Indian Times*, 4 December 2011.

Siwach, Sukhbir (2013) "Khaps Custodians of Social customs, says retd. Gen. Vats." *Times of India*, 8 November, 2013, p. 3.

Warrick, C. (2005), "Vanishing Victim: Criminal Law and Gender in Jordan", *Law and Society Review*, Vol. 39, No. 2, 2005, pp. 315-348.

JURISPRUDENCE

Arumugam Servai vs. State of Tamil Nadu.

Bhagwan Das vs. State (NCT of Delhi) 2011 6 SCC 396.

K. Belal alias S.K. Raja and Others vs. State of Orissa and Others II (1994) DMC 327.

Lata Singh vs. State of UP, 2006, 5 SSC 475.

Manoj and Babli Murder case 2011.

Muhammad Akram Khan vs. The State PLD 2001 SC 96; para. 3 p. 100.

R. vs. Nahar, 2004 BCCA 77.

R. vs. Sadiqi, 2009 Can LII 37350 (ON SC).

Sushma Prabhu vs. State of Maharashtra.

REPORTS

Amnesty International Reports.

Law Commission Report 2012.

Palestinian Independent Commission for Human Rights Report 2012.

UNITED NATIONS DOCUMENTS

Commission on Human Rights Report (E/CN.4/2002/83).

Convention on the Elimination of All Forms of Discrimination Against Women (1979).

Declaration on the Elimination of Violence Against Women (1993).

International Covenant on Civil and Political Rights. Adopted and opened for signature, ratification and accession by General Assembly resolution 2200A (XXI) of 16 December 1966.

Fourth World Conference on Women General Assembly Resolution 55/66.

International Covenant on Civil and Political Rights (1976).

Report of the Special rapporteur on extra-judicial summary or arbitrary executions, UN Doc. E/CN.4/2000/3, 25 January 2000, para. 78.

Report of the special Rapporteur on violence against women, its causes and consequences, UN doc. E/CN.4/1999/68 10 March 1999, para. 18.
Universal Declaration of Human Rights, available at: http://www.un.org/en/documents/udhr/

NEWSPAPERS

Hindu (Delhi; Chennai)
Hindustan Times (New Delhi)
Indian Express (New Delhi)
Times of India (New Delhi)
Tribune (Chandigarh)

Index

STUDIES IN ZOOLOGY

STUDIES IN ZOOLOGY

Part II

Dr. P. Raikumar Singh

AKANSHA PUBLISHING HOUSE
NEW DELHI • GUWAHATI • VISAKHAPATNAM

AKANSHA PUBLISHING HOUSE
4649-B/21, Ansari Road
Daryaganj, New Delhi-110002
Phones: 23268193, 09435116718
Email: ektabooks@yahoo.com
visit us: www.akanshapublishinghouse.com

Studies in Zoology (Part II)

First Published 2010

ISBN 978-81-8370-243-0

PRINTED IN INDIA

Published by Akansha Publishing House, New Delhi-110002 and printed at Harmain Offset Printers, Delhi.

CONTENTS

CONTENTS

Foreword

This book is my humble presentation as a tribute to my late husband Dr. P. Raikumar Singh who has authored this book during his mundane existence. He was an academician and a dedicated teacher whose sole aim in life was the welfare of the students. His love and concern for his students was so intense that he could write six Textbooks and guides in his favourite subject Zoology in spite of his busy schedule.

After his retirement from govt. service in 1996, he wrote a book entitled 'Studies in Zoology," keeping in view the needs of B.Sc. students. But unfortunately, he died before the book could be published. He left the manuscript in his own beautiful hand writing and the same have been printed without any addition/deletion/modification.

Zoology is a very significant discipline of study in understanding human nature. Its applications find it way into medical practices and for the improvement of health and care of patients.

Researches in the field of Zoology is now being conducted widely and there is no dearth of books and research papers on this subject. And in such a present scenario or simple book like the present one would hardly matter. Yet I sincerely hope that the book will be useful to students of undergraduate standard. I am aware of the shortcomings of the publication as the book is being produced when the author is no more. I hope and trust that all the omissions and commissions in this publication may be excused.

I would be failing in my duties unless I record my deep sense of gratitude to Dr. Ayekpam Chinglenkhomba Meetei for his untiring work in reading the manuscript and making improvement in the book with appropriate diagrams which he did as a labour of love for his teacher-oja Raikumar.

Jamini Devi
Formerly Chairperson
Manipur State Women's Commission
Imphal, Manipur

UNIT – I
CHORDATES

1

PRINCIPLES OF CLASSIFICATION

History of Animal Classification

Classification is the ordering of organisms into groups on the basis of similarities of characters. There are many different sorts of living creatures in the Universe. Some of them are represented by numerous numbers and others are extremely few. In order to gain a perspective and understanding of these diversified forms of animals, it is essential that they are easily identified, suitably named and properly classified into groups or sets. Identification means ascertaining whether a particular thing is a new one or already known one.

Several early Greek scholars, notably Hippocrates (460-377 B.C.) and Democritus (465-370 B.C.) studied different kinds of animals, but there is no indication of a useful classification in their works. Aristotle made the first attempt to classify plants and animals in the 4th century B.C. He indicated that the animals might be grouped according to their characters. He also established numerous collection categories, or genera, using as differentiating characters such as blooded or bloodless; two-footed or four-footed; hairy or feathered; with or without an outer shell and so forth. Aristotle suggested to naturalists the idea of arranging all animals in a single graded nature according to their degree of perfection. This led to the endeavour to classify animals into those that are 'lower' and those that are 'higher', at the grade of organization.

John Ray (1627-1705) was the first biologist to give a modern concept of species. However, it was Linnaeus (1707-1778) who laid the real basis for modern classification and nomenclature. Linnaeus is called the "father of nomenclature and classification." He made the first enumeration of all known animals in 1758 and included 1,29,370 kinds. Many animals have lived in the past ages but died out. Today, it is estimated that about one million kinds or species of animals are existing in our earth.

In the tenth edition of the *Systema naturae* (1758) of Linnaeus, the binomial system of nomenclature was for the first time consistently applied to animals and this work of Linnaeus became the foundation of modern Systematic Zoology. In addition, his work was characterised by clear cut species diagnosis and by the adoption of a hierarchy of higher categories, genus, order and class. This eminently practical system was quickly adopted, expanded and elaborated because of his great personal prestige and the influence of his followers. The Linnaean philosophy dominated taxonomy for the next century and most of the essentials of his methods are still components of the modern taxonomy.

Charles Darwin (1809-1882) during his voyage of the Beagle, encountered various phenomena of distribution, variation, structure and adaptation which caused him to think of evolutionary interpretation. Darwin stressed that the separation of taxa must be based on branching (propinquity of descent), but that in the ranking of these taxa into various categories due consideration must be given "to the different degrees of modifications which they have undergone".

Cuvier (1829) divided animals into 4 branches that is, Vertebrata, Mollusca, Articulata and Radiata. Others who advanced the scheme of classification include Lamarck (1812), Leuckart (1848), Owen (1855), Edwards (1855) and Agassiz (1859).

Ernst Haeckel (1834-1919) introduced the method of representing phylogeny by means of trees or branching diagrams. This method was useful and stimulating and provided the taxonomists with a graphic means for expressing supposed relationship. Haeckel in 1864 and Lankester in 1877 outlined the principle features of the classification that is used today.

Concept of Species

Animals closely resembling one another, by reason of their origin from a common stock, and showing constancy in physical characters, are included in one species. From earlier times many attempts were made to define a species, but most of these attempts did not succeed. And so, inspite of the importance of the species, there is at present no general agreement regarding the exact manner in which a species should be defined. The basic unit or "building stone" in biological classification is the species. On this line, species can be defined as a group of individuals (population) having many characters in common, capable of reproducing themselves, differing from all other forms of life in one or more ways. The individuals of a species are all derived from a common ancestry, related by "blood" , and can breed with one another to produce fertile offsprings that resemble the parents. Concisely, the species may be defined as a group of interbreeding individuals in nature having close similarities and common ancestry.

The species breed among themselves but not with another species, and this becomes one of the criteria for determining the limit of a species. The horse if crossed with the ass gives birth to the mule. It is not a species distinct from the species horse or the species ass, and it is infertile and cannot reproduce individuals of the same type. The concept of species was based on types which were individual specimens, from which a few were selected and labelled as types for purpose of writing a description of its morphological characters or distinctive feature suitable for identification of the species. Such concept is said to be typological. Since the philosophical tradition is sometimes referred to as essentialism, the typological definition is also sometimes called the essentialist species definition. Typological species concept is now only of historical significance.

Morphological species definitions sometimes run into difficulties. There are many individuals which show striking differences in structure owing to age, sexual dimorphism, polymorphism and environmental influence though they belong to the same species or are conspecific. Biological species or sibling species though may be morphologically identical nonetheless are separate species.

Biological species concept is also known as Newer Species concept. By late 18th century, it is realised that the medieval species concepts as described earlier were not applicable to biological species. Therefore, new species concept emerged. It was K. Jordan (1905) who first of all clearly formulated this biological species concept in all of its consequences. It combines elements of the typological and nominalistic concepts by stating that species have independent reality and are typified by the statistics of populations of individuals. The biological species concept solves the paradox caused by the conflict between the fixity of the species of the naturalist and fluidity of the species of the evolutionist. The biological species combines the discreteness of the local species at a given time with an evolutionary potential for continuing change.

Populations which are mutually exclusive geographically are called allopatric as opposed to two or more populations which occupy identical or broadly overlapping geographical areas and known as sympatric. The Indian species of Lion and the African are examples of allopatric species. In fact, the concept is based on population studies with reference to localities or geographical areas in which they are found. If the local populations are sufficiently distinct from each other they are called subspecies. The subspecies differ from one another in minor charaters rather than absolute characters like the English and the Egyptian sparrows which respectively are scientifically *Passer domesticus domesticus* and *Passer domesticus niloticus*.

Allopatric populations are often so distinct from each other that there is a little doubt about their having reached species level. Such groups of allopatric species are called superspecies. According to Mayr (1931) a superspecies is a monophylectic group of closely related and largely or entirely allopatric species.

A species consisting of two or more subspecies is called polytypic species. The sparrow, likewise the lion and the tiger, are polytypic species.

Some reproductive isolating mechanisms seem to be more dependent upon the environment, and therefore, more easily modified by external influences, than others. Ecospecies are groups of populations which are able to exchange genes freely without loss of fertility or vigour in the offspring; while cenospecies consists of ecospecies which may exchange genes among themselves to a limited extent through hybridization.

If there be deviations in form and colour, from the specific type, such varying forms are indicated as varieties of the species. Variations in species may occur in different directions. Not with standing the variations, the species remain separate and distinct from one another. Two or more species agreeing in many fundamental characters are put together into a genus.

Variation is the result of imperfect manifestations of the idea implicit in each species. This was the species concept of Linnaeus and his followers. Species was supposed to be fixed or static unit which did not change and as such existed permanently and forever.

The individuals of a species of animals recognize each other as potential mates and seek each other for the purpose of reproduction. The species is also an ecological unit which, regardless of the individuals composing it, interacts as a unit with other species with which it shares the environment.

Species is also a genetic unit consisting of a large, intercommunicating gene pool, whereas the individual is merely a temporary vessel holding a small portion of the contents of the gene pool for a short period of time.

Principles of Classification

The purpose of classification is two fold: (i) identification of the animal and to arrange different types of animals into groups; (ii) to express degree of genetic relationship or affinity between the different types of animals. There is hardly any single method of classification to satisfy both purposes.

The systems of classification may be artificial, natural or phylogenetic. Artificial (or practical) is based on external characters useful for distinguishing one animal or rather one species from another and grouping the different types or basis of common characters. Such arrangement sometimes bring together animals otherwise greatly different as in the classification of flightless birds under Ratitae.

More than ninety-nine lacs of different species of animals are existing on the surface of the earth. There are filter-feeders like the sponges and the mussels which live a sedentary life under water, tentacle feeders like Hydra and the fast swimmers like the carnivorous shark and the whale. There are vegetable feeders and also blood suckers like the mosquito. These have to be arranged or classified, in one way or the other. The accepted principle of classification is based on Organic Evolution which states that all organisms had a common ancestor in the past and are related. The object of classification is to express the degree if relationship or affinity.

Natural system of classification is based on available data on structure, life history, breeding experiments, ecology and paleontology, and it reflects phylogenetic affinity. It shows the course of evolution from single celled animals to multicellular animals called Metazoa, acoclomate to coelomate, non segmented coelomate to segmented and the latter into non chordates, chordates and vertebrates from fiish to mammalia. It is a fact that more related the animals are, closer become the resemblance in form and structure ; the children of the same parentage have common physical features, by which they can be distinguished from those of another parentage. In pursuance to this argument, classification is based upon structural similarities and differences. Of a number of characters that make up the animal body, relatively more stable characters, like the skeletal, the nervous and the genital organs, are used as a guide or key in classification. However, the morphological resemblances do not always reflect blood relationship or phylogeny. Therefore, the avowed aim of classification to reflect phylogeny is not always realised. This classification is a compromise between purely practical classification based on morphology and the classification that expresses phylogeny. Structures, however cannot be permanently stable for all the time, in course of long time, the stability is disturbed under the influence of surroundings or the environment, or on account of a change in the constellation of genes, and the characters are modified so much so, that it often becomes difficult to assign an animal to a group or to a family to which it belonged. This is generally the case with parasites which suffer degeneration in parts or whole, and the characteristic features are so obliterated that only by tracing their early developmental history, true affinity is discovered. Saculina is a bag of reproductive cells, parasitic on crabs, but its larval form shows that it is a Crustacea. The Tunicate did not reveal its chordate character till its developmental stages were studied.

Importance of Classification

There is extreme need to classify the animals in tune with the modern ways of thinking. Classification is for convenience of identification and future reference. Classification provides a vocabulary for writing and talking about plants and animals. Classification helps in the discovery of new knowledge. The most important object of classification is to trace out the degree of relationship or affinity between diverse forms of plants and animals.

Binomial nomenclature

It is a scientific method of naming organisms by the use of two separate words. This binomial method of nomenclature was first established by Carolus Linnaeus in 1758 and finally settled by the International Zoological Congress held at Berlin (1901) and Paris (1905).

Each animal is named by two Latin or Latinised words, the first of which is called the generic (derived from the word genus which in Latin means a race) and the second the specific name. The first letter of the generic name is written in capital letter. It is a noun, while the specific name which is placed after it, is an adjective qualifying this noun in number and in gender. Both are written in italics. This in scientific language our common toad is called *Bufo melanostictus*.

The generic name is a matter of opinion, and therefore may suffer change, as better knowledge as to the relationship between animals is obtained. In other words, if a species formerly included under a particular genus, is considered to be belonging to another genus, the original generic name of that animal is changed. Since the species is a fact, the original specific name of an animal as given by the author who first reported this species, is not altered unless this specific name was preoccupied, not with standing any change in the generic name. Moreover, the name of the author who first described the species, is shown by inserting it after the specific name. The author's name is written in abridged form. If the same animal happens to be described by two or more authors under different names, these names are sunk as synonymous, priority being given to the author who described it first. Thus, the cat was named by Kerr, as *Felis bengalensis*, and the same name was called by Gray *Felis chinensis*. Later as this genus was revised, the same species of the cat was renamed *Prionailurus bengalensis* (Kerr.), Linnaeus in 1766 named the lion, *Felis leo*, the tiger *Felis tigris*, the leopard, *Felis pardus*, the domestic cat, *Felis domestica*. He considered all these species as belonging to the genus *Felis* because all of them had the common characters : a short head, retractile claws and similar type of dentition (teeth). With advance in knowledge, the reasons for retaining the lion and the tiger, likewise the cat, in the same genus, became untenable, and the generic names underwent a change The lion was named *Panthera leo* (Linn.), the tiger *Panthera tigris* (Linn.), the leopard *Panthera paradus* (Linn.).

International Code of Zoological Nomenclature

At the Fifth International Congress, which met in Berlin in 1901, the International Rules for Zoological Nomenclature were adopted to establish policies leading to stable and dependable names for organisms. Although the original rules are nearly all in effect, some modifications have been made at subsequent meetings. The International Rules, sometimes called the International Code, consist of a series of rules and recommendations of such importance that all who plan to enter into the field professionally should be familiar with them, at least in broad outline. Those who describe species should be familiar with them in detail. The major objectives of the rules are to: (a) ensure that no two different species shall have the same name, (b) ensure that no one species shall have more than one "right" or "valid" name, and (c) ensure that the one valid name will be permanently applied in the same species.

One of the rules is that no species name shall be considered valid if some other species belonging to the same genus bears that name. If someone should accidentally give a new species a name previously used within the genus, the two identical names are homonyms. The first species given the name retains it, and the second must be given a new name. When all or parts of two genera are combined, homonyms may be created.

To make sure that every species will have only one valid name where several have been used, the rule of priority applies. The first adequate description of a species takes preference and the name used in this description is the valid name.

Other Rules

Obviously, all must agree on the kind of notice a systematist must present if his names are to be recognized officially. Names used in a letter or newspaper article would never be seen by most students and are not valid. Adequate publication may be written in any of several languages, requires the use of reasonably permanent paper, and requires that the publication be offered for general sale.

It is worthwhile to study the rules in detail, for they are an invaluable guide to taxonomic practices. Even with the rules, it is no easy to keep names and references straight. When a name has been changed, not everyone will be aware of it, and the older name will often be used. Field workers often report specimens under invalid names because they cannot be specialists in all of the groups occurring in the habitats they study. In other cases, honest difference, of opinion develop, so that for a time no one is certain of the valid name for a species. But with all its problems, the taxonomist has in his system of nomenclature a remarkably flexible tool, capable of change where needed and yet with stability as its goal. Without it, scientific work on animals would be well not impossible.

ADDITIONAL EXAMINATION STYLE QUESTIONS & ANSWERS

Q.1. What is classification?

Ans. Classification is the ordering of organisms into groups on the basis of similarities of characters. There are different sorts of living creatures in the universe. Some of them are represented by numerous numbers and others are extremely few. In order to gain a perspective and understanding of these diversified forms of animals, it is essential that they are easily identified, suitably named and properly classified into groups or sets.

Q.2. Write one use of classification.

Ans. Classification provides a way of grouping the taxonomic units (species) on the basis of resemblances and relationships into higher categories.

Q.3. In what respect, natural system of classification is more advantageous than the Artificial system?

Ans. Natural system of classification increases the amount of information available from the groupings.

Q.4. What is binomial nomenclature? Discuss the importance of binomial nomenclature.

Ans. It is a scientific method of naming organisms by the use of two separate words. Each animal is named by two Latin or Latinised words, the first of which is called the generic and the second the specific name. The first letter of the generic name is written in capital letter. It is a noun, while the specific name which is placed before it is an adjective qualifying this noun in number and in gender. Both are written in italics.

Importance: Binomial nomenclature gives the correct identity of the plant or animal throughout the world. It is the method of naming plants and animals that is, every plant or animal has two Latin names: a generic name designating its genus, and a specific name indicating the species. The binomials are more definite and precise than common names. They are mainly derived from Latin or Greek, since these languages are internationally known by scholars. They are frequently descriptive of the organisms. They aid the taxonomists in finding the original and subsequent descriptions which indicate the systematic relationships.

Q.5. Define the International Code of Zoological Nomenclature. Write the important features of it.

Ans. The International Code of Zoological Nomenclature is the system of rules and recommendations adopted by International Congress of Zoology.

Important features

1. The system of nomenclature adopted must be the binomial system to indicate the species name and trinomial system for subspecies name.
2. The scientific names of animals must be Latin or Latinized and underlined when typed or handwritten.
3. The name of the genus is a single word in a nominative singular and always beginning with a capital letter. The specific name may be single or compound word and should begin with a small letter.
4. The name of the author who first publishers the name when describing it should be written after the species name.
5. The generic or specific name first published is the only one recognized.
6. In the animal kingdom, no two genera can have the same name, and within a genus, no two species can have the same name.
7. The family name is formed by adding – *idae* to the name of one of the genera included in it and the sub family name is formed by adding – *inae* to the same generic name.

Q.6. A pair or groups of very similar and closely related species which cannot interbreed are –

(A) Biological species (B) Sibling species
(C) Evolutionary species (D) Genetical species. **Ans.** (B).

Q.7. The concept of species having the properties that it is a reproductive community, an ecological unit and a genetic unit is called the --

(A) Biological species concept
(B) Nominalistic species concept
(C) Typological species concept
(D) Evolutionary species concept. **Ans.** (A).

Q.8. A species is the –

(A) basic unit in the taxonomic hierarchy
(B) stage in which evolutionary process begins and ends
(C) group of organisms sharing the same ecological niche
(D) geographical isolated population of living organisms.

Ans. (A).

Q.9. Natural classification of organism is based on their –

(A) natural history (B) utility to man
(C) morphological similarity (D) zoogeography.

Ans. (C).

Q.10. The species inhabiting same geographical areas are called–

(A) allopatric species (B) sympatric species
(C) symbiotic species (D) sibling species. **Ans.** (B)

Q.11. The highest taxonomic category in modern classification of animal is –

(A) Class (B) Phylum
(C) Order (D) Family. **Ans.** (B).

Q.12. The species which are closely related but reproductively isolated are called as –

(A) allopatric (B) sympatric
(C) sub-species (D) sibling species. **Ans.** (D).

Q.13. Define species.

Ans. Species can be defined as a group of individuals (population) having many characters in common, capable of reproducing themselves, differing from all other forms of life in one or more ways.

Q.14. Give an example of trinomial nomenclature.

Ans. *Cervus eldi eldi.*

Q.15. What is the suffix added to designate a family in the animal classification ?

Ans. *idae.*

Q.16. Define cytotaxonomy.

Ans. The classification which is based on the study of cellular structure especially the chromosomes is called cytotaxonomy.

Q.17. What is taxon ? Give the role of taxon in taxonomy and relation of taxonomy and classification.

Ans. *Taxon:* It is a taxonomic group of any rank that is sufficiently distinct to be worthy of being distinguished by name and to be ranked in a definite category. According to Simpson taxon is "a group of real organisms recognised as a formal unit at any level of a hierarchic classification".

Taxon is used to represent the actual biological objects included in the rank or category in taxonomy and classification. Taxonomic categories like species, family, order and class are abstract terms representing only a rank or a level in taxonomic hierarchy. They do not represent a living organism. For example, all tigers form the species taxon *Panthera tigris.* All cat like species of animals constitute the family taxon Mammalia. All vertebrate animals constitute the sub-phylum taxon vertebrate.

Q.18. Distinguish between binomial nomenclature and trinomial nomenclature.

Ans. Binomial nomenclature is the method of naming plants and animals introduced by Linnaeus in the mid 18th century. Every plant or animal has two Latin names : a generic name designating its genus and a specific name indicating the species. For example, *Panthera tigris* ; it means Panthera is generic name and tigris is the specific name.

Trinomial nomenclature is a scientific name of an animal or plant consisting of three terms, the first indicating the genus, the second the species, and the third the sub-species or variety ; example, *Cervus eldi eldi.*

Q.19. All classification systems whether of books or automobiles or of plants and animals are based on one fundamental principle. What is it ? The common name of plant that is, mango is simpler than its technical name *Mangifer indica* (Linn.). Why technical name has the advantage ? Give the significance of the word 'Linn'.

Ans. The fundamental principle is naming (nomenclature). Technical name has the advantage that is, it is universally used for a particular species or a particular group of animals.

The word 'Linn' means Linneus indicates the first author who described the species *Mangifera indica.*

Q.20. Explain briefly the underlying idea of chemotaxonomy.

Ans. The classification of organisms by their chemical constituents.

Q.21. Distinguish between systematic and taxonomy.

Ans. Systematic is the scientific study of the kinds and diversity of organisms and of any and all relationships among them. Taxonomy is the theoretical study of classification including its bases, principles, procedures and rules. Ernst Mayr has defined taxonomy as "the theory and practice of classifying organisms".

Q.22. Describe the uses of biological classification.

Ans. (1) Biological classification recognises and describes as completely as possible the basic taxonomic units or species.

(2) It provides a way of grouping the taxonomic units (species) on the basis of resemblances and relationships into higher categories.

(3) This classification makes the study of the animals simpler and easier.

2

PHYLUM CHORDATA

Introduction

Among the milestones of the modern evolutionary advances undergone by the animals, the position of Vertebrates or more comprehensively the Chordates stand forth as one of the commanding highest rank amongst the animal group.

The Phylum Chordata (Lat., 'Chordatus' meaning having a cord, and GK, 'Chorde' meaning cord or string, referring to the notochord) is perhaps the most diversified and heterogeneous among animal phyla. When Ernst Haeckel first introduced the term 'Chordata' in 1874, it embraced three groups of animals, viz., Urochordata, Cephalochordata, and Vertebrata. Kowalewsky (1871), in his embryological researches, demonstrated the affinity of the Urochordata with the Vertebrata, with which they were then amalgamated under the name Chordonia. Most German Authorities also adopt the term Chordonia in place of Chordata. With this change in name, the Chordonia included only the three groups as shown by Ernst Haeckel. The combined effort of these authorities is an attempt to found the classification of animals on an embryological basis. This is a good thing.

However, there is no harm in keeping up the customary term Chordata to include large polyphyletic (heterogeneous) group of animals.

The Phylum Chordata now includes the lowly tongue worms (*Balanoglossus* and its allies), tunicates (Acidians), and lancelets (Ámphioxus), and Vertebrate animals (Cyclostomes, Sharks and other fishes, Amphibians, Reptiles, Birds and Mammals) and a number of marine forms that are not well established. In the scale of organization, the tongue worms, tunicates and lancelets are considered to be of lower grade and primitive in nature, and the remaining other Chordates are higher and more advanced in the same sense. Majority of the lower Chordates are marine, though some of the tunicates are sessile and they are mostly of small size. Higher Chordates are strictly non-parasitic, rather they are free-living. The Vertebrates comprise practically of all living animals of medium to large size. They are distributed in almost all the habitable places of the earth. There are some kinds of fishes, birds and mammals which are gregarious, but most of the Vertebrates adopt solitary habit. Many Vertebrates are of great importance in human affairs while very little of them do harm to us.

General Characters of Chordates

The chordates (including Vertebrates) have the following three most unique characters:

1. Notochord
2. Pharyngeal gill-slits
3. Dorsal, tubular, hollow nerve cord.

In addition to the above big three characters, chordates possess a large number of other features, which along with the 'big three', are described below.

1. Axiate organization

Like some invertebrate fellows, the members of the Phylum Chordata are bilaterally symmetrical. Typically, a chordate animal moves in one direction with one side constantly presented upwards. Assuming the animal to be standing on a horizontal substratum, a vertical or sagital plane will divide each into equal and opposite right and left halves, each of which is, as if, it were the mirror image of the other. In such animals the part that ordinarily preceding information (an usually, contains the mouth) is termed the head-end or 'anterior' (cephalon) and the opposite end is termed the 'posterior' or tail-end (cauda); the axis running from head to tail-end is most commonly called the antero-posterior axis (longitudinal axis); the back or the upper surface is termed dorsal (dorsum), and the under surface, usually toward the ground of locomotion is called the ventral (venter), and the sides are laterals.

The Chordates (especially the higher chordates) exhibit three body axes : an antero-posterior axis, a dorsoventral axis, and a left-right axis.

It may be said that the axiate organizations of Chordates through seems to be, at least superficially, similar to that of many of the higher invertebrates, there are a large number of fundamental differences between the two groups so that they can be considered as analogous rather than homologous.

2. Metamerism

Metamerism or segmental organization implies not only the serial repetition of homologous parts within the body, but each of these parts is working in co-ordination with all others for the upliftment of the activities of the body as a whole. The segmental structures, here, are functionally interdependent and integrated, as such the individuality of the body is not disturbed.

Metamerism, though present in the Chordates is very often masked externally; it is visible only internally in higher Chordates. In Chordates segmentation is showing in the nervous system, gill-slits, vertebral column, ribs and breast bone, and in the muscles of the trunk.

3. Position of the mouth

In Chordates the position of the mouth differs fundamentally from that of the invertebrates in that the initial position of the gut is not surrounded by any circum and ring of nervous material but than the entire nervous system is on one side of the body and dorsal to the mouth, whereas in the invertebrates the initial position of the mouth is surrounded by a circum oral ring of nervous material and the brain is placed more or less above the mouth.

4. Post end tail

The post end part of the body is distinguished as the tail which is the continuation of the body-axis posterior to the anal aperture. In Chordates the posterior part of their body usually takes the form of a post-end tail which is metamerically segmented. Further the tail of the Chordates has been developed probably in adaptation to aquatic habit long time ago. This may persist throughout life in different forms (such as Protocercal, Homocercal, Heterocercal, Pre-hensile, etc.) or it may be an embryonic structure which is lost in the adult condition. In higher Chordates the tail usually possesses vertebrae, muscle segments, nerve cord, and blood vessels but not visceral organs. It is extremely flexible and muscular and its original function seems to have been that of aquatic locomotion. This is clearly shown by the tail fin of fishes and the locomotor tail of tadpole larvae and the many tailed amphibians. However, in Reptiles and Mammals the tail is insignificant as locomotor organs. Earliest known birds even preserved tail, though the modern birds have reduced the tail region to a nubbin. Majority of the Mammals exhibit elongated, prehensile tails (as in Monkeys), foreshortened tails (as in Hamsters), fly-swatters (as in Cattle), balancers (as in Squirrels), and as organs of defense (Procupines). The highest vertebrate, the man himself although appears to be a tail-less creature, exhibits a tail in early embryonic stages. Vestigial reminiscence of this tail may be observed on the skeleton of any human being as the coccys.

The gradual reduction of tail from aquatic to land life is explained by the fact that in land forms the trunk decreases in importance as an element in locomotion; the limbs assume the primary role, and the originally stout trunk musculature is reduced, hence the tail is no longer of importance in population in land life and it suffers heavy reduction but is retained generally as a vestigial reminiscence of the ancestors.

5. Paired appendages

The higher forms of Chordates have appendages, either fins or limbs, four in number, arranged in two pairs. They are composed of tissues derived from several segme.

6. Cephalization

The anterior end of the Chordate body is specialized to form the "head" into which the brain and all the important sense organs become concentrated. In the lower Chordates including Amphioxus, the head, if at all present, is poorly developed and not sharply marked off from the trunk. But from the Cyclostomes onwards upto man, there is a steady increase in relative size and specialization of the head and its sense organs. This steady trend toward greater and greater prominence and domination of the head over the rest of the body is called cephalization.

7. Coelomate

Coelom or body cavity in Chordates is lined with epithelial cells of mesodermal in origin. Generally it lies in between the body wall and the alimentary tract. This cavity communicates with the exterior by the excretory and the reproductive ducts; further the reproductive elements are derived from the epithelial lining of the cavity.

The coelom of Chordates is different from that of most invertebrates and it cannot be considered as homologous with that of the invertebrates.

In higher Chordates (especially in fishes, amphibians and reptiles) the coelom becomes divided into two compartments : a pericardial cavity housing the heart, and a pleuroperitoneal cavity, occupied by most of the other viscera including the lungs. These two compartments are separated by septum transversum, a membranous partition. Again, coming to Birds and Mammals, the pleuroperitoneal cavity becomes subdivided into two which the two lungs are sheltered. Here the septum transversum is supplemented by additional septa, one of which is that found in Birds, called the oblique septum which separates the pleural and the peritoneal cavities. Further, still in Mammals the diaphragm, which is partly derived from the septum transversum, demarcates the peritoneal cavity from the pleural and pericardial cavities.

8. Pharyngeal gill slits

The pharynx is the anterior enlarged region of the alimentary canal, and in all chordates it acquires a somewhat complicated structure. In invertebrates the pharynx remains as a muscular tube primarily meant for feeding.

The pharynx of the chordates is an integral part of the alimentary canal as well as respiratory apparatus. The lateral wall of the pharynx in chordates is always (at least in the embryonic condition) provided with a series of paired openings called gill-slits which communicate with the exterior. The number of gill-slits ranges from one pair (*Cephalodiscus*) to 180 pairs (Amphioxus). In aquatic forms like the fishes this number is not necessarily more than four or five pairs.

In development, each gill-slit is formed by an outpouching of the pharyngeal endoderm and a corresponding impouching of the body ectoderm; later on the intervening thin wall breaks through and a continuous passage, called the gill-slit is produced. Typically in the fish each slit is fringed with many slender filaments containing blood vessels, forming a gill with which the respiration is carried out. Such gill-slits appear during the development of every Chordate animals but by no means always retained their ancient respiratory function with the higher chordates. Respiration by gills takes place from tongue worms to amphibians. However, the amphibians which transform from aquatic larvae to air breathing adults, abandon the gills at metamorphosis. The embryo of Reptiles, Birds and Mammals possess several pairs of gill-slits, but these are without gill-lamellae; they are never functional and they soon close up, most of them completely disappear later on. Specially in Mammals (including man) when the number of gill-slits becomes reduced into only one pair, these then form the eustachian tubes which serve to equalize the air pressure on either side of the eardrum. In the embryos of Mammals the blood is however, aerated by aid of the foetal sac known as the allantois; and after birth the individuals breathe by lungs.

9. As the progressive organization of the digestive tract takes place in the chordates, the stomach with its internally developing glands, the dorsal wall of the abdomen. The liver also arises as a special diverticulum of the gut and occupies a distinct position.

10. Notochord

The most important distinguishing character of a chordate is the possession of a notochord. The notochord (Gk. noton, back; chorde, cord or string) is also the most primitive internal skeleton of the chordate body. It is the notochord that has bestowed the name chordata to the group. The notochord is the first longitudinally directed, stiff but flexible axial rod acting as a fulcrum for the segmental muscles to drag against locomotor movements. The notochord is situated in the mid-dorsal line and typically extending along the whole length of the animal being placed a little below the ventral edge of the nerve cord but above the gut, with paired muscle segments to left and right of it. Anteriorly it terminates in the head somewhere near the base of the brain (or near the pituitary when it is developed) and posteriorly to the end of the tail. Anatomically, it is a rod composed of large vacuolated cells, the cavities of which are so distended with fluid as to render the whole structure turgid, resistant to pressure, but highly elastic; and the rod itself is covered by one or two sheaths of tough connective tissue (elastic external and fibrous sheath). Ontogenetically, the notochord is the first endoskeletal element to differentiate, and Goodrich has stated that "the notochord invariably develops from the dorsal wall of the archenteron as a thickening or upfolding which becomes nipped off from before backward, and continues to grow at its posterior end as the embryo lengthens".

The notochord persists throughout life in the lower chordates. In the tongue worms (Balanoglossus) the anterior dorsal side of the gut, over the mouth, forms a short skeletal outgrowth into what is called the proboscis. This outgrowth has been awarded the same name as the notochord, on the theory that it represents the anterior portion of that structure. In the Amphioxus and Cyclostomes, it persits throughout their life as the main axial support, but in the fishes to mammals it is later enclosed by cartilages or bony vertebrae, or else completely replaced by the vertebral column. The backboned animals or vertebrates are chordates in which the notochord develops in the embryo but later becomes enclosed by cartilage or bone or both to form vertebral column fully formed vertebral column is made up of a number of serially arranged logamental bones or cartilages that are organized about the notochord. Cartilage cells reinforce and penetrate the notochordal sheaths and partially or completely displace the notochordal tissue to construct the vertebral column. The vertebral column extends from the base of the brain-box to the extremity of the tail. Two pairs of appendages, viz., the fins of fishes and limbs of terrestrial forms, with jointed skeletal support, are joined to the vertebral column.

11. Blood vascular system

In the blood vascular system of higher Chordates, the blood is red due to the presence of red blood corpuscles or Erythrocytes, which take their origin from different sources in the body, but generally from the red bone marrow. The circulatory system as a whole is a closed system and the direction of blood-flow is forwards ventrally and backwards dorsally (which is the reverse of the invertebrate condition). Moreover in chordates the circulation of the blood in the blood vascular system is maintained by a central muscular propulsive organ, the heart. The heart in chordates is morphologically nothing but a specialised region of the main ventral vessel and consequently ventral in position. Whereas in invertebrates, the heart, if present, is usually a modified part of the dorsal vessel and consequently dorsal in position. In the higher chordates the heart becomes many chambered and is contained within the pericardial cavity, the bounding wall of the heart being called the pericardium.

12. A series of endocrine glands occur in most chordate animals. The glands provide internal secretions or hormones, transported by the blood stream, that regulate bodily processes growth and development.

13. Dorsal tubular nerve cord

In chordates the nervous system consists of an unpaired longitudinally directed nerve cord (trunk) lying above the notochord and internally containing a central cavity (neurocoel). The nerve cord may remain as a very simple structure (as in the lower chordates), or again its anterior region may increase and develop to enter a new milieu until in its highest expression, the human brain, it has appeared what is plausibly the most complicated thing in nature.

In all chordates, however simple or intricate the brain may be, the neurocoel persists, though exceptions may be said to occur in the adult tunicates, which are nothing but striking instances of degeneracy resulting from sedentary habit. From Cyclostomes onwards the nerve cord (ultimately the spinal cord) later becomes surrounded by neural arches of the vertebrae that protect it from mechanical injury, nerve cord (spinal cord) is housed in a brain box (cranium or skull).

The brain, together with the spinal cord constitute the mid-dorsally located central nervous system, from which nerves originate to supply the various organs of the body. The nerves, along with the associated ganglia, form the so called peripheral nervous system.

The dorsal origin and position of the nerve cord in chordates are attributable to the fact that the ancested chordates adopted pelagic habits receiving their chief stimulation from the sea surface above them and consequently the concentration of nerve cells to form a central nervous system took place in relation to the direction from which came the maximum stimulation.

14. Eyes if present in the chordates are always developed as outgrowths from the brain. Compound eyes of some invertebrates are never present in the chordate animals.

ORIGIN OF CHORDATES

Time of origin of Chordates

The Chordates are a very ancient race, dating back probably to the beginning of Paleozoic time, although the tangible record of their existence commences with the fragmentary remains of armoured "fishes" (Ostracoderms) found in the Middle Ordovician rocks near Canyon city, Colorado, in the Big Horn Mountains of Wyoming, and in the Black Hills of South Dakota. But these relics are those of creatures which had already travelled far along the evolutionary road and, according to most authorities, do not represent the most primitive members of the chordate stem. Hence we may safely say that the time of origin was not later than the beginning of the Ordovician, and probably long before. The earliest were probably soft-bodied, without hard skeletal elements likely to be preserved. The first Vertebrates are several groups of fishes in Silurian and Ordovician time. Thenceforth, Vertebrates are common and often dominant elements in the record of animals of the past and show a progressive series of developments toward the living types of the present day.

The earliest sharks and bony fishes appear in fresh water deposits, and later both groups invaded the seas. The amphibians probably derive from the Crossopterygian fishes. They appear first in Devonian rocks and were differentiated into 3 orders by Carboniferous times. The first Salamanders (Cretaceous) and frogs (Jurassic) are distinct, like their modern successors. Reptiles appeared in Permian time and expanded widely into a great variety of dominant types in the Mesozoic era, then most of the Orders died out at the end of the Cretaceous. The first bird (Archaeopteryx) appeared in the Upper Jurassic; it was bird-like, with feathers and wings, but had teeth and other reptilian features. The Mammals arose from the Reptiles, beginning in the Triassic, and differentiated widely in the early Tertiary period. The Cenozoic, terminating with present times, is a comparatively short era, but one of great importance, for it was during this time that there took place the interesting evolutionary history of the Mammals and man himself appears in the first stage of Cenozoic history.

Place of Origin of Chordates

For want of direct evidence, we cannot exactly give the real place of origin of Chordates. The most primitive chordate existing today – Tunicates, Amphioxus, etc. – are marine, inhabiting for the most part the flat sea, where they lead a wholly or partially sedentary life. In the Ordovician times, we find the first faint traces of the oldest known of our vertebrate kinsmen in the shape of small flakes of bone in rock deposits apparently formed in a shallow bay in an old sea. It is probable that the oldest Vertebrates were inhabitants of fresh waters, and most of the older rocks are marine deposits. Hence it is only when remains were carried by rivers to the sea that we can obtain any record of the early presence of backboned animals.

Vertebrate ancestry

Another problem confronted to us is the mystery as to how the vertebrates have originated. During the course of organic evolution innumerable varieties of animals ranging from the simplest Amoeba to the most complicated forms, such as we are, have arisen. Some 550 million years back there was apparently a revolution in the general organization of the animal body with the consequent emergence of vertebrate body.

One of the earliest to explain the origin of chordates was made by E.G. st. Hillaire (1818). According to him a vertebrate represents an insect lying on its back. If an insect turns this way and swims naturally the ventral nerve cord becomes dorsal and the heart ventral. St. Hillaire believed that a new mouth was formed on the ventral side after the old one had degenerated. Cuvier however, showed that there were many notable objects to this theory. This idea of reversal of an invertebrate body was applied by many other workers with different details. Prominent workers among these were Dohrn (1875), Semper (1875-76), Minot (1897), Patten (1891-1912), Owen (1883), Gaskell (1896, 1898-1906). All of them suggested that one or another type of jointed invertebrate with ventral nerve-chain and a dorsal heart was transformed into a vertebrate in which the heart is on the functionally ventral side and the nerve tube on the back. After more than a century of debate the methods remain fundamentally the same and the amount of details has become enormous. The present position is different and most of the great phyla of typical invertebrates have been eliminated from the list of the possible ancestors of Vertebrates. It is, however, necessary to sum up all these theories only because of their historic standpoint before the present solutions are discussed.

Coelenterate theory

The three-layered (triploblastic) vertebrates are supposed to have involved from 2-layered (diploblastic) Coelenterates. Masterman (1877) assumed that "the bilaterality and triploid subdivision of an early embryonic stage of Amphioxus has been derived directly from the secondary bilaterality of a circular coelenterate, resulting from contact with the substratum and from subsequent efforts to creep forward".

Nemertean theory

Hubreacht (1887) compared the proboscis and its sheath and cephalic pits of Nemerteans to the notochord and gill-slits, respectively, of Chordates. Some paired lateral nerve trunks of the worm are assumed to have migrated dorsally to form a single dorsal cord, while one pair remained lateral, as are lateral branches of the vagus nerve in Chordates.

This theory is however, not supported by any evidence and intermediate stages are unknown, hence it is given up.

Annelid theory

Semper (1875-76), Dohrn (1875) and Minot (1877) independently attempted to demonstrate the origin of Chordates from Annelids.

Both annelids and chordates are coelomate and metameric; both elongate by means of terminal growth; circulatory and urinogenital systems are fundamentally similar; both have dorsal and ventral longitudinal blood vessels interconnected around the pharynx by aortic arches. If the dorsal and ventral sides of the annelid are reversed, the flow of blood is similar, and the contractile dorsal vessel of the worm becomes the heart of the vertebrate. The heart of Amphioxus and that of vertebrate embryos is, as would be expected from the Annelid theory, a median longitudinal tube. Further, resemblances of nervous and muscular systems may be found in both ; and the differences between annelids and chordates may be interpreted as Coenogenetic.

Semper, in supporting the annelid theory, laid great stress upon the similarity of segmental tubes in Annelids and Chordates. The protonephridia of Amphioxus are identical with those of Annelids, and the Coelomducts of Annelids resemble the renal tubes of Vertebrates both in development and metameric relations. Some Annelids have both nephridia and coelomducts in the same metamere. Apparently, nephridia have persisted in Cephalochordates and coelom ducts in Vertebrates.

The presence of a longitudinal collecting duct, into which the nephridia open in such Annelids as Allolobophora, has been cited as evidence in support of the Annelid theory. But this evidence, instead of supporting the Annelid theory actually weakens it, since it shows that structures not genetically related by closely resembling one another.

The attempt has been made to compare the mesodermal bonds of Annelids and Chordates. In Annelids, these arise from a pair of teloblastic cells located in the posterior end of the body. In Amphioxus which is usually taken as the prototype of Chordate development, the anterior portion of the mesoderm arises as an outpocketing of the primary endoderm.

One of the most striking contrasts between Annelids and Chordates is afforded by the notochord. If Chordates are the descendants of Annelids, it is necessary to assume either that the notochord is a novelty or that an homologous structure is present in Annelids. Some morphologists prefer the first alternative. Others assume that the notochord has developed from the "Faserstrag" of Annelids, which is a bundle of connective tissue fibres extending along the ventral nerve cord.

Again, the absence of gill-slits in Annelids and their presence in Chordates has led to considerable speculation on the part of supporters of the Annelid hypothesis. The most plausible guess as to their origin has been that the gill apertures have arisen from paired diverticula of the pharynx, which reached the skin and become perforated. It has also been suggested by Dohrn that nephridia have been converted into gill-slits by the attachment of their inner ends to the pharynx, and subsequent shortening. The elongated tubular ectodermal passages of the gills of Myxinoids have been mentioned as evidence in support of this assumption.

Since, however, the gills of Cyclostomes are wholly ectodermal, and since in all Vertebrates the development of gills is initiated by endodermal pouches, the suggestion that ectodermal nephridia have been converted into gill-slits seems quite incredible.

Dohrn (1875) and Marshall (1879) regard the olfactory pits of Vertebrates as the anterior most pair of pre-oral gill-pouches, and hence unlike any structures in Annelids. Balfour (1881) and Gegenbaur (1887), however, opposed the assumption that olfactory pits are gill-pouches, on the ground that olfactory pits are ectodermal, while gill-pouches are endodermal.

Eisig (1887) believed that the lateral line organs of Vertebrates are represented in Annelids by certain sense buds found in Capitellid worms, in which these sense organs are metamerically arranged (in Annelids) as are the lateral line organs of Telecosts embryos. The intestinal muscles of Annelids are arranged like those of Chordates in circular and longitudinal layers. Annelids have longitudinal metameric muscles on both dorsal and ventral sides of the body. In the trunk region of chordates, muscles are primarily lacking in the ventral half of the body, but are secondarily supplied by migration from the dorsal side. Acceptance of the Annelid theory, therefore, makes it necessary to assume that the dorsal muscles of Annelids have disappeared in the course of phylogenesis.

Objections to the Annelid Theory

I. In 1895, Goette found the difference in the fate of the blastopore, an inseperable objection to the Annelid theory. Since in Annelids the blastophore becomes, at least in part, the mouth, while in Chordates it becomes the anus, or lies near the anus. It was this difference which led Grobben to classify animals into two great groups – Protostomians and Deuterostomians.

Supporters of the Annelid hypothesis minimize the importance of the blastopore and assert that even in different genera of the same phylum the fate of the blastopore may differ, so that its fate cannot have a phylogenetic significance.

II. Second objection was put forward by Leydig in 1864, who suggested that the oesophagus formerly passed through the vertebrate brain in the region of the 4th ventricle, between the "crura cerebri". In his support Dohrn stated that the embryo of a vertebrate is almost completely formed, that all other organ systems are developed, while in invertebrates the mouth is one of the first formed organs.

Speaking about the Annelid hypothesis, Minot (1897) says – "As regards the head, however, even theories have hitterto failed us, and no hypothesis as to the evolution of the Vertebrate head from the annelidan type has been brought forward, which could not be shown to encounter insuperable objections, or at least which appeared insuperable to those who opposed to the Annelid theory". His assumptions were –

1. The preservation of the ectodermal stomodaeum of annelids as the naso-hypophysial invagination of Vertebrates.
2. The formation of the vertebrate brain from several of the post-oral ganglia of the ventral chain.
3. The conversion of the visual apparatus and supra-oesophageal ganglia, which are prevented from fusing in the median line by the

enlargement of the vertebrate brain, into the vertebrate retina. He further explains the absence of eyes in Amphioxus as the result of degeneration.

Delsman's Theory

Delsman (1913) put forward a modification of the Annelid theory. The gist of his theory is that the neural tube of Vertebrates was originally a part of the alimentary canal of invertebrates and that it corresponds to the ectodermal stomodaeum of invertebrates as the Annelids.

As additional proof of this theory, he stated that the stomodaeum of Annelids, like the neural tube of a young Amphioxus, is ciliated. Morgan found that the neural tube of frog is ciliated. Another statement put forward by Delsman is that he assumes Amphioxus as intermediate between Annelids and Vertebrate, but he is confronted with the difficulty explaining the absence of well marked spinal ganglia in Amphioxus in which they should be more evident than in Vertebrates. Another suggestion of Delsman is that the characteristic differences which separate phyla, such as the Chordates, Annelids and Molluscs, may have arisen by changes in the region of growth by which a larval form like the Trochophore is converted into an adult. The suggestion that 3 great phyla may have arisen from a simple larval form like a Trochophore sounds attractive. Delsman suggests that just as the elongated Annelid develops from the Trochophore by the elongation of the region posterior to the blastopore separating mouth and anus as far as possible from one another at opposite ends of the body, precisely so Molluscs and Chordates may have originated from a Trochophore like ancestor by change of the growth centre.

Arachnid Theory

Some authors such as Gaskell, reasonably enough, sought the vertebrate ancestors among the Arthropods. The insects and crustaceans, most numerous, among arthropods, have not been given serious consideration in this case, nor have the Centipedes and their relatives been considered. A more worthwhile case has been made out for Arachnids, the forms that include not only the Spiders, Mites and Scorpions but also the horse-shoe Crabs (Limulus), and a number of Paleozoic relatives of this type, the Eurypterids or Scorpions. Patten devoted much of his time to they theory of Vertebrates descent from the Arachnid stock. The Eurypterids, like other Arthropods were armoured types, with an external rather than an internal skeleton. But some of the earlier Vertebrates were also armoured and also possessed some deeper lying skeletal structures. The fact that the Eurypterid armour resembled the armour of the early Vertebrates (Ostracoderms) cannot be denied. The degree of likeness is often so great that it becomes a difficult task for the Paleontologist to adjust whether a particular fossil is that of a fish or of the Arthropod. Patten made ingenious use of the available paleontologic evidence in favour of his Arachnid theory. This theory emphasises that the living Limulus is the nearest living survivor of the invertebrate ancestors of Vertebrates.

The resemblances between Limulus and the larval Lamprey (Ammocoetes) was described by Gaskell in 1908 and Patten in 1912. Remarkable is the presence of pineal gland which is all that remains of a pair of median eyes of Erypterid ancestor of the Vertebrates. One of these is still functional in the Ammocoetes. The Ostracoderms, the earliest fossil fishes, also show two median and two lateral eyes like those of Limulus or allied forms. The composition of the internal cartilaginous elements of Limulus and Ammocetes is similar. Such similarities have been traced in the case of respiratory and olfactory organs also. Gaskell's theory grew primarily out of his amazing detailed comparison of the cranid nerves of the larval Lamprey, with those of Scorpions, of Limulus and other Arthropods.

However, there are objections to these views. It cannot be explained as to what happened to the jointed appendages of the Arthropods. There is no trace of them in the Vertebrates. Further, in the above, it is the top of the vertebrate which is derived from the top of the Arachnid, but here to nerve cord is on the underside as in the Annelids. If the animal is turned up-side-down then most of the resemblance is destroyed. Besides this now the anatomy of some of the oldest and suningly most scorpion like Vertebrates, is well known and there are no features suggestive of Arachnid relationship. Gaskell's Ammocoetes-Limulus theory was also bitterly criticised by his co-workers. Although the views of Gaskell and Patten are interesting but now they do not find any positive support. The basic designs of the two phyla are so different that mere correspondence in either position or function between particular parts cannot be accepted as relationship.

Echinoderm Theory

Some zoologists believe that the place of the ancestors of the Vertebrates is among the Echinoderms such as the Starfishes, Sea-urchins, Sea-lilies and the like. No typical chordate characters are found among these radially symmetrical animals, and they have no internal skeleton and have too many peculiar and complicated organs of their own. At the first sight, therefore, this group seems to be the most unpromising of all as a place for the potential ancestor of the Vertebrates. Inspite of the extreme similarity between the Echinoderms and the Chordates, all these are enterocoelic type of animals. The early embryo of Echinoderm is tiny free-swimming creature and it floats freely in water. Unlike the adult it is bilaterally symmetrical suggesting that the radial symmetry of the starfish is a secondary affair. This larva resembles that of the acorn worm (Balanoglossus) called the Tornaria larva. The type of development of certain of the body cavities is identical with that found in the embryos of some primitive vertebrates. What seem to be the most primitive known Echinoderms, the Cambrian and Ordovician Carpoidea might be conceived Tornaria-like forms which had begun to settle down the sedentary like, acquiring an exoskeleton of many plates, together with a water pore system developed out of ciliated grooves.

According to Willey, "Echinoderms are descended from bilaterally symmetrical ancestors represented in their development by such larval forms as the Bipinnaria and Auricularia; the general likeness between the Echinoderm, Auricularia and Tornaria larva of Balanoglossus is so great that it can only be accounted for on the ground of genetic affinity. Balanoglossus is a Protochordate supplied with gill-slits and dorsal tubular nervous system, and requires only the notochord and segmental myotomes to approximate the Amphioxid type. Larval forms represent past ancestral forms, and the evolutionary sequence is worked out accordingly". The evidence from the larvae strongly suggests that in the dawn of the world, there existed some type of small, bilaterally symmetrical animal of very simple structure possessing many of the features of the larval Echinoderms or Acorn worm but lacking the specialization of either Vertebrate group or Echinoderm. But from these very forms arose types that retained their original bilateral symmetry, and which developed specialized breathing organs in the form of gill-slits, better possibilities of motility with the development of comparatively powerful musculature and a notochord for its support and better nervous control of activity through the development of a dorsal nerve cord. From this line, it is believed that the Chordates appeared and these finally gave rise to the true Vertebrates.

Neotenous larva theory

Garstang (1894) was the first "to look for the race of an ancestor of the Vertebrates in early instead of the adult stages of invertebrates; and he focussed his attention on the larvae of Echinoderm (Starfish, Sea Urchin, etc.). He showed that if the ciliated bands on the larva (Auricularia) of a sea-cucumber were to become accentuated and rise of as ridges leaving a groove between them, and if these ridges were to fuse, converting the groove into a tube, a structure would be produced which has all the relations of the vertebrate nervous system, including such details as the newcoenteric canal". De Beer points out that this view about the origin of the vertebrate nervous system has several advantages. Garstang's theory further asserts that if the larval form of such animals persisted and they become sexually mature they would provide "exactly the necessary material for the evolution of the chordates".

Still there are some workers who regard the similarity between the larval forms because of similar ecological factors. H.B. Fell (1948), for instance, shows that parallelism in development has often taken place among the different subclasses of the Echinoderms and he concluded that the similarity of the free swimming larvae of certain Echinoderms and Balanoglossus supplies no trustworthy evidence of common ancestry. Gregory (1951) says, "we may even concede, at least provisionally, that Balanoglossus may not be a chordate at all and that its bag-like, ciliated swimming larva is merely a parallel adaptation among different groups for securing a wide distribution in the search for suitable localities for the sessile or slow moving adult".

From this it becomes apparent that no final agreement has been reached. However, there is no dispute on the point that whatever the actual type of the ancestor might have been, it must have necessarily been bilaterally symmetrical and metameric moving in a cranio-caudal direction.

N.J. Berill (1955) in his book, "The Origin of Vertebrates", has suggested the following larval sequence "echinoderm – auricularia- hemichordate – tornaria – protochordate – ascidian tadpole – permanently free swimming chordate. On this theory the ascidian tadpole becomes essentially an interpolation in the ascidian life-cycle; and by the suppression of metamorphosis and through further evolution it gives rise to the Vertebrate as a whole. This view finds its expression in Garstang's theory also. Berill agrees with this view but not with the manner in which Gasrstang supposes the changes to have taken place. However, this view places the ascidians in the main line of the chordate origin; at least as larvae, although not necessarily as the basic stock in other ways.

CLASSIFICATION OF CHORDATA

The phylum Chordata has been divided into four subphyla.

Sub-phylum I Hemichordata (Adelochordata)

The hemichordates are worm-like soft-berlied, sea animals. The body is not metamerically segmented but is divisible into three regions – a pre-oral lobe (proboscis), a collar and a trunk. The post and tail is absent for the anus is terminal. The notochord is short and is restricted to the proboscis region. The pharynx bears numerous paired gill-slits which open to the exterior on either side behind the collar. The central nervous system mainly consists of a dorsal and a ventral nerve cord. The coelom is divided, occurring in proboscis, collar and trunk.

Class I. Enteropneusta

1. Body is worm-like with three regions-proboscis, collar and trunk.
2. The anterior part of the body bears numerous gill-slits which open dorsally. The gill slits increase in number during life.
3. The mesoderm arises by the outgrowth to five coelom pouches from the archenteron. An unpaired anterior pouch forms the pre-oral or proboscis cavity of the adult ; there are two collar cavities and two trunk cavities.
4. Notochord lies in the proboscis.
5. There is a dorsal tubular nerve-cord connected by a ring round the pharynx with a ventral cord. The skin possesses nerve plexus.
6. Sexes are separate. Examples – *Balanoglossus, Dolichoglossus,* etc.

Class II. Pterobranchia

1. They are small colonical marine forms, reproducing by budding and sexually, and often living in tubes formed by the proboscis which is usually flattened to form the buccal shield or disc.

2. The collar is prolonged into paired tentacle bearing arms.
3. Trunk is shortened.
4. Digestive tract is U-shaped.
5. Gill slits are reduced to one or none.
   Examples – *Cephalodicus, Rhabdoplura.*

Sub phylum II Urochordata (Tunicata)

The Urochordates are found attached to the rocks on the sea-shore. The body is sac-like in the adult and is enclosed in a tough leathery covering known as tunic or test consisting largely of cellulose. In the adult the nervous system is reduced to a ganglion and the notochord too is practically absent. Sexes are united. Reproduction is either sexual or asexual by budding. The larva is free-swimming resembling a tadpole. It possesses a dorsal tubular nerve cord, a well defined notochord in the tail region, and pharyngeal gill-slits. The ventral heart is tubular. The larva undergoes retrogressive metamorphosis to become the adult.

Class 1. Larvacea

1. They are free-swimming, small in size and pelagic.
2. Notochord is persistent in the adult which has a tail.
3. The pharynx opens to the exterior by two gill apertures, and there is no atrial chamber.
4. Individual at times secretes a gelatinous tunic.
5. There is no budding, and development is without metamorphosis.
   Ex.– Apendicularia, Oikopleura, etc.

Class 2. Thalliacea

1. They are free-swimming, pelagic forms, which may be either single or "social", and in the adult are never provided with tail or notochord.
2. The test is transparent, and the muscles are in the form of distinct circular bands.
3. Mouth and atrial aperture are at opposite ends.
4. Alternation of generations (metagenesis occurs) the adult (sexual form) produces by budding a chain of sexual individuals. In some (Doliolum) the eggs develop into a tailed larval stage, in others (Salpa) no tailed larval stage.

Ex.– Doliolum, Salpa, Pyrosoma, etc.

Class 3. Ascidiacea

1. They are fixed or free, simple or colonial but the individuals are not surrounded by a common gelatinous mass, each individual having its tunic.
2. Adults have no tail and no trace of notochord.
3. There is a large branchial sac opening by many slits into the atrial chamber, which communicates with the exterior by a single aperture.
4. Many of them form colonies by budding, and there is sometimes alternation of generations.
5. Often there is a larval stage with tail and notochord and undergoing retrogressive metamorphosis to form the sessile adult form

Ex.– Ascidia, Ciona, Botryllus, etc.

Sub-phylum III Cephalochordata (Acrania)

They are small fish like animals but without paired fins, jaws, vertebrae, skull and brain. Epidermis is single layered, but no scales. Notochord is present throughout the entire dorsal length of the body. There are no paired eyes and auditory organ. Pharynx is large and provided with numerous gill-slits opening into the atrium that surrounds the pharynx. Circulatory system is present but without heart, and the blood is colourless. Liver is a hollow pouch of the intestine. Muscles and gonads are metamerically arranged. Gonads have no ducts. Nephredia are U-shaped tubes with solenocytes. Coelom is well developed. The larval form is asymmetrical and the larval period is prolonged. The Cephalochordates occur near the coasts in warm and temperate seas.

Ex.– Amphioxus (Branchiostoma)

Sub-phylum IV Vertebrata (Craniata)

They are higher Chordates with vertebral column or backbone and a definite brain which is enclosed in a cranium (hence Craniata). There is a very high degree of cephalisation, so that a proper head region can be recognised. In them, the integument becomes a stratified epithelium of epidermis, having many mucous glands in aquatic forms. The skin becomes protected by scales, feathers or hairs. The endoskeleton is of cartilage or bones. The digestive tract lies ventral to the vertebral column. The organs of nitrogenous excretion are kidneys which occur in various types. A true muscular heart provided with valves is differentiated from part of the ventral vessel. Heart is 2, 3, or 4 chambered. Respiration is generally by gills and lungs. Brain becomes differentiated into regions. Endocrine glands (pituitary, thyroid, etc.) provide internal secretions or hormones.

The sub-phylum Vertebrata consists of two branches:

Branch A. Agnatha

They are vertebrates without jaws and paired appendages. This branch includes two classes :

Class 1. Ostracodermi

They are now extinct. They are the oldest vertebrates without jaws but had a head shield and an armoured body. Ostracoderms were very heavy creatures and were probably relatively inactive.

Ex. – Cephalaspis, Pteraspis.

Class 2. Cyclostomata

1. Body is elongate, cylindrical.
2. Skin is soft, slimy because of the abundance of mucous glands. Scales are absent.
3. The mouth is round (hence Cyclostomata) and is not bounded by jaws (hence Agnatha). The mouth is suctorial and fringed with horny teeth.
4. There is a single median nasal aperture.
5. Notochord is persistent; skull and visceral arches are cartilagenous.
6. There are no paired fins.
7. There are 6-14 pairs of gills ; gill pouches are paired.
8. Heart consists of a sinus venosus, single auricle, single ventricle from which a ventral aorta arises giving off blood vessels to gill pouches.
9. The brain is primitive and parts of its roof are composed of non-nervous material.

10. The adult kidney (a mesonephros) is not a compact organ, but consists of segmentally arranged tubules.
11. The larva of living representatives of the class has an endostyle and other ciliated tracts in the pharynx.
    Ex. – Petromyzon, Myxine.

Branch B. Gnathostomata

They are vertebrates with jaws and usually with paired limbs. The premandubular visceral arch is possibly represented by the trabeculae. The greater part of the respiratory epithelium of the gills is of ectodermal origin, and the nerves and blood vessels supplying the gills pass down on the outside of the visceral arches. The brain is more advanced in structure than in the Cyclostomes. The nostrils and olfactory organs are paired structures. There are 3 semicircular canals in the ear. The glands associated with the alimentary canal are very well specialised than in Cyclostomes.

The branch Gnathostomata is divided into five classes : Pisces, Amphibia, Reptilia, Aves and Mammalia.

Class 1. Pisces or Fishes

Fishes are "cold-blooded" primarily aquatic vertebrates. They form the first markedly successful class of Vertebrates. They are found in ponds, lakes, rivers, seas, etc.

General characters of Fishes :

1. Body is streamlined (spindle-shaped), divided into head, trunk and tail.
2. Mouth is provided with jaws and teeth. The position of the mouth is either terminal (situated at the terminal end of the head) or sub-terminal (situated behind the head on the ventral side).
3. Both paired and unpaired fins are present. The paired finds include a pair of pectorals and a pair of pelvics. The unpaired fins comprise of the dorsal and the ventral, and the caudal fins. The fins are cutaneous expansions of the body and supported by skeletal structures called fin-rays.
4. Eyes are paired and without eye-lids (except a few). A fish can see in water.

5. Nostrils are paired. They do not communicate with the buccal cavity or pharynx (except in lung fishes and lobe-finned fishes).
6. Opercula or gill covers are present on the posterior sides of the head of bony fishes but absent in cartilagenous fishes, such as shark.
7. The body has a covering of scales which are of different types. In some fishes the body is invested with dermal denticles horny plates. All such outer hard coverings constitute the exoskeleton of the fish. There are some fishes (example, Magur, Singhara) in which the scales are entirely absent.
8. Lateral lines containing sense organs are present on the two sides of the body. They are enclosed in close canals sunk beneath the surface, with open pores.
9. The skin is attached tightly to the muscles by connective tissue and is said to be living. Slime glands are present in the skin.
10. The voluntary muscles are divisible into myomeres the dermis lacks muscular elements.
11. The cranium (skull) completely envelops the brain. The cranium is made up of many lobes. In some fishes cartilogenous condition is maintained and in most cases one occipital condyle is present in the skull.
12. The teeth are not planted in sockets. They are simple and similar in structure (homodont). The teeth are derived from dermal denticles.
13. The vertebrae usually possess amphicoclous centre (amphi-double, having cavity at each end of the centrum).
14. The caudal vertebra fuse to produce the caudal skeleton.
15. The ribs are present in one form or the other.
16. Pectoral girdle (supporting the pectoral fin) is simple and represented by scapula, coracoid, mesocoracoid, supra-clavicle, post temporal and post clavicles.
17. The alimentary system is simple (but more specialised than the lower forms). Tongue, when present, is used for holding and catching the prey. Pharynx is greatly shortened up. Small intestine is not differentiated into three parts, the rectum is the only part of the

intestine. Cloaca is sometimes absent. Pancreas is not superficially visible (except in some). Salivary glands are absent.

18. Pharynx is perforated by gill-slits. Gills are the chief organs of respiration; number of gill-slits never more than seven pairs and usually with only five pairs.

19. The air bladder functions as a lung in "Lung fishes" but in most cases its respiratory significance is slight. Accessory breathing organs may be present.

20. In the circulatory system, the blood cells are nucleated and oval in shape. The heart is tubular consisting of sinus venosus, one auricle, one ventricle, and filling with the impure or venous blood. Arising from the ventricle is a ventral aorta which gives off paired oxygenation in the gills is collected by paired efferent branchial vessels to a single dorsal aorta. The hepatic portal and renal portal systems are developed.

21. The brain is small but the olfactory and optic lobes are well developed. Brain gives rise to 10 pairs of cranial nerves.

22. The internal ear has three semi-circular canals. There is no eardrum, nor ear ossicles.

23. Generally there is no urinary bladder.

24. The kidney is mesonephros.

25. Sexes are separate. Usually fishes lay eggs. Excepting a few, fertilization takes place in water.

   Ex. – Acanthodes, Torpedo, Osteolepis, Dipterus, Acipenser, Amia, etc.

Class 2. Amphibia

1. They live partly in water and partly on land. They are the lowest tetrapods, having two pairs of limbs with moist glandular skin and without external scales.

2. The skin serves as a respiratory surface and is richly supplied with blood vessels. The larva respires through gills.

3. The paired nostrils open into the buccal cavity and take part in respiration.

4. There is a cloaca which has a voluminous diverticulum, the bladder. This is considered to be homologous with the allantois of the amniotes.
5. The kidney is a mesonephros.
6. The heart consists of a sinus venosus, two auricles and a single ventricle.
7. In the skull there are two occipital condyles. The vertebrae are usually procoelous.
8. The middle ear apparatus has a single auditory ossicle. External ear is absent.
9. Lateral line organs are present in the larvae and in the adults of aquatic forms.
10. Fins, if present, are not supported by skeletal structures.

Ex. – Bufo, Rana, Proteus, Salamanders, etc.

Class 3. Reptilia

1. They are cold-blooded, terrestrial or aquatic vertebrates. The reptiles living at the present day are but the insignificant survivors of a group which evolved towards the end of the Palaeozoic.
2. The skin is dry, cornified, usually with epidermal scales. Bony plates may also be present.
3. The skull is larger than in Amphibia. The skull articulates with the vertebral column by a single condyle. The vertebral column is usually long and flexible.
4. In many reptiles the outer casing of dermal bones over the cranium is incomplete owing to the presence of temporal vacuities. The number of temporal vacuities and their relations to the dermal bones of the skull provide a basis for the classification of the group.
5. They respire exclusively by lungs.
6. The heart is imperfectly 4-chambered (2 auricles and partly divided ventricle). The aortic arches spring directly from the ventricles.
7. The kidney is a metanephros.
8. There is a cloaca.

9. External ear is absent, but the lagena is often large and coiled.
10. There are 12 pairs of cranial nerves.
11. Fertilization is internal. The eggs are laid on dry land. The embryo is enclosed in embryonic membranes.

    Ex. – Turtles, Tortoises, Lizards, Snakes, Crocodiles, Alligators, Sphenodon, etc.

Class 4. Aves (Birds)

1. The birds are warm-blooded, bipedal vertebrates. They have become so adapted to flying that in many ways they are now the most specialised of all craniate classes.
2. The feathers cover the surface of the body. Feathers may be wing feathers (flight feathers or remiges) provided with barbs and barbules, steering feathers (rectrices) on tail, contour feathers, filoplumes and down feathers. Feathers give heat insulation and also give planing surface to wing for light.
3. The fore-limbs are modified as wings for flight; hind limbs are covered with scales and armed with claws.
4. The mouth is toothless. It is provided with a sharp projection called the beak or bill.
5. The neck is long and flexible.
6. Nostrils are oblique slits surrounded by swollen skin called the cere.
7. The skull has only one occipital condyle. The entire skeleton is light and spongy (pneumatic).
8. In the alimentary canal there is a crop and a muscular gizzard; the rectum opens into a cloaca; there is no urinary bladder ; the urine is semi-solid and is removed along with the faecal matters.
9. Respiration is effected by means of lungs and air sacs.
10. Heart is 4-chambered : 2 auricles, 2 ventricles. There is no sinus venosus; right auricles receives venous blood, left auricles receives oxygenated blood from lungs. There is a single aortic arch on the right; red blood corpuscles are nucleated.
11. The brain is large, especially certain regions of it. There are 12 pairs of cranial nerves.

12. Voice box or syrinx is present as an enlargement at the lower end of trachea.
13. Eyes are with sclerotic plates, eyelids and nictitating membrane.
14. Auditory aperture is behind the eye, sunk deep hidden by feathers; there are 3 semicircular canals.
15. Kidney is metanephros.
16. Female birds have only the left ovary and left oviduct.
17. Eggs with large yolk covered by a hard shell.

    Ex. – Pigeon, Swan, Peacock, Goose, Fowl, Crow, etc.

Class 5. Mammalia

1. Mammals are warm-blooded, quadrupedal animals which have attained the most complete structural, developmental and physiological adaptation to terrestrial life. A few have successfully reconquered the sea and fresh water and have become modified accordingly. Mammals are characterised by their great activity, high rate of metabolism, "intelligence", and by their display of parental care.
2. Body is covered with hairs or furs; except in whales, in which hairs are temporarily formed in the embryo. In Porcupines the hairs are modified into quills, in the Ant eater into scales. In Rhinoceros the horn is made of matted hairs.
3. The skin possesses different glands such as sweat, sebaceous, odoriferous and mammary glands.
4. The four limbs are usually pentadactyl. In Cetacea (Whales) hind limbs are absent.
5. There is a muscular partitioning wall called diaphragm separating the chest cavity from the abdominal cavity.
6. The ears are provided with external fleshy pinna. Internal ear is with spirally coiled cochlea. Middle ear is with three ear ossicles.
7. Eyes are with eye-lids and often with eye-lashes.
8. Larynx is provided with vocal cords.
9. Teeth are usually heterodont and implanted in sockets or alveoli in jaws. Teeth may be absent in some (example ant-ear).

10. There are two occipital condyles in the skull. A bony palate formed of the premaxilla, maxilla and palatines, cuts off the nasal passage from the buccal cavity. The cranial cavity is large. The lower jaw consists of one bone only, the dentary, which articulates with the squanosal.
11. Centrum of the vertebra is usually flat on the anterior and posterior surfaces. Cervical vertebrae seven in number, excepting a few. (E.g., Sloth and few other species).
12. Heart is 4-chambered (2 auricles and 2 ventricles), but the sinus venosus is reduced. There is a single aortic arch curving to the left.
13. The brain has corpus callosum, corpora quadrigemina, and Pons varolli. Cerebral hemispheres are large with convoluted surface.
14. Urinary bladder is present. In the male urinary bladder opens into urinogenital passage or urethra which receives the vasa differentia and opens into the exterior through the penis. In the female the unirogenital passage is the vestibule.
15. Female mammals pass through oestrus cycle or heat period.
16. Fertilization is internal. The period of gestation varies from mammal to mammal.

    Ex. – Squirrel, House rate, Tiger, Rabbit, Guinea-pig, Bat, Mouse, Brow-antlered deer, Zebra, Monkey, Man, etc.

BALANOGLOSSUS

Structure, Life History and Affinities

Balanoglossus belongs to the Sub-phylum Hemichorda, Class Enteropneusta. It is a worm like marine animal, found burrowing in sand under water. The body consists of an anterior muscular proboscis, a short cylindrical region called the collar and a long trunk and posteriorly ending at the anus. Both proboscis and collar are used in burrowing. The proboscis first makes its way into the sand or mud by to and fro movements and then the collar follows and by distending, gives a purchase for drawing forward the trunk.

On the ventral side between the overlap of the collar and the proboscis stalk is a wide aperture, the mouth which is incapable of closing completely and whose lips are the ventral edges of the collar region. At the base of the proboscis next the collar is a small opening on the dorsal side called the "dorsal pore" or "proboscis pore".

The trunk is coiled in some species and as a whole irregularly ringed; this annulation is however superficial and does not correspond to the internal segmentation. The trunk may be subdivided into the front branchio-genital part, the hepatic region, and the rear abdominal genitial part (tail end). On the dorsal surface of the anterior branchiogenital region is a double row gill slits, each row situated in a longitudinal furrow; these slits increase in number throughout life. In the region of the gills and a little behind it, the trunk has a pair of prominent flattened areas or lateral ridges also called genital ridges. A number of prominences called hepatic diverticula, arranged in two rows are also present in the anterior abdominal part of the trunk.

Skin and muscles (Body wall)

The skin has the outer epidermis composed of a single layer of cells resting on a basement membrane. The epidermis as a whole is ciliated and it contains unicellular gland cells. The glands secrete mucous. Sand particles adhere to mucous forming a kind of dwelling tube in sand. Below the basement membrane lies the musculature

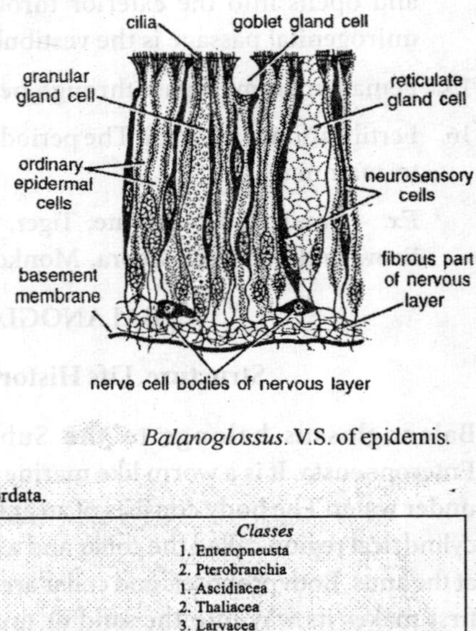

Balanoglossus. V.S. of epidemis.

Table : Outline Classification of Phylum Chordata.

					Classes	
Phylum Chordata	*Group* Acrania or Protochordata (Lower Chordata)	Subphylum *Hemichordata			1. Enteropneusta	
					2. Pterobranchia	
		Subphylum Urochordata			1. Ascidiacea	
					2. Thaliacea	
					3. Larvacea	
		Subphylum Cephalochordata			1. Leptocardii	
	Group Craniata or Euchordata (Higher Chordata)	*Subphylum* *Vertebrata*	*Division* Agnatha		1. Ostracodermi	Anamniota (Lower Vertebrata)
					2. Cyclostomata	
			Division *Gnathostomata*	*Superclass* Pisces	3. Placodermi	
					4. Chondrichthyes	
					5. Osteichthyes	
				Superclass *Tetrapoda*	6. Amphibia	
					7. Reptilia	Amniota (Higher Vertebrata)
					8. Aves	
					9. Mammalia	

* Subphylum Hemichordata is now considered to be an invertebrate group.

comprising an outer layer of circular muscle fibres and an inner layer of longitudinal fibres. Usually, the circular muscle fibres are weak while the longitudinal fibres are tough and strong so that they bring about the contraction of the body as and when required.

Coelom (Body cavity)

The coelom consists of five distinct parts, all of which are lined by mesoderm, and arise as pouches from the archenteron. The first coelom is the proboscis coelom situated in the proboscis. This opens to the exterior on the dorsal side of the proboscis by the single proboscis pore. The next cavity is situated in the collar; collar contains one cavity, or two (right and left) cavities separated from one another by dorsal and ventral mesenteries and completely cut off from the proboscis cavity. The collar cavity communicates with the exterior by a pair of collar pores. The third cavity is the paired trunk cavities which do not open to the exterior. All the cavities are filled with water. In burrowing through sand or mud, water is taken in through the pores and again expelled from the pores.

Skeleton

The skeleton structures of Balanoglossus comprise of the notochord, the proboscis skeleton, gill bars and pygochord.

The notochord is a hollow dorsal outgrowth of the alimentary canal of the collar region. It is composed of large vacuolated cells, but since it also shows topographical relations with the mouth, some authors call it as "stomochord" or "oesophageal diverticulum". It extends forwards into the basal (posterior) part of the proboscis, through the neck, into the proboscis coelom, ending blindly in front.

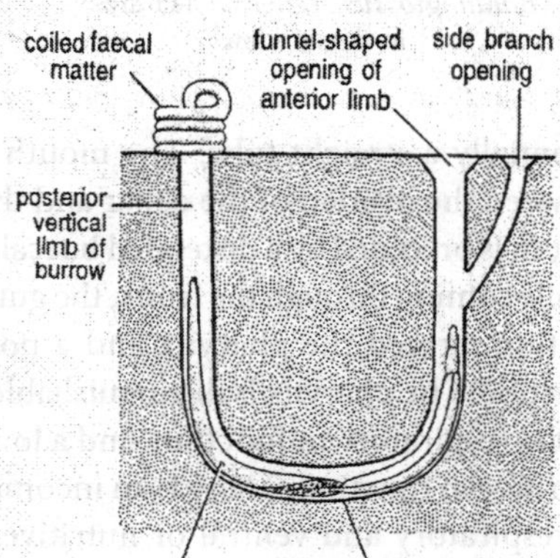

Balanoglossus clavigerous in U-shaped burrow

The notochord supports

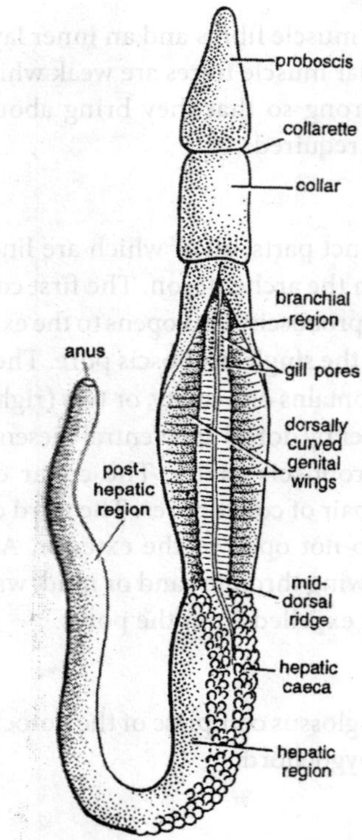

Balanoglossus, External features in dorsal view

the proboscis. Most of the longitudinal muscles of the proboscis are attached to it.

The proboscis skeleton (nuchal skeleton) is the main support of the proboscis stalk. This is a cartilagenous Y-shaped organ whose median part lies beneath the base of the notochord and the diverging arms or cornea extend backwards along the outer side of the alimentary canal of the collar.

The pygochord is a hard rod-like structure found in the caudal region of the body. This is a median derivative of the alimentary canal on its ventral side.

The gill-lamellae are supported by two rods of gill bars called primary and secondary gill-bars.

Digestive System

The alimentary canal is essentially a straight tube. The mouth is situated ventrally in a groove between the overlap of the collar and the proboscis stalk. Posteriorly the mouth is preceded by a distended buccal cavity running through the collar. While coming through the trunk, the gut is distinguishable into an anterior portion termed the pharynx and a posterior prolongation termed the intestine. The pharynx is distinguishable into an upper or dorsal chamber that is respiratory in function, and a lower or the ventral chamber that is nutritive in function. There is an incomplete partition between the dorsal or respiratory and ventral or nutritive regions. The sides of the dorsal chamber is perforated by numerous apertures called the gill-slits which open to the exterior. The lower chamber contains on its ventral surface a

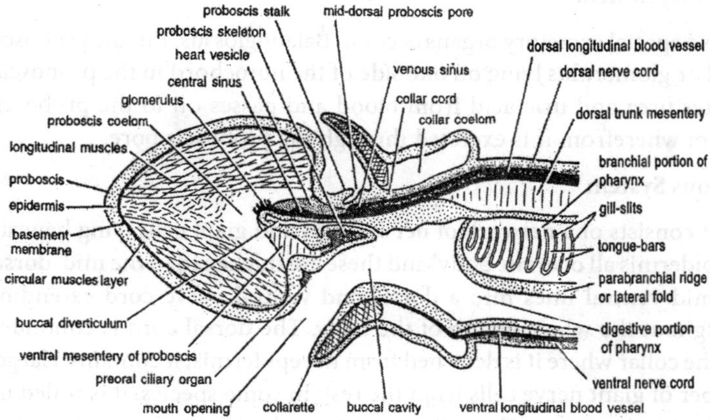

Balanoglossus, V.L.S. Anerior region to show the alimentary canal

longitudinal groove through which mud is taken in as food by the mouth. The intestine which starts from the end of the pharynx courses backward through the trunk; it receives openings of a number of hepatatic coaca. Anus is terminal.

Respiratory System

The respiratory system consists of many pairs of ciliated gill-slits, situated in the upper chamber of the pharynx. These gill-slits are developed as paired outgrowths of the alimentary canal, and more and more gill-slits are formed at the posterior end (of the branchial region) with advancing age. The gill-slits open dorsally by minute pores behind the collar. Water passes in by the mouth and out by the gill-slits, where it washes branches of the dorsal blood vessel.

Circulatory System

The circulatory system consists of two main blood vessels – the dorsal and ventral longitudinal trunks. The dorsal vessel at its anterior end forms a heart lying above the notochord. This is covered by a vesicle called the pericardium. From the heart a tiny blood vessel comes out so as to enter a glandular organ, called the "glomerulus", situated at the front end of the notochord. Blood in the dorsal vessel flows towards the anterior direction but that in the ventral blood vessel towards the posterior direction. The blood is a colourless fluid.

Excretory System

No special excretory organs occur in Balanoglossus. But the proboscis gland or glomerulus lying on one side of the notochord in the proboscis, secretes urea and uric acid from blood and passes on to the proboscis coelom wherefrom it is excreted through the proboscis pore.

Nervous System

It consists of a network of nerve fibres and giant cells lying beneath the epidermis all over the body' and these are thickened in the mid-dorsal and mid-ventral lines into a dorsal and ventral nerve cord extending throughout the whole length of the body. The dorsal cord is continued into the collar where it is detached from the epidermis; it contains a larger number of giant nerve cells from the rest; in some species, it is rolled up in this anterior part of the collar so as to enclose a canal, the neurocoel, opening in front and behind. From the neurocoel, dorsal nerve roots are given off to the skin of the collar. At the posterior extremity of the collar the dorsal and ventral nerve cords are connected by a ring-like thickening and there is a thickening also round the neck of the proboscis.

There are no special sense organs in the adult; but certain cells on the proboscis and collar seem to be of the nature of sensory cells. In the larvae of some species there are two eye-spots.

Reproductive System

Sexes are separate in Balanoglossus. Gonads lie within numerous little sacs situated within the trunk behind the gastric coeca. These project into the coelom but, they are separated out from the general coelomic cavity. They lie ventral to the gills extending along a ridge on either side of the trunk. The gonads, when ripe, open in the gill pouches by special pores. From here the sex cells pass out to the exterior where fertilization takes place.

Development

The course of development differs in different species of Balanoglossus. In some there is direct development into adult form while in others, the embryo passes through a larval stage – Tornaria larva, which metamorphoses into adult form.

I. *Direct Development*

In the direct development, for example, *Balanoglossus kowalevskii*, as contrasted with indirect development, for example, *Balanoglossus biminiensis,* the eggs are large. Impregnation in both methods is external. Segmentation or cleavage is complete that is, it affiets the entire substance of the egg.

The first cleavage begins about 2 hours after fertilization and produces two generally but not invariably equal cells. The second cleavage is also like the first and produces usually approximately equal cells. As a result of the third cleavage two tiers of cells are produced, a tier of four animal cells and a tier of four larger vegetal cells. Division continues. The mass of cells so formed is called morula. Further changes in the cell division of the morula gives rise to a hollow sphere called blastula. The blastula encloses a cavity internally. This is the blastocoel. Earlier stage of blastula is rounded, but gradually it begins to flatten at the vegetal or posterior end. The flattened area of the hollow blastula becomes pushed inwards or invagenated; a double-walled cup-gastrula being formed. The inner wall is endoderm and the outer wall, ectoderm which is highly ciliated; the internal cavity of the gastrula is the archenteron. The aperture of invagination the blastopore closes and the ectoderm and endoderm become completely separate.

The embryo at this stage being freed from egg-envelope, and moves about the bottom of water. It elongates and a transverse groove appears. From the primitive gut or the archenteron, there arises 5 coelomic pouches which become completely separated off and subsequently become the coelomic cavities of the proboscis, the collar and that of the trunk.

Mouth is perforated in the position of the transverse groove. Anus develops in the position previously occupied by blastopore. A second transverse groove arises and the body is divided into three parts – the beginning of proboscis, collar and trunk. Two gill-slits appear and others follow throughout life.

II. *Indirect development (development through metamorphosis)*

In the indirect development, the embryo assumes a larval stage – Tornaria larva, which resembles to some extent an Echinoderm larva

Tornaria larva

Tornaria larva is bell-shaped or avoid. The ventral mouth opens into a curved gut which is differentiated into oesophagus, stomach, intestine, and a terminal anus. A looped ciliated band traverses the anterior surface, resembling Echinoderm larva.

Running along the posterior part is tolotroch – another band of cilia. Below it in some cases there may be a secondary tolotroch. In the middle of the pre-oral lobe of the anterior end there is an apical plato or an ectodermal thickening with nerve cells and eye spot.

Metamorphosis

After a free period of pelagic life, the larva becomes smaller and opaque. Ciliated bands and apical plate become lost. It sinks to the bottom. An outgrowth gives rise to proboscis, and a constriction separates it from the collar. Hind part elongates to form trunk. A series of perforations from the external side (of the foregut) give rise to gill-slits. Collar-cord is formed along the middle line from the ectoderm by delamination. The notochord grows out from in front. There is an elongation of the post-oral region, and the body begins to elongate to the worm-like adult form.

Affinities of Balanoglossus

There may be differences of opinion as to the mechanism of evolution but not about the evolution of the higher forms from the lower ones. The chordates must have had an invertebrate ancestor and a primitive member through which the invertebrate-chordate line must pass. This primitive position is claimed by various lower chordates of which the claim of Balanoglossus in one which demands much consideration.

Though *Balanoglossus* was discovered in 1825 by J.F. Eschschotz in Marshal Islands, the name 'Balanoglossus' was first introduced by Delle Chiaje in 1829. Larval affinities between Echinoderms and *Balanoglossus* was first observed by Johannes Muller in 1846. But Metschnikoff recognized its true systematic position in 1870. It earned the rank of a chordate when Huxley and Bateson pointed out its chordate resemblances in 1885. Earlier to him, however, Sedgwick hinted its affinities with chordates.

Balanoglossus has got affinities with various groups of animals – both invertebrates as well as other chordates.

Affinities with Invertebrates

1. With Annelida

Annelid affinity of Balanoglossus was first furnished by Prof. Spengel.

Similarities

A. *Larval (between Tornaria and Trochophore) :*

1. Both are pear-shaped.
2. Presence of post-oral circlet of cilia.
3. Presence of anteriorly placed apical plate.
4. Presence of alimentary canal (similar arrangement).

B. *Adult :*

1. Vermiform body.
2. Straight alimentary canal.
3. Heart dorsal to the gut.
4. Body cavity formed from segmentally arranged coelomic pouches.
5. Collar of Balanoglossus is represented by clitellum of some Annelids.
6. Typhlosole of Annelid is represented by pygochord in Balanoglossus.
7. Feeding habit of *Balanoglossus* (burrowing, food capture, through permanently open mouth), the extraction of the nutrient matter in the gut, leaving off the refuse behind, suggest an earthworm

Dissimilarities (Adult and Larval)

1. In Annelids, the cleavage pattern is 'spiral' through which the fate of successive blastomeres can be determined
2. Origin of coelom and mesoderm differs in both markedly.
3. Anterior band of cilia unrepresented in Trochophore.
4. Nephridia of Trochophore unrepresented in Tornaria.
5. Double nervous system of Balanoglossus is absent in Annelid where double ventral nerve cord is the rule.
6. Absence of gill-slits in Annelids.
7. Absence of notochord in Annelids.

From the above differences between Annelid and *Balanoglossus*, especially in the absence of the nephridia which are usually present in Annelida, it thus points their restricted origin from common stalk. If there be any relationship with the Annelids, it seems to be very distant one.

2. With Nemertinia

Willy and others have suggested that indications exist of a relationship between the Nemertian and *Balanoglossus.* The features which are supposed to indicate this are : (1) Vermiform body with ciliated glandular skin. (2) Straight alimentary canal. (3) Nature of nerve cord. (4) Notochord of *Balanoglossus* corresponds to the Nemertian proboscis. (5) Unsegmented musculature.

Remark

The resemblances are entirely superficial. The absence of notochord in Nemertina and different arrangement of gonads are important points of differences which justify Long's statement that the affinities of Balanoglossus with Nemertinia is a rather complicated and highly problematical one.

3. With Phoronida

According to Masterman there are some features which are common to both Actinotroch larva of Phornois and *Balanoglossus.* The common features are :

1. A pair of gastric diverticula of the Actinotrocha larva may be compared to the notochord of *Balanoglossus.*
2. Nephridial pores of Actinotroch larva resemble collar pores of *Balanoglossus.*
3. Actinotrocha larva possesses 5 coelomic pouches like Tornaria larva of Balanoglossus.
4. Both the larvae possess ring of cilia membranullae.

Remark

Workers in this field have challenged Masterman's accuracy of work and have shown that he based his view on a rather insufficient ground (Goodrich, Ikada and others).

4. With Echinodermata

According to Metschnikoff, supported by Gotte, Korschette and

Hinder, the Tornaria larva of *Balanoglossus* exhibits striking likeness to the Auricularia and Bipinnaria larvae of Echinodermata in the following features :

1. General shape and external appearance.
2. Ciliated bands.
3. Development and 5 divisions of coelom.

In fact, the similarity between a young Tornaria larva and a young Bipinnaria larva is so great as to have misled even Johannes Muller who regarded it (Tornaria) as the larva of a starfish.

Furthermore,

(a) The anterior pouch of *Balanoglossus* has been compared with the beginning of the water vascular system in Echinoderms.

(b) The 'proboscis pore' of *Balanoglossus* has been compared with the water pore or outlet of the water system of Echinoderms. It is because of this point that some authors have even visualised the beginning of the Echinoderm water vascular system in the Hemichordates.

(c) A more significant resemblance is the arrangement of the coelomic cavities and especially of the *Balanoglossus* that exhibit direct development.

Remark

The resemblances in external appearance and in ciliated bands are only superficial. Apical tuft of the cilia and heart of the Tornaria are unparallel in Auricularia and Bipinnaria. According to Korschelte and Hinder, the resemblances between the larvae do not establish any near connection, but it suggests that Tornaria is the type nearest to the Echinoderm larvae. And basing on this latter idea a plausible theory of the origin of the vertebrates from Echinoderm line has been suggested.

Affinities with Vertebrates

Balanoglossus fulfits some characteristics of a typical chordate and that is why authorities like Bateson, Huxley, Gegenbaur placed it under the Phylum Chordata. However, the chordate affinities of *Balanoglossus* was first hinted by Sedgewick and later emphasised by Bateson in 1885 for the following reasons.

1. Notochord

In *Balanoglossus*, a solid rod-like outgrowth (notochord) from the anterior mid-dorsal region of the alimentary tract grows forward for a short distance into the proboscis. It has got some relation to the skeletal function. Histologically, cells are somewhat vacuolated as that of vertebral column. As a whole this notochord of *Balanoglossus* may be compared with the notochord of other chordates. Newman says that the so called notochord of *Balanoglossus* is at best an example of far-fetched homology and probably will soon cease to be regarded as a notochord at all

2. Gill-slits

In *Balanoglossus* numerous gill-slits open from the anterior region of the gut to the exterior, and are separated from one another by skeletal bars, which in someways resemble the framework of the respiratory pharynx in Amphioxus. Further, these gill-slits are developed as in Vertebrates, as paired outgrowths of the alimentary canal, and new gill-slits are constantly being formed with the advancing age. Also, *Balanoglossus* agrees with Amphioxus in the indefinite number of gill-slits. Gegonbaur went further comparing the ventral nutritive section of pharynx of *Balanoglossus* with the endostyle of Amphioxus.

3. Nerve cord

In *Balanoglossus*, the nerve cord is formed in the plan of nerve-principle. Two main nerve plexuses in thick forms, dorsal and ventral forming that may be called the nerve cords. In the dorsal region of the collar the main nerve trunk tends to be folded in the form of a tube from a short distance.

Remark

Newman says "all three of the alleged chordate characters of *Balanoglossus* (gill-slits, notochord, and dorsal tubular nerve cord) seem to be decidedly questionable. To the same extent the claims of Enterropneusta to full chordate status are no less so. Nevertheless there are cogent reasons for regarding the Hemichordates as at least distantly related to the true Chordates.

Affinities of *Balanoglossus* with Urochordata (Huxley and Gegenbaur)

Similarities

1. Presence of notochord.
2. Presence of respiratory pharynx.
3. More or less ciliary mode of feeding.
4. Some relation of heart and pericardium.

Dissimilarities

1. Notochord is a larval structure in Urochordata.
2. Absence of restrogressive metamorphosis in *Balanoglossus.*

With Cephalochordata

1. Segmentation of eggs was sketched by Davis.
2. Presence of notochord.
3. Presence of respiratory pharynx.
4. Presence of enterocoelic pouches.
5. Presence of series of paired gonads.
6. Presence of dorsal tubular hollow nerve cord.

Remark

Both of them differ in many respects, especially in the detailed structure of the gills.

Criticism by Newman

"Very many doubtful homology have been introduced into the fabrics of Phylogenetic Biology. One need only to mention the two so called notochord and central tubular nervous system". Tunicates which are closely related to Branchiostoma than are the Hemichordata exhibit no such resemblance to Amphioxus in architecture or development of gill-slits. It is questionable whether the gill-slits are really pharyngeal clefts, since they belong actually to trunk. If there is any region in *Balanoglossus* that deserves to be called the head, that region is the collar plus the proboscis. If the branchial region of the alimentary tract is really a pharynx, the latter must be extensive for in one species of *Balanoglossus* there are as many as 700 pairs of gill-slits, which extend far down the trunk. But that as it may, it was the discovery of the close analogy between the gill-slits in

Balanoglossus and Amphioxus that stimulated a search for additional chordate characters in *Balanoglossus*.

Conclusion

The review of the above considerations leads us to associate *Balanoglossus* with the Chordate. It fulfils some characteristics of a typical chordate and that is why authorities like Bateson, Huxley, Geganbaur placed it under the Phylum Chordata. But the problem is not yet solved as to its exact position in the evolutionary tree of chordates, if at all be a chordate, is still in the open field.

A careful study of the adult anatomy and the larval stages ultimately brings to light some resemblances. Between *Balanoglossus* and true chordates, but it seems in some instances that the principle of homology has been strained almost to breaking point. There can be little question that the Hemichordates (*Balanoglossus*) are fully accepted chordates, and are related, however, distantly and have been derived from the same ancient ancestral stock.

Newman prefers to separate Hemichordata to chordata as a separate Phylum and to arrange them at the end of a side branch of the ancestral tree that would come off the main stem somewhere between the Echinodermata and the true chordate.

Although *Balanoglossus* and its allies are considered or are not admitted by many zoologists to be related to the Vertebrates, there can be no question that their respiratory organs closely resemble gill-slits. Since, however, they possess structures which can be regarded with a fine amount of probability as agreeing in essential respects with the notochord and the tubular dorsal nervous system of vertebrates, it appears justifiable to include them in the Chordata, assuredly below the rank of Amphioxus in the level of their organization, but on the other hand, having a common ancestral tree with the Echinoderms.

Hemichordata
Urichordata
Cephalochordata
Ancestral fish-like vertebrates
Echinoderms

Ancestral Trochophore like animals

Comment: *Balanoglossus* is at the most the much modified modern representative of the extinct forms which are also to ancestors of modern vertebrates.

CEPHALODISCUS AND RHABDOPLEURA

Cephalodiscus and Rhabdopleura are the two genera of the Order Pterobranchia, Class Hemichordata. They are colonial animals, possessing the power of budding. They inhabit in tubes secreted by ectoderm of the flattened proboscis. Although they possess many similar characters yet their morphological and anatomical differences are not less in any way. Both of them diverged from the common stalk at a very early period. They gradually changed their constitution and features according to diversities in environmental adaptation. The similarities and dissimilarities of *Cephalodiscus* and Rhabdopleura are given in a tabulate form below.

Cephalodiscus

A. External features

1. Measures 2.3 mm. in diameter in broadest region.
2. No muscular stalk.
3. The body has an investment in the form by a branching gelatinous structure.

B. Nature of Colony

4. Though a large number of individuals live in a single gelatinous investment, yet they have no organic continuity. Thus it is an association of house and colony.

C. Proboscis

5. It is a shield-shaped lobe overhanging and concealing the mouth.
6. The proboscis cavity (unpaired) communicates with exterior by 2 proboscis pores. There is a pigment band on proboscis.

D. Collar

7. Collar region has 8-16 arms, each with numerous fine tentacles and contain a prolongation of collar cavity.

Cilia occur only on the arms, proboscis and lateral lips.

8. A pair of collar cavities open to the exterior by a pair of pores.
9. Arms generally end in a swollen bulb and have ventral grooves along which food particles travel to the mouth by ciliary currents.
10. On the ventral side of the nerve strand which is situated on the dorsal side of the collar below the epidermis, is a slender cylindrical cellular cord-notochord. This is homologous with the diverticulum of the *Balanoglossus*.

E. Trunk

11. Behind the collar region on each side is a small area in which body wall and that of pharynx coalesce. This is perforated by a pair of gill-slits only through which the water of the feeding current drawn in by the cilia of the tentacles, passes out.

F. Alimentary system

12. It is a U-shaped tube differentiated into a narrow ventral mouth, muscular pharynx, a short oesophagus and a bulging stomach, a tubular bend intestine, and a dorsal anus in the anterior end of the body (near the mouth).

G. Blood vascular system

13. Central nervous system consists of a nerve-strand, the dorsal ganglion or collar rod. It is prolonged into the dorsal surface of proboscis and arms. It is not hollow.

I. Reproductive system

14. Sexes are separate (except in a few cases where they are united). Presence of a pair of ovaries in between the pharynx and last part of intestine, a pair of oviducts opening to the exterior or dorsal side.

J. Development

16. Development takes place in the passage of investment, and there is a larval stage.
17. Asexual method of reproduction also takes place by budding which is somewhat similar to that employed by the nurse generation of the

Salpians (Urochordata). A process of the body wall called stolon grows out at right angles from the ventral side of the trunk region from the end of the stunk region from the end of the stolon new individuals are budded off, which become detached after they have attained a certain age (or before they are mature) and thus add in the multiplication of the colony.

Rhabdopleura

1. Body comparatively very slender.
2. Stalk muscular and subject to contraction and retraction.
3. Gelatinous investment is in the form of creeping stolon. Each individual exhibits in a delicate flexible tube into which the body is withdrawn.
4. They live in colonies of zooids and organically connected together, enclosed in an investment.
5. Comparatively smaller.
6. Proboscis cavity communicates with exterior by proboscis pores. There is no pigment band on proboscis.
7. Collar bears a pair of hollow arms each carrying double row of slender tentacles. The whole is supported by firm internal rods.
8. Collar cavities and their openings are same as in *Cephalodiscus*
9. Arms do not end in a swollen bulb.
10. More or less same as in *Cephalodiscus.*
11. Gill-slits absent; their place being taken over by a pair of ciliated grooves.
12. More or less same as in *Cephalodiscus,* but pharyngeal region absent.
13. Blood vascular system is similar to that of *Cephalodiscus.*
14. Blood vascular system is more or less similar to that of *Cephalodiscus,* only slightly differing in detail structure.
15. Sexes are united.
16. Not known.

17. Asexual reproduction gives rise to buds which retain their organic continuity with colony and thus true colony is formed.

Affinities of *Cephalodiscus*

A. Polyzoan affinity

In *Cephalodiscus*, the gut is curved, the anus being beside the mouth, beneath which are 4-6 pairs of arms with ciliated tentacles.

This character in *Cephalodiscus* may perhaps be adaptations to sedentary life.

B. Affinity with *Balanoglossus* (Enteropnuesta)

Cephalodiscus shows in the following points a remarkable agreement with the *Balanoglossus*.

1. The body is divided into 3 sections, one pre-oral and two post-oral. The pre-oral section, the so called buccal shield, corresponds with the proboscis, the middle section with the collar, and the larger posterior section and the pedicle with the trunk of Enteropnuesta.
2. Each of the three regions contains a coelomic cavity, the most anterior being single, while the other two are divided by a median partition.
3. The anterior pre-oral cavity opens to the exterior by two pores (comparable to the proboscis pore of *Balanoglossus*).
4. In the collar region the dorsal nervous system corresponds with the collar cords of the Tenropneusta.
5. The anterior diverticulum of buccal cavity corresponds with the proboscis diverticulum (notochord) of the Enteropneusta.
6. The anterior region of the gut is perforated by a pair of lateral gill-slits.
7. The gonads lie between the anus and pharynx. Buds are given off from a lateral stalk.

Dissimilarities with *Balanoglossus*

1. Alimentary canal is bent on itself in *Cephalodiscus* so that the anal opening is situated not far from the mouth.

2. Presence of arms bearing tentacles arising from the collar in *Cephalodiscus.*
3. The general crowling together of the most important external organs at the most anterior part of the body.
4. Presence of pedicle or stalk in *Cephalodiscus.*
5. Comparatively small size of the proboscis in *Cephalodiscus.*
6. Absence of blood-vascular system in *Cephalodiscus.*
7. Small number of gill-slits and genital organs in *Cephalodiscus.*

Remark

In the position of the central nervous system in the skin of the collar, *Cephalodiscus* appears to be more primitive than *Balanoglossus* as has been pointed out by Morgan. It is not impossible that the presence of one pair of gill-slits in *Cephalodiscus* indicates that this animal diverged from the ancestors of *Balanoglossus* before the gill-slits were metamerically repeated.

However, the differences existing between *Cephalodiscus* and *Balanoglossus* may well be attributed, at least in part, to the tubucolous, half sedentary manner of life of the former.

UNIT – II
ENVIRONMENTAL BIOLOGY

3
ECOSYSTEM

Ecology and Concept of Ecosystem

Ecology is that branch of biology which is concerned with principles or fundamentals common to life. Ecology deals with the study of the inter-relationships that exist between the living organisms and their environment. The term "ecology" was first coined by Ernst Haeckel in 1869. Ecology is concerned with the biology of individual organisms and with such groups of organisms as populations and communities. It is, therefore, subdivided into autoecology and synecology. Autoecology is the study of the interrelationships of a single species of organism and its environment. Synecology deals with the study of groups of organisms such as populations, biotic communities, and ecosystems. Hence, ecology may also be subdivided into species ecology, population ecology, community ecology and ecosystem ecology.

The organism is a self regulating and self perpetuating physiochemical entity. It is always in a state of perfect balance with the environment. The term environment refers to the things around the organism which have a direct influence on the activities of the organism. Organism and environment are two inseparable factors. The organism depends upon its environment for its sustenance while the environment provides the organisms with the substratum or the medium for their various activities.

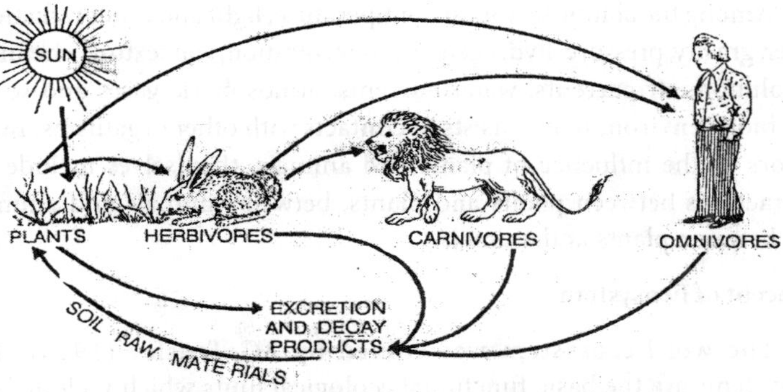

A generalised scheme of nutritional relationships among different biotic components of an ecosystem

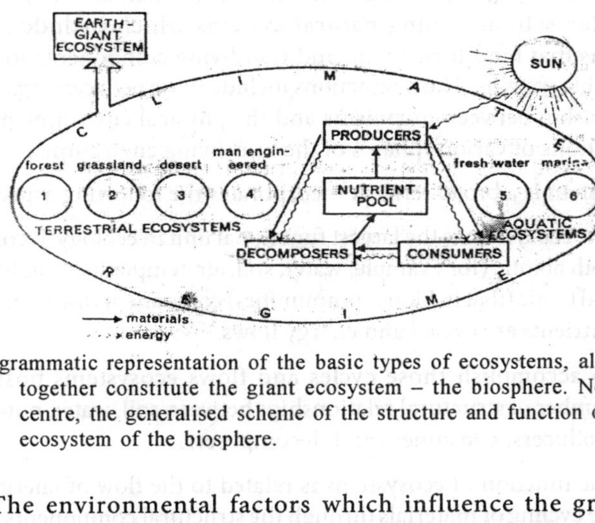

Diagrammatic representation of the basic types of ecosystems, all of which together constitute the giant ecosystem – the biosphere. Note, in the centre, the generalised scheme of the structure and function of any unit ecosystem of the biosphere.

The environmental factors which influence the growth and distribution of living organisms may be subdivided into two groups, the abiotic and biotic factors. A biotic community and its non living or abiotic environment form the largest functional unit in ecology, which is called the ecosystem or ecological system. The part of the earth in which ecosystems exist is called the biosphere. The biosphere is subdivided into three principal habitat called biocycles. These are the terrestrial marine, and fresh water biocycled. Each biocycle has its own types of ecological featured and its own associations of plant and animal organisms.

Among the abiotic factors are temperature, light and other radiations, water, gravity, pressure, hydrogen ion concentration, soil texture, chemicals in solution, air currents, water currents, atmospheric gases and so on. The biotic environment consists of contacts with other organisms. Biotic factors or the influence of plants and animals, themselves include the interactions between plants and plants, between animals and animals, and between plants and animals.

Concept of Ecosystem

The word ecosystem was coined by AG Tansley (1935). The ecosystems are the basic functional ecological units which include both the organisms and the non-living environment, each influencing the properties of the other and both necessary for maintenance of life. They are complex self-sustaining natural systems which include all the interactions that bind their living and non-living components together into the stable systems. The interactions include those between organisms, the relationship between organisms and the physical environment, and the interactions of various phases of the non-living environment.

Ecosystem is a broad term. It incorporates the following aspects :–

1. The ecosystem is the largest functional unit in ecology. It contains both abiotic (for example, water, soil, air, temperature, light, etc.) and biotic (that is, biotic communities) components through which nutrients are cycled and energy flows.

2. To accomplish those cycles and flows ecosystems possess a number of structural relationships between soil, water, nutrients, producers, consumers and decomposers.

3. The function of ecosystems is related to the flow of energy and the cycling of materials through the structural components of the ecosystem.

4. The total amount of energy that flows through a natural system depends upon the amount fixed by plants or producers. As energy is transferred from one feeding level to another, a considerable portion is lost for further transfer. This limits the number and mass of organisms than can be maintained at each feeding level.

5. The sequence of plant and animal associations, or biotic communities, which replace one another in a given community is called an ecological succession. The transient communities in an ecological succession is termed seral communities. A succession may be primary or secondary. Early stages of succession are characterised by an excess of potential energy and a relatively high energy flow per unit of biomass. There is less waste and less accumulation of energy in mature ecosystems because the energy flows through more diverse channels.
6. The biotic community is composed of small units of intimately associated members called populations. Populations have characteristics or attributes such as density, birth rate, death rate, age distribution, dispersal, dispersion, and so on, which are unique to the groups and not to the individual members of the group.
7. Both the environment and the amount of energy fixation in any given ecosystem are limited. When a population reached the limits imposed by the ecosystem, its members must stabilize.
8. The distribution of ecosystem on earth is relatively small in geographical extent when compared with the total volume of the earth. What we term the biosphere is divided into three principal habitats called biocycles. These are the terrestrial, marine, and fresh-water biocycles. Each biocycle has its own types of ecological features and its own associations of plant and animal organisms.

Abiotic and Biotic components and their roles in Ecosystem

Abiotic components : These constitute the non-living components of the ecosystem and are composed of inorganic materials such as soil, water, air, carbon dioxide, oxygen, nitrogen, calcium, phosphorous, etc. Soil is the upper part of the surface layer of the earth in which are found freely divided rock-derived material containing an admixture of organic matter capable of supporting vegetation. The chemical composition of the soil is an important factor in determining the presence of plants and certain animals. The texture of the soil is also important since it regulates the moisture conservation and availability and the presence of burrowing animals. Water is an important medium in which majority of animals live. Water is an important constituent of protoplasm which forms the physical basis of life. Water performs several functions inside the body of the animals. Whether an animal lives in the water, in the soil, or on land, the water balance in its body must be maintained. Air is the gaseous substance that envelops the earth and forms its atmosphere. It is a mixture of gases, the most abundant of which are nitrogen and oxygen (approximately 78 parts nitrogen, and 21 parts oxygen. The remaining 1 percent includes small amounts of carbondioxide, ozone, argon, neon and krypton).

Producers: Producers are those living members of ecosystem which are capable of synthesizing food from inorganic or organic compounds. In any ecosystem the producers are largely composed of photosynthetic plants. The microscopic plants and the rooted or floating plants in ponds and lakes; the algae in the ocean; the grasses in the grass lands and the trees in the forests are examples of producers.

Consumers: Consumers are the living members of the ecosystem which consume the food produced by the producers. Under this category are included all the different kinds of animals found in the ecosystem. The herbivores are dependent upon the plants for their sustenance and they are the primary consumers in an ecosystem. A deer is a primary consumer in a forest while the bison is one on a prairie. Similarly the protozoans, crustaceans and molluscs which feed on the floating algae found in ponds and seas are primary consumers in their respective habitats. Insects, rodents and ruminants are the major herbivores on the terrestrial environment. The entire life of any ecosystem revolves around the presence of these herbivores and hence Elton refers to them as 'key industry animals'. The herbivores form the food of primary carnivores which in their turn form the food of secondary carnivores.

Decomposers: Decomposers are also living components of ecosystem and are largely composed of micro-organisms such as bacteria. These act on the dead bodies of producers and consumers and are responsible for breaking up complex materials into simple substances. These substances which are released into the environment are consumed by the producers.

Light: Light is an important ecological factor which influences the growth and distribution of plants and the formation of plant communities. Different kinds of plants have different light requirements. The different responses of various plants to differences in light intensities are important in the establishment of a given species in a given area. The reproductive cycle of many species of plants is affected by duration of light or length of day. Light affects animals indirectly by determining their food supply and directly by altering their physiological activities and certain structural features. Light plays an important role in determining the periods of activity of animals.

Temperature : Temperature is an important factor in the distribution of plants animals because of its effects on physiological processes Many animals and plants become dormant during periods when the environmental temperature is unfavourable. Adjustments to temperature in animals may involve changes in both structure and behaviour. The seasonal development of subcutaneous fat, fur, or feathers, migration to another region where conditions are more tolerable, and hibernation are adjustments to cold.

Biotic or Living Components

In the biotic environment there is a delicate balance between the members of the same species, (intera-specific relationship) and between the members of different species (inter-specific relationship). The delicate balance that exists between the members of the same species is known as intra-specific relationship. The following factors affect the intraspecific relationships :

(i) *Reproduction:* In sexual reproduction two or more individuals are always involved. Over production leads to competition for food and space to live in.

(ii) *Assistance:* This involves protection given to the helpless young ones by the parents.

(iii) *Competition over food:* Over production of animals and the decrease in the rate of food production leads to competition for food among animals. It may either be active or passive.

(iv) *Definite hostility:* This involves conflicts over territorial rights as well as in the selection of mates. During the struggle the ill adapted ones are eliminated. There is a tendency for stronger ones to prevail over the weaker ones.

Interspecific relationship: The relationship that exists in different species is known as inter specific relationship. The following factors affect the interspecific relationship.

(i) *Competition for food:* This is very fierce among the different species. It is due to overproduction on the part of animals.

(ii) *Prey-predator relations:* Many organisms feed upon others. The predators can maintain themselves only when the prey is present.

(iii) *Host-parasite relations:* A parasite lives partly or wholly at the expense of the host or a parasite may be completely dependent on the host. The most successful parasite is one which does not harm its host.

(iv) *Commensalism:* It is a relationship between two different species in which neither is dependent upon the other.

(v) *Symbiosis:* It is a close physiological relationship that exists between two different species dependent on each other.

(vi) *Slavery:* Certain social animals may capture other animals and utilize their services for their benefit.

(vii) *Mutualism:* A relationship between two dissimilar organisms that are mutually beneficial is called mutualism. The association may be continuous, transitory, obligate or facultative. The relationship is between plant-plant, animal-animal or plant-animal relations.

Energy Flow in Ecosystems

Energy is the capacity to do work, whether that work be on a gross scale as raising mountains and moving air masses over continents, or on a small scale such as transmitting a nerve impulse from one cell to another. Energy may be potential energy and kinetic energy. Potential energy is energy at rest. It is capable of and available for work. Kinetic energy is due to motion, and results in work. Work that results from the expenditure of energy can both store energy (as potential energy) and arrange or order matter without storing energy.

The expenditure and storage of energy is described by two laws of thermodynamics. The first law is known as law of conservation of energy. It states that energy is neither created nor destroyed. It may change forms, pass from one place to another, or act upon matter in various ways, but regardless of what transfers and transformations take place, no gain or loss in total energy occurs.

Energy is simply transferred from one form or place to another. When wood is burned the potential energy present in the molecules of

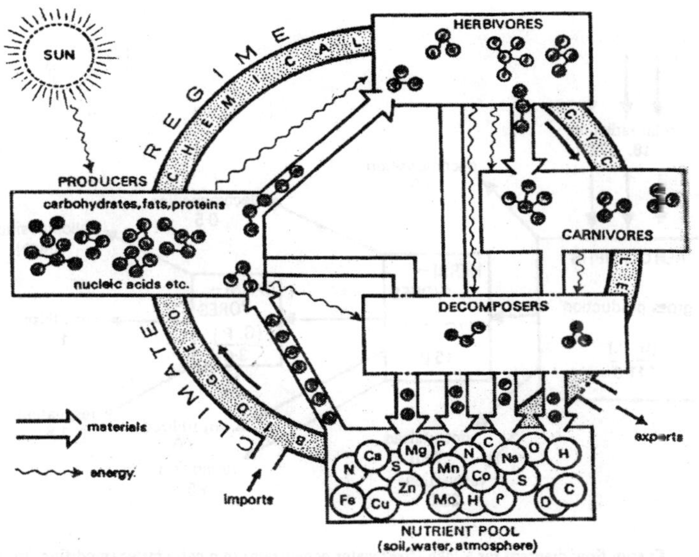

A generalised model of an ecosystem to show its structure and function. Note, the biogeochemical cycles superimposed on the various components of the ecosystem; movement of materials in cyclic manner, and that of energy in non-cyclic (unidirectional) manner.

wood equals the kinetic energy released, and heat is evolved to the surroundings. This is an exothermic reaction. In an endothermic reaction energy from the surroundings may paid into a reaction. For example, in photosynthesis, the molecules of the products store more energy than the reactants. The extra energy is acquired from the sunlight, but even than there is no gain or loss in total energy. Further though the total amount of energy involved in any chemical reaction, such as burning wood, does not increase or decrease much of the potential energy stored in the substance undergoing reaction is degraded during the reaction into a form incapable of doing any further work.

The second law of thermodynamic states that whenever energy is transformed from one kind to another, there is an increase in entropy and a decrease in the amount of useful energy. Thus when coal is burned in a boiler to produce steam, some of the energy creates steam and performs work, but part of the energy is dispersed as heat to the surrounding air. The same thing happens to energy in the ecosystem. As

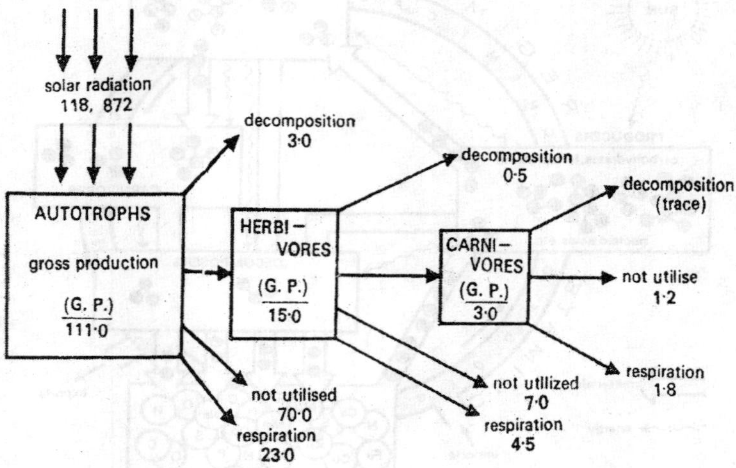

Energy flow diagram for a lake (freshwater ecosystem) in g cal /cm²/yr (modified from Lindeman, 1942)

energy is transformed from one organism to another in the form of food, a large part of that energy is degraded as heat and as a net increase in the disorder of energy. The remainder is stored in the living tissues.

Three sources of energy account for virtually all the work of the ecosystems : gravitation, internal forces within the earth and solar radiation. The last is very significant for ecosystem. The solar radiations which originate from sun is the source of energy for life and life is what sets the ecosystem apart from other natural system.

Energy in an Ecosystem

Living organisms can use energy in several forms, but all can be grouped under one of two headings – a radiant and fixed. Radiant energy is in the form of electromagnetic waves such as light. Fixed energy is potential chemical energy bound up in various organic substances which can be broken down or reacted with something else in order to release their energy content.

Only a small fraction of the light energy reaching the earth is trapped.

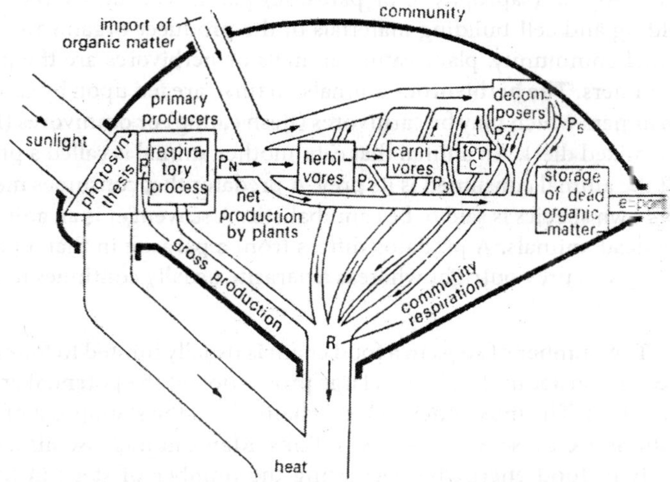

The relationship between flow of energy through the grazing food chain and detritus pathway (After E.P. Odum, 1956)

Considerable areas of the earth have no plants, and plants can utilize in photosynthesis only about 3 per cent of the incident energy. The radiant energy of sun is converted into chemical or potential energy by photosynthesis in plants.

The reaction is catalyzed by certain pigments (for example, chlorophylls) in the cells. The product of this reaction is carbohydrate such as sugar (glucose). Oxidation of sugar or any other organic molecule to get usuable energy by organism is called respiration. The energy released by respiration is lost permanently to the ecosystem.

Food Chain

A food chain is a group of organisms in which there is a transfer of food energy. The energy is transferred from its primary source in plants, through a series of organisms, each feeding on the organism before it in the group of series. Green plants, in which the energy of the sunlight is converted to a biologically useful form, constitute the base of a food chain consisting of animals and plants linked together by their nutritional relationships. The autotrophic plants may be considered the producer organisms in such a chain. Consumer organisms, such as animals and heterotrophic (saprophytic or parasitic) plants, can utilize the energy-yielding and cell-building materials of the producer organisms. In any animal community, plant-eating animals or herbivores are the primary consumers. The herbivorous animals, in turn, are fed upon by secondary consumers which may be carnivores (flesh eating) or omnivores (feeders on a mixed diet). An animal that eats another animal is called a predator, and the animal consumed is its prey. A predator that consumes members of its own species is said to be cannibalistic. A scavenger is an animal that eats dead animals. A predator differs from a parasite in that a predator destroys its prey outright whereas a parasite usually continues to live in/ on its host.

The number of steps in a food chain is usually limited to four or five. At each transfer in the chain, a large proportion of the potential energy is lost as heat. The most efficient food chains from the standpoint of energy relations are those with the fewest links. Man can increase his available supply of food energy by decreasing the number of steps in his food chain.

There are three types of food chains : predator, parasitic and saprophytic. A predator chain starts with a a plant base and goes from smaller to larger animals. A parasitic chain goes from larger to smaller organisms. A saprophytic chain goes from dead organic matter of decaying animal or plant bodies to microorganisms.

A pyramid of numbers exists in the various populations in the food chain of a community. An enormous number of plants, which first synthesize food, utilising the energy of the sun is located at the base of each pyramid of numbers. Next are fewer numbers of herbivorous animals which eat these plants. The herbivorous animals are, in turn, eaten by a still smaller number of other carnivorous animals. In addition to the pyramid of numbers, there is a pyramid of protoplasm. The total amount of protoplasm in the plant life at the base of a food pyramid is greater than the total amount of protoplasm of the primary consumers or herbivorous animals. The total amount of protoplasm of the primary consumer animals is greater than that of the forms which prey on them, and so on. This is due to the energy relations involved in a food chain. Special adaptations have occurred in different species of animals for securing food.

POND ECOSYSTEM

Ponds are shallow standing water bodies, generally characterised by relatively quiet waters and abundant vegetation. There may be three types of ponds : (i) Ponds derived from large lakes; (ii) Ponds which never have had any connection with lakes and which have been quite small right from the beginning of their origin and (iii) Artificial ponds (due to activities of man).

Based upon the seasonal duration, ponds may be temporary or permanent. In temporary ponds, water is present at certain seasons only while at other times dry. The ponds which exist in the spring are referred to as vernal ponds. If the ponds contain in the spring which subsequently dry up in the summer and then once again if they are filled up with water in the autumn they are called Vernal autumnal ponds. Some water persists right throughout the seasons and if it freezes up during winter such ponds are referred to as Aestival ponds. Permanent ponds are those which contain water throughout the year.

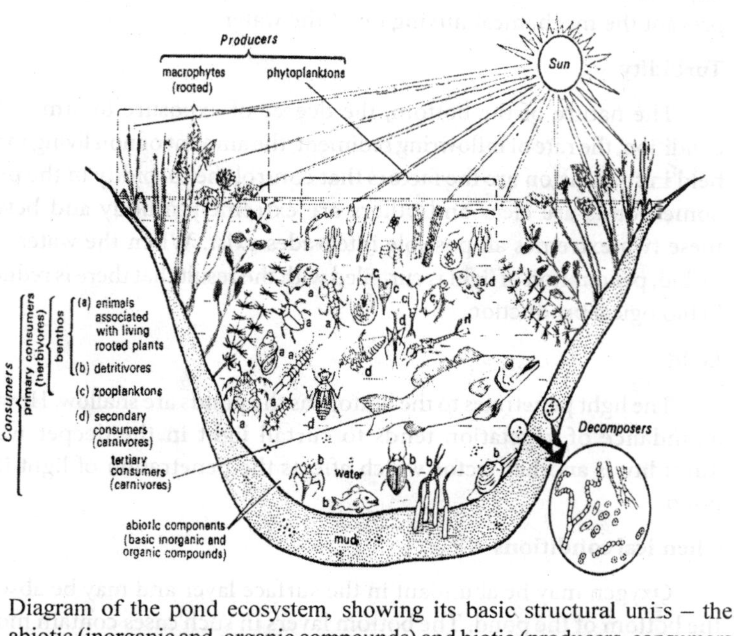

Diagram of the pond ecosystem, showing its basic structural units – the abiotic (inorganic and, organic compounds) and biotic (producers, consumers and decomposers) components.

Physical Conditions

The movement of water in the pond is minimal. Wave action is very light. The movement of water in ponds is restricted due to luxuriant vegetation. The ponds often contain rich vegetation and this increases with the age of the ponds. In many of the older ponds because of the abundance of both rooted and floating type of plants there is very little open surface in the centre of the pond. The bottom of the pond may be either sandy or rocky or marshy in its nature.

Temperature

The temperature of the pond because of its relatively shallow depths tends to fall in line with the changes in the atmospheric temperature. In summer the temperature of a pond may rise up to 30°C or more. The daily variation of temperature is noticed clearly in places where the days are warm and the nights are cool. Even in summer in ponds containing vegetation, the upper surface tends to be warm whereas that of the bottom layers are relatively cool. This is due to the presence of plants which prevent the mechanical mixing up of the water.

Turbidity

The nature of the bottom, the degree of exposure to atmospheric condition, the rate of inflowring sediment, the amount of non living matters held in suspension are the factors that control the turbidity in the ponds. Some ponds are clear and others are extremely muddy and between these two extremes all possible integrades exist. When the water is too turbid, penetration of light is curtailed with the result that there is reduction in biological production.

Light

The light penetrates to the bottom as the ponds are shallow. However, abundance of vegetation tends to curtail light in the deeper waters. Turbidity is another factor which affects the penetration of light in the ponds.

Chemical conditions

Oxygen may be abundant in the surface layer and may be absent in the bottom of the pond. The bottom layers in such cases contain more of carbondioxide and other decomposed gases.

Dissolved nutrients

Phosphates and nitrates are very essential for the production of fish in the ponds. In all natural waters the nutrients are found in varying quantities dissolved in the surrounding soil. If the nutrients are deficient, production and growth of organisms in the water are affected.

Pond Vegetation

The vegetation in the pond is arranged in three distinct zones : (i) marginal zone composed of emergent plants, (ii) middle zone composed of floating plants which include the rooted and rootless forms and (iii) the zone consisting of submerged plants.

The pond flora includes – (1) Phytoplankton, such as Volvox, Eudorina, Clasterium, Oscillatoria, Euglena, Ceratium, etc.; (2) Filamentous algae, such as Spirogyra, Oedogonium, Chara, etc.; (3) Marginal and emergent plants such as Ipomea, Typha and Acorus; (4) Surface floating plants, such as Pistia, Lemna, Walffia and Eichornia; (5) Submerged plants which are rooted to the bottom such as Vallisneria, Patamogeton, Naias and Otellia.

Pond Fauna

Pond animals include – (1) Plankton which float on the surface and they are invariably provided with floating devices, for example, Dinoflagellates, Heliozoans and Copepods; (2) Necton which move actively being provided with definite locomotor organs, for example, insects; (3) Benthos which live at the bottom and they may be seen crawling or attached to the bottom, for example, Lamellidens, Planarians, etc.

Pond dwelling animals are represented by almost all phyla of invertebrata. Among the protozoans several species of Amoeba, Actinophrys, Difflugia, Euglena, Pandorina, Paramecium, Vorticella etc. are found. The sponges are represented by Spongilla. Among the Coelenterates, Hydra is common. Platyhelminthes is represented by turbellarians. Rotifers are also commonly found. The annelids are represented by aquatic earthworms, leech, etc. Among the Arthropoda, Daphnia, Miona, Ceriodaphnia, Cyclops, etc. are common. The molluscs are represented by Lamellidens, Limnaea, Physa, Pila, etc. The vertebrate fauna is limited in ponds, Catla, Labeo, Cirrhina, Barbus Macropodus, Chela, Barilius, etc. are commonly met within ponds.

POPULATION

A population is defined as a group of plant or animal organisms of the same (or similar) species that occupy a given area at a given time. Clarke distinguishes two types of population namely (i) single-species population and (2) mixed or multi-species population. Single species population is composed of a single species. Under natural conditions several species of plants and animals go to form a population called mixed population. Communities are formed of complex population groups. Populations have characteristics or attributes such as density, birth rate, death rate, age distribution, dispersal, dispersion, and so on, which are unique to the group and not to the individual members of the group.

Density

The density of a population is the number of individuals in relation to unit area or unit volume – for example, the number of squirrels per square mile, the number of earthworms per acre, or the number of phytoplanktonic organisms per liter of sea water. When individual size in a population is highly variable, some type of biomass or live weight measure is often a more satisfactory measure of density than is the number of individuals. There are two ways of expressing the density of a population, crude density and ecological density.

Crude density is the number of individuals or the biomass per unit of total area or total volume. Ecological density is the number of individuals or the biomass per unit of habitable area or volume. When only a fraction of a total area or volume is suitable habitat, ecological density is a better measure of population density than is crude density. Various measure are used to determine population density – total count, sampling methods, tagging – recapture methods and so on. In the tagging – recapture method which is applicable to larger animals, a definite number of animals such as squirrels are captured, tagged, and released. At a subsequent time, the same number of squirrels are captured, the number of tagged squirrels in the group is determined, and from the proportion of tagged squirrels to untagged squirrels, the total population of squirrels is determined.

For many organisms, it has been found that increased density slows population growth. Usually it is the amount of food available that explains how density affects the population. The Kaibab deer illustrate this principle. Destruction of the predators of the deer resulted in a considerable increase in the deer population on the Kaibab plateau. The carrying capacity of the vegetation was exceeded and a large percentage of the deer starved to death.

Natality or Birth-rate and Mortality or Death-rate

Birth rate (natality) can be defined as average number of offspring produced per unit of time. The maximum rate of reproduction for a given species under ideal conditions is known as potential natality. This is never attained in nature because all females are not equally fertile, all the eggs that are produced do not hatch and all the larvae produced do not develop into the adults for they encounter several hardships before natality. The normal birth rate that prevails is known as realised natality. The maximum birth rate and the actual birth rate are compared and the information obtained is used as a device for predicting the rate of increase in a population.

Mortality rate of a population is the number of individuals which die in a given period of time. Minimum mortality refers to those that die from old age. The actual death rate is known as realised mortality. In general, mortality rate decreases as the rate of population increases. Decreasing or increasing mortality during the period of high vulnerability produces marked effect on the future size of the population.

The biotic potential rate is the innate capacity of a population to increase under optimal surroundings and staple age ratios. The biotic potential rate of increase is very great and if it is not checked by nature's balance it would lead to an increase of particular groups of animals. The rise in numbers is controlled by a number of factors such as density, competition, mortality rate, scarcity of food supply, etc. Small forms usually have faster birth rate when compared with large organisms, but even the slowest breeders multiply quickly if conditions are fully favourable. The delicate balance that exists in nature between the biotic potential and the environmental resistance determines the actual rate of increase of a population.

Age Distribution

Age distribution is the number or the percentage of individuals in a population in the different age groups. The ratio of young to older individuals provides an index to the population trend. A high percentage of young individuals is usually characteristic of a rapidly expanding population, whereas a low percentage of young individuals is generally characteristic of a declining population. Death and birth rates usually vary with the age group distribution of the population.

In general, asexual forms begin to multiply much earlier than the sexual forms and the rate of reproduction is equally high. Likewise many sexual forms attain sexual maturity a few days after hatching while in others it takes several months or even years. The middle aged groups usually have the highest reproductive capacity. Young members predominate in rapidly growing populations while in stationary populations prevails an even age distribution. Age distribution serves as an index to indicate the stability or fluctuality of the population. Fluctuation in numbers, a common feature of animal population may be either regular or irregular. If the fluctuations are small than the population curve is flat. If it is large and regular the curve is termed as cyclic or if it is highly irregular it is known as irruptive type. The cause of these fluctuations in some cases seems clear whereas in others the various explanations are not in agreement. There is a regular nine-to-ten-year fluctuation in the snowshoe hare and lynx population in Canada, apparently unrelated to seasonal or early changes. The lynx population peak occurs about a year or more after the peak of the snowshoe hare population. The hare serves as prey for the lynx, and hence the cycles are related. The lemming population in the northern tundra reached a peak every three or four years. During high peaks of population, increased migration occurs.

Some population (for example, snowshoe hare), even in the absence of disease and predation, continue to fluctuate. When carrying capacity (amount of food available) is exceeded, they die off in large numbers.

Individuals or their reproductive products move into or out of populations. This movement is called population dispersal. Plants spread, with few exceptions, by passive dispersal of their seeds, fruits or spores. Some animals also are passively spread, but the majority of them disperse through their own locomotor activity. The major barrier to plant dispersal is climate. The major barrier for animal dispersal, especially in larger mammals, is geographic (oceans, deserts, etc.).

Dispersal should not be confused with dispersion which is the mode of distribution of individuals in a population. The individuals in a population may be clumped, uniform, or random in their distribution. Random distribution seldom occurs in nature. The most common type of

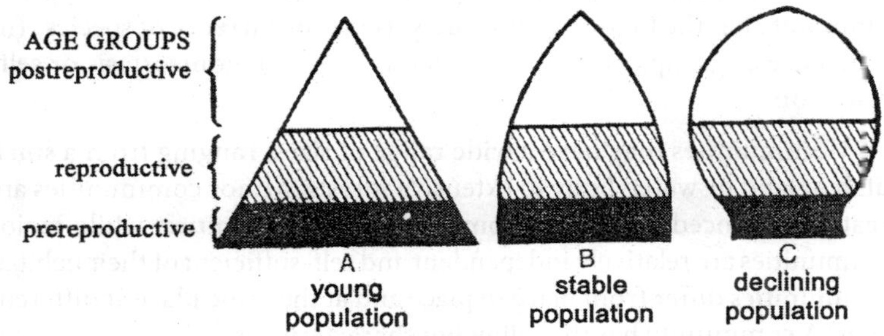

Hypothetical diagram showing different types of age pyramids

internal distribution pattern in a population is clumping. Aggregation of individuals to produce clumping may be the result of reproductive urges or social attractions or the response to weather changes or local habitat differences. Among animals with more complex behaviour patterns, such as the higher invertebrates and the vertebrates, territoriality is common.

The characteristic growth of a population is represented by population growth curve. Such a curve can be plotted if the numbers of the animal is noted against time factor. If the population does not meet with much resistance either from the biotic or abiotic environments, it increases in size and the curve grows steemply upwards. Such curves are noted only for a brief period and these growth curves are similar for all types and sizes of animals. When the population encounters environmental resistance, growth rate slows down and becomes stationary.

Overcrowding in a population seems to affect the members in several ways. For example, in fishes it leads to cannibalism. In the case if certain birds like English Sparrow which are accustomed to breeding in large areas fail to breed in small areas. Thus each organism requires a definite area to live in comfortably. Otherwise it affects the population growth.

BIOTIC COMMUNITY CONCEPT

The populations which occupy a given geographic area or habitat form a unit known as biotic community. Such a community includes all the animals and plants in a given area. All the organisms of a community live together, share same habitat, influence each other's life directly or indirectly and have reached a survival level within a given radiant energy. A community has the following attributes : (i) co-occurrence of species, (ii) recurrence of groups of the same species, and (iii) homeostasis or self-regulation.

Communities may have a wide range of sizes, ranging from a small patch of land or water-body to extensive forests. Minor communities are greatly influenced by inputs from adjacent communities, while major communities are relatively independent and self-sufficient of their habitat. Communities differ from place to place and at the same place at different times. A community has the following characteristics :

1. Species diversity

Various species of plants and animals living in a community exhibit species diversity. For animal communities, a study of age structure and growth pattern is important, while for plant communities floristics, study of taxonomy of life forms such as herbs, shrubs, climbers, trees are important. Since seasonal changes occur in the appearance of plant structure and growth, periodicities and phenology are significant parameters.

2. Growth form and structure

The type of the community is described by major categories of growth forms (for example, trees, shrubs, herbs, mosses, etc.). These different growth forms determine the stratification, or vertical layering of the community.

3. Dominance

Among several species present in a community, a few exert a major controlling influence by virtue of their size, numbers, or activities. These are called ecological dominance or dominant species.

4. Relative abundance

Different populations in a community exist in a relative proportions and this idea is called relative abundance.

5. Trophic structure

The feeding relations of the species in the community will determine the flow of energy and materials from plants to herbivorous animals to carnivorous animals.

Based on the general growth, composition, shape, etc., of vegetation, and organisms associated with them, communities may be classified as forests, deserts, grasslands, tundra and so on. Further, according to the amount of water in the habitat, communities may be divided as hydrophytic, mesophytic, xerophytic.

All the plants and animals in the world constitute the global community which includes the continental communities and oceanic communities.

Composition of community

1. *Size:* Communities may be large or small. Larger one extends over areas of several thousands of square kilometers, as forests, others such as deserts, etc. are comparatively smaller with dimensions in hundreds of kilometers. Very small-sized communities are the groups of microorganisms in such microhabitats as leaf surface, fallen log, litter, soil, etc.

2. *Number of species:* The number of species and population abundance in communities vary greatly. Charles Elton (1927) calculated that the communities of certain British rivers included 131 species of invertebrates in addition to fish, amphibians, populations of algae, protozoa, bacteria, and rooted aquatic plants. M.C. Dash and his coworkers studied the composition of a biotic community in some tropical pastures of Sambalpur, India and found that it consisted of 22 grass and other herbaceous species (the primary producers), 5 species of earthworms, 25 of test-bearing protozoa, 15 of nematodes and 7 of microarthropods, 16 of nematodes, 32 of phytoplankton, 20 of zooplankton and 7 of fish.

3. *Dominants:* There are diverse species in each community. In most of the communities, only a single species is particularly conspicuous and dominant and in such case the community is called by the name of dominant species. If the dominant individuals are removed for any reason, dominance is usually assumed by another species and the character of the community changes completely. This extensive change does not occur when nondominant species are removed, for with the dominants intact the same community may regenerate itself. Plants are usually the major dominants in land communities. However, in some cases, as when the vegetation is small, animals may be major dominants.

4. *Ecological amplitude:* The range of environmental conditions which a taxon can tolerate is called ecological amplitude. The composition of a

biotic community in any habitat is dependent upon the frequency of environmental conditions in that habitat and the ecological amplitude of species populations. In this way, the climate and other abiotic and biotic factors of a habitat determine the type of community which survives and develops.

Stratification of Community

The arrangement of populations in a community in vertical layers is called stratification. The layering occurs in the two broad basic strata of both terrestrial and aquatic communities, in the upper sunlight or euphotic zone and in the lower subeuphotic zone. A forest has characteristic animals associated with the treetops, with the lower branches of the trees, with the fallen leaves on the soil, and with the soil. In an aquatic habitat, such as a lake, where there is stratification of physical factors such as light and temperature, there are surface dwellers, bottom dwellers, and dwellers in intermediate depths. The members of a single class of organisms, such as fish, because of differences in temperature tolerance, may occupy different strata in a lake in the summer time where the upper water is warm and oxygen-rich, the deeper noncirculating water being colder and neatly depleted of oxygen.

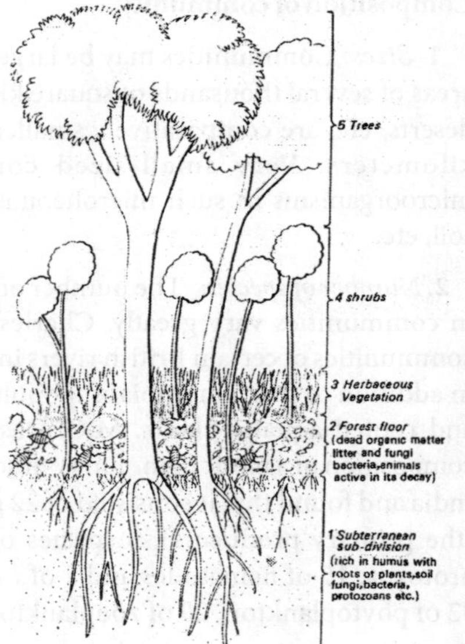

Diagrammatic representation of a complex deciduous forest community showing stratification, where five vertical sub-divisions of different vegetational types (subterranean, forest floor, herbaceous vegetation, shrubs, and trees) may be easily distinguished.

Ecological Succession

The sequence of plant and animal associations, or biotic communities, which replace one another in a given community is called an ecological succession. The transient communities in an ecological succession are termed seral communities. The final or relatively permanent community is called the climax. A climax community tends to persist. A succession may be primary or secondary. Succession which starts in an area like a plowed field or a cutover forest which already contains some organisms is termed secondary succession. Secondary succession has fewer stages than primary succession and the climax is reached more quickly. Plants play the primary role in the development of a succession, but a succession involves changes in both plant and animal life in an area. Animal succession is associated with plant succession.

The causes of ecological succession are intricate and not completely known. Physical and biotic factors play a role. The end results of succession vary in different climates ; but since succession continues when the climatic pattern remains the same in a given area over a long period of time, climate cannot be the cause. The nature of the community itself, a biotic factor, is important in directing a succession. The action of each seral community on the habitat makes the area a less favourable habitat for itself and a more favourable habitat for other species until the climax community is reached. Species suitable for one type of habitat may be entirely unadapted when the habitat undergoes alteration into a different one.

Plant succession on bare rock surface without any pockets of accumulated soil begins with some species of crustose lichen as the pioneer stage. The lichens produce acids that broing abut dissolution of the rock. The decay of the older parts of the lichens results in the formation of small amounts of humus. The humus together with the rock particles becomes a trace of primitive soil. The crustose lichens may be succeeded by foliose forms which grow on the trace of soil. The lichens are followed by mosses. As the mosses become established, they shade the lichens and compete with them for water and nutrients. The lichens are crowded out. The older mosses die ; decay and sufficient soil have now accumulated to support herbaceous seed plants such as hardy grasses. The next stage is dominated by shrubs which shade the plants of the precceding stage, and the latter tend to disappear. The shrubs bring about conditions favourable for the development of the tree stage in the succession, and thus the succession ends with the development of a forest. The first tree invaders may not be the climax species. Trees such as pines and oaks, which can endure exposure to light, appear first in the succession. Their seedlings are shade intolerant and will not thrive in the shade of the parent trees. The seedlings of beech and maple grow successfully since they are shade tolerant. As the pines and oaks die and decay, they are replaced by the beeches and maples. The earlier stages in the succession just described may be bypassed when small amounts of soil are present in rock crevices.

Excessive studies in ecological succession have been made along the southern shores of Lake Michigan. The retreat of the lake to its present boundaries has left successively younger and younger sand dunes, and the stages in a succession can be observed as one proceeds away from the lake. The order of the communities as one goes inland is cotton wood beach grass, jack pine forest, black oak dry forest, oak and oak-hickory moist forest, and finally the beach-maple forest. Each stage in the succession was preceded by the one before it. Thus the jack-pine forest was preceded by the cotton wood beach grass stage, and so on with the others.

Along with the succession of plants, there is a corresponding succession of animal communities. Each plant community in a succession is inhabited by a characteristic group of animals.

Succession occurs in human communities. Some old cities which have not changed significantly for many years have reached a relatively stable or climax stage. Others are in a state of constant expansion and are in various seral stages. Succession in human communities is a problem in human ecology.

Ecological Niche

Every species has a specific position within the community designated as ecological niche, and this very often stand for the functional status or total role of the species within the community. The niche comprises all the bonds between the population and the community and ecosystem in which it is found. These bonds include factors such as the tolerance ranges, and optima for all abiotic environmental factors, the sorts of organisms that can be utilized for food by the population, as well as the organisms that feed upon it, the areas in which the species can live, and the population structure of the species. Every population has an ecological niche and this niche is the major determinant of structural, physical and behavioural adaptations of the population. The concept of niche has been extended to categories such as spatial niche or habitat niche, trophic niche.

1. *Spatial or habitat niche*

This type of niche pertains to the physical space occupied by an organism. O'Neill (1967) has cited a good example of spatial niche in the distribution of seven species of millipeds in forest floor of a maple-oak forest. All the seven species, occur in the same general habitat that is, forest floor and all belong to the same basic trophic level. Each species of millipeds predominates in its own specific different microhabitat.

2. *Trophic Niche*

In this case two species live in the same habitat but they occupy different trophic niches, because of differences in food habits. For instance, two aquatic bugs, Notonecta and Corixa live in the same pond but occupy different trophic niches. Notonecta is an active predator that swims about grasping and eating other animals, but Corixa feeds mainly on decaying vegetation.

Different communities in ecosystems characterized by similar environments are often exceedingly similar in their structure, and they may contain one or more niches that are essentially identical. The adaptations of populations inhabiting these niches may also be exceedingly similar, even though they are totally unrelated. The phenomenon of similar but unrelated species in different geographical areas is called ecological equivalence. In order, for two unrelated species to have evolved to a point of ecological equivalence, the niches to which they are adapted must be essentially identical, even though they may be separated by many thousands of miles. Clearly, the structure of communities set in similar environments is so similar that essentially identical niches can develop in them.

On the other hand, no two species populations can occupy the same niche in a single community. In such a case, one will always be superior and derive the other into local extinction through competition. If different species are to survive within a single community, thee must be some difference between their niches. Of the six species of parasitic Hymenoptera attacking the cocoons of the sawfly, the four indigenous species overlapped in their distribution although each species occupied one position in the niche space. If the amount of overlap is very small then the two populations can exist simultaneously in essentially separate niches. If the overlapping is virtually complete, then the population that is more successful in exploiting the environment will drive the less successful population into extinction through interspecific competition. Abundance of food supply in situations where the same food resource was exploited by different species, averted competitive exclusion. Many closely allied herbivorous fishes coexist in the same habitat utilizing the same food and this is attributed to the sumptuous supply of algae, generally among two populations.

The number of potential niches in the community is a function of the degree to which the development of community under a given environmental regime leads to a divergence or separation of partially overlapping niches. If the tendency for separation is high then the community will be more complex than if it is low. Stable environments which are characterized by communities having a large number of separate niches, foster the separation of niches, whereas harsh environments characterized by communities with fewer niches, tend not to foster niche separation. The mechanism for niche separation is natural selection.

HABITAT

Habitat refers to the place where the animal lives. The word habitat is derived from a Latin word which means "it dwells". The entire space occupied by living organisms is termed biosphere. The primary or basic unit in the biosphere is spoken off as a biotope. Plant and animal life met with one another on land as well as in the water. The habitat contains different types of niches. The zebra and the African lion are found to inhabit the same habitat namely, tropical grass lands but their niches are different. The zebra is a herbivore feeding on vegetation while the lion is a carnivore feeding on the herbivores including the zebra. The total mass of life which may be termed the biomass, is different in different biotopes. The community forms present in a biotope is called biocoenoses. Just as species are regarded as the basic units of classification the biotope forms the basic unit of biosphere. The biochores are grouped together to form the biocycles. The biosphere is divided into three principal divisions or habitats: (1) Fresh-water, (2) Marine, (3) Terrestrial. Each of these provides certain special habitat conditions to the animals inhabiting it.

Fresh water (Limnobiotic) habitat

The fresh water habitat is limited in its extent when compared with halobiotic (marine) and geobiotic (terrestrial) realms. The fresh water habitat includes the lakes, rivers, rivulets, streams, streamlets, brooks, brooklets, ponds, pools and puddles. The fresh water environment includes (i) standing water formations or lentic environment and (ii) running water formations or lotic environment. The lentic habitat includes lakes, ponds, swamps or bogs. The lotic environment includes the river systems such as spring, stream and the rivers.

Fresh water is characterised by low salinity. The salt content averages 1.8$\%_0$ (18 parts per thousand). In rain water there are 30 to 40 parts of solutes per million parts. Calcium, magnesium and carbondioxide are abundant in hard water whereas soft water contains very little of the above mentioned substances. The richness of fauna in any fresh water formation is mainly dependant upon the presence of oxygen and carbondioxide. If sufficient amount of sunlight, oxygen, carbon dioxide, nitrates and phosphates are available in the fresh water habitat it will be able to support a luxuriant plant life. The temperature often acts as a limiting factor for fresh water organisms. Temperature changes result in the circulation and stratification of water which seem to influence considerably the aquatic life. Light can penetrate in the deep lakes than in turbulent turbid waters of the stream. Turbidity is often a limiting factor in the development and distribution of plant and animal life in fresh waters. Stagnationand the fouling of water is another feature which also effects the fresh water inhibitants. The fresh water fauna include amphibians, sponges, bryozoans, coelenterates, larvae of the damsel and dragon flies, stone flies, may flies, caddis flies, dipteran larvae (mosquito and chironomus), etc.

Fresh water plants and animals have certain special characteristic features which fit them to their habitat. Many adaptive features are met with in fresh water animals to tide over the adverse environmental conditions such as desiccation, fouling of water, extremes of temperature etc.

Lotic habitat (Running water formation)

Lotic habitat includes springs, streams and rivers. Streams exhibit two major habitats namely rapid streams and pools. Current is a major factor in the rapid streams and if the bottom is composed of stones or pebbles, it affords favourable location for the organism to live in. In soft bottomed pools the burrowing forms predominate, for example, Fresh water mussel. The plants or animals are permanently attached to some immovable objects in the substratum such as stones, logs, etc. The algae and mosses are generally found attached to the stones and logs. Fresh water sponges and the larvae of trichoptera are permanently fixed to the stones.

On account of the abundance of oxygen and food supply, animal life is always rich in the lotic habitat. Among the rapid moving streams, the nymphs and the larvae of caddish flies, may flies, stone flies, beetles and black flies predominate.

Marine habitat

The ocean constitutes 71% of the earth's surface and as a habitat it provides an unusual stability in temperature, salinity and gaseous contents. The marine realm provides the largest inhabitable space for living organisms.

The most characteristic feature of sea water is its high salt content. The salinity is relatively constant in different oceans. As the range of salinity in the open sea is rather small, a salinity of 3.5% is taken as an average for all oceans. The constancy of composition in the different oceans is mainly due to the result of circulation and mixing up of water

caused

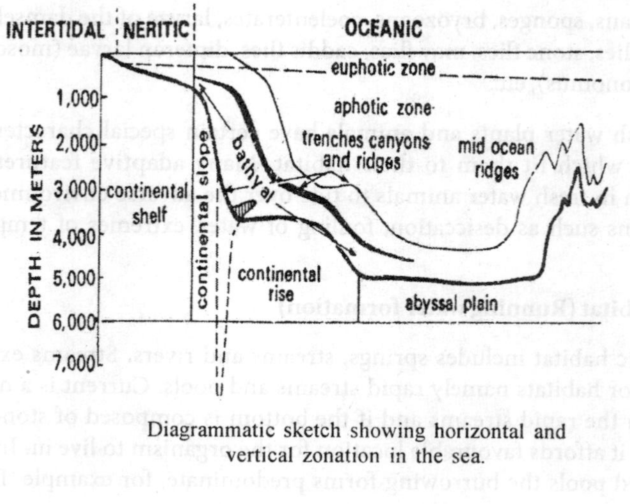

Diagrammatic sketch showing horizontal and vertical zonation in the sea.

by oceanic currents. The temperature ranges from 2^{0}C at the bottom to about 30^{0}C at the surface. The atmospheric pressure at the sea level is 15 lbs per sq. inch. The pressure increases at the rate of one ton to the sq. inch for every 1,000 fathoms. The light intensity varies from brilliant sunlight at the surface to absolute and perpetual darkness in the deeper layers. The water is kept in motion for the most part, and it helps in the dispersal of waste products produced by the animals as a result of katabolism, in the dispersal of nutrient materials.

Marine environment may include two zones : pelagic and benthic. The pelagic region includes the sunlit surface waters while the benthic zone includes the ocean floor.

The pelagic area of the sea can be divided into the neritic province and the oceanic province. The neritic province consists of water upto a depth of 200 meters and it is close in the land mass. The oceanic province extends from the continental shelf to the archi-benthic level (about 1,100 meters). Pelagic organisms are generally classified into two major groups – plankton and necton. The plankton organisms are generally microscopic in size except for jelly fishes and pyrosomes. The planktonic organisms may be phytoplankton and zooplankton. The phytoplankton includes many protozoans ; jelly fishes and siphonophores, many worms, a large number of small crustaceans, a number of molluses, etc.

Neritic plankton are those which inhabit the coastal water and extend only for a short distance sea-ward. The neritic plankton is composed of the larvae of the benthic invertebrates, fish eggs and fish larvae. Copepods seem to predominate in the neritic plankton of the different parts of the world. The characteristic forms of the oceanic plankton includes Velella, Ianthina, Calanus, Sapphivina.

Planktonic animals exhibit many structural adaptations. Some of the diatoms are either bladder like, needle like, hair like. The ciliates, ctenophores, trochophores and other larval forms depend upon the activity of the cilia for movement.

Necton is composed of swimming animals found at the surface waters and they are provided with efficient locomotor organs. Streamlined bodies, well developed musculature, nervous system, sense of vision are the notable adaptations found in nektonic animals.

The pelagic animals are diverse and are specialised in many ways. A common feature of all the pelagic forms is their ability to maintain themselves in the open waters without sinking to the bottom. Pelagic fauna is mostly composed of the larvae of many animals which live as adults in the benthic zone.

The benthic biotic environment is concerned with ocean floor and forms two main zones: (i) the lighted zone or Littoral benthal and (ii) the lightless Archibenthal and Abyssal benthal forming the so called deep sea systems. The littoral zone extends from the high tide level to about 250 miles off the shore and roughly to about 200 meters depth. The Archibenthal zone extends from 200 meters to 1000 meters depth. The abyssal zone covers the ocean bottom running upto 6000 meters. The animals of the littoral zone have different modes of life. Some of them are adapted for crawling (worms and molluses), some others for burrowing (crustaceans, molluses, and worms) and yet others are sessile (crinoid, bryozoans and corals).

Biomes

A biome is a large community unit characterized by the kinds of plants and animals present. In each biome the kind of climax vegetation is uniform – grasses, conifers, deciduous trees – but the particular species of plant may vary in different parts of the biome. The kind of climax vegetation depends upon the physical environment and the two together determine the kind of animals present. Biomes may include the following:

1. *Tundra Biome:* Tundra presents the most common example of "fragile ecosystem". Tundra lies largely north of latitude 60^0N (that is, between the Arctic ocean and polar ice – caps and the forest of the south) and is characterized by the absence of trees, the presence of dwarfed plants, and an upper ground surface that is wet, spongy and uneven. The characteristic arctic tundra plant is the lichen. The animals that have adapted to survive in the tundra are Caribou or reindeer, musk ox, the arctic hare, arctic fox, polar bear, wolves, lemmings, snowy owls, mosquitoes and a host of migratory birds.

The region of mountain above the timber line contains a distinct flora and fauna and is referred to as the alpine zone. The alpine zone includes a sub-snow zone immediately below the snow zone, a meadow zone in the centre and a shrub zone which gradually merges into the timber zone. Many invertebrates of alpine zone are predatory and occur in lakes, streams and ponds. Among vertebrates, fishes and amphibians are totally lacking. A large number of insects and arachnids remain best adapted to Himalayan alpine zone.

2. Forest Biomes: The forest biomes include a complex assemblage of different kinds of biotic communities. Optimum conditions of temperature and ground moisture responsible for the growth of trees contribute greatly to the establishment of forest communities. The nature of soil, wind and air currents determine the distribution of forest vegetation. Forest biomes may be divided into coniferous forest, tropical forest and temperate forest. Cold regions with high rainfall and strongly seasonal climates with long winters and fairly short summers are characterized by boreal coniferous forest. In the northern coniferous forest (which stretches across both North America and Eurasia), the characteristic flora include evergreen plant species such as Spruce (*Picea glauca*), fir (*Abies balsamea*) and pine trees ; the fauna include snow shoe hare, lynx, wolf, bears, red fox, porcupine, squirrel, amphibians like Hyla and Rana, etc.

The temperate rain forest is a colder ecosystem than any other rain forest. Rainfall is high, but fog may be very heavy and actually more important as a source of water than rainfall. The diversity is much lower, both in plants and animals, in comparison to warmer rain forests. The dominant trees are coast redwood and the alpine ash. Epiphytes and lianas are common. The animals of rainforests are similar to those of deciduous forests.

Tropical rainforests occur near the equator in Central and South America, Central and Western Africa, South east Asia (parts of India and Malaysia). Tropical rainforests are among the most diverse communities on earth. Both temperature and humidity are high and constant. The flora is highly diversified. The extremely dense vegetation remains vertically stratified with tall trees. The common invertebrates of tropical rainforests are worms, snails, millipeds, centipeds, scorpions, isopods, spiders, insects, planarians and leeches. The common vertebrates include arboreal amphibians, aquatic reptiles, chameleons, agamids, geckos, and many species of snakes, birds and a variety of mammals.

3. The *grassland biome* is found where rainfall is about 25 to 75 cm. per year. It includes tall grass prairies, short grass prairie and arid grassland. Typical animals of grasslands tend to be quite small.

4. The *desert biomes* are formed in the driest of environments. Low abnormal precipitation coupled with soil and air temperature that are extremely high by day and drop abruptly by night, low humidity, and high isolation are the major desiccating environmental factors to which desert vegetation and animals have adapted. The animals present in the desert are reptiles, insects and burrowing rodents.

5. *Wetland Biomes* are submerged or water saturated lands, natural and artificial, permanent or temporary with water that is static or flowing and fresh, brackish or saltish. They are characteristic transitional conditions between terrestrial land and deep water bodies and are represented by swams, marshes, fens, peatlands, lagoons. Wetlands are also represented by paddy fields, fishery ponds, riverine flood plains, etc. Rice is best grown in wetlands.

ECOLOGICAL PYRAMIDS

The different modes of nutrition that are found in animals occupying different trophic levels in an ecosystem can well be illustrated by constructing what are known as ecological pyramids. In many ecological pyramids, the producers form the base and the successive trophic levels make up the apex. Communities of terrestrial ecosystems and shallow water ecosystems contain gradually slopping ecological pyramids because these producers remain large and characterized by an accumulation of organic matter. This trend, however, does not hold for all ecosystems. In such aquatic ecosystems as lakes and open sea, primary production is concentrated in the microscopic algae. These algae have a short life-cycle, multiply rapidly, accumulate little organic matte - and are heavily exploited by herbivorous zoo-plankton. At any one point in time the standing crop is low. As a result, the pyramid of biomass for these aquatic ecosystems is inverted ; the base is much smaller than the structure it supports.

Three different types of pyramidal relationships exist among organisms namely, the pyramid of numbers, the pyramid of energy, and the pyramid of biomass.

1. Pyramid of Numbers

The pyramid of numbers was advanced by Charles Elton (1927), who pointed out the great difference in the numbers of the organisms involved in each steps of the food chain. It serves to illustrate the population density relationships within and between the trophic levels. The number of individuals decrease at each trophic level due to differences in population growth rate and due to predation upon small organisms by larger ones. This principle may be best illustrated by taking a lake as an example. The lowest trophic level is occupied by the diatoms and they are numerically more abundant in the ecosystem. The lowest trophic level is occupied by the diatoms and they are numerically more abundant in the ecosystem. The second trophic level is occupied by the copepods which are less numerically abundant. The third and the fourth trophic levels are occupied by the smaller and larger fishes respectively. There is a considerable reduction in the number of individuals and an increase in the size of the body in the trophic levels from base to top of the pyramid. The pyramid of numbers ignores the biomass of organisms and it also does not indicate the energy transferred or the use of energy by the groups involved.

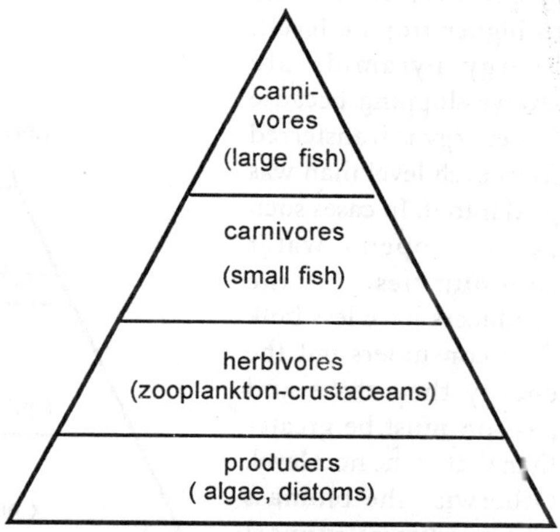

A pyramid of numbers in a lake ecosystem

2. Pyramid of Energy

The pyramid of energy clearly indicates the reduction in the availability of energy between the different trophic levels. Greater amount of energy is available at the producer level, than in the herbivore (primary consumers) trophic level. The energy production of the primary consumers is greater than that of primary carnivores forming the second link in the consumer level (secondary consumers). The least amount of energy production is noticed among secondary carnivores (tertiary consumers). It may be noted that the percentage loss of energy by respiration increases progressively from lower to higher trophic levels. Energy pyramids are always slopping because less energy is transferred from each level than was paid into it. In cases such as in open water communities the producers have less bulk than consumers but the energy they store and pass on must be greater than that of the next level. Otherwise the biomass that producers support could not be greater than that of the producers themselves.

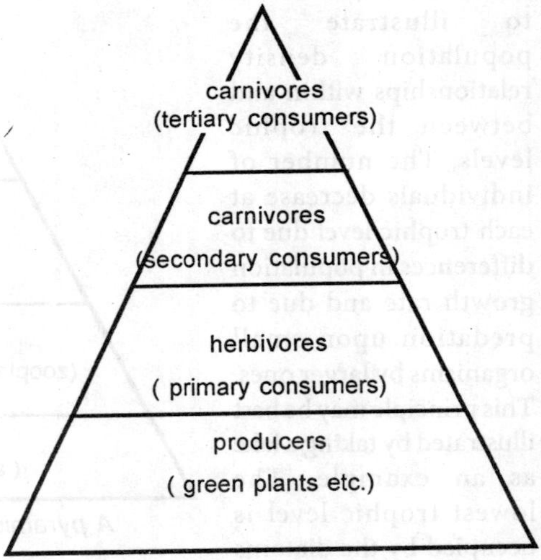

Energy pyramid of an ecosystem

3. Pyramid of Biomass

The biomass of the members of the food chain present at any one time forms the pyramid of the biomass. The pyramid of biomass clearly shows a decrease in the biomass (total amount of living material) from the lower to the higher trophic levels. This principle can be illustrated by taking the examples of the biomasses of the marine and terrestrial environment. The basic trophic level in the pyramid of biomass of the marine environment is occupied by

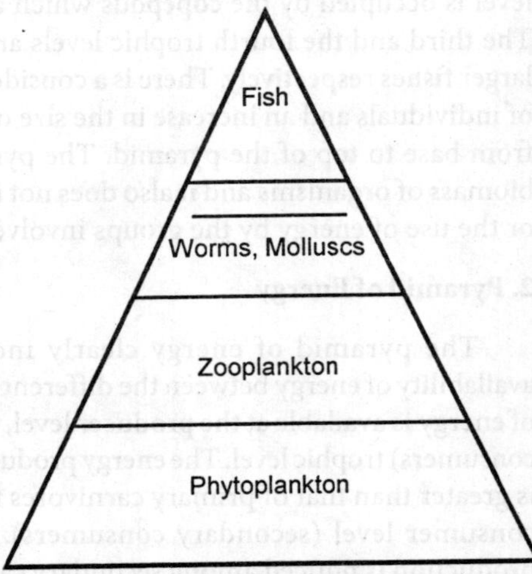

Pyramid of biomass in a marine ecosystem

the phytoplankton. The next trophic level is occupied by the zooplankton. The third and the fourth are occupied by the worms, molluscs and fishes respectively. In the terrestrial environment the basic trophic level is occupied by the autotrophic plants. The next trophic level is occupied by the herbivores. The 3rd, 4th and 5th are occupied by the primary, secondary and tertiary carnivores respectively. In the above mentioned examples the biomass falls in a graded manner from the basic to the higher trophic levels.

BIOCHEMICAL CYCLES

The cyclic movements of chemical elements of the biosphere between the organism and the environment are referred to as biogeochemical cycles.

Water Cycle

Living organisms, atmosphere and earth maintain between them a circulation of water a moisture which is referred to as water cycle or hydrologic cycle. Water forms a very significant factor of environment and without the cycling of water, biogeochemical cycles could not exist, ecosystems could not function, and life could not be maintained. Water is the medium by which nutrients are introduced into autotrophic plants ; it is an important part of living tissue, it serves as a means of thermal regulation for both plants and animals ; it is the medium by which sediments are removed from or added to local ecosystem ; it is the dominant feature of all aquatic ecosystems.

The hydrolic cycle is driven by solar energy and gravity. More than 80 percent of the total isolation that is not lost immediately as electromagnetic radiation goes to evaporate water. The atmospheric water vapour produced by this means can then condense around particles of dust in the atmosphere. The atmosphere possesses a limited capacity for holding water vapour. Almost 95 per cent of the total water on earth is chemically bound into rocks and does not cycle. Of the remainder about 97.3 percent is in the ocean, about 2.1 percent exists as ice in the polar caps and permanent glaciers, and the rest is fresh water, present in the form of atmospheric water vapour, ground water, soil water or inland surface water.

The rate of cycling of water between surface and atmosphere is very rapid. The amount of water vapour in the atmosphere is sufficient, on the

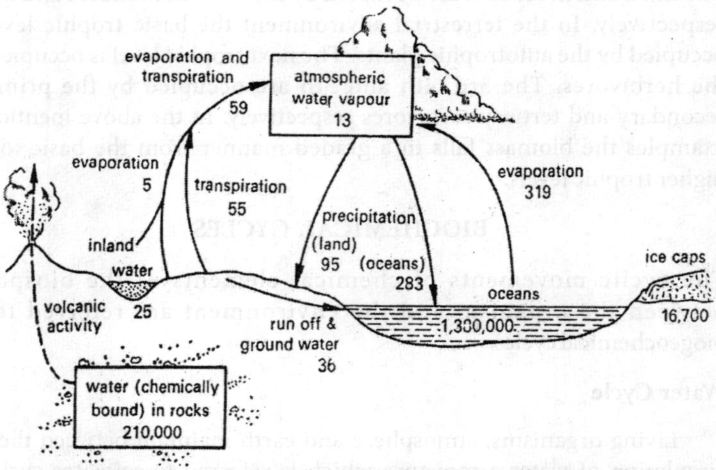

Global hydrological cycle. Most of the storage is in the oceans, but most of the flux is to and from the atomosphere. Units : stores, 10^{18}g: fluxes, $101^{8}g^{a-1}$ (Modified from Rickelfs, 1979).

average, to cover the entire earth to a depth of 2.25 cm. But the average annual rainfall for the earth is about 81.1 cm. and in some places it ranges upto 1200 cm. The distribution of evaporation and rainfall is quite uneven.

The water is evaporated from the surface of the ocean and water vapours form the clouds which when cool down precipitate the water as rain fall. The routes of hydrologic cycles on land can be divided into (i) evapotranspiration, (ii) surface runoff and (iii) ground water. In evapotranspiration, the water is evaporated directly from any surface. The main effects of direct evaporation are to moderate the temperature of local area and to allow the hydrologic cycle to continue. In some ecosystems, evaporation also leads to a concentration of salts in the water of soil. Transpiration is the process of loss of water in the form of water vapour by from the surface of leaves of plants. Transpiration acts to move the biogeochemical cycles for all mineral nutrients that enter the food chain via the roots of plants.

If transpiration is related to the mechanism of nutrient uptake, the gross movement of soluble and solid particles in the ecosystem is accomplished largely by runoff. Nutrients that have accumulated in sediments or soils can be *eroded* by streams and removed altogether from a local ecosystem, or soluble nutrients may be carried by soil seepage into surface waters, where they are removed from the area. Moving water acts as an agent of erosion which removes soil and allows weathering of the underlying rock to make their nutrients available to plants.

Ground water is water that saturates either sediment or rock below the water table in general. It is an important reservoir for water which moves from one place to another. In general it is not trapped by plants for transpiration and it is too deep to be directly evaporated from the soil surface. The area where the net water movement is from the surface into the ground water systems is termed catchment area ; areas where ground water reaches the surface and runs off are termed springs.

Oxygen Cycle

Oxygen is the by-product of photosynthesis. It is involved in the oxidation of carbohydrates with release of energy, carbon dioxide and water. Its primary role in biological oxidation is that of a hydrogen acceptor. Hydrogen is removed by enzymatic activity from organic molecules in a series of reactions and is finally accepted by the oxygen, forming water.

The major supply of free oxygen which supports life occurs in the atmosphere. There are two sources of atmospheric oxygen. One is the photodissociation of water vapour in which most of the hydrogen released escapes into outer space. The other source is photosynthesis. Photosynthesis and respiration are cyclic, and involve both the release and utilization of oxygen. The main non-living (abiotic) oxygen pool consists of molecular oxygen, water, and carbon dioxide, all intimately linked to each other in photosynthesis and other oxidation-reduction reactions.

Oxygen cycle is very complex. As a constituent of CO_2, it circulates freely throughout the atmosphere. Some carbon dioxide combines with calcium to form carbonates. Oxygen combines with nitrogen compounds to form nitrates, with iron to ferric oxides, and with many other minerals to form various other oxides. In these states oxygen is temporarily withdrawn from circulation. In photosynthesis the oxygen freed is split from the water molecule. This oxygen is then reconstituted into water during plant and animal respiration.

Carbon Cycle

Carbon is a basic constituent of all organic compounds and a major element involved in the fixation of energy by photosynthesis. The source of all the fixed carbon both in living organisms and fossil deposits is carbon dioxide, found in the atmosphere and dissolved in the waters of the earth. During photosynthesis, carbon from atmospheric CO_2 is incorporated into the production of the carbohydrate, glucose that subsequently may be converted to other organic compounds. The organic compounds containing carbon are stored in different plant tissues as food and from them the carbon is passed on to the trophic levels of herbivores or phytoparasites, or retained by the plant until it serves as food for decay organisms. The carbon dioxide which is released as the by

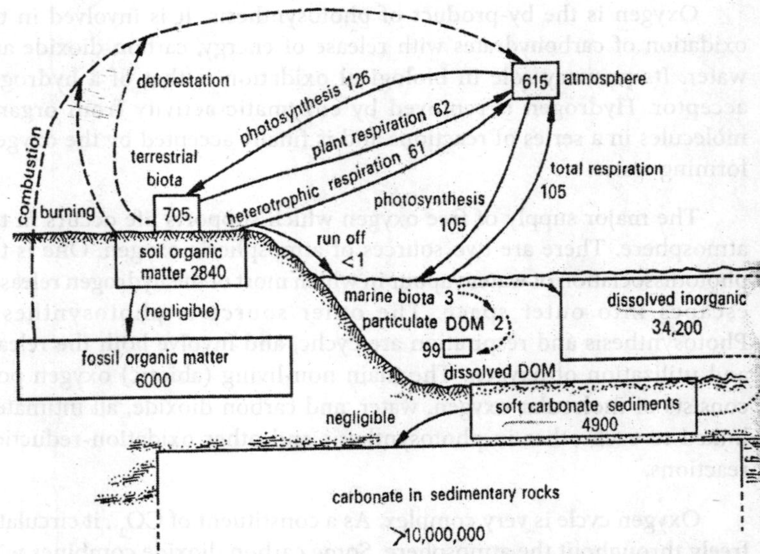

Global carbon cycle. Storage in 10^{15}g carbon; fluxes, $10^{15}g^{a-1}$ carbon. Solid lines indicate the cycle in balance, with dotted lines being the complex marine intractions between water, biota and sediments, which are not well quantified. Dashed lines are fluxes resulting from human activities that have thrown the cycle out of balance DOM = dead organic matter (Data from Bolin *et al* 1979).

product of plant respiration is again used by plants in photosynthesis. This is the basic carbon cycle.

Carbon taken up by herbivores or phytoparasites may travel in different routes. It may be incorporated into protoplasm and stored until the organism dies, where upon it is utilized by decomposers.

Nitrogen Cycle

Nitrogen forms the major constituent of the atmosphere, comprising about 79 percent of it. To be used biologically, the free molecular nitrogen has to be fixed and fixation requires an input of energy. This fixation comes about in two ways: one is by high energy fixation such as cosmic radiation, meteorite trails and lightening that provide high energy needed to combine nitrogen with oxygen and hydrogen of water. The second method of nitrogen fixation which contributes 90 percent of fixed nitrogen of earth, is biological. Some bacteria, fungi, and blue-green algae can extract molecular nitrogen from the atmosphere and combine it with hydrogen to form ammonia. Some of the ammonia is excreted by the nitrogen-fixing organisms.

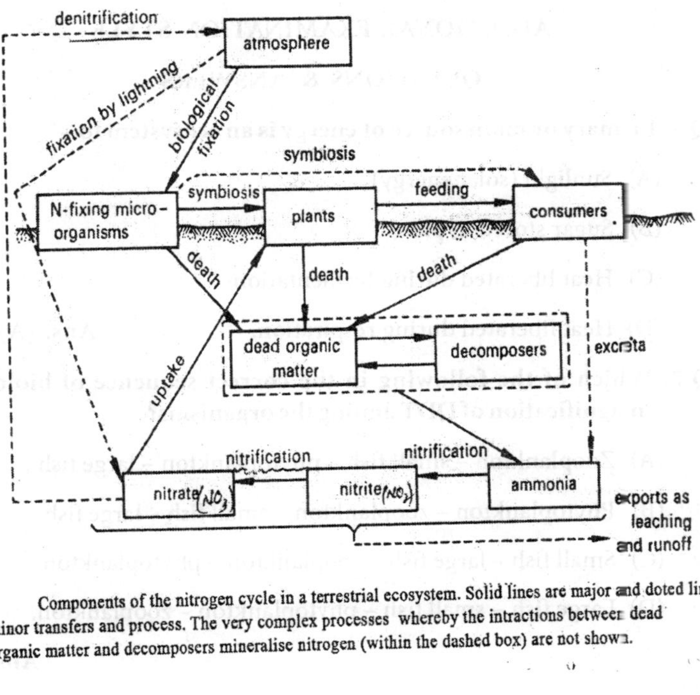

Components of the nitrogen cycle in a terrestrial ecosystem. Solid lines are major and doted lines minor transfers and process. The very complex processes whereby the intractions between dead organic matter and decomposers mineralise nitrogen (within the dashed box) are not shown.

soil and water is one source of nitrogen. Another source is organic matter. In nitrification process, ammonia is oxidised to nitrate and nitrite yielding energy. This energy is used by the bacteria to make their organic materials directly from carbondioxide and water.

The source of inputs of nitrogen under natural conditions are the bacterial fixation of atmospheric nitrogen, addition of inorganic nitrogen in rain from such sources as lightning fixation and fixed "juvenile" nitrogen from volcanic activities, ammonia absorption from the atmosphere by plants and soil, and nitrogen accretion from withdrawn aerosols, which contain both organic and inorganic forms of nitrogen. In terrestrial ecosystems, nitrogen, largely in the form of ammonia and nitrates is taken up by plants, which convert it into amino acids and proteins. Animals excrete several kinds of nitrogen containing wastes – urea, uric acid. Ammonia may be lost as gas to the atmosphere, may be acted upon by nitrifying bacteria, or may be taken up directly by plants. Under natural conditions nitrogen lost from ecosystems by denitrification, volatilization, etc. is balanced by biological fixation and other sources.

ADDITIONAL EXAMINATION STYLE QUESTIONS & ANSWERS

Q.1. Primary or main source of energy is an ecosystem to –

(A) Sunlight (solar energy)

(B) Sugar stored in plant

(C) Heat liberated during fermentation

(D) Heat liberated during respiration. **Ans.** (A).

Q.2. Which of the following in the correct sequence of biological magnification of DDT among the organisms?

(A) Zooplankton – small fish – phytoplankton – large fish

(B) Phytoplankton – zooplankton – small fish – large fish

(C) Small fish – large fish – zooplankton – phytoplankton

(D) Large fish – small fish – phytoplankton – zooplankton.

Ans. (B).

Q.3. Which of the following represents correct sequence of food chain

(A) Tiger – Fox – Mouse – Grass

(B) Fox – Tiger – Mouse – Grass

(C) Grass – Mouse – Fox – Tiger

(D) Mouse – Grass – Tiger – Fox **Ans.** (C).

Q.4. Rain forest occurs in which of the following areas of India.

(A) Western and Central Himalayas

(B) Deccan plateau

(C) Western Ghats and Eastern Himalaya

(D) Gangetic plain. **Ans.** (C).

Q.5. Grasshopper in grassland ecosystem is –

(A) Carnivore (B) Insectivore

(C) Herbivore (D) Cannibalistic. **Ans.** (C).

Q.6. Which of the following represents an ecosystem ?

(A) Grass (B) Grassland

(C) Tree (D) Insect. **Ans.** (B).

Q.7. The term Ecosystem was introduced by –

(A) Friederich (B) Thienman

(C) Tansley (D) Odum. **Ans.** (C).

Q.8. In which Tropical level in the grassland ecosystem does the Rabbit belong ?

(A) Primary producer (B) Herbivore

(C) Carnivore (D) Top carnivore. **Ans.** (B).

Q.9. While practising jhum (shifting) cultivation, the most harmful effect is produced due to –

(A) Cutting trees at ground level (B) Removal of tree roots

(C) Burning of vegetable cover (D) Langerhum cycle. **Ans.** (C).

Q.10. Which of the following represents the correct sequence of food chain in the ecosystem ?

(A) Mouse – rich – tiger – fox (B) Rice – mouse – fox – tiger

(C) Fox – tiger – mouse – rice (D) Tiger – fox – rice – mouse.

Ans. (B).

Q.11. The heterotroph is an organism which

(A) depends on plants food (B) can live in water

(C) can manufacture its food (D) does not require food.

Ans. (A).

Q.12. Ecological studies at the species level is known as

(A) Monoecology (B) Autoecology

(C) Synecology (D) Bioecology. **Ans.** (B).

Q.13. The term ecology was first coined by

(A) Lamarck (B) Haeckel

(C) Von Baer (D) Hygo de Vries. **Ans.** (B).

Q.14. The ecology of the soil is of the vital importance to the life of organism. Which of the following deals such a science ?

(A) Autoecology (B) Synecology

(C) Pedology (D) Palaecology. **Ans.** (C).

Q.15. Define ecology *Or* give the meaning of ecology.

Ans. Ecology is that branch of biology which is concerned with principles or fundamentals common to life. It deals with the study of the inter relationships that exist between the living organisms and their environment. Ecology is concerned with the biology of individual organisms and with such groups of organisms as populations and communities.

Q.16. What do you mean by trophic level ?

Ans. Each successive level of nourishment as represented by links of the food chain is known as trophic level. The first trophic level in an ecosystem is occupied by the plant producers, the second trophic level by the herbivores and the third by the primary carnivores.

Q.17. Define biotic component of an ecosystem.

Ans. Biotic component of an ecosystem is all the living beings of different species found in an ecosystem.

Q.18. Define a food web.

Ans. Food web is a network of food chains which become interconnected at various trophic levels so as to form a number of feeding connections amongst different organisms of a biotic community.

Q.19. Distinguish between a food chain and a food web.

Ans. A food chain is a group of organisms in which there is a transfer of food energy. The energy is transferred from its primary source in plants, through a series of organisms, each feeding on the organism before it in the group or series. On the other hand, food web is the interlocking pattern formed by a series of interconnected food chains.

Q.20. Name the main components of ecology.

Ans. Abiotic and biotic components.

Q.21. What do you mean by pyramid of energy ?

Ans. It is a graphic representation of amount of energy trapped per unit time and area in different trophic levels of a food chain. Greater amount of energy is available at the producer level, than in the herbivore (primary consumers) trophic level. Energy pyramids are always slopping because less energy is transferred from each level than was paid into it.

Q.22. What is decomposer ? Give its role in an ecosystem.

Ans. Decomposers are living components of ecosystem and are largely composed of micro-organisms such as bacteria. These act on the dead bodies of producers and consumers and are responsible for breaking up complex materials into simple substances. These substances which are released into the environment are consumed by the producers. Plants are the predominant producers, the animals are the consumers while the micro-organisms are the essential decomposers.

An ecosystem may sometimes lack one or another of the components. For example, the depths of the ocean are without producers but their place is taken by the dead and the decaying protoplasm that sink from the surface. The producers include the plants which are of two main types viz., (i) the rooted and the floating plants and (ii) the phytoplankton. In certain of the large ponds the phytoplanktons are essential producers because of the absence of the rooted plants. The primary consumers namely the herbivores are dependent upon the living plants or the plant remains. They are of two types viz,, zooplankton and the bottom dwellers such as molluscs and certain other insects. The secondary consumers namely the carnivores such as fishes and insects feed on the primary consumers. The pond decomposers include the bacteria and other fungi. Decomposers decompose the dead body of plants and animals and absorb some of the decomposed products and release most of the inorganic compounds to the environment. They make the entire biochemical cycle complete.

Q.23. Which of the following is regarded as the renewable sources of energy ?

(A) Biomass (B) Water

(C) Coal (D) Electricity. **Ans.** (B).

Q.24. In an aquatic ecosystem which is the primary producer.

Ans. Phytoplankton.

Q.25. What is ecological niche ?

Ans. Every species has a specific position within the community designated as ecological niche and this very often stand for the functional status or total role of the species within the community. The niche comprises all the bonds between the population and the community and ecosystem in which it is found. This bonds include factors such as tolerance ranges, and optima for all abiotic environmental factors, the sorts of organisms that can be utilized for food by the population, as well as the organisms that feed upon it, the areas in which the species can live, and the population structure of the species.

Q.26. Distinguish between habitat and ecological niche.

Ans. Habitat refers to the place where the animal lives. The word habitat is derived from the Latin word which means "it dwells".

The ecological niche refers to animal's place in the biotic environment and its relation to its food and enemies.

4

ENVIRONMENTAL POLLUTION

The term pollution is used to refer to harmful, foreign substances introduced by man into the environment. Pollution is an undesirable change in the physical, chemical or biological characteristics of our air, water, land that may or will harmfully affect human life or that of desirable species, our industrial processes, living conditions and cultural assets.

It is considered that human population explosion is associated with the pollution problem. With the increasing number of population there is more sewage, more solid wastes, more fuel being burned, more fertilizers and insecticides being used to produce more food for hungry mouths. In countries where there have been the greatest technological advances, the worst pollution occurs. Urban, industrial, and most technologically advanced society dispose of certain kinds of by-products and waste products which when are injected into the biosphere affect the normal functioning of ecosystems and have an adverse effect on plants, animals, and man. Nitrogen and phosphorous are essential nutrients for living organisms, and are extensively used in agriculture to increase crop yields but they can also cause pollution in lakes and rivers when found in excess.

Pollutants may be (i) natural pollutants, and (2) synthetic, man-made pollutants. Certain pollutants such as carbon dioxide, carbon monoxide, sulphur dioxide, lead, mercury, and other trace elements are the consequence of life processes being produced through respiration, faeces, urine and body decomposition. A vast array of synthetic pollutants are increasing continuously with urbanization and industrial growth. They include pesticides, detergents, pharmaceuticals, cosmetic products, organic acids, aerosols, and metals, etc. Several of these compounds pose serious environmental hazards.

Air Pollution

Air pollution is the presence in the atmosphere, or injection into it, of substances that are not present naturally, or present naturally but is in much smaller concentrations, and they may harm living organisms directly or indirectly. But, due to some natural processes or human activities the amount solid waste or concentration of gases other than oxygen in the air which normally has constant percentage of different gases in it, the air is said to be polluted and this phenomenon is known as air pollution. Air pollution is a dangerous environmental pollution. Air pollution occurs in many industrial towns and metropolitans of India and abroad.

Source of Air Pollution

Nature adds few natural pollutants such as pollen, hydrocarbons released by vegetation, dusts from deserts, storms, and volcanic activity. Volcanic eruptions may eject large amounts of gases and particulate matter. Settling volcanic ash can kill vegetation by coating leaves and preventing photosynthesis and transpiration. Fine particles, mainly of sulphates, may penetrate the stratosphere. Dust storms sometimes carry fine sand and pollute the atmosphere.

Industries are also potent sources of air pollution. Petroleum refineries are also the major sources of gaseous pollutants. Industrial processors such as metallurgical plants and smelters, chemical plants, petroleum refineries, pulp and paper mills, sugar mills, cotton mills and synthetic rubber manufacturing plants are responsible for about one fifth of the air pollution. Cement factories emit plenty of dust, which is potential health hazard. Stone crushes and hot mix plants also create a menace. Chemical manufacturing industries emit acid vapour in air.

The chief pollutants of coal burning are fly ash, SO_2 and other gases (CO, NO_2) , aldehydes and hydrocarbons. The transportation industry also contributes the same type of pollutants. The vehicular exhausts are toxic being a source of considerable air pollution, next only to thermal power plants. The exhaust produces many air pollutants including unburnt hydrocarbons, CO, NO and lead oxides. There are also traces of aldehydes, esters, ethers, peroxides and ketones. Due to volatine nature of petrol evaporation from fuel tank goes on constantly and results in emission of hydrocarbons.

The other types of air pollutants include carbon compounds, sulphur compounds, nitrogen oxides, ozone, flurocarbons, hydrocarbons, metals, photochemical products, particulate matter and toxicants. If the pollutants are injected into the atmosphere, they enter the biochemical cycles by different routes. The air above many cities can assimilate and disperse great quantities of fine particulate and gaseous pollutants as long as air can move and disperse. But if air masses over cities become stagnant, pollutants accumulate quickly and deteriorate air quality which cause many respiratory diseases in man and other animals.

Gaseous pollutants like sulphur oxides and hydrogen sulphide are released by the biological decomposition and from volcanic eruptions. Artificially they are also released due to human activities such as smelting of sulphide – containing ores, combustion of sulphur – containing fuels. Sulphur dioxide pollution causes various types of injuries in man, such as eye irritation, chest constriction, headache, vomiting and death from respiratory ailment. Sulphuric acid also causes many respiratory diseases in man and also produces acid rainfalls over parts of the earth.

Carbon monoxide is also released chiefly from gasoline engines and burning of coal in the defective furnace. This gas produces headache, dizziness, nousea, heart palpitation, etc. in man. Nitrogen dioxide is a pungent gas. It causes nose and eye irritation and pulmonary discomfort in man. Levels of ozone may rise in atmosphere due to human activities. Ozone near the earth's surface in the atmosphere creates pollution problem.

Many other gaseous pollutants like Hydrogen fluoride, Hydrocarbons, Hydrogen chloride, Ammonia, Tabacco smoke, Fluorides, etc., adversely affect flora, fauna and climate of a given area.

Air pollution causes contamination of the upper atmosphere and the alteration of weather and climate. Air pollution affects weather on a continental or global basis. The simultaneous cooling and heating effects of air pollution on earth have increased variability in the world wide weather patterns which may be a serious threat to global food production.

Water Pollution

Water pollution is a type of aquatic contamination between two extremes : (1) a highly enriched, over productive biotic community, such as a river or lake with nutrients from sewage or fertilizer, or (2) a body of water poisoned by toxic chemicals which eliminate living organisms or even exclude all forms of life. Normally water contains two types of impurities – dissolved and suspended. Dissolved impurities are gases

(H_2S, CO_2, NH_3, etc.) and minerals (Ca, Mg, Na, salts). Suspended matter includes clay, silt and sand and even microbes. Polluted waters are turbid, unpleasant, foul smelling, unfit for drinking, bathing and washing or other purposes. They are harmful and means of many diseases as cholera, dysentery, typhoid, hepatitis, etc.

Water pollution may be surface water pollution, ground water pollution, soil water pollution, etc. ; the habitat in which they occur such as river pollution, lake pollution, estuarine pollution, coastal water pollution, open ocean pollution, etc. ; and source or type of contamination, such as nutrient pollution, bacterial pollution, viral pollution, metallic pollution, petrochemical pollution, pesticide pollution, thermal pollution, radioactive pollution, etc.

Pollutants entering water sources may be of the following types : domestic sewage and oxygen-demanding wastes ; infectious agents ; plant nutrients ; chemicals such as insecticides, herbicides, and detergents ; other minerals and chemicals ; sediment from land erosions ; radioactive substances ; and heat from power and industrial plants.

Aquatic pollutants come from many sources. Extensive nutrients, such as nitrates and phosphates, commonly originate in domestic sewage. Toxic chemicals as agents of water pollution originate in industrial operations, acid mine drainage, surface erosion from strip mines, washing of herbicides and insecticides, radioactive fall out from atomic explosion, and commercial accidents such as oil spills or the rupture of chemical tanks.

Water pollution affects the abiotic and biotic factors of different aquatic systems in different degrees. Some of the well known ecological effects of water pollution are the following:

1. Sewage Pollution

Sewage includes mostly biodegradable pollutants such as human faecal matter, animal wastes, and certain dissolved organic compounds (for example, carbohydrates, urea, etc.) and inorganic salts such as nitrates and phosphates of detergents and sodium, potassium, calcium and chloride ions. When the biodegradable pollutants accumulate in large quantities, they create problem.

Marine pollution is most evident in coastal waters and estuarine areas. The oceans have become the final settling basing for millions of tons of waste products from human activities. For example, in the late 1960s West Germany was dumping 375 tons of sulphuric acid, 750 tons of iron sulphate, 20 tons of chlorinated hydrocarbons and 16,000 tons of gypsum wastes into the North Sea and North Atlantic Ocean every day.

Petroleum and its distillates, halogenated hydrocarbons including pesticides, organic compounds including detergents, domestic raw sewage, agricultural run-offs, inorganic chemicals including metals such as mercury, lead and copper, dumped containers, radioactive wastes, etc. are the major pollutants entering the sea. These pollutants affect the health and integrity of the world's ocean.

In order to control water pollution, most cities of the world have evolved certain engineering systems such as septic tanks, oxidation ponds, filter beds, waste water treatment plants and municipal sewage treatment plants.

Noise Pollution

Noise is a 'sound without value'. Noise is undesired by the recipient. Noise levels in many urban-industrialized situations are known to be deleterious to human health and efficiency, with effects on the sense organs, cardiovascular, glandular and nervous systems.

Noise pollution or high intensity sound is produced by many machines which are invented by man. There exists a long list of sources of noise pollution including different machines of numerous factories, industries and mills, different kinds of auto and motor vehicles such as scooters, motorbikes, cars, tempos, buses, trucks, tractors, aircrafts, motor boats, ships, loud speakers, social gatherings, loud pop-music, supersonic aircrafts, etc. Noise is not only annoying but if continued for a long time can also result in emotional and behavioural alterations in man.

Noise pollution has certain well evident ecological and pathological effects on biota and human beings. Noise causes disturbance in the atmosphere which in turn interferes with the systems of communication. Noise affects our peace of mind, health and behaviour. Sudden loud note can cause acute damage to the ear drum and the tiny hair cells in the internal ear, whereas prolonged noise results in temporary loss of hearing or even permanent impairment. It causes headache, irritability, etc. Noise is also known to flush the skin, constrict stomach muscles and produces ulcers, heart diseases, high blood pressure, nervousness, etc.

The means of noise control are (i) to manipulate the source so as to reduce the noise at its origin ; (ii) to interrupt the path of transmission, and (iii) to protect the recipient. Nobody should be permitted to create noise in silent zones or during night. Noise producing traffic vehicles should be prevented from plying on the roads and their use of pressure horns should be entirely checked.

The path of the sound can be interrupted by using various materials which absorb the sound energy. Under noisy situations, one may hold his hands over his ears or may run away from the source, or may simply stuff a bit of cotton or ear plugs in the ears to reduce much hazards of noise pollution.

ADDITIONAL EXAMINATION STYLE QUESTIONS & ANSWERS

Q.1. Which of the following can be degraded by the action of microbes ?

(A) Plastic bags (B) DDT (C) BHC (D) Plant root.

Ans (D).

Q.2. Carbon dioxide saturation in the air is about

(A) 0.3% (B) 0.03% (C) 0.003% (D) 0.0003%

Ans. (B).

Q.3. One of the pollutants below cause nervous disorder and is collected in the bones

(A) CO_3 (B) SO_3 (C) PCB (D) Pb. **Ans.** (D).

Q.4. The substance which is harmless when present in small amount but causes harmful effects when present in higher amount is called

(A) Qualitative pollutant (B) Quantitative pollutant

(C) Degradable pollutant (D) Non-degradable pollutant.

Ans. (B).

Q.5. Which of the following pollutants in highest quantities, will be produced due to the use of bio-fuels in the automobiles ?

(A) Carbon dioxide (B) Sulphur dioxide

(C) Lead (D) Aldehydes. **Ans.** (A).

Q.6. Ozone containing zone of atmosphere is known as

(A) Ionosphere (B) Troposphere

(C) Biosphere (D) Stratosphere. Ans. (D).

Q.7. The pesticide, DDT and BHC are categorised under

(A) Carbonate (B) Organophosphate

(C) Organochlorines (D) Pyrethroids. Ans. (C).

Q.8. The critical level of noise in decibels for human ear damage is

(A) 160 (B) 85 (C) 60 (D) 30. Ans. (B).

Q.9. Which of the following substance is associated with the formation of photochemical smog ?

(A) 2.4-D (B) CFC (C) PAN (D) DDT. Ans. (C).

Q.10. The ozone layer of the earth is destroyed by one of the chemicals released from refrigeration, air conditioning, etc.

(A) Organophosphates (B) Fluorochromes

(C) Organochlorines (D) Chlorofluorocarbon. Ans. (D).

Q.11. Gamma radiation can destroy living cells by a process of

(A) Electrolysis (B) Ionization

(C) Scattering (D) Excitation. Ans. (D).

Q.12. Which of the following is a quantitative pollutant ?

(A) SO_2 (B) Helium (C) Nitrogen (D) CO_2.

Ans. (A).

5

WILDLIFE MANAGEMENT

(*With Reference to India*)

Wildlife management is concerned with assuring the maximum possible populations of game animals consistent with other land uses in the same area and with the number that the given habitat will support. This is attained by manipulating the balance of nature in such a way that the desired game species are favoured. Successful game management depends upon a number of factors including an understanding of ecological principles, and appreciation of the conflicts between game species and agricultural uses of land, and educating both the landowner and the hunter concerning the objectives, techniques and limitations of game management.

India is unique in possessing a rich and diverse wild life fauna. According to an estimate, in India, there are 400 species of mammals, 1200 species of birds, 350 species of reptiles and more than 29,70,000 species of insects. Black buck, Nilgiri tahr, pigmy hog, golden langur, lion-tailed macaque, etc. are unique to India. Other wild animals of India include : elephant, rhinoceros, mouse deer, swamp deer, dancing deer, hog deer, thamin, Kashmir stag ; antelopes such as black buck, four-horned antelope, Indian gazelle, and blue bull ; bison ; wild buffalo ; wild goat ; wild boar, wild ass ; carnivores such as lion, tiger and leopard, striped hyaena, jackel, wolf, desert cat, desert fox ; bears such as black Himalayan bear and sloth bear, monkeys and apes such as Nilgiri langur, lion tailed monkey, rhesus monkey and Hanuman monkey (Semnopithecus) ; Indian grant squirrel; desert hare ; porcupine ; pangolin ; birds such as pea fowl, jungle fowl, partridge, quail, great Indian bustard, duck, pigeon, sandgrouse, storks, and egrets, pelican, eagle, crane, owl, hornbill, etc., and reptiles such as crocodiles, gharials, lizards and enormous varieties of snakes.

Wildlife management is a branch of conservation. The conservation of wild life is required for the following benefits : (i) The wildlife helps us in maintaining the balance of nature. If this equilibrium is disturbed it causes many problems. The destruction of carnivores or insectivores often leads to the increase in herbivores which in turn affects the forest vegetation or crops. (2) The wildlife can be used commercially to earn more and more money. It can increase our earning of foreign exchange, if linked with tourism. (3) The preservation of wildlife helps many naturalists and behaviour biologists to study, morphology, anatomy, physiology, ecology, behaviour biology of the wild animals under their natural surroundings. (4) The wildlife provides best means of sports and recreation. (5) The wild life of India is our cultural asset and has deep-rooted effects on Indian art, sculpture, literature and religion.

For the wildlife management, the following measures have been taken in India.

1. Protection by Law

The Wild Birds and Animals Protection Act was passed in India in 1887 and repealed in 1912. For game protection in the States, in 1927, the Forest Act XVI was enacted. Indian Board for Wild Life was established in 1952 and this was followed by setting up of Wild Life Boards in different States. In 1972, new Wild Life Protection Act was passed under this Act, possession, trapping, shooting of wild animals alive or dead ; serving their meat in eating houses ; their transport and export are all controlled and watched by special staff. This Act prohibits hunting of females and young ones. Under this Act threatened species are absolutely protected and the rest afforded graded protection according to their state of population size.

Protected species of Indian Wildlife

The following wild animals are enlisted as threatened and protected species : White eyed buck, Indian antelope, Four-horned antelope, Bharal, Swamp deer, Eastern pangolin, Elephant, Indian gozelle, Musk deer, Serow, Tahr, Golden cat, Snow leopard, Great Indian bustard, Pink headed duck, Pea fowl, Monal pheasant, Koklas pheasant, Chir pheasant, Horned pheasant, Monitor lizard, Water lizard, Gharial, Marsh crocodile, Python, and Leathery turtle.

Establishment of Sanctuaries and National Parks

Under the Wildlife Protection Act, 1972, national parks and sanctuaries could be created in order to protect, preserve and propagate rich natural bounty. Thus, in India about 450 national parks and sanctuaries have been established. A national park is an area which is strictly reserved for the betterment of the wild life and where activities such as forestry, grazing or cultivation are not permitted. There are almost 100 national parks in the country which are spread over an area of 33,988.14 square kilometres. Sanctuaries are places where the killing or capturing of any animal is prohibited except under orders of the authorities concerned. Sanctuaries provide protection and optimum living conditions to wild animals.

Some of the well known wildlife sanctuaries and national parks of India are as follows :

1. *Kaziranga Wildlife Sanctuary :* – This was set up in 1926 in Sibsagar district, subdivision Jorhat (Assam) on the south bank of the Brahmaputra river. It occupies 430 sq. km. of forest grasslands and swamps. It supports 700 rhinoceros, besides elephant, wild buffalo, bison, tiger, leopard, sloth bear, sambhar, swamp deer, hog deer, wild boar, gibbon and birds such as pelican, stork and ring-tailed fishing eagles.

2. *Manas Wildlife Sanctuary :*– It is located in district Kamrup in Assam. It has an area of 540 sq. km. and is situated at an altitude of 80 metres. River Manas passes through it. It supports tiger, panther, wild dog, wild boar, rhinocerous, gaur, wild buffalo, sambhar, swamp deer and golden langur.
3. *Jaldapara Wildlife Sanctuary :*– It is in the Jalpaiguri district of West Bengal. It is a 65 sq. km. stretch of grassland. Its wild life fauna includes rhinoceros, gaur, elephant, tiger, leopard, deer, and a variety of birds and reptiles.
4. *Palamau National Park :*– It is situated in Daltongunj district in Bihar. It has an area of 345 sq. km. Its flora is thick tropical forests. The fauna of this park includes tiger, panther, sloth bear, elephant, chital, gaur, nilgai, chinkara, chow singha and mouse-deer.
5. *Hazaribagh National Park :*– It was established in 1954 in Bihar. It has an area of 184 sq. km. of thick tropical forests. Its fauna includes wild boar, sambhar, nilgai, tiger, leopard, sloth bear, hyena and gaur.

6. *Simplipal National Park :–* It lies in the district Mayuri Bhanj in Orissa. It has an area of 2750 sq. km. It is covered over by dense sal forests. Its typical fauna includes tiger, elephant, deer, pea fowl, talking mynas, chital, sambhar, panther, gaur, hyena and sloth bear.
7. *Chilka Lake:–* This is a large inland lake occupying an area of 1000 sq. km. and is about 100 km. from Bhubaneshwar (Orissa). Its typical fauna includes water fowls, ducks, cranes, ospreys, gold plovers, sand pipers, stone curlews, flamingoes, etc.
8. *Kolameru Bird Sanctuary:–* This is a small bird sanctuary near Tadepallegudum in Andhra State. It is a breeding place for pelicans. Many marine birds visit this place.
9. *Vedanthangal Bird Sanctuary :–* It extends over a lake of about 0.30 sq. km. South of Madras. Many migratory birds regularly visit this lake. The regular visitors of this lake are birds such as spoon bill, open billed stork, egrets, ibis, cormorant, grey heron, pelican, snipes, etc.
10. *Guindy Devi Park :–* It is situated near Madras city. It has chitals, black bucks, albinos, etc.
11. *Point Calimera Wildlife Sanctuary :–* It is situated at the southern tip of Thanjavur district of Tamil Nadu. Its fauna includes visiting flamingos, pelicans, chitals, wild bears.
12. *Mundanthurai Sanctuary :–* It is in the Tirunelveli district of Tamil Nadu. It has an area of 520 sq. km. It has evergreen forests. Its fauna includes panther, tiger, sambhar, chital.
13. *Periyar Wildlife Sanctuary :–* It is situated in Kerala state. It has an area of 777 sq. km. Its fauna includes wild elephants, gaurs, leopards, sloth bear, sambhars, barking deer, wild dogs, wild boars, black langur and water birds such as grey hornbills, egrets.
14. *Mudumalai Wildlife Sanctuary :–* It was established in 1940 in North Western part of Nilgiris in Tamil Nadu. It has rich forests. Its fauna includes wild elephant, gaur, sambhar, chital, barking deer, mouse deer, four-horned antelope, tiger, panther.
15. *Ranganthittoo Bird Sanctuary :–* It includes a series of islands in the Cauvery river 15 km. off the Banglore-Mysore Road, near Shrirangapattnam. Its avial fauna includes open bill stork, white ibis, egret, spoon bill, wild duck, peafowl, night heron birds.

16. *Bandipur Wildlife Sanctuary :-* This was established in 1941. It is situated 80 km. south of Mysore city enroute to Octacamund. It has an area of 874 sq. km. and is at an altitude of 1454.4 meters. It has thick forest. Its rainfall is high. Its wild life fauna includes gaurs, elephant, leopard, sloth bear, wild dog, chital, panther, barking deer, porcupine and langur.

17. *Cotigo Wildlife Sanctuary :-* It is situated in South Goa. It has an area of 105 sq. km. It has wet evergreen forest of Elve and Berla trees. It has the following fauna : gaur, sambhar, chital, hog-deer, barking deer, wild boar, hyaena, panther, jackal, otter, porcupine and birds such as parakeet, woodpecker, king fisher, bulbul, jungle fowl, egrete, etc.

18. *Bhagwan Mahadev Wildlife Sanctuary :-* It is situated in North Goa. It has an area of 240 sq. km. It supports fauna almost similar to Cotigo Wild Life Sanctuary.

19. *Sesar Gir :-* It is situated in Gujarat state, 468 km. from Ahmedabad and 43 km. from Veraval. It has an area of 1295 sq. km. It has deciduous trees. Its fauna includes Asiatic lion, spotted deer, blue bull, four-horned antelope, chinkara, striped hyena, wild boar, porcupine, langur, python, crocodiles and birds such as green pigeon, partridge, rock-grouse, etc.

20. *Kanha National Park :-* It was established in 1955 in former Banjar Valley Reserve (Madhya Pradesh). It has an area of 939.94 sq. km., and includes hilly terrains and streams. It has forests of sal trees. Its fauna includes tiger, chital, panther, sambhar, black buck and bara singha.

21. *Tandoba National Park :-* It is in the chandrapur district (Maharastra). It has an area of 116 sq. km. Its fauna includes tiger, sambar, sloth bear, bison, chital, chinkara, barking deer, blue bull, four-horned deer, langur, pea fowl and few crocodiles.

22. *Sariska :-* It is situated in Rajasthan near Alwar. It has an area of 800 sq. km. It has dense Dohokra and Solar forests. Its fauna includes tiger, leopard, spotted deer, jungle cat, four-horned antelope, langur, porcupine, hedgehog, peafowl, etc.

23. *Bharatpur Bird Sanctuary :-* It is in the Bharatpur (Rajasthan). It has an area of 29 sq. km. It has many kinds of indigenous nesting water birds, water side birds, migratory birds, spoon bills, white ibis, Indian darters, egrets, painted storks, open billed storks, great black necked

storkes, etc. Drier parts of this marshy sanctuary have animals like spotted deer, black buck, sambhar, blue bull, wild boar and python.

24. *Sultanpur Lake Bird Sanctuary :-* It is located at Gurgaon district (Haryana) about 30 km. from Delhi. Its avian fauna includes crane, sarus, spot-bill, drake and rudyshel.

25. *Shikari Devi Wildlife Sanctuary :-* It is in the Mandi district of Himachal Pradesh. It has an area of 213 sq. km. It has the following animals : snow leopard, flying fox, black bear, barking deer, musk deer, chakor, partridge, etc.

26. *Bir Motibagh Sanctuary :-* It is situated near Patiala in Punjab. Its fauna includes black buck, blue bull, hog deer, hare, jackal and birds such as peafowl, partridge, sparrow, babbler, myna, parakeet, pigeon, dove, etc.

27. *Dachigam Wildlife Sanctuary :-* It was established in 1951 in Kashmir 26 km. away from Srinagar. It has an area of 89 sq. km. It has two levels : Upper Dachigam at 3692.3 meters altitudes and Lower Dachigam at 1846.2 meters altitudes. It preserves hangul or Kashmir stag, musk deer, leopard, black bear, brown bear and baboon.

28. *Corbett National Park :-* It was established in 1935 as the first national park of India. It is situated between Nainital and Garhwal districts in Utter Pradesh. It has an area of 525 sq. km. and is located within west to south bend of river Ramganga. Its fauna includes tiger, panther, sloth bear, hyaena, elephant, blue bull, swamp deer, barking deer, Indian antelope, porcupine, birds such as bulbul, woodpecker, barbet, babbler and bee eater, and reptiles such as crocodile, python, etc.

29. *Shivpuri Sanctuary :-* It is in the Madhya Pradesh. It supports tigers.

30. *Anamalai Sanctuary :-* It was established in 1972 in the southern part of Coimbatore District in Tamil Nadu. It has an area of 958 sq. km. It supports the following animals : elephant, gaur, sambhar, spotted deer, barking deer, Nilgiri tahr, lion-tailed macaque, tiger, panther, sloth bear, langur, porcupine and pangolin.

Conservation Measures

In order to preserve wild life, the following measures are necessary.

1) For the preservation of species, wildlife management staff should have a correct idea about the exact habitat which the species under consideration needs.

2) Natural habitat of wild animals should be carefully protected.
3) Habitat of wildlife should be improved by constructing water holes, saltlicks and by raising plantation of better and nourishing fodder grasses and trees.
4) Effective means of census operation should be adopted to measure population sizes of various wild animals.
5) The enforcement of Wildlife Protection Acts should be observed strictly.
6) Shooting and hunting of endangered species should be totally banned.
7) Veterinary efforts should be made to take care of wildlife in case of epidemics.
8) Public should be educated about the advantages and disadvantages of wild life.
9) Research works should be encouraged to understand the biology and behaviour of wild animals.

Endangered Species

These are species or taxa, which are in danger of extinction and which may not survive if the adverse factors continue to operate. The species whose population have been seriously decreased and whose ultimate security is not assured and also those whose populations are still abundant but are under threat throughout their range. The species whose numbers have been reduced to a critical level or their habitats have been drastically reduced in such a way that they are in the instant danger of extinction. Due to limited shelter and food supply, deforestation, urbanisation, mass hunting, etc. there has been a great reduction in the number of *Sangai* or brow antlered deer (*Cervus eldi eldi*) of Manipur. It is at the verge of extinction.

Importance of wildlife fauna of Manipur

Manipur has very rare and endangered species of wild life. At the beginning of the 20th century, the Javan Rhinoceros (*Rhinoceros sondaicus*) was found along the Khuga river valley, but such a species are altogether extinct from Manipur now a days. South East Asian deer includes three sub-species. Burmese sub species (*Cervus eldi thamin*) occurs in upper and lower Pourma and also in parts of Thailand. Siamese Eld's deer (*Cervus eldi siamensis*) is found in Thailand, Kampuchea, Vietnam and Henam island of China. The third species is Manipur thamin or "Sangai" or Brow antlered deer (*Cervus eldi eldi*). The Brow antlered deer is the rarest amongst the three species. This deer is found only at Keibul Lamjao National Park. It is in great danger of extinction because of intensive hunting. In Ukhrul district of Manipur, the amphibian species, Salamander or Himalayan Newt (*Tylototriton verrucosus*) is found. Among the birds, the white winged wood duck, the pink headed duck, the grey leg goose, the white ibis, the glossy ibis, the open bill stork, the blacknacked stork, the Eastern White stork, etc. are a few species that have been extinct or have become very rare at present. The Sabeng (*Capricornis sumatraensis*), the Banteng (*Bos banting*), the Sambar (*Cervus unicolor*), the Goral, etc., are now facing extinction due to habitat destruction. The Hog deer (*Axis porcinus*) is at present confined to the swamps of Keibul Lamjao National Park. The Golden cat, the clouded Leopard are also on the verge of extinction. The Malayan Sun bear has become extremely rare, probably is extinct in Manipur. The Gharial was found in the Barak river drainage, particularly in the Maku river, but now a days it is not to be seen. Keilam hill range in Churchandpur district of Manipur is the home of Hornbill and some other important animals. The Great Indian horn bill, the Wreathed horn bill, the Brown backed horn bill are now facing the human pressure. Besides these, a number of wild birds and animals including the Clouded Leopard, Golden Cat, Marbled Cat, Hoolock Gibbon, Pig tailed monkey, Porcupine are also inhabiting the area. Herds of Indian elephant have been reported to frequently roaming of Dzuko Valley area, the northern side of Manipur.

A large number of valuable wild life, some rare and endangered species such as Slow loris, Gharial and Elephant, Himalayan black bear, Spotted linsang, Blyth's tragopan, Hume's bar tailed pheasant, etc., occur outside the conservation area of the State.

A wildlife sanctuary is at Yangangpokpi Lockchao in Chandel District with Burma in the east, and Mizoram in the South proposed to preserve the wild animals like Barking deer, Sambar Serow, Clouded leopard, Golden cat, Jungle cat, Jackal, Elephant, Tiger, Pythons, King cobra, Burmese pea fowl, etc. This sanctuary was established in 1989 as a Wild Life Sanctuary and it covers an area of 184.8 sq. km. The Siroi National Park in Ukhrul District has been declared as a proposed National Park in 1984 by the Government of Manipur. It is the home of some rare animals like Himalayan black bear, Malayan Sun bear, Leopard Cat, Sambar, Barking deer, Tragopan sp. and Salamanders, etc.

ADDITIONAL EXAMINATION STYLE QUESTIONS & ANSWERS

Q.1. The most common Amphibian found in Manipur is

(A) *Bufo bufo* (B) *Bufo melanostictus*

(C) *Rana tigrina* (D) *Rana cynophycta.* **Ans.** (B).

Q.2. Which of the following is a game bird ?

(A) Duck (B) Bublul (C) Dove (D) Parrot. **Ans.** (D).

Q.3. The place where animals are kept in very restricted enclosures is known as

(A) Sanctuary (B) National Park

(C) Zoological garden (D) Zoological Park. **Ans.** (B).

Q.4. The Brow antlered deer (*Sangai*) of Keibul Lamjao is

(A) *Cervus devauceli* (B) *Cervus eldi eldi*

(C) *Cervus eldi thamin* (D) *Cervus eldi siamensis.* **Ans.** (B).

Q.5. Which one of the following is an extinct bird belonging to Manipur?

(A) Pink headed duck (B) Blyth's tragopan

(C) Porachminy duck (D) Indian Bustard. **Ans.** (A).

Q.6. The IUCN's Red Data Book contains –

(A) all national parts of the world

(B) the tiger reserves in India founded by IUCN

(C) the lists of endangered species

(D) the NGOs in nature conservation. **Ans.** (C).

Q.7. Nandan Kanon is a famous zoological park. It is located in which state of India

(A) West Bengal (B) Orissa

(C) Andhra Pradesh (D) Maharastra. **Ans.** (B).

Q.8. What is wild life conservation ?

Ans. Wild life conservation means the use and preservation of natural resources available on earth and their protection against destructive forces, fire, waste, decay or any misuse.

Q.9. Name an avian threatened species which visits Manipur.

Ans. Osprey (*Pandion haliactus haliactus*)

Q.10. Give the scientific name of Asian Urodela.

Ans. *Tylototriton verrucosus.*

Q.11. What is Red Data Book ?

Ans. This is a Book containing the record of threatened animal or plant species.

Q.12. What is the long term of IUCN ?

Ans. International Union for Conservation of Natural Resources.

Q.13. Write the scientific name of a dominant wild life species found in Kaziranga National Park.

Ans. *Rhinoceros unicornis.*

Q.14. Why do we conserve wild life ?

Ans. In order to conserve nature and natural resources.

Q.15. Give the scientific names of the following animals and write where they are found more commonly in India.

Ans. The Great Indian Bustard – *Ardeotis nigriceps* or *Choriotis nigriceps,* found in Ahmadnagar, Maharastra ; Siberian crane – *Grus leucogeranus,* found in Kedadeo Ghana National Park, Bharatnagar, Rajasthan ; Wild Yak – *Bos mutus,* found in Changchenma Valley in Ladakh.

Q.16. For what particular animals mainly the following are famous for Kaziranga, Gir Forest, Sunderban, Kaladeo Ghana Sanctuary, Keibul Lamjao and Corbett National Park.

Ans. **Kaziranga :** Great one horned Rhinoceros (*Rhinoceros unicornis*) ; **Gir Forest :** Indian Lion (*Panthera leo persica*); **Sunderban:** Tiger

(*Panthera tigris*) ; **Kaladeo Ghana Sanctuary :** Siberian crane (*Grus leucogeranus*) ; **Keibul Lamjao National Park :** Brow antlered deer (*Cervus eldi eldi*) ; **Corbett National Park :** Tiger (*Panthera tigris*).

Q.17. Write short note on endangered animals of India.

Ans. These are species or taxa, which are in danger of extinction and which may not survive if the adverse factors continue to operate. The species whose populations have been seriously decreased and whose ultimate security is not assured and also those whose populations are still abundant but are under threat throughout their range. The species whose numbers have been reduced to a critical level or their habitats have been drastically reduced in such a way that they are in the instant danger of extinction. Due to limited shelter and food supply, deforestation, urbanisation, mass hunting, etc., there has been a great reduction in the number of *Sangai* or Brow antlered deer of Manipur. It is at the verge of extinction.

Q.18. The Keibul Lamjao National Park is said to be one of the unique Parks in the World. In what character it is unique ?

Ans. The Keibul Lamjao is the floating national park and it is only one of its kind in the world.

Q.19. Write the scientific or zoological name of – Wild Ass, Great Indian Bustard and Indian Lion.

Ans. Wild Ass – *Equus hemianus kiang ;* Great Indian Bustard – *Ardeotis nigriceps ;* Indian Lion – *Panthera leo persica.*

Q.20. Write the scientific names of the following animals, their specific locality or habitat along with their native state – Asiatic lion, Rhinoceros and Bison.

Ans. Asiatic lion – *Panthera leo persica,* Gir lion Gujarat Sanctuary; Rhinoceros – *Rhinoceros cenicornis,* Kaziranga, Assam National Park; Bison – *Bos gaurus,* Itanagar Arunachal Pradesh Sanctuary.

Q.21. How does Wild Life (Protection) Act, 1972 help in the conservation of endangered animals in Manipur ?

Ans. The Wild Life Protection Act prohibits hunting of females and young ones, and threatened species are well protected.

Q.22. Suggest one of the most important necessity for wild life conservation. Why is it so ?

Ans. The conservation of wild life is required to maintain the balance of nature.

The various food chains and cycles constitute the life support system essential for survival of the living world. If alteration takes place in any one of these, there results serious disturbances in the balance of nature and may threaten the very existence of man himself on the planet.

Q.23. Name at least six importances of wild life.

Ans. (i) For maintaining the balance of nature ; (ii) commercial values ; (iii) scientific values ; (iv) drugs and medicines ; (v) game values ; (vi) aesthetic values.

Q.24. What is wild life ? Write the important wild life fauna of Manipur.

Ans. The flora and fauna which are non-domesticated are the wild life.
Importance of wild life fauna of Manipur :

Manipur has very rare and endangered species of wild life. At the beginning of the 20th century, the Javan Rhinoceros (*Rhinoceros sondaicus*) was found along the Khuga river valley, but such a species are altogether extinct from Manipur now a days. South East Asian deer includes three sub-species. Burmese sub species (*Cervus eldi thamin*) occurs in upper and lower Pourma and also in parts of Thailand. Siamese Eld's deer (*Cervus eldi siamensis*) is found in Thailand, Kampuchea, Vietnam and Henam island of China. The third species is Manipur thamin or "Sangai" or Brow antlered deer (*Cervus eldi eldi*). The Brow antlered deer is the rarest amongst the three species. This deer is found only at Keibul Lamjao National Park. It is in great danger of extinction because of intensive hunting. In Ukhrul district of Manipur, the amphibian species, Salamander or Himalayan Newt (*Tylototriton verrucosus*) is found. Among the birds, the white winged wood duck, the pink headed duck, the grey leg goose, the white ibis, the glossy ibis, the open bill stork, the blacknacked stork, the Eastern White stork, etc. are a few species that have been extinct or have become very rare at present. The Sabeng (*Capricornis sumatraensis*), the Banteng (*Bos banting*), the

Sambar (*Cervus unicolor*), the Goral, etc., are now facing extinction due to habitat destruction. The Hog deer (*Axis porcinus*) is at present confined to the swamps of Keibul Lamjao National Park. The Golden cat, the clouded Leopard are also on the verge of extinction. The Malayan Sun bear has become extremely rare, probably is extinct in Manipur. The Gharial was found in the Barak river drainage, particularly in the Maku river, but now a days it is not to be seen. Keilam hill range in Churchandpur district of Manipur is the home of Hornbill and some other important animals. The Great Indian horn bill, the Wreathed horn bill, the Brown backed horn bill are now facing the human pressure. Besides these, a number of wild birds and animals including the Clouded Leopard, Golden Cat, Marbled Cat, Hoolock Gibbon, Pig tailed monkey, Porcupine are also inhabiting the area. Herds of Indian elephant have been reported to frequently roaming of Dzuko Valley area, the northern side of Manipur.

A large number of valuable wild life, some rare and endangered species such as Slow loris, Gharial and Elephant, Himalayan black bear, Spotted linsang, Blyth's tragopan, Hume's bar tailed pheasant, etc., occur outside the conservation area of the State.

A wild life sanctuary is at Yangangpokpi Lockchao in Chandel District with Burma in the east, and Mizoram in the South proposed to preserve the wild animals like Barking deer, Sambar Serow, Clouded leopard, Golden cat, Jungle cat, Jackal, Elephant, Tiger, Pythons, King cobra, Burmese pea fowl, etc. This sanctuary was established in 1989 as a Wild Life Sanctuary and it covers an area of 184.8 sq. km. The Siroi National Park in Ukhrul District has been declared as a proposed National Park in 1984 by the Government of Manipur. It is the home of some rare animals like Himalayan black bear, Malayan Sun bear, Leopard Cat, Sambar, Barking deer, Tragopan sp. and Salamanders, etc.

UNIT – III
STRUCTURE OF A CELL

6

INTRODUCTION TO CELL

The cell is the fundamental unit of any living organism. The term cell owes its name to the honey-comb like chambers with thick walls as seen in sections of old plant tissues. In plants the thick walls of the chambers are made of lifeless substance made of cellulose. In animal cell, unlike a plant cell, has no thick boundary wall, and instead of it, has a tough protoplasmic membrane which forms the outer part of the cytoplasm.

That the tissues are made of cells was first discovered by the English microscopist, Robert Hooke who used the term cell in 1665 to describe the hollow spaces bound by cork in thin slices of cork. Schleiden discovered that all tissues of plants are made of cells. In the same year, Schwann arrived at the same conclusion for animals. This concept was thin applied to all living organisms. This generalization, that all animals and plants are made of cells and cell products, is known as the cell theory.

Some workers concentrated their attention practically on the distinct cell wall, possibly because the transparent protoplasm escaped their notice. Felix Dujardisv appreciated the importance of cell contents to which he applied the term 'Sarcode'. Huge von Mohl recognized the importance of the living contents and he gave it the name protoplasm. Thomas Henry Huxley in 1868 described it as "the physical basis of life". Hanstein in 1880 proposed the term protoplast for a cell.

A cell shows activities characteristic of life. It absorbs nutriment, respires, grows and reproduces by dividing itself into two halves each of which grows into a daughter cell. Life is treated as a property of the cell system as a whole.

There are millions of cells in the body of a multicellular animal. In the unicellular animals, a single cell represents the body. A cell has length, breadth and thickness.

Shape: The shape of the cell is variable that is constantly changing, for example, Amoeba or leucocytes or fixed. In the latter case the cell may be flattened, for example, squamous epithelium, endothelium and upper layers of the epidermis; cuboidal, for example, in thyroid gland follicles; columnar for example, the cell lining the intestine, discoidal, for example, erythrocytes; spherical, for example, the eggs of many animals; spindle shaped, example, smooth muscle fibres; elongated, example, nerve cells, or branched, example, pigment cells of the skin.

Size: The size of the cell also varies from the very small cells of bacteria (0.2 to 5.0 m) to the very large egg of the Ostrich (6″). The human red blood corpuscle which is a type of cell measures 7.8 m. The factors governing the size of the cell are – nucleocytoplasmic ratio, or the ratio between the volume of the nucleus and the cytoplasm; the ratio of the cell surface to the cell volume; and the rate of metabolism.

Schwamn conceived very definite conclusions regarding the morphology and physiology of cell. He divided the cellular phenomenon into two groups – the plastic phenomenon and metabolic phenomenon. His plastic phenomenon corresponds with the modern term cellular morphology while metabolic phenomenon deals with results from "chemical changes whether the particles that compose the cell itself or in the surrounding cytoblastima".

Prokaryotic and Eukaryotic cells

Organisms in which the nuclear material is not bounded by a definite nuclear membrane are known as prokaryotes, for example, bacteria, blue green algae. On the other hand, the organisms in which the nucleus has a definite nuclear membrane are called eukaryotes, example, all other plants and animals.

In prokaryote cells, the DNA is segregated into discrete masses the chromatin bodies or genophores, composed of a network of very fine, relatively non-opaque fibrils. The chromatin bodies are tangled masses of fine fibres which probably represent strands of DNA, giving the appearance of whorls. There are frequent invagination of the cell membrane, forming lamellae which lie close to the outer surface of the cell. The outer cell wall projects occasionally into an invagination of the plasma membrane, forming a septum. The invagination of the cell

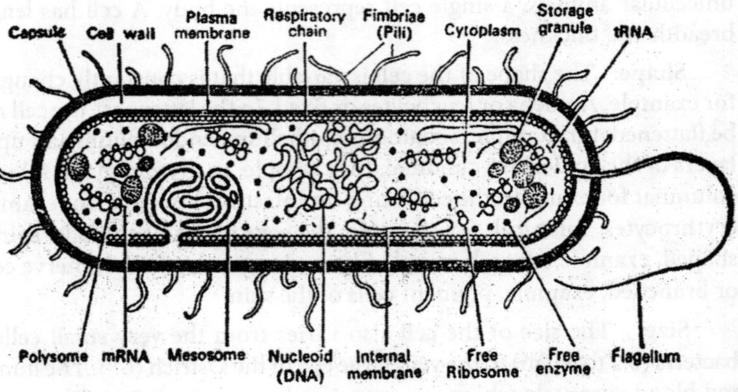

Generalized diagram of a bacterium.

membrane may extent beyond the edge of the edge of the septum, forming a highly organized villous structure called a mesosome to which a chromatin body is frequently attached. The cytoplasm of prokaryotic cell is filled with dense granules many of which are ribosomes. The granules don't appear to be associated with any membranous structure. In the photosynthetic bacteria there are vesicular infolding of the cell membrane in which pigment is located. These are called chromatophores. Prokaryotic cells have no endoplasmic reticulum, Golgi complex, mitochondria, lysosomes or centrioles. The enzymatic functions of the mitochondria are carried out by the cell membrane. The cell wall of prokaryotes contains amino sugars and muramic acid.

In eukaryotes the nucleic acid (DNA) is associated with proteins to form definite bodies called chromosomes. Eukaryotic cells have definite internal membranous structures like the endoplasmic reticulum. Golgi complex, mitochondria and lysosomes. The flagella and cilia of eukaryotes have a definite structure consisting of two central and nine peripheral fibrils.

Eukaryotic cells may be of the following types :

1. *Epithelial cells :* These may be flat or squamous cuboidal or columnar. These may occur in single layer or in multiple layers. Epithelial cells usually line the surface of the organism.

2. *Connective tissues :* These are found in the spaces between the organs.
3. *Macrophages cells :* These are found free in connective tissue or relatively fixed in the wall of blood and lymph vessels of the liver, spleen and lymph node.
4. *Muscle cells :* These are smooth muscles of the walls of gut, blood vessel, heart. These are also found attached to the parts of the skeleton, and used for movement.
5. *Nerve cells :* These are long possessing appendages which are involved in the detection or transmission of nerve impulses.
6. *Blood cells :* These occur in the form of a dense suspension of separate cells in plasma. They are red cells, white cells and platelets.
7. *Bone cells :* Bone contains relatively few cells in a complex matrix in which calcium salts are deposited.
8. *Adipose cells :* They form the fatty tissues of the organism. They consist of a thin layer of cytoplasm surrounding a huge fat droplet.
9. *Gland cells :* These cells perform secretary activities. These may be exocrine gland cells and endocrine gland cells.
10. *Ciliated and flagellated cells :* Many cells such as Euglena, Paramecium, Trypanosoma, Opalina and sperms may contain elongated thread-like flagellum or a number of small cilia.

An animal cell is more complex than a plant cell. The protoplasm constituting the cell is differentiated into two parts, viz., cytoplasm or cytosome and nucleus. The nucleus lies suspended within the cytoplasm having its own definite membrane – the nuclear membrane. Cytoplasm is more of the liquid mass of protoplasm outside the nucleus. It has also a definite membrane (cell membrane) which forms the covering of the cytoplasm on the cell as a whole.

Component parts of the cell

1. *Plasma membrane (cell membrane) :* It is the outermost part of the cell. It is very thin, delicate and elastic. It is formed by the specialization of the superficial protoplasm. It is a living part. Its thickness varies from 75 Å to 215 Å. It consists of two dense outer layers of protein molecules and two light middle layers of lipid molecules. Each of the protein layers is 35 – 50 Åthick. The two protein layers surround the middle layer on both sides. The lipid molecules are arranged in parallel chains. Their outer ends remain linked with the molecules of protein layer

through hydrogen bonding, and their inner non-polar ends are held together by Vandar Waal's Forces.

Chemically, plasmamembrane contains carbon-hydrates (about 5%), lipids (20 to 40%) and protein (60 to 80%). The entire plasmamembrane is not a smooth layer. Here and there it gives rise to projections called microvilli. These are about 0.6 to 0.8 mm long and about 100 mm in diameter. They enhance the absorptive area of the cell. Sometimes the plasmamembrane becomes thicker in certain regions to form a fastening body, called desmosome which is supported inside by fine tonofibrils.

Besides its limiting function, the cell membrane serves to absorb, secrete and regulate the inflow and outflow of certain substances like gases and liquids, at the sometime it acts as a barrier to certain others. The plasma-membrane also gives an identity to the cell. It protects the cell organelles and helps in the formation of cytoplasmic organelle. Plasma-membrane is often called a permeable membrane.

2. *Cytoplasm:* The general protoplasm excluding the nucleus is commonly distinguished as the cytoplasm. This is the main substance of the cell. In the case of one-celled animals like Amoeba, the cytoplasm is divisible into and outer denser part called the ectoplasm and an inner more fluid granular part called the endoplasm. Again, the ectoplasm modifies to form the plasmalemma which is very thin, transparent and elastic outermost layer. In such case, the endoplasm consists of an outer stiffer plasmagel and an inner fluid plasmasol. In the case of many-celled animals, this distinction of the cytoplasm is not noticed.

   As a whole, the cytoplasm is obviously similar to protoplasm in all its physical, chemical, biological and other properties. In living cells, the cytoplasm appears to be semi-transparent, semi-fluid, slimy, viscous and elastic substance. It is not altogether homogenous. A large number of living and non-living bodies are embedded in it. Some of these are big and visible. Others are small enough not to be seen under the microscope and are of the nature of colloids having much affinity for water. Both living and non-living bodies found in the cytoplasm are in common termed cytoplasmic inclusions.

3. *Cell centre (or centrosome) :* It lies usually nearer to the nucleus at one side. It has a clear and rounded or oval cytoplasmic area called centrosphere enclosing one or two dot-like bodies called centrioles

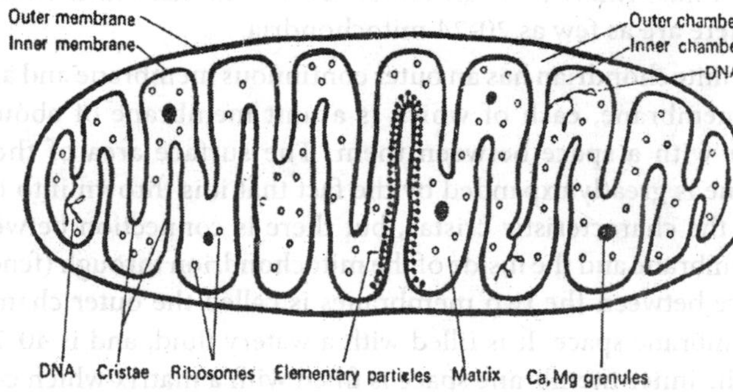

Section through mitochondrion (diagramatic). The elementary particles have been shown on only one crista.

or central bodies. Under electron microscope, the centriole looks like a small rod bearing nine fibrils in a ring. The centriole has a diameter of 0.15–0.25 mm, and a length of 0.3 – 0.7 mm. It is not yet certain whether centrioles have DNA and RNA. Functionally, centrosome is said to initiate Mitosis. It is also concerned with the formation of astral rays and spindle fibres in the cytoplasm. In the living state centrosome undergoes repeated division to form granules associated with the bases of flagella and cilia in those flagellated and ciliated cells. Flagella and cilia are cytoplasmic protrusions having slight variations among themselves.

4. *Mitochondria (or Chondriosomes)*: These occur in various parts of the cytoplasm in clumps or in a scattered state. Mitochondria appear as minute granules, vesicles, rodlets, filaments and the like. If a filamentous mitochondrion swells at one end it gives a club-shaped appearance. If the swollen end hollows out then the appearance is that of a tennis racket. Pleomorphic forms may contain swelling at both ends.

Mitochondria are present in all cells which respire aerobically. However, the number of mitochondria varies in different cells types. Mitochondria are absent in bacteria. Cells with high metabolic activity have a high number of mitochondria, while those with low metabolic activity have a lower number. In a normal liver cell there are 1000-1600 mitochondria. Large sea urching eggs have 13,000-14,000. In the giant

Amoeba, *Chaos chaos*, there are about 500,000 mitochondria while in the sperm there are as few as 20-24 mitochondria.

The mitochondrian has an outer continuous membrane and an inner double membrane, each of which is a unit membrane of about 75 Å diameter with a space between them. The surface area of the inner membrane is greatly expanded by the fact that it is thrown into folds to produce the characteristic cristae, but there is connection between the outer membrane and the inside of the mitochondrion through (fenestrae). The space between the two membranes is called the outer chamber or inter-membrane space. It is filled with a watery fluid, and is 40-70 Å in width. The inner membrane space is filled with a matrix which contains dense granules, ribosomes and mitochondrial DNA. The granules consist of insoluble inorganic salts. In some cases they apparently contain polymers of sugars. The side of the inner membrane facing the matrix is called M-side, while the side facing the outer chamber is called the C-side. Two to six circular DNA molecules have been identified within the mitochondrion. These rings may either be in the open or in the twisted configuration. They may be present free in the matrix or may be attached to the membrane. The enzymes of the Krebs cycle are located in the matrix. The inside of the inner membrane and the outside of the outer membrane bear a number of particles of 90-100Å diameter. The particles on the outer surface are in the form of a pimpled appearance on the mitochondrial surface. Each particle on the inner surface possesses a base, a stalk and a spherical head. The stalk is 50Å long and 33Å wide, whereas the base and the head have the equal diameter of 80Å.

The life span of a mitochondrion is 5-10 days. There are three views regarding the origin of mitochondria.

(i) *Origin from various membranes*

Robertson (1964) postulated that mitochondrion in muscle cells arises by an infloding of the plasmamembrane, into which passes a projection from an adjacent part of the membrane. This would result in a double-membraned vesicle. In growth of cristal from the inner membrane would give rise to the mitochondrion.

(ii) *By division of fully formed mitochondria*

Luck and Rich (1964) stated that mitochondria arise by growth and division of pre-existing mitochondria.

(iii) *De novo origin*

Harvey (1951) gave evidence for de novo synthesis of mitochondria. Sea-urchin eggs were centrifuged into two halves. The halves containing nuclei generated mitochondria.

Mitochondria perform several important functions such as secretion of enzymes, oxidation, dehydrogenation, oxidative phosphorylation and respiratory chain of the cell. Mitochondria are also known as "power hoses of the cell" because they synthesize energy rich compound Adenosine Triphosphate (ATP). The ATP molecules produced as a result of cellular respiration accumulate in the mitochondria.

Golgi bodies (Golgi complex or Golgi apparatus)

These were first discovered by the Italian neurologist Camillo Golgi in 1898 in the nerve cells of Barn Owl. These are found round about the centrosome of the cell in the form of a network or granules. Sometimes they are found scattered throughout the cytoplasm.

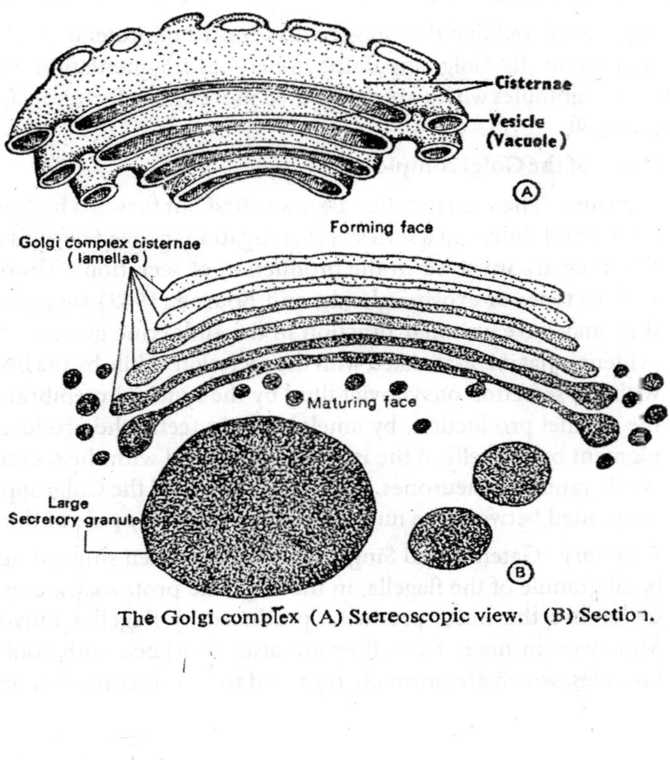

The Golgi complex (A) Stereoscopic view. (B) Section.

The Golgi complex is generally a single large structure. There are two large Golgi complexes in Paramoeba species, while in the Amoeba, Stereomyxa there are many Golgi complexes. Nerve cells, liver cells and most plant cells have multiple Golgi complexes.

The Golgi complex is large in nerve and gland cells, but small in muscle cells. Electron microscopy studies have revealed the structure of Golgi apparatus to consist of three membranous components : (i) flattened sacs or cisternae, (ii) small tubules and vesicles, and (iii) large vacuoles filled with an amorphous or granular substance.

The cisternae are the most constant elements of the Golgi complex. They consist of flattened, parallel sacs piled one upon the other to form stacks. The number of cisternae in a stack varies from species to species. The small vesicles are 400-800 Å in diameter. They are intermately associated with the cisternae and may show continuity with them. The small vesicles arise from the cisternae by budding. Large vacuoles generally lie at the edge of the Golgi complex. They represent modified and expanded cisternae and contain clear material which reduces metallic salts.

It is considered that the Golgi bodies consist of proteins and lipoids. In cell division the Golgi apparatus undergoes fragmentation into fine particles or granules which are distributed more or less fortuitously to the daughter cells.

Functions of the Golgi complex

(i) *Secretory:* The secretory function was first put forward by Nassanor (1923) and Bowen in a series of investigations proved beyond doubt, that they are involved in the production of secretion - droplets in various types of exosine glands, and Bourne (1942) suggested that they may have a similar function in the endocrine glands. There is evidence that it is associated with the secretion of bile by the liver, and with the secretion of synovial fluid by the synovial membrane with the enamel production, by ameloblasts in teeth, the production of pigment by the cells of the iris epithelium and with the secretion of Nissl granules in neurones. In each secretory cell the Golgi apparatus is oriented between the nucleus and the excretory pole of the cell.

(ii) *Excretory:* Gatenby and Singh believed that when situated near the basal granule of the flagella, in the flagellate protozoans, they serve to remove the waste products, produced by flagellar movement. Moreover, in many cases they are also associated with contractile vacuoles, which are normally regarded to be excretory in function.

(iii) *Absorptive:* The absorptive function has also been ascribed to the Golgi bodies from time to time. Alttussaini (1949) working on the gut epithelia of fishes, found that the Golgi element disintegrates during fat absorption.

(iv) *Synthetic:* The Golgi bodies appear to be intimately associated with cellular synthesis, so that they are specially active during histogenesis. Bourne suggests that they very likely contain enzyme or can synthesize them; from cytoplasm or absorb them on their surface. Without doubt the Golgi apparatus acts as an important condensation membrane, absorbing vitamin C and perhaps other substances both fatty and proteid which may pass through to the Golgi internum and play a part in cellular synthesis. Dalton (1951) states that it serves as an area for the segregation and accumulation of the products of the secretory or excretory activity of the cell.

(v) *Acrosome formation:* It is claimed that the acrosome of the sperm is formed directly out of the part of the Golgi bodies, the rest of which is sloughed off along with the residual cytoplasm of the spermated.

(vi) The Golgi bodies are associated with the formation of the vacuoles in some manner.

(vii) The Golgi apparatus appears to have some function in the carbohydrate and fat metabolism.

(viii) Gatenby showed that the Golgi bodies are directly concerned with the formation of the yolk spheres.

(ix) *Lysosome formation:* Novikoff proposed that the primary lysosomes are formed by the Golgi complex.

(x) In many mammalian tumour and cancer cells the Golgi complex has been described as the site of origin of pigment granules.

Endoplasmic reticulum (ER)

This is a sort of diffused reticulum spreading all through the cytoplasm. It occurs in the cytoplasm in three principal forms, viz., cisternae (lamellae), vesicles and tubules. The cisternae are broad, flat membrane bound spaces arranged parallel to each other to form lamellae. They are inter connected with each other. The tubules are 50-100Å in diameter. The vesicles or sacs appear as membrane bound, isolated globose cavities. The tubules have many branches and these together with cisternae and vesicles constitute the reticular system inside the cytoplasm. The cisternae, vesicles and the tubules of the endoplasmic reticulum are bounded by a thin membrane which has the same structure as that of the plasma membrane. However, the endoplasmic reticulum is only 50-60Å thick. Some of the endoplasmic channels are connected with the nuclear membrane and Golgi bodies while others open at the plasma membrane.

The endoplasmic reticulum may be of two types, those with smooth walls and without ribosomes in them are called a granular or smooth endoplasmic reticulum, and those having rough walls and possessing ribosomes are known as granular or rough endoplasmic reticulum and is predominant in cells which actively synthesize proteins. The smooth endoplasmic reticulum is characteristic of cells in which synthesis of non-protein substances takes place.

The endoplasmic reticulum performs a variety of functions, such as secretory, storage, circulatory, and ultrastructural skeletal framework to the cell. Ribosomes attached to the endoplasmic reticulum are used during protein synthesis.

Ribosomes

These are oblate spheroid particles of 150 to 250Å in diameter. Each ribosome consists of a smaller and a larger subunits. The smaller subunit lies above the larger one forming a cap. The ribosomes may occur freely in the cytoplasm or remain attached to the endoplasmic reticulum. They consist of proteins and ribosomal RNA. The ribosomes are regarded as protein factories. In protein synthesis, they operate in groups or clusters called polyribosomes.

Microsomes

They are bits and pieces of endoplasmic reticulum lying freely in the cytoplasm. They are very small and they contain proteins and lipids and are concerned with protein synthesis.

Lysosomes

They are tiny, membrane bounded, fluid-filled vesicles. They vary in size from 0.4 m to 6 m in diameter. On the basis of their functions, four types of lysosomes are recognized. Primary and secondary lysosomes, residual bodies and cytolysosomes. They are involved directly or indirectly in the intra-cellular digestion.

Metaplastic bodies of the Cytoplasm

These are non-living inclusions and are in the form of yolk-granules, fat granules, pigment granules, excretory secretory granules, glycogen, etc. Certain small cavities called vacuoles may also be found in the

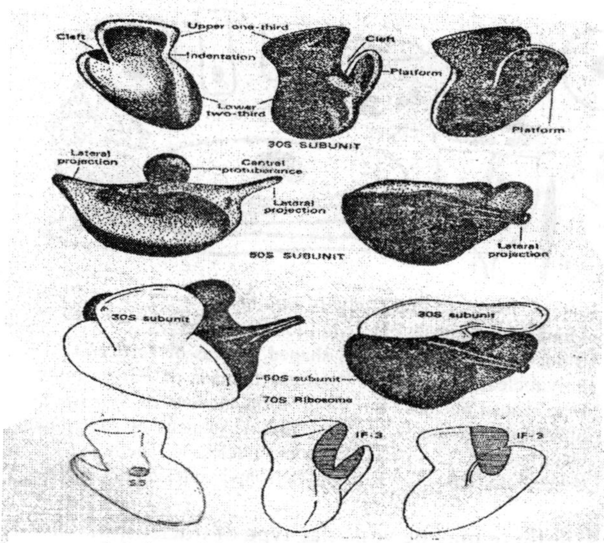

Lake's model of the 70s *E. coli* ribosome.

cytoplasm. The vacuole is filled with water, gas or some other materials. Each vacuole is enclosed by a thin hyaline layer of the cytoplasm called tonoplast or vacuolar membrane. The various non-living inclusions are formed during metabolic activities of the cell.

Nucleus

Nucleus usually lies in the centre of the cell. Very often the nucleus is spherical or oval but it may assume different forms according to the shape and necessity of the cell.

Variations of Nucleus in Animals

The presence of nucleus is diagnostic of all known organisms. Sometimes a definite and well organized nucleus may be wanting in micro-organisms. But then, representation of nuclear material is invariably found even in the bacteria and viruses. Red blood cells (corpuscles) of the blood of mammals do not have nucleus in the full grown condition but present in their early stages. Striped muscle fibres have got more than one nucleus in each case. Certain unicellular animals (Protozoa) also have many nuclei in each. Further, among Protozoa two types of nucleus are distinguished according to the function and size, viz., micronucleus (smaller) and meganucleus (bigger). According to the materials with which the nucleus

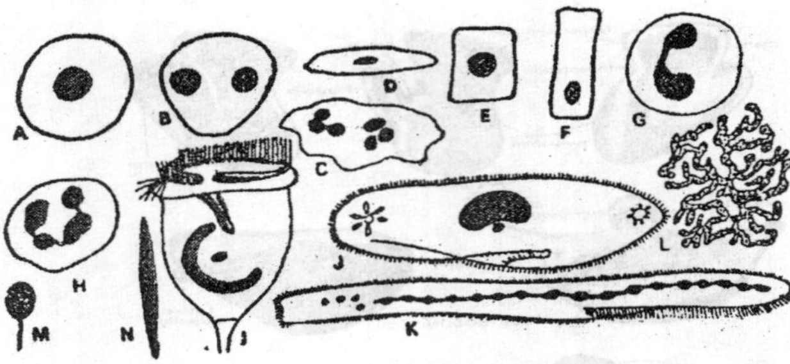

Number and shape of nuclei

A. Mononucleate cell.
B. Binucleate cell.
C. Polynucleate cell.
D. Disc shaped nucleus.
E. Spherical nucleus.
F. Oval nucleus.
G. Bilobed nucleus.
H. Multilobed nucleus.
I. C-shaped nucleus of *Vorticella.*
J. Pyriform nucleus of *Paramecium.*
K. Moniliform nucleus of *Spirostomum.*
L. Labyrinthine nucleus of *Platyphylax.*
M. Elliptical nucleus of sperm.
N. Spindle shaped nucleus of sperm.

is composed of, there may be vesicular type of nucleus, massive type of nucleus, compact type of nucleus, and so on.

Component Parts of the Nucleus

Essentially, the nucleus is the specialized mass of protoplasm but is denser than the surrounding cytoplasm. A nucleus has the following parts:

(i) *Nuclear membrane :* This is the semipermeable membrane covering the nucleus. It delimits nucleus from the cytoplasm. It consists of two unit membrances : each membrane is about 70 to 80Å thick. The two membraned are separated by a perinucleus space of 150-300Å wide. The outline of nuclear envelope is smooth but is not continuous, being interrupted by pores. It disappears and reappears during cell division. Enclosed by the nuclear membrane is the nucleoplasm.

(ii) *Nucleoplasm (Nuclear sap or karyoplasm) :* This is the specialized kind of protoplasm inside the nucleus. It is a clear fluid but different from cytoplasm in its physical and chemical properties. Embedded in the nucleus are nuclear or chromatic reticulum and one or more nucleoli.

(iii) *Nuclear or chromatin reticulum :* This is a network of slender fibres consisting of deeply staining protein materials of a variety of kinds, collectively called the chromatic (or karyotin). During cell division the chromatin materials in the nucleus become condensed and resolved into semi-solid threads of chromatin called chromosomes. The

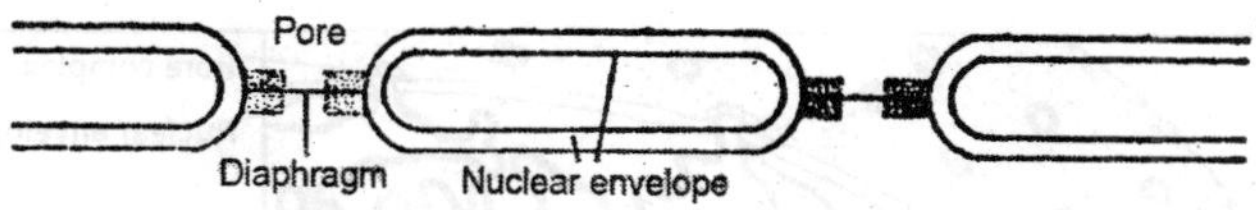

The structure of the nuclear pore (Afzelius, 1955)

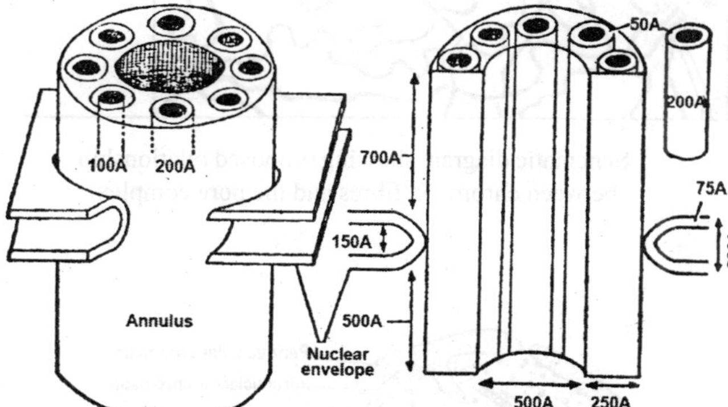

Witschnitzer's model (1958) of the nuclear pore and annulus (cylindrical model).

chromosomes carry the hereditary units called genes. Chromosomes are not visible at the interphase or resting stage. For every species of plant or animal there is a fiscal number of chromosomes, for example, there are 23 pairs of chromosomes in the human body cell.

(iv) *Nucleoli :* These are small rounded refractile bodies embedded in the nucleoplasm, sometimes attached to one or two of the chromosomes. Usually two types of nucleoli are distinguishable – one type has great affinity for acid dyes and known as plasmosome, and the other stains more readily with basic dyes. Hence called karyosome. Nucleoli contain protein and RNA and so nucleoli are concerned with the synthesis of residual RNA and protein.

Chemistry of Nucleus

The chemical composition of nucleus is very complex. It contains the following :-

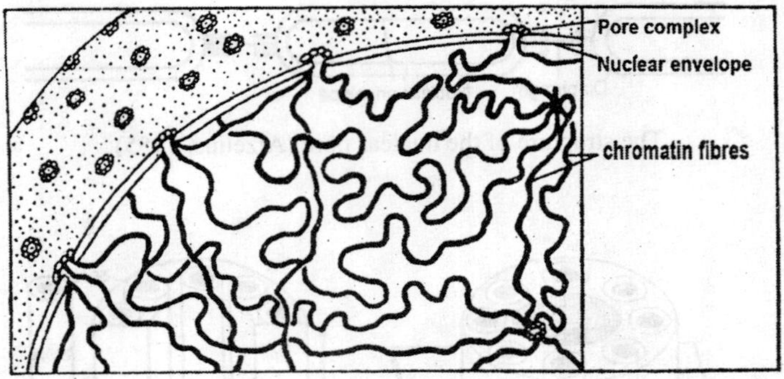

Schematic diagram showing proposed relationship between chromatin fibres and the pore complex.

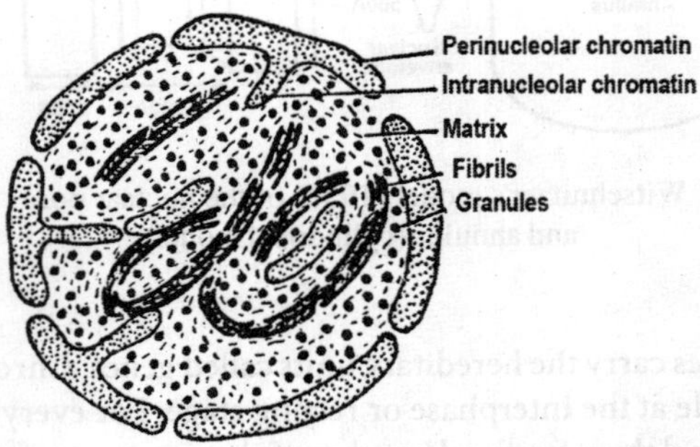

Schematic representation of the ultrastructure of a tpical vertebrate nucleclus.

(a) Basic proteins (protamines and histones).

(b) Non histone acid proteins of large molecular weight.

(c) Nucleic acids comprising DNA and RNA.

(d) Inorganic enzymes.

(e) Nuclear enzymes.

Function of Nucleus

As a whole nucleus is regarded as the dynamic centre of the cell. It initiates and controls all the vital activities of the cell. Nucleus controls RNA synthesis. If a cell is divided into two parts, one including the nucleus and the other only with the cytoplasm, the one without the nucleus cannot develop into the original, whereas the other nucleated half will grow to full size. Moreover, cytoplasm without the nucleus shows the katabolic activity. Transmission of hereditary characters from parents to offspring is effected through nucleus. However, the nucleus and the cytoplasm are both essential for the life of the cell.

NUCLEIC ACIDS

Nucleic acids, like proteins, are macromolecules ranging in molecular weight from about 30,000 to several millions. They are present in all living cells as a major component of the nucleus and also as a component structures such as the ribosomes. They are generally associated with proteins to form nucleoproteins. Nucleic acids prepared from plants resembled yeast nucleic acid whereas those prepared from animal tissues resembled thymus nucleic acid.

Nucleic acids are of two types, deoxyribose nucleic acid (DNA) and ribose nucleic acid (RNA). DNA occurs predominantly in the nucleus, while RNA is predominant in the cytoplasm. In most organisms including viruses, DNA is the genetic material. However, some viruses have RNA as their genetic material.

Nucleic acids are the master molecules in the cell and the primary genetic link between generations of organisms. Friedrich Miescher was the first to discover acid substances associated with proteins of the cell nucleus. Nucleic acids are also the molecules that exert primary control over the basic life processes in all organisms. Nucleic acids are also found in other parts of the cells such as mitochondria, chloroplast, etc.

Chemically, the nucleotides are the basic chemical sub-units of the nucleic acids, the structural relationship of the two being analogous to that of the amino acids and proteins. Each nucleotide consists of three elements. These are – (i) a heterocyclic ring containing nitrogen and referred to as the base; (ii) a five carbon sugar or pentose, and (iii) a phosphate groups.

The bases of common occurrence in nucleic acids are five in number. They are – (i) Purine bases, (ii) Pyrimidine bases. The pyrimidines are 6-membered rings while the purines consist of fused 5-and 6- membered rings. The two principal purine bases are adenine (A) and Guanine (G). The pyrimidines are uracil (U), Cytosine (C), and Thymine (T), which differs from Uracil only in having a methyl substituent in the C_5 position. In the ribonucleotide series the sugar is ribose. In the deoxynucleotide series, the sugar is deoxyribose, which differs from ribose. The bases commonly occurring in RNA are adenine, uracil, cystocine and guanine. In DNA, uracil is replaced by thymine.

Deoxyribose nucleic acid (DNA)

DNA is present in the cells of all plants and animals, prokaryotes and viruses. In the eukaryotes it is combined with proteins to form nucleoproteins. In prokaryotes, example, Escherichia coli (a bacterium) the genetic material consists of a single giant molecule of DNA, about 1,000 microns in length, without any associated proteins.

The DNA of all plants and animals and many viruses is double stranded. Watson and Crick (1953) proposed that the molecular model of DNA is the double helix structure. The DNA molecule consists of two helically twisted strands connected together by 'steps'. Each strand consists alternating molecules of deoxyribose (a pentose sugar) and phosphate groups. The purine and pyrimidine bases are connected to deoxyribose sugar molecules. The two strands are tightly coiled and the turning and the steps or bases are many. The steps or bases contain adenine and thymine, guanine and cytosine. There is a hydrogen boarding between purines and pyrimidine bases. The sequence of bases in one strand determines the sequence of the other and the two strands are complimentary. If adenine occurs in one strand, thymine is present in the complementary strand. Guanine is paired with cytosine. Two strands separate, and each strand forces the synthesis of an image of itself in the complementary strand. In this way replication takes place. The result is the formation of two molecules of DNA that are identical with the first. The base pairs may be compared to genetic alphabets, a combination of which forms a 'word' and many words can be formed by varying the combination. Such a word is the genetic code or information and this is transferred to RNA which acts like a messenger and moves away from the nucleus to the cytoplasm at the sites of synthesis of proteins from amino-acids.

Replication of DNA takes place during the interphase between two mitotic cycles. There is no replication of DNA during intackenesis between the first and second meiotic divisions. There are three types of replication of DNA, viz., semi conservative, conservative and dispersive. According to the semi conservative mode proposed by Watson and Crick, each

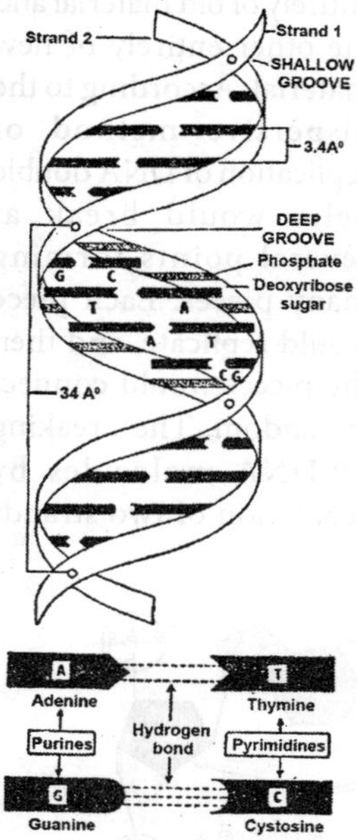

The DNA double helix.

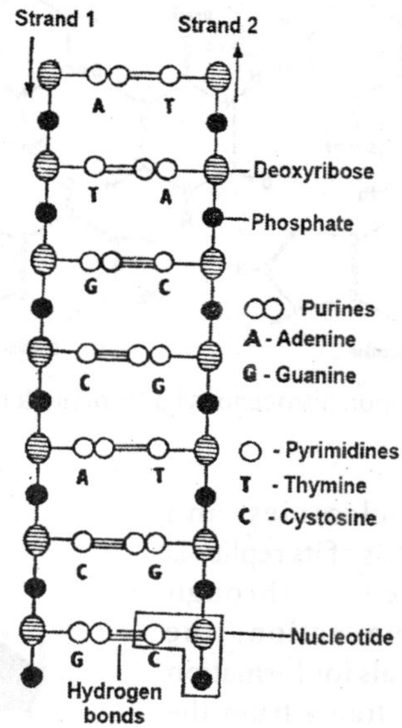

Diagramatic representation of the DNA molecule

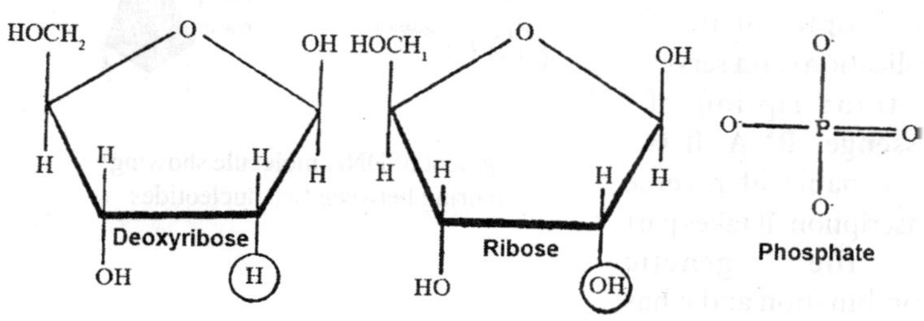

Deoxyribose, ribose and phosphate.

strand of the two double helices formed would have one old and one new strand. According to the conservative mode, of the two double helices

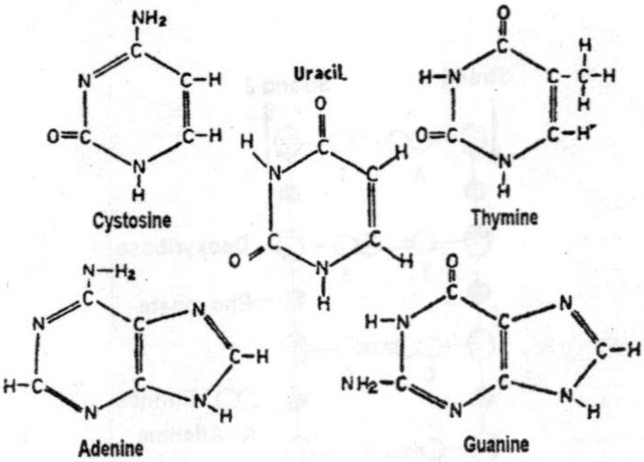

Common nitrogenous bases of nucleic acids.

formed one would be entirely of old material and the other entirely of new material. According to the dispersive method of replication of DNA double helix would break at several points forming many pieces. Each piece would replicate, and then the pieces would connect at random. The breaking of DNA molecules by separation of two strands of nucleotides and synthesis of its replica is effected through enzyme action, the materials for formation being drawn from the pool of the bases.

DNA is the genetic material of most organisms. It can make exact copies of itself (replication) and serves for transcription of messenger RNA. It is also capable of reverse transcription. It takes part in the genetic recombination and it has the ability to repair itself.

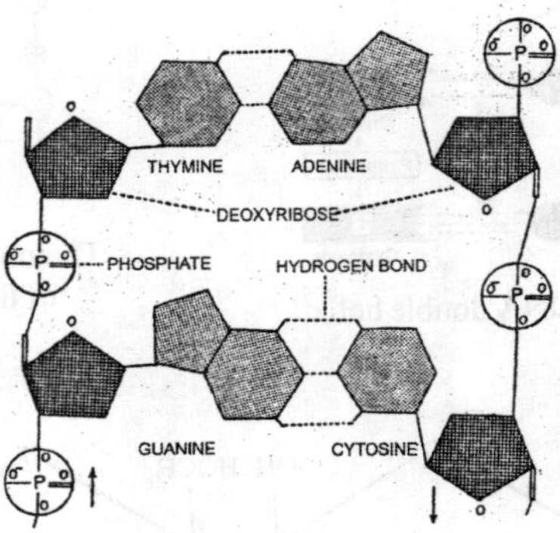

Segment of DNA molecule showing pairing between two nucleotides

Ribose Nucleic Acid (RNA)

Ribose nucleic acid usually occurs in nature as long unbranched polymeric molecule made up of a single chain or helix of polynucleotide strand. It is generally present in the cytoplasm and the nucleolus. RNA is composed of pentose sugars, phosphoric acid and nitrogenous bases.

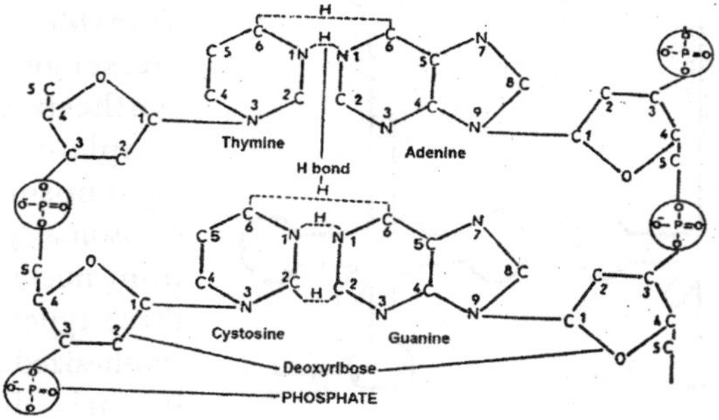

Two pairs of nucleotides showing bonding between phosphate, deoxyribose and nitrogenous bases

Ribose sugar forms the backbone along with phosphoric acid for the attachment of nitrogenous bases. On the basis of phosphate or phosphoric acid, the chemical constituents of RNA can be written as follows :

Nitrogenous base + Ribose sugar + Phosphate ¾® Nucleotide

Nitrogenous base + Ribose sugar ¾® Nucleoside

The nitrogenous bases of the ribonucleic acid are the purine and pyrimidine. Purine bases comprise mainly adenine and guanine, while pyrimidine bases comprise cytosine and uracil.

Three types of cellular RNA have been distinguished : messenger RNA (mRNA) or template RNA, ribosomal RNA (rRNA) and soluble RNA (sRNA) or transfer RNA (tRNA). Ribosomal and transfer RNA comprise

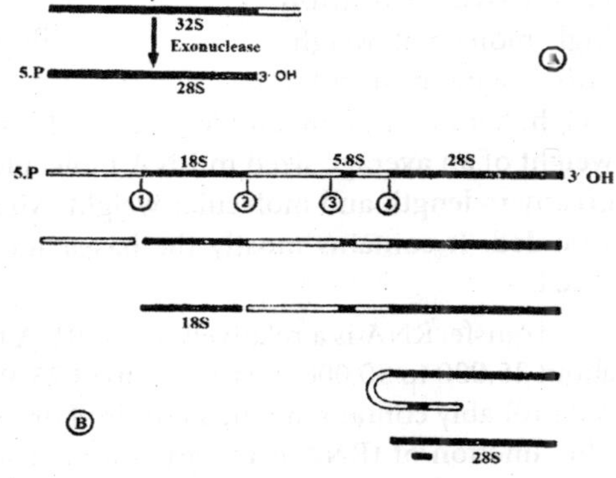

Two schemes for processing eukaryote 45S RNA to yield 28S, 18S and 5–8 rRNA.

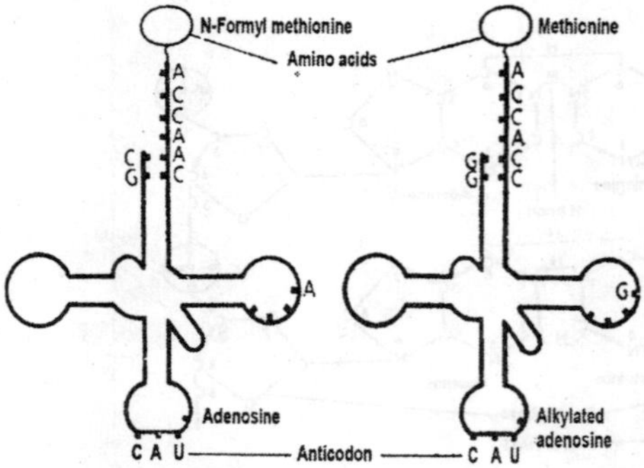

Diagram showing differences between N-formyl-met-tRNA and met-tRNA.

about 90% of all RNA. Transfer RNA and messenger RNA are synthesized on DNA templates of the chromosomes, while ribosomal RNA is derived from nuclear DNA. The three types of RNA are synthesized during stages in early development. Most of the RNA synthesized during cleavage is mRNA.

Synthesis of tRNA occurs at the end of cleavage and rRNA synthesis begins during gastrulation.

In Eukaryotes, ribosomes are formed in the nucleolus. The ribosome consists of proteins and RNA. There are three types of ribosomal RNA, viz., high molecular weight rRNA over a million high molecular weight rRNA with molecular weight below a million and low molecular weight rRNA. The molecular weight of an average sized m RNA molecule is about 500,000 and varies greatly in length and molecular weight. MessengerRNA is always single stranded. It contains mostly the bases adenine, guanine, cytosine and uracil.

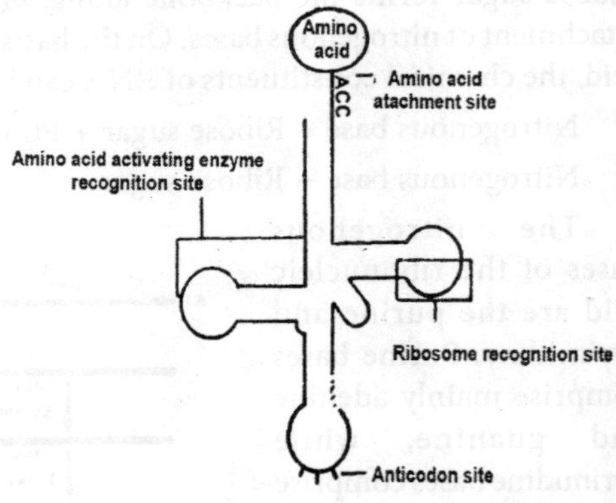

Recognition sites on tRNA

TransferRNA is a relatively small RNA having a molecular weight of about 25,000 to 30,000. It is made up of 73-93 nucleotides. Each bacterial cell probably contains about a hundred or more different types of tRNA. The function of tRNA is to carry aminoacids to mRNA during protein synthesis. Transfer RNA is synthesized in the nucleus on a DNA template. The transfer RNA molecule consists of a single strand looped about itself. According to cloverleaf model the single polynucleotide chain of t RNA is folded upon itself to form 5-arms. An arm consists of a stem and a loop. Transfer RNA acts as an acceptor for the activated amino acids and as an adopter for carrying the amino acids to the site of protein synthesis.

The messenger RNA is present in nuclear region as well as in cytoplasm and it is derived from the nucleolar DNA. The amount of mRNA is about 5-10% of the total RNA present. mRNA has an affinity for hybrid formation only with DNA from the same or from genetically closely related organisms. mRNA does not show any secondary or double helical structure at all. It forms a template for protein synthesis. Ribosomal Ribonucleic acids (r RNA) are small particles of about 200 Å to 250 Å in diameter, and are generally present in the cytoplasm. Ribosomal RNA from most organisms is relatively rich in guanine and cytosine.

The RNA molecules move to associate with amino acids which are then synthesized by formation of peptide bonds into protein. Thus nucleic acids (nucleotides) are the masters of protein manufacture. Nucleic acid, attached by bonds with protein, forms nucleoprotein which is found in all living organisms – virus, bacteria, plant and animal cells and in fair concentration in the nucleus, chromosomes and genes.

7

CHROMOSOMES

Chromosomes are thread like bodies found within the nucleus of the cell. These thread like bodies were first detected by Hofmaster in 1848. Waldeyer in 1888 coined the term chromosomes to these thread like structures. The chromosomes are constant in the somatic nuclei of all the individuals of the species. All the chromosomes that are present in the somatic nucleus are collectively referred to as chromosome compliment. The lowest chromosome complement in animals is two, which is seen in *Ascaris megalocephala* (Horse round worm). The highest chromosome compliment recorded is 1600 in Aulacantha, a Protozoan species. The chromosomes in the somatic nucleus are even and they occur in different pairs. The two members of a pair are similar in shape and size. These are called homologous chromosomes. The homologous chromosomes during meiosis undergo synapsis. One member in the homologous pair is maternal in origin while the other is paternal. Thus in the somatic nucleus there are two sets of chromosomes. One set is maternal in origin, the other is paternal. A set of chromosomes which are inherited as a unit is known as genome. Thus in the somatic nucleus there are two geneomes. The organisms having two genomes in their somatic nucleus are known as diploid organisms.

Out of the different homologous pairs, one pair are known as the sex chromosomes and they take part in the determination of sex. The other pairs of chromosomes are collectively known as Autosomes. In most of the females the sex chromosomes are similar and they are by XX. In

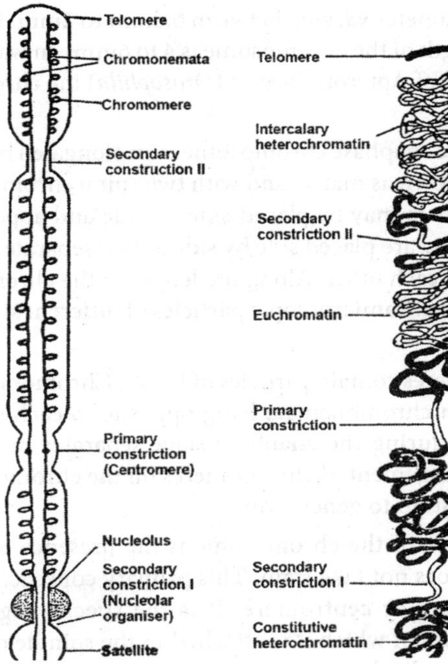

Fig.1: Structure of a typical chromosome.
Fig. 2: Model of constitutive heterochromatin in the metaphase chromosome of a mammal.

males, one chromosome is X and its partner differs in size and shape. This is known as Y chromosome. The sex chromosomes in the males are thus represented by XY. In some diploid organism the chromosome number is uneven in one sex, example, Prryhocoris (Bug). The male has 23 chromosomes (22A + XY) and the female has 23 chromosomes (22A+XX). One chromosome in the male is not having its partner and this chromosome is known as the odd chromosome. The odd chromosome is nothing but the sex chromosome (X). In humans the somatic or diploid number of chromosome is 46.

Chromosomes are the carriers of hereditary characters. They reproduce by longitudinal division and pass from generation to generation, yet they maintain their integrity and individuality. These are clearly seen during metaphase and anaphase stages. They greatly differ in size in different organisms. The length of a chromosome may vary from 0.1mm to 50mm, and the diameter varying between 0.2mm to 2mm. In humans the approximate length of the chromosome is 4 to 6mm . In water lili and in the salivary glands of Apterous insects (*Drosophila*) the chromosomes are very large.

A typical somatic anaphase chromosome is an elongated body with a ground substance known as matrix and with two spiral chromonematea. The two chromonemata may be placed side by side and appear to be a single structure or they are placed side by side as two separate structures and they twist round each other. Along the length of the chromonemata there are a number of ultramicroscopic particles of different sizes known as chromomeres.

The chromosomeres contain particles of DNA . Chromomeres occur in pairs, one on each chromonemata lying opposite to each other. The two chromonemata during the anaphase stage separates out into two chromatids. The arrangement of chromomeres on the chromonemata is constant from generation to generation.

Another character of the chromosome is the presence of primary constriction which does not take stain. This primary constriction is also known as kinotochore or centromere. It is the special organ of the chromosome by means of which it is attached to the spindle during the metaphase, hence it is also known as spindle attachment. In some cases the centromere is seen to consist of a small granule known as knosome. This will take stain while the centromere does not take stain. Darlington regarded the kinosome as a real organ of attachment during metaphase and he called it as the attachment chromomere.

Generally there is a single centromere in a chromosome and this chromosome is known as monocentric chromosome. But in some cases there may be more than one centromere in each chromosome and such a chromosome is described as Polycentric, for example, in Ascaris megalocephala, the normal long chromosome contains 16 centromeres in the middle of each chromosome.

The shape of the chromosome is determined by the position of the centromere on it. Depending upon the position of the centromere, the chromosomes are classified as follows:

(i) *Acrocentric chromosomes:* When the centromere is situated near the end of the chromosome (subterminal) it appears rod-shaped and is known as accrocentric.

(ii) *Metacentric chromosomes:* If the centromere is near the middle of the chromosome, the two arms of the chromomere nearly equal. The chromosome appears V-shaped during anaphasic movement. Such a chromosome is called metacentric.

(ii) *Submetacentric chromosomes:* If the centromere is located some distance away from the middle, one arm of the chromosome will be shorter than the other. Such a chromosome will appear L-shaped during anaphasic movement and is called the submetacentric.

(iv) *Telocentric:* If the centromere is truly terminal that is, situated at the lip of the chromosome, the chromosome is said to be telocentric.

(v) *Polycentric chromosomes:* In some plants and animals, the centromere is not located in one position but lies in a diffused state along the length of the chromosome. In such cases the centromere is called a diffuse centromere, and the chromosome is said to be polycentric.

(vi) *Acentric chromosomes:* Sometimes a chromosome may undergo a break into two, so that only one part has the centromere while the other is without the centromere. The part lacking the centromere is called acentric fragment.

The ratio of length of the long arm to the short arm of a chromosome is called the arm ratio. It is characteristic for each single chromosome. In chromosomes where the centromere is nearly terminal (example, accrocentric chromosome) the arm ratio is high. Chromosomes in which

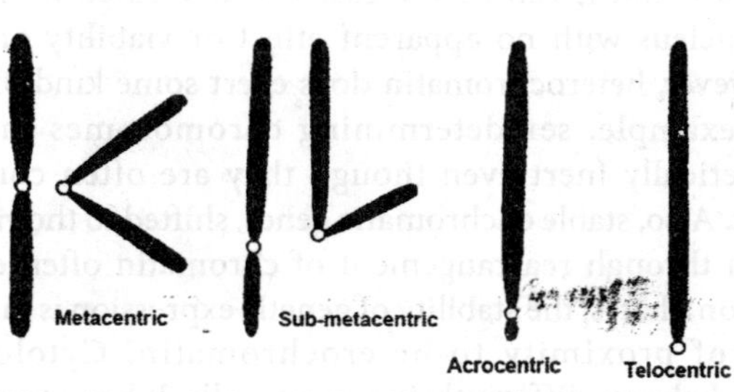

Types of chromosomes based on the position of the contromere.

the centromere is located in or near the middle have a low arm ratio. The arm ratio is useful in distinguishing chromosomes which are similar in total length. In humans metacentric chromosomes have arm ratios ranging from 1.07 to 1.95, submetacentrics from 2.05 to 3.75 and acrocentrics from 5.00 to 11.94.

The chromosomes are differentiated lengthwise into regions or segments of heterochromatin and euchromatin. The heterochromatic region is thicker and takes up deep staining. Heterochromatin does not bear any genes and the earlier term used for it was prochromosome. The euchromatin region consists of genes of major effect. The euchromatin region is also known as genetically active region while the heterochromatin region is known as genetically inert region. The sex chromosome termed the Y chromosome contains only heterochromatin and it does not bear any gene. It is inert for inheritance of characters. Heterochromatin, however, may have some influence over chromosome metabolism. Euchromatin sums to be heavily coated with nucleic acid (DNA). The difference in chemical composition between heterochromatin and euchromatin is quantitative rather than qualitative, and one may be derived from the other. During metaphase and anaphase the euchromatin regions take stain while the heterochromatin regions are colourless. In most of the animals the Y-chromosome is having a large heterochromatin region. In Drosophila the Y chromosome is completely heterochromatin, and such a chromosome is known as inert chromosome. Heterochromatin differs from euchromatin in several ways. Cytologically euchromatin goes through the regular cycle of coiling and uncoiling during cell division, and is usually so diffused during interphase as to be difficult to detect. Heterochromatin, on the other hand, is usually but not always devoid of mendalizing genes, and it can be increased or decreased in moderate amounts in a nucleus with no apparent effect or viability or genetic expression. However, heterochromatin does exert some kind of genetic influence. For example, sex determining chromosomes cannot be considered genetically inert even though they are often completely heterochromatic. Also, stable euchromatic genes, shifted to the vicinity of heterochromatin through rearrangement of chromatin often exhibit a variable expression, that is, the stability of genetic expression is influenced by the degree of proximity to heterochromatin. Cytologically, heterochromatin behaves differently in various cells. It has a tendency to amalgamate into an amorphous chromocenter in salivary gland cells. It exhibits a kind of pairing quite different from the highly specific pairing of euchromatin. In other cells it is indistinguishable from euchromatin at metaphase, but in interphase it remains a condensed state while the euchromatin is dispersed. The condensation undoubtedly results from a differential coiling of the heterochromatic regions. Heterochromatin is delayed in its synthetic processes, as indicated by the fact the radioactive level incorporated at the end of the period of DNA synthesis is located only in the heterochromatic regions. It is suggested that euchromatic DNA consists of adenine, thymine, cytosine, guanine nucleotide pairs arranged in a great variety of sequences while heterochromatic DNA consists largely of one kind of nucleotide pair only.

Another character of the chromosome is heteropyknosis. Heteropyknosis is defined as the difference in the density in the chromosomal parts. The body of the chromosome is not dense throughout its length. Some regions are however, dense. This is due to the high coiling of the chromonemata in that region. In most of the cases, heterochromatic regions are heterophyknotic.

Chemical analysis of the chromosomes indicates that they consist of two main nucleic acids and two types of proteins. DNA is the main nucleic acid. It is the hereditary material of the chromosome. Recent experimental evidence is that the genes are made up of particles of DNA. DNA is protein molecule consisting of deoxyribose sugar, phosphoric acid and bases of two kinds, viz., purines and pyrimidines. The alternating phosphate and deoxyribose form the outer boundary of the molecule. The bases linked the two boundaries of the molecule. The right and left halves of the molecule are united together by the Hydrogen bond. According to Watson and Crick DNA is in the form of a double helix, that is, a sort of spiral, stair case in which phosphate and deoxyribose represent the boundaries.

POLYTENE CHROMOSOMES
(SALIVARY GLAND CHROMOSOMES)

The polytene chromosomes were first observed by E.G. Balbiani (1881) in the salivary glands of the midge chironomous, and are hence called salivary gland chromosomes. They may reach a size upto 200 times (or more) the size of corresponding chromosomes at meiosis or in the nuclei of ordinary mitotic cells. Another characteristic of these giant chromosomes is that they are somatically paired. Consequently the number of these giant chromosomes in the salivary gland cells always appear to be half of the normal somatic cells.

Occurrence

Salivary gland chromosomes occur only in the Order Diptera of insects in the salivary glands, gutepithelia, Malpighian tubules, glandular cells of the proventriculus, etc. But they attain their maximum development in the salivary glands.

Structure

The salivary gland chromosome is peculiar in as much as it shows along its length distinctive pattern of transverse bands or discs of varying thickness which are placed at certain distances from each other. The bands consist of alternating chromatic (stainable) and achromatic (non stainable) areas and these may be hundreds in number in a single chromosome. The achromatic bands represent areas which are supposed to be locus of gene and represent euchromatic regions and the chromatic the hterochromatic regions. Moreover, the chromosome is not of uniform width, it contains along its length waists or narrow portions. The bands vary in thickness, spacing, shape and fine structure so that it is possible for each band to be specifically identifiable. The bands have greatly helped in the mapping of the chromosomes in cytogenic studies. The bands occasionally form reversible "puffs", known as "chromosome puffs" or "Balbiani rings", which are associated with differential gene activities. The puffs represent regions where the tightly coiled chromosomal fibres open out to form many loops. Thus puffing is due to unfolding or uncoiling of individual chromomeres in a band. The puffs are active genes and represent sites of RNA synthesis.

The salivary gland chromosomes represent a bundle of fibrils which arise by repeated cycles of endo-reduplication of single chromatids. Endo-reduplication means that the chromatin replicates without cell division, as a result of which the number of chromonemata keeps on increasing. This is why these chromosomes are also popularly known as polytene chromosomes. The number of chromonemata (fibrils) per chromosome may reach upto 2000 in extreme cases.

It happens in *Drosophila* that the centromeric regions and pericentric heterochromatic regions of all the chromosomes fuse together to form a spherical mass, the chromocenter, from which all the chromosomes appear to radiate out. Thus in Drosophila metanogaster 6 arms radiate out from the chromocenter, something like a 6-limed ophiuroid. One of these limbs is very short and represents the small dot like IV chromosomes. One long strand corresponds to the X chromosome and the remaining four long strands are the arms of II and III chromosomes. In the male flies the Y chromosome is also found fused within the chromocenter. The size of the chromocenter is determined by the extant of the pericentric heterochromatin.

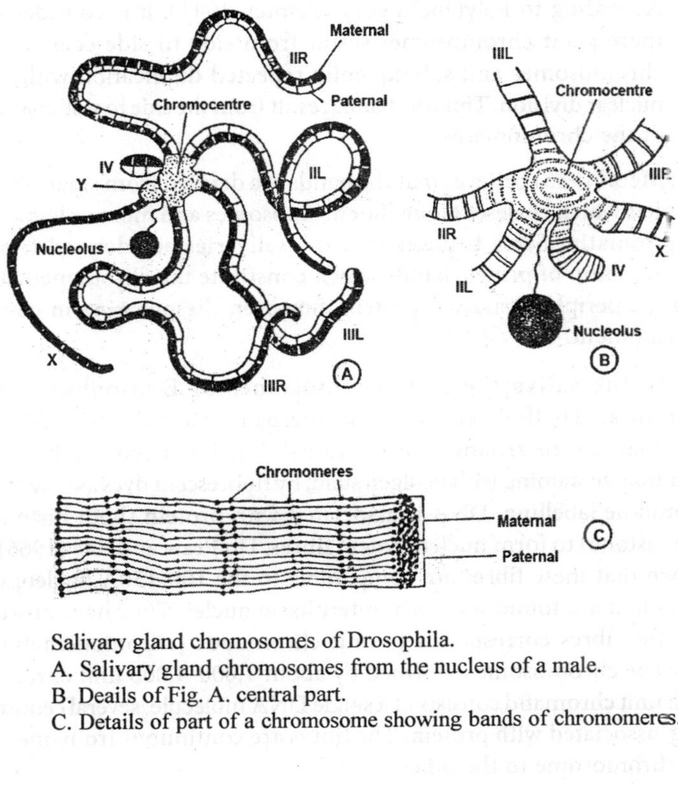

Salivary gland chromosomes of Drosophila.
A. Salivary gland chromosomes from the nucleus of a male.
B. Deails of Fig. A. central part.
C. Details of part of a chromosome showing bands of chromomeres.

Nature of the salivary gland chromosomes

1. Salivary gland chromosomes are the result of several cycles of intracellular chromosomal reproduction, and it consists of bundles of the folded ordinary chromosomes.
2. Kodani (1942) and Darlington (1949) considered that salivary

chromosomes are paired chromosomes which have enormous length and width by addition or incorporation of extra material not present in ordinary chromosomes.

3. Salivary chromosomes consist of bundles of chromonema, their size is due at least in part to the accumulation of extramaterial in the centre of chromosomes.

4. According to Polytene theory (Painter, 1941), it is considered that these giant chromosomes result from side to side coalescence of chromosomes and subsequently repeated duplication without any nuclear division. Thus the bands result from the side to side coalesconic of the chromomeres.

Metz (1935) believes that the bands are derived from small alveoli or droplets which coalesce along the chromosomes and more or less charged of chromatin. Serra believes that the salivaries are derived from the reduplication of proteic bands which constitute the chromonemata, the original peripheric nucleo-protein, however, disappearing in course of development.

In the salivary gland chromosomes of Drosophila DNA is concentrated in the bands while the interbands have very little DNA. The fact that the interbands do contain DNA has been established by quantitative staining with Feulgen stain, by fluorescent dyes and by tritium-thymidine labelling. DNA is associated with protein (both histone and non histone) to form nucleoprotein fibres. Du Praw and Rae (1966) have shown that these fibres are comparable to the 100-150A nucleoprotein fibres that are found in typical interphasic nuclei. They have postulated that the fibres corresponds to unit chromatids (chromonemata). The polytene chromosome is formed by about 1,000-4,000 unit chromatids. Each unit chromatid consists of a single DNA molecule, several centimeters long, associated with protein. The fibres are continuous from one end of the chromosome to the other.

The giant chromosomes occur in pairs like the homologous chromosomes at synapsis at pachytene stage of meiosis. The giant chromosomes of the salivary glands in the larva can be distinguished into autosomes and sex chromosomes either in the form of X-chromosome or Y chromosome according to sex of the individual.

LAMPBRUSH CHROMOSOMES

Lampbrush chromosomes have been defined as "germ line chromosomes with laterally projecting loops". The qualification "germ line" is needed because the Balbiani rings of polytene chromosomes are also thought to consist of lateral loops.

Lampbrush, chromosomes were first recorded by Flemming in 1882 but it was J. Ruckert (1892) who named them "Lamp brush chromosomes" due to their brush-like appearance. Lampbrush chromosomes are found in the telolecithal primary oocytes of many vertebrates and a few invertebrates. They are exceptionally very large, hence called giant chromosomes. They are even longer than the longest salivary gland chromosomes, but unlike the latter, they are no greater in number of strands than more typical chromosomes. The stage of female meiotic prophase during which the lateral loops are conspicuous may, to a first approximation, be described as diplotene and thereafter the chromosomes begin to revert to a more typical aspect, until by first metaphase they are quite usual in appearance. The largest lampbrush chromosomes so far known are present in Urodela (Amphibia). In some Salamander oocytes the lampbrush chromosomes may reach a length of 5,900 microns. In many other animals lampbrush chromosomes may be more than 1,000 microns in length and 20 microns in width during early prophase I. Towards the end of prophase I (diakinesis), however, the chromosomes contract and are greatly reduced in size. Lampbrush chromosomes are very elastic, and can be stretched upto about two times before they break.

Organisation

Lampbrush chromosomes are described as having a central chromosome axis from which project a series of lateral loops. The main axis is composed of 4 chromatids or two bivalent chromosomes. The chromonema of these chromatids give out fine loops at the lateral sides which impart characteristic brush-like appearance. The loops are of various sizes ranging from 39 Å – 50 Å in diameter. Each loop varies in thickness at different regions. The loops are extensible and elastic, and as a chromosome is stretched, pairs of loops become widely spaced along the axis but the bases of the loops do not open out appreciably.

Chromosomes which are small dense granules containing DNA and basic protein, are present wherever loops are attached to the chromosome axis. When chromosomes are stretched beyond the elastic limit, breakage occurs transversely across the chromomeres in such a way that the break comes between the left and right insertions of a pair of lateral loops in a chromomere. Attached to certain chromomeres are the "spheres" which are round Feulgin-negative structure.

There are two regions in the smallest lampbrush chromosome (XII) of Triturus cristatus and Triturus marmoratus where the axis is unquestionably double. In double axis region chromomeres bear single loop, not pairs, and when stretched and broken a single loop spans each break.

Ris (1957), by electron microscopic observations of loops has revealed that they are composed of many submicroscopic fibrils. Large normal

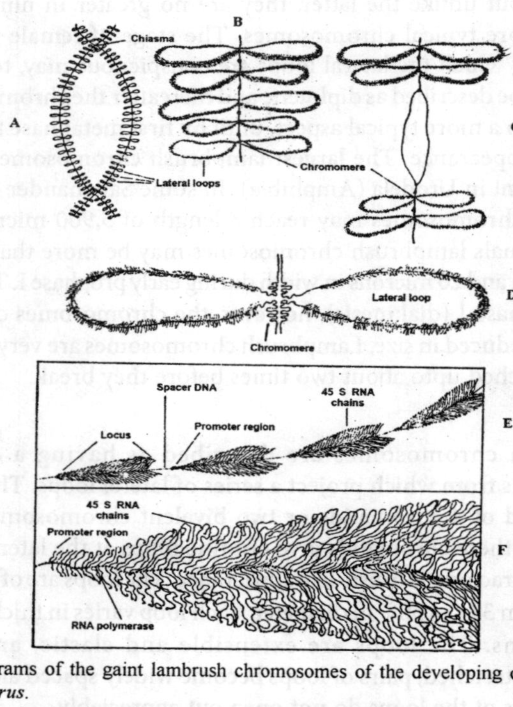

Diagrams of the gaint lambrush chromosomes of the developing oocytes of the new *Triturus*.

A. A pair of meiotic chromosomes joined by two chaiasmata.

B. A part of the chromosome enlarged showing the lateral loops.

C. Stretching of the chromosome shows that the loops are continuous with the axis of the chromosome.

D. A part of axis and a pair of loops. Note the RNA-protein fibrils being transcribed on the DNA thread.

E. Diagram of a tandem series of genes.

F. One gene locus enlarged.

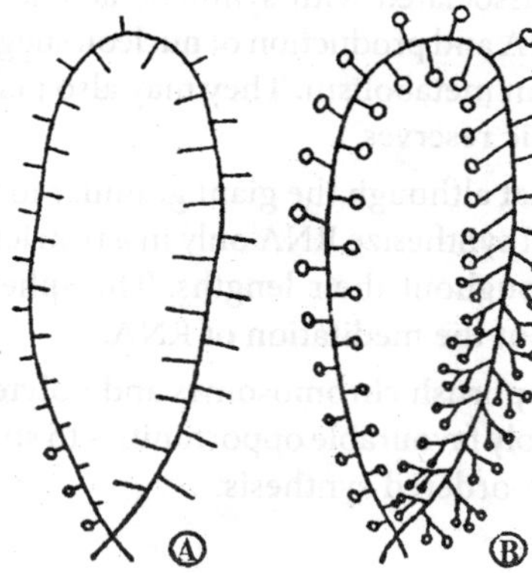

Lateral loops.
(A) Typical loop, (B) Special loop.

loops show signs of possessing an axis with many fine fibres projecting radially from it. Each normal loop is asymmetric in the sense that one of its insertions in the chromomere is bare of fibres; as one follows rounds the loop from its bare end, the fibres become progressively longer. Broadly speaking all lateral loops other than the normal ones are distinguished by the accumulation of 'matrix', and by the form. The matrix is distinctive of loops and it occupies different sites. The matrix accumulating loops may be classified into the "granular" loops, the "fusing" loops, the "lumpy" loops, the "giant fusing loops", etc. Although asymmetry is especially evident in granular loops, certain granular loops on chromosome V and VIII of Triturus cristatus are remarkable for their symmetry.

Chemical Properties

The parts of the lampbrush chromosome, except chromomeres are Feulgen-negative and so are all free aggregates. Chromomeres contain basic protein. Lateral loops and all free aggregates, except spheres, contain RNA. Spheres presumably contain an acidic protein. Callan and Lloyd (1960) suggested that there was a continuous transfer of DNA thread from the left to the right components of a chromomere, or vice-versa.

Polarity of lateral loops

Constant polarity is one of the characteristics of a pair of loops at a given site on the chromosome. There is also evidence for constant polarity of hereditary material from strictly genetic studies (Lissonba, 1960).

The loop is believed to represent one longoperon consisting of a series of identical copies of the same structural genes (cistrons). Callan and Lloyd (1960) suggested that each pair of loops is associated with the activity of a specific gene. Each loop is supposed to contain repeating DNA sequences arranged in a series.

Functional significance

Lampbrush chromosomes are associated with synthetic activity in growing oocyte. Their presence of RNA and production of nucleoli suggest that they are the sites of nucleoprotein metabolism. They may also play a role in the formation of deutoplasmic reserves.

Gall and Callan (1962) found that although the giant granular loops of Triturus cristatus chromosome XII synthesize RNA only in a restricted region, they synthesize protein throughout their lengths. The spheres appear to synthesize a protein without the meditation of RNA.

Recent studies indicate that lampbrush chromosomes and polytene chromosomes both provide remarkably favourable opportunities to study the mechanism responsible for gene-ordered synthesis.

8

CELL DIVISION

Introduction

For many years it was believed that new cells originated spontaneously by a process of crystallization. The real nature of the cells was understood only after the invention of the microscope. It is now known that cells are never formed de novo or afresh but they come into being by the division of the pre-existing cells.

New cells so formed serve in the general growth of the living body and in the repair of its injured portions. The cells constituting the body of the organism that is, the body cells or somatic (or vegetative) cells have a limited growth, and when they grow to the maximum size, they divide, each into two daughter cells. Thus the living organisms grow bigger in size mainly by the multiplication of more and more body cells which are formed as a result of repeated division of the "pre-existing" cells. In every kind of cell a fixed relationship exists between the size of the nucleus and the volume of the cytoplasm. This is known as "Kern-plasma ratio" (K-P ratio). Hertwig, who has introduced this term, claims that whenever there is a disturbance between the K-P ratio by relative increase of the bulk of the nucleus, the cell responds by dividing into two daughter cells.

There are various processes by which the cells divide. The chief methods are – direct cell division or amitosis, indirect cell division or mitosis, and reduction division or meiosis. Other methods are free cell formation, budding or gemmation.

Direct Cell Division (Amitosis)

This occurs in the simplest group of animals, namely, Protozoa (e.g., Amoeba) and in some very old and abnormal cells of Metazoa. In this, the nucleus first elongates and assumes the form of dumb-bell or hour glass and later on becomes completely separated into two daughter nuclei of approximately equal size. Consequent upon the division of the nucleus, the cytoplasm also constricts in the middle part in such a way that the ingrowing depression passes between the two daughter nuclei, and the mass of cell ultimately becomes divided into two parts, each containing a nucleus. There is no formation of the spindle, and chromosome formation is also not visible.

The direct type of cell division described above shows some modifications in some type of cells. Usually when the nucleus is divided, the cytoplasm also becomes divided. Sometimes the division of the nucleus is not followed by the division of the cytoplasm. The result of this is that the cell has got a common mass of cytoplasm containing more than one nucleus. This condition is called syncytial condition.

Indirect Cell Division (Mitosis)

Mitosis is the usual type of cell division, occurring universally amongst the body cells (somatic cells) of all multicellular organisms. During mitosis, the dividing cell undergoes a series of complicated but orderly changes both in the nucleus and in the cytoplasm effecting thereby in the equal distribution of cell inclusions between the two resulting daughter cells. The changes undergone by the nucleus during the process of mitosis was discovered by Walther Flemming in the year 1882.

Nuclear changes involve formation or appearance and movement of chromosomes in a definite number and orderly manner, ultimately dividing the nucleus into two identical daughter nuclei. Such a division of the nucleus is karyokinesis.

Consequent upon the nuclear division, there is in the cytoplasm, in a similar way, various changes going on, resulting in the formation of astral and spindle fibres and ultimate division of the cytoplasm into two parts. Such a division of the cytoplasm is called cytokinesis.

As a whole, the various complicated processes of mitosis can be conveniently described under five phases, viz., Interphase, Prophase, Metaphase, Anaphase and Telophase. These phases of mitotic division of a cell are continuous processes, having no clear line of demarcation between themselves, each phase merging into the next.

1. Interphase

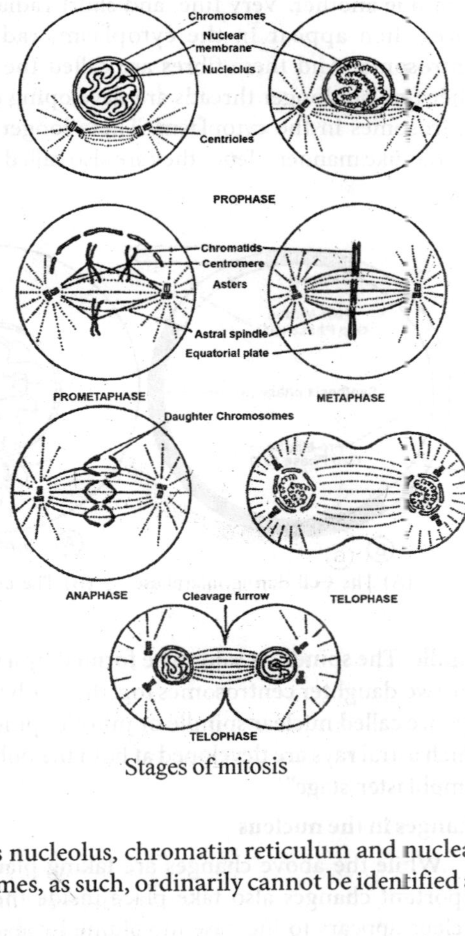

Stages of mitosis

A cell which is not actually in the process of cell division is described as a cell in the interphase. The term "resting stage" has also been applied to it because of its lack of visible nuclear changes, in contrast to the obvious cycle of visible changes in mitotic cells. This latter term, however, is regarded as a misnomer, because the modern physiological research has exposed the fact that a living cell is never taking "rest" but that various metabolic activities are going on in it. Thus the term 'interphase' is preferable to 'resting stage'.

A cell in the interphase is marked by the presence of a quiescent centrosome, a prominent nucleus with its nucleolus, chromatin reticulum and nuclear membrane. The chromosomes, as such, ordinarily cannot be identified at this stage.

2. Prophase

In this stage changes in the cytoplasm and in the nucleus take place in the following manner.

Changes in the cytoplasm

The centrosome inaugurates the cell division. The centrosome contains two centrioles; if it has but one, this divides and then the two halves of the centrosome move in the cytoplasm in opposite sides of the nucleus and reach the opposite poles of the cell lying approximately 180^0 from one another. Very fine, and short radiating protoplasmic, gel-like fibres then appear in the cytoplasm, radiating around each such centrosome. And these fibres are called the astral rays. Again, certain other fine but longer threads are developing extending between the two centrosomes in the cytoplasm. These longer threads are arranged in a spindle-like manner. Hence they are also called spindle fibres or achromatic

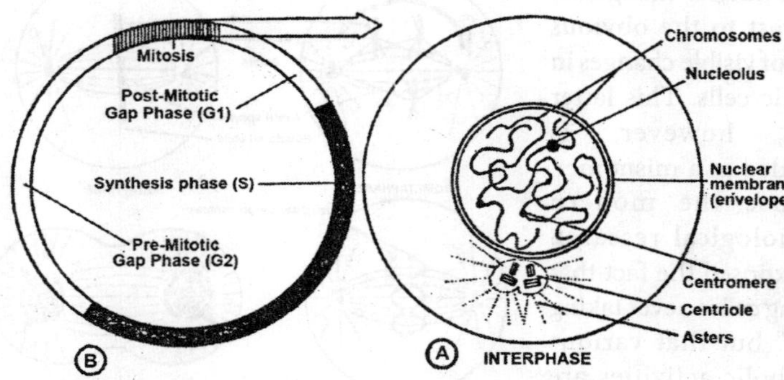

(A) The Cell during interphase (B) The cell cycle

spindle. The spindle is said to be formed by a gelation of the nuclear sap. The two daughter centrosomes together with the spindle fibres and astral rays are called nuclear spindle or mitotic spindle, and the condition with which astral rays are developed at both the poles of the cell is described as "Amphiaster stage".

Changes in the nucleus

While the above changes are taking place in the cytoplasm, other important changes also take place inside the nucleus. First of all, the nucleus appears to increase in volume by absorption of water from the cytoplasm. The chromatin into threads of chromatin. These threads are called chromonemata or genomemata or gene strings, because the swellings or dense masses on the chromonemata are said to be associated with chromomeres. The chromomeres are deep staining particles of chromatin. The hereditary units or genes are said to be located in linear order within these chromomeres. Each pair of chromonemata together with the chromatin material covering them constitute a chromosome.

The two chromonemata of each chromosome are united at one point known as centromere. When the chromosomes are first formed inside the nucleus; they assume the form of very thin and much coiled threads.

As the prophase advances four stages in the chromosomes gradually become clearly evident, viz., increasing dehydration, increasing aggregation of chromatin materials, shortening and thickening due to condensation or contraction and eventually a desparalization that is, unwinding of the chromosomes due to shortening and thickening. As a result of these changes, the chromosomes become distinctly visible.

Toward the end of the prophase, there is a tendency for the individual chromosomes to move to the periphery of the nucleus and to arrange themselves on the inner surface of the nuclear membrane. All the while each chromosome has been split up lengthwise, but the centromere has not yet been divided so that the two halves of the chromosomes form two parallel rods or loops in close contact with one another and but uniting only at the point of the centromere. The nucleolus and the nuclear membrane gradually disappear and the nuclear material mixes with the cytoplasm. With these changes, the cell becomes almost completely disorganised and enters the metaphase.

3. Methaphase

Prophase is followed by the metaphase. During metaphase all the chromosomes of the dividing cell arrange themselves in a single plane at the equator of the spindle, forming the so called 'equatorial plate. All the chromosomes spoilt (if not already splitted) longitudinally to form chromatids, but both the chromatids thus formed by one chromosome remain attached with each other by centromere till late metaphase where each centromere divides into two. The arrangement of chromosome at the equator of spindle is not of one type in all organisms, as the arrangement depends upon the shape, size and number of chromosomes.

The chromosomes lying in the equatorial plane are associated with the spindle. They are equally spaced around the periphery of the spindle. Attachement of each dividing chromosome to the spindle is made by a particular region of the chromosome, the remaining unattached portion of the chromosome floating in the cytoplasm as if hanging from the middle of the spindle. The position of the centromere in the chromosome varies in different chromosomes, but it is constant for each particular chromosome. It may be subterminal, median or in any other position, which determines the shape of the chromosome. If it be median in position,

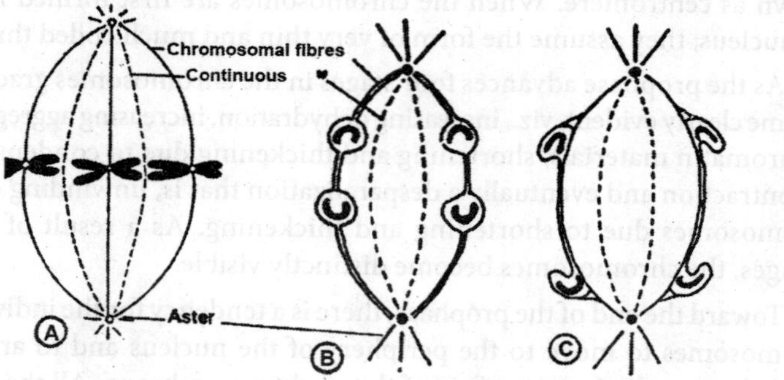

(A) Metaphasic spindle (B) Direct spindle (C) Indirect spindle

the chromosome is V-shaped, and the apex of the V contains the centromere. If it be subterminal the chromosome may be hook-shaped and the two limbs of the chromosome are unequal.

4. Anaphase

During this phase, the daughter chromosomes migrate to the opposite poles that is, one daughter chromosome of each chromosome migrates to one pole and the other daughter chromosome migrates to the other pole. And thus the respective daughter chromosomes become associated with the centrosome of that aside. During the migration, the half chromosomes bend in the shape of 'V' or 'U' or 'J' with the centromere leading the path to destination. In the case of V-shaped chromosomes the apex of the V which contains the centromere is first pulled apart along the spindle fibres, when the spindle elongates, as if by traction of its fibres. The daughter halves of each V-shaped chromosome as they move apart, open out in the form of < >, that is, two arrowshaped daughter chromosomes. The rod shaped chromosome may open out as hookshaped. A cluster of daughter chromosomes is formed at each pole of the cell. If there were four chromosomes in a resting cell, this number was doubled by longitudinal division of each chromosome, and, after separation, each cluster then has four daughter chromosomes.

5. Telophase

When the groups of daughter chromosomes reach the opposite poles, they unite, and eventually by a process of rehydration the entire chromosome material of each of the two groups slowly assume the arrangement of a network or reticulum. At last, around each such group of reticulum a nuclear membrane and nucleolus appear. Meantime the spindle fibres also disappear, the centriole at each pole becomes divided into two.

While all these changes are taking place, the cytoplasm becomes constricted in the middle part. As the constriction finally passing right through the cytoplasm between the two daughter nuclei, two daughter cells are produced each having its own nucleus. Here ends the mitosis.

The duration of mitosis may vary from nine minutes to several hours, depending upon the species of the animal or plant and the kind of cell. Nerve cells divide slowly while the embryonic cells divide rapidly. Some factors such as temperature affect the rate of mitosis.

Mitosis maintains the constant diploid chromosome number from one cell generation to another in the body, and brings about an increase in the number of cells. Mitosis also brings about asexual reproduction. Mitosis is a part of the process of growth in metazoan animal.

MEIOSIS

Meiosis has been defined by Darlington as "occurrence of two divisions of nucleus accompanied by one division of chromosome". White has defined meiosis as "the special process of nuclear division which reduces the normal number of chromosomes to one-half. Meiosis was first discovered by Weismann in 1887 when he was working in fertilization. It was previously forecasted by O. Hertwig that the fusion of nucleus during fertilization involves some other different types of division of chromosome other than mitotic or somatic. Von Beneden discovered the actual mechanism of meiosis.

Stages of Meiosis

Meiosis involves two complete cell divisions : the first division is reductional, resulting in two haploid daughter cells; the second division is equational, dividing each haploid cell into two similar haploid cells. Meiosis can be described in two parts namely, first meiotic division, and second meiotic division

First Meiotic Division

It can be distinguished into four phases as the mitotic division : Prophase I, Metaphase I, Anaphase I, and Telophase I.

Prophase I : It is prolonged and rather complicated one. It is again sub-divided into four stages viz., Leptotene, Zygotene, Pachytene, Diplotene and Diakenesis.

Leptotene (Leptonema) : In this the chromosomes are thrown into loops of delicate threads so as to form a tangled mass. The ends of slender chromosomes are drawn together at one side of the nuclear membrane near which the centrosome is situated and are so oriented as to give formation of Bouquet (flower), the loops extending into the nuclear cavity.

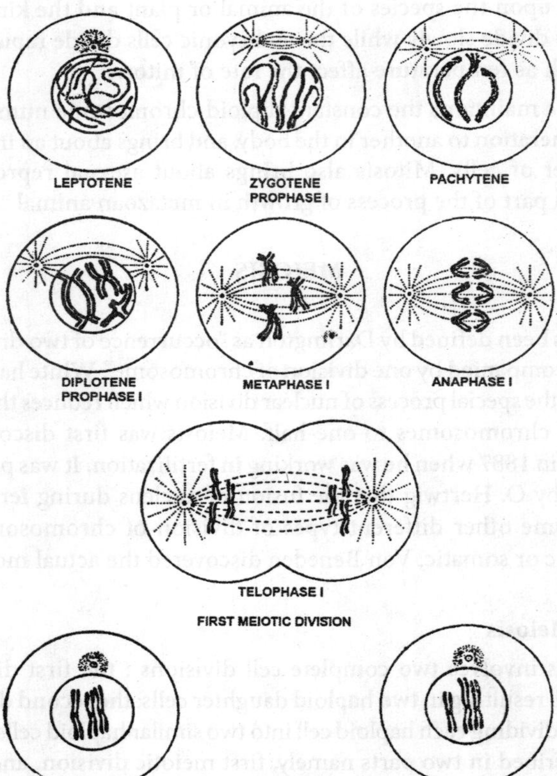

The first meiotic division and interkinesis.

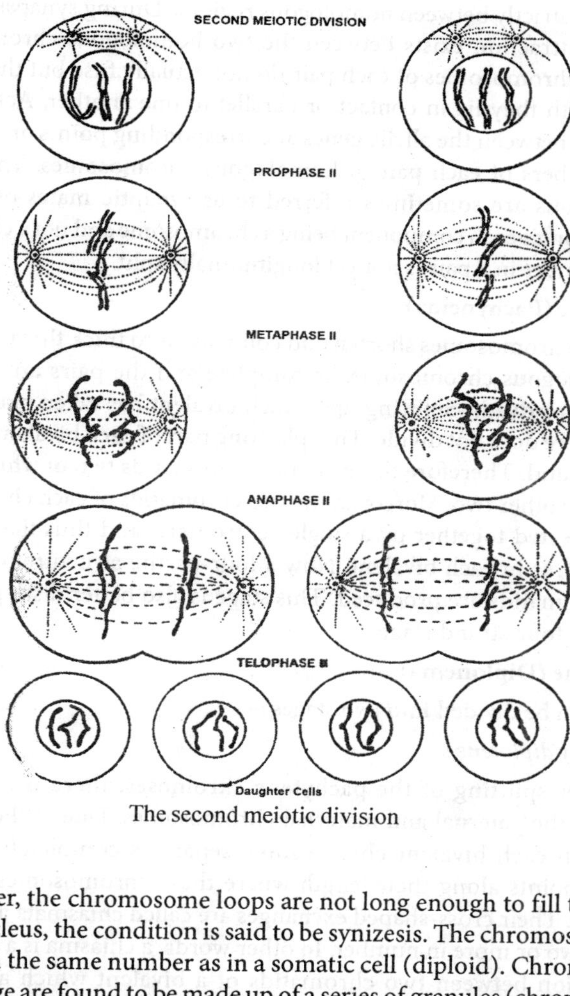

The second meiotic division

If, however, the chromosome loops are not long enough to fill the cavity of the nucleus, the condition is said to be synizesis. The chromosomes are present in the same number as in a somatic cell (diploid). Chromosomes at this stage are found to be made up of a series of granules (chromomeres, or according to some, genes) connected by non-staining materials. These granules are of unequal size and they live at unequal distance. The chromosomes are not longitudinally split.

Zygotene (Zygonema)

Homologous threads or chromosomes now come to lie side by side and are said to pair; and this phenomenon is known as synapsis or pairing.

Pairing is strictly between homologous regions. During synapsis, mutual force of attraction exists between the two homologous chromosomes. The two chromosomes of each pair do not actually fuse but throughout their length they lie in contact or parallel to one another. Actually, the pairing is between the allelic genes at corresponding points or loci in the two members of each pair of homologous chromosomes. The pairing homologous are sometimes referred to as synaptic mates or bivalent chromosomes each component being a chromosome and not a chromatid. Each member in a pair is not yet longitudinally split.

Pachytene (Pachynema)

The chromosomes shorten and condense into thick threads. Pairing of homologous chromosomes is complete and the pairs are called the bivalents or dyads. Splitting up of each bivalent has taken place but the centromere does not divide. The sploitting part of each bivalent is known as chromatid. Therefore there are four chromatids two of which wound round the other two. Moreover, the two chromatids of each chromosome are connected together by a single centromere, and thus there are two centromeres in each bivalent. Now a four-partite structure or tetrad of four chromatids are produced. This stage is also better distinguished as tetrad or four strand stage.

Diplotene (Diplonema)

It can be divided into two stages :–

Early diplotene :

After splitting of the pachytene chromoses, there is a repulsion between the paternal and maternal chromosomes. Due to the excessive repulsion each bivalent chromosome separates completely except at certain points along their length where these chromosomes exchange partners. Their cross-shaped exchanges are called chiasmata and may lie one or two or more in number. In other words, a chiasma is a cross-arise connection between two chromatids of a bivalent which are not the daughter strands of one original chromosome. Chiasma does not occur between the two chromatids of a single chromosome. Chiasmata are due to breakage and reciprocal rejoining between the two chromatids of the partner chromosomes.

Late diplotene :

Chromatids shorten and thicken. Two arms of the cross of chiasmata rotate through about 180^0 in case of a single chiasma and through about

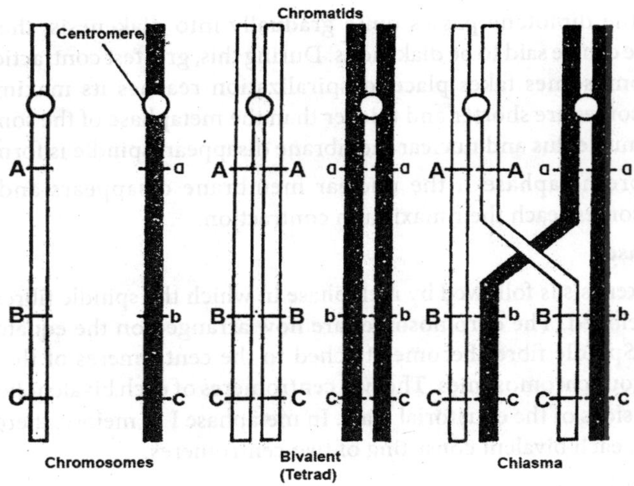

Chiasma formation

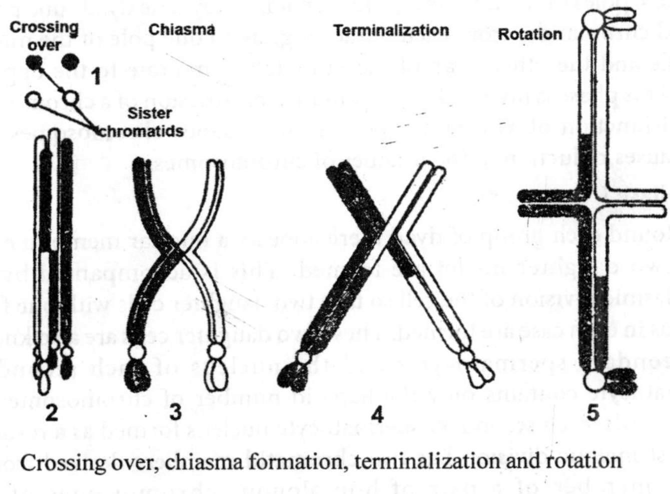

Crossing over, chiasma formation, terminalization and rotation

90^0 in case of several chiasmata. This phenomenon is rotational coiling. Terminalization takes place and due to this, exchange of paternal and maternal chromatids takes place.

Diakenesis

As the diplotene passes quite gradually into diakenesis, the late diplotene can be said to be diakenesis. During this, greatest contraction of the chromosomes takes place; despiralization reaches its maximum; chromosomes are shorter and thicker than the metaphase of the somatic mitosis; nucleolus and nuclear membrane disappear; spindle is formed.

In prometaphase I, the nuclear membrane disappears and the chromosomes reach their maximum contraction.

Metaphase I

Diakenesis is followed by metaphase in which the spindle fibres are well developed. The chromosomes are now arranged on the equator of the cell. Spindle fibres become attached to the centromeres of the two homologous chromosomes. The two centromeres of each bivalent lies on opposite sides of the equatorial plate. In metaphase I of meiosis there are bivalents, each bivalent consisting of two centromeres.

Anaphase I

Each of the tetrad breaks into two dyads which separate and move to opposite poles of the division spindle, that is to say, one dyad (one pair of united chromatids) from each tetrad migrate to one pole of the nuclear spindle and the other dyad of the same tetrad migrate to the opposite pole. This phase is involved not in longitudinal division of a chromosome but disjunction of associated pairs of homologous chromosomes, and this causes reduction in the number of chromosomes.

Telophase I

Round each group of dyad there appears a nuclear membrane and thus two daughter nuclei are formed. This is accompanied by the cytoplasmic division of the cell so that two daughter cells with one fresh nucleus in each case are formed. These two daughter cells are also known as secondary spermatocytes and the nucleus of each secondary spermatocyte contains only the haploid number of chromosomes. In other words, each secondary spermatocyte nucleus formed as a result of the first meiotic division has two chromatid members derived from a single member of a pair of homologous chromosomes of the spermatogonium. Separation of the chromatids into pairs, representing an original member of a pair of homologous chromosome, reduces the numbers of chromosomes in each secondary spermatocyte.

Second meiotic division

The second meiotic division is essentially similar to mitosis, as the chromosome number is not changed during the second meiotic division. In the second meiotic division, the chromosomes are present in a haploid number. Chromatids are widely separated, exhibiting no coiling with each other. The second meiotic division can be distinguished into four phases.

Prophase II: The centriole and centrosphere divide and move towards opposite poles, each surrounded by astral rays. The nucleolus and nuclear membrane disappear. Each centromere still has two chromatids attached to it.

Metaphase II: During this stage the chromosomes become arranged on the equatorial plane. Spindle fibres appear between the two centrioles and the centromeres get attached to them at the equatorial plane.

Anaphase II: Each centromere divides and separates the two chromatids which are now called chromosomes and they move to the poles.

Telophase II: During this stage, the groups of chromosomes are covered by the fragments of endoplasmic reticulum. At this stage each daughter nucleus is haploid in nature. New nucleolus is also developed. After the formation and appearance of nuclear membrane and nucleolus respectively, cytokinesis takes place and two cells are formed from each cell passing through anaphase II, each is having haploid set of chromosomes in the nucleus. Thus four cells are formed, two by the 1st meiotic division and two by the 2nd meiotic division. All these four haploid daughter cells are formed from a single diploid cell.

Conclusion

The meiotic division or reduction division always occurs in germ cells. It is responsible for the formation of haploid gametes which, after fertilization, restore the constant diploid number in the zygote. Thus, it helps to maintain the constant chromosome number from one generation to another in a species. The homologous chromosomes separate (segregate) and pass on to different daughter cells, resulting in new combinations of chromosomes, and hence genes, in them. This too brings about new combinations of characters in the offsprings.

UNIT – IV
GENETICS

9

HISTORY OF GENETICS

Genetics is the science which tries to explain the resemblances, differences, their source and their development due to heredity. It is because of heredity that the organisms resemble each other. But heredity does not necessarily imply that parents and their progeny are identical in all their traits or characters. The unlikenesses which exist are termed variations.

The science of Genetics should have come into being in 1865 when Father Gregor Mendel (1822-1884), the abbot of an Augustinian monastery in Brunn in what is now Czechoslovakia, read a manuscript entitled "*Experiments in Plant Hybridization*" before the members of the Brunn Society of Natural Science. The paper was forgotten until 1900, when three European botanist – De vries in Holland, Tschermak in Austria, and Correns in Germany independently rediscovered and verified the experiments of Mendel. Sixty years later Genetic has developed into a massive body of knowledge which has been integrated with the other biological sciences.

Since the discovery of the findings of Mendel, a vast amount of meticulous work has been done by geneticists working with both plants and animals. Of especial importance has been the use of the tiny fruit fly, Drosophila mealogaster. A large share of genetic knowledge has been obtained through the use of this insect.

The use of Drosophila in genetic experiment was begun about 1910 by T.H. Morgan and his associates at Columbia University. By 1915, the Columbia group (Morgan, Sturdevant, Bridges, and Muller) published the mechanism of Heredity. This was the first attempt to explain the problems of genetics on a chromosomal basis. Drosophila was shown by these investigators to be an important laboratory animal for genetic investigations.

The term Genetics, coined by William Bateson in 1906, has its origin in the Greek language and means the science of coming into being. Genetics today is doubtlessly the most significant branch of Modern Biology. Genetics has a wide scope. It covers heredity as well as its variations.

Horses and cattle were bred and domesticated by Babylonians and assyrians hundreds of years before the Christian era. Barley grains, found in cases of mummies, indicate that Egyptians cultivated them as far back as 4000 B.C. There is evidence that the Chinese grew rice of different varieties as early as 500 years back.

Aristotle (384-322 B.C.) gave a theory of Heredity. He was of the opinion that the offspring, was produced by the mixing of man's and women's blood during coition. An important stage in the discovery of the true physical basis of the Heredity was reached in the seventeenth century.

Heredity includes those traits or characteristics which are transmitted from generation to generation and is, therefore fixed for a particular individual. Variations on the other hand, are mainly of two types, namely (i) hereditary and (ii) environmental. Hereditary variations refer to the differences which are are inherited by the progeny from their parents. Such variations are found not only in the progenies of different parents but also among the progeny from the same parents. The traits which are present in parents can reassort and give rise to different combinations, which are responsible for hereditary variations within the same progeny. Identical twins, however, is an example, where no hereditary variation exists. Enviromental variations are those which are merely due to environment. The study of genetics, therefore, should enable us to differentiate between hereditary variations and environmental variations. Hereditary variations within a progeny result due to sexual reproduction.

J.B. Lamark (1809) came up with the idea that characters, which an individual acquires during his life time, affect his reproductive cells which consequently transmit those characters to the offsprings. Charles Darwin (1838) carried this idea further by proposing a mechanism by which acquired characters are inherited.

Weismann referred to the reproductive cells as germplams and the rest of the body as somatoplasm. He advanced the idea that germaplasm forms the bridge of life passing from generation to generation. In each generation, it produces somatoplasm and yet remains unaffected by changes in the latter. This theory of continuity of germplasm gave a death blow to the various theories on inheritance of acquired characters and established a landmark in the history of Genetics.

Mendelian Inheritance Pattern

The principles which form the very basis of Heredity were formulated by Gregor Johann Mendel in the second half of the nineteenth century. Mendel was deeply interested in Darwin's work on Evolution. He knew that a proper understanding of Evolution was not possible without a clear conception of inheritance. In 1857, Mendel started his own breeding experiments which were intended to give information on inheritance and evolution.

It is highly fruitful and instructive to consider the technique Mendel adopted in his experiments. It may be summarised as follows:

1. A clear, well thought out plant of work;
2. Careful choice of experimental material. These must possess : (I0 constant differentiating characters, (ii) the hybrids of such plants must be protected from foreign pollen or be easily capable of such protection;
3. The hybrids and their offspring should suffer no marked disturbance in their fertility in the successive generations;
4. Object of experiment was to observe the variations "in the case of each pair of differentiating characters and to deduce the law according to which they appear in successive generations, that is, just as many experiments as there are constantly differentiating characters transmitted in the experimental plants";
5. Healthy vigorous plants to be chosen since "weakly plants always afford uncertain results";
6. Reciprocal crosses done in such a way that the variety which served as seed parent in the experiment was used in the other as pollen parent;
7. Control plants maintained in each experiment and
8. Record of all observations and counts of progeny kept.

Mendel considered his experimental plants as composed of a number of differentiating characters. Each character was a unit. He studied each unit character for a period of two years to prove that they were constant. Out of 34 samples collected he selected seven constant differentiating characters for his study.

By contrasting characters is meant the different expressions of a character which can be sharply distinguished. For example, black colour is contrasting to white, similarly heavy and light wood, broad and narrow leaves, coloured and non-coloured flowers, tall and dwarf men. Here in each case it is colour, weight, length, or width that is involved. Thus if there are more inches and feet added it is called tall, if there are fewer of them it becomes dwarf. A character may have two or more opposing, expressions, for example, colour may be black, brown, red, yellow, green or white.

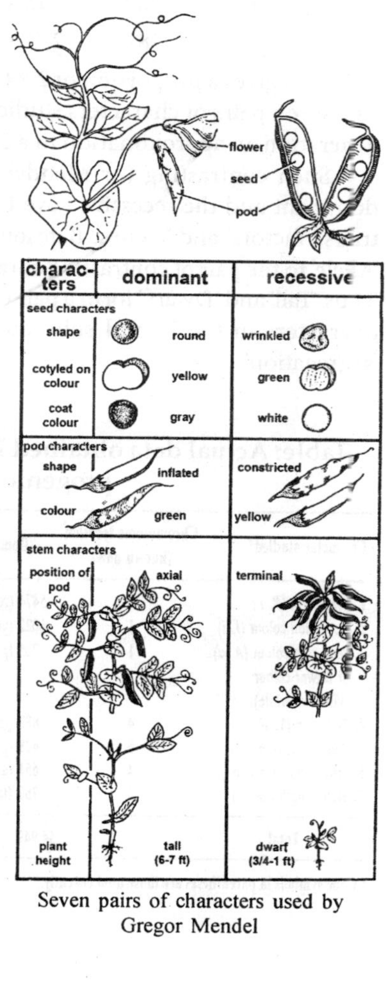

Seven pairs of characters used by Gregor Mendel

While studying height of plants Mendel crossed long plants with short plants (P to 1@ foot length) and found that the hybrids exceed the length of parental stems. This he ascribed as due to luxuriance which is exhibited in all parts of plants when plants of different lengths are crossed. Mendel gave the name "Dominant" to such characters as are stransmitted entirely unchanged and form the character of the hybrid, and to those that become latent as "Recessive". In the above experiment the character long plant is dominant, while short is recessive.

For clarity the two parents are indicated as P_1 and P_2, while the offspring by F_1 (first filid generation). Out of 1,064 plants raised from the seeds of the F_1, 787 were long stemned and 277 short ones. This generation is termed as F_2 generation. Each generation is thus indicated by number as F_1, F_2, F_3, F_4 and so on. Crossing is usually indicated by the symbol X. The above experiment may be represented as :–

P_1	Tall	X	Short P_2
F_1		Tall	
F_2	Tall	Short	Total population
	787	277	1,064

This gives a proportion of 2.84 : 1 of long and short stemmed plants. The seven pairs of characters studied by Mendel each time gave in the F_2 generation an approximation to a 2.98 to 1 or 3:1.

Such contrasting (or Mendel's differentiating) characters like the dominant and the recessive have been variously called ad 'determiners', traits', 'factors' and 'Genes'. Bateson proposed the name 'Allelomorph' or 'Allele' to the pair of contrasting chracters – the dominant and its recessive. Thus 'Tall' and 'Dwarf' form a pair of alleles. The separation of the parental characters in the F_2 and subsequent generations has been termed as 'segregation'.

Table: Actual data obtained by Mendel in F_2 segregating progenies in pea.

Character studied*	Chromosome location (known now)	Dominant	Recessive	Total	Ratio
1. Seed form (*R, r*)	7	5474 (round)	1850 (wrinkled; rugosus)	7324	2.96 : 1
2. Cotyledon colour (*I, i*)	1	6022 (yellow)	2001 (green)	8023	3.01 : 1
3. Seed coat colour (*A, a*) or flower colour (violet *vs* white)	1	705 (grey)	224 (white)	929	3.15 : 1
4. Pod form (*V, v*)	4	882 (inflated)	299 (constricted)	1181	2.95 : 1
5. Pod colour (*Gp, gp*)	5	428 (green)	152 (yellow)	580	2.82 : 1
6. Flower position (*Fa, fa*)	4	651 (axial)	207 (terminal)	858	3.14 : 1
7. Stem length (*Le, le*)	4	787 (tall)	277 (dwarf)	1064	2.84 : 1
Total		14,949	5010	19,959	2.98 : 1

* Gene symbols in parentheses are those used curently.

In describing the experiment above, it was mentioned that the differentiating characters of the parents must be constant. This means that when the parents, say tall plant, is protected from outside pollen and the seeds obtained from such protected plants are sown, only tall plants arise. When in an experiment the stigma from a flower is pollinated with pollen from the anther of the same flower or sometimes from another flower of the same plant, the pollination is known as "self polination" or in short "selfing" and the seed setting "self fertilization" or "selfed". When the same character appears generation after generation in such selfed progenies the plant is said to be "homozygous". Seed to seed forms a generation. On the other hand when as in the hybrid of tall X short, after selfing, plants with different characters appear in the progeny, the parent plants are said to be "Heterozygous".

The pattern of inheritance observed in all the seven cases is summed up as follows :

(1) For any character the F_1 individuals derived from crosses, between two diffrent varieties having alternative characters, showed only one of the traits and never the other.

(2) It did not matter which parent variety provided the pollen and which provided the eggs; the results are always the same. In other words, the reciprocal crosses gave the same results.

Mendel's interpretations of results of his crossing experiments on pea plants are summed up as Mendel's Laws or Principles of Heredity.

Mendel's Laws

1. Every individual biparental in origin receives contribution of factors (alleles or genes) from each parent.
2. In the germ cells (gametes) of hybrids there is free seperation of factors (segregation of genes in meiosis) contributed by two parents without regard to which parent supplied them.

The principles involved in these laws are based on : (i) the concept of unit character (as determined by a pair of alleles), (ii) concept of dominance (the effect of recessive gene present but not being expressed in F_1 or hybrid generation), and (iii) concept of segregation and independent assortment of factors (gene-bearing chromosomes). The inheritance of characters in the above examples is autosomal and is said to be Mendelian inheritance. Mendelian inheritance did not include inheritance of sexlinked chracters through X chromosomes. It is to credit of Mendel that he discovered laws before chromosomes were known, and his concept of segregation which is the best part of his theory, stands valid.

Quantitative Inheritance

Variations such as those in stature, weight, or intelligence in man, econimically important traits in domestic animals and cultivated plants such as yield of fruits, seeds, or eggs and amount of milk or meat produced, do not usually fall into clear cut classes. These characters are quantitative rather than qualitative. All gradations occur between large and small, heavy and light, high-yielding and low-yielding. Mendel's methods of analysis are hard to apply to such continuously varying traits, because they seem to mix or blend, instead of segregate, in the offspring of hybrids.

Nilsson Ehle (1908) showed that the colouration of the wheat endosperm was due to operation of duplicate genes. The red colour was not completely dominant over white. Hence the F_1 showed intermediate intensities of colour. The same character gave also a monogenic difference that is, there were both 3:1 and 15:1 segregations. In the dihybrid F_2 progeny intermediates as to colour could be recognized. The same character was found by him to exhibit also triplicate factor difference, viz., 63:1. Here the range in intensities of the red colour was greater. The intermediates gave a great uniformity in character. That these are Mendelian is proved by the occurrence of 3:1 and 15:1 ratios in further breeding. Nilsson Ehle proposed the hypothesis of Multiple factors to explain the above segregations. This hypothesis assumes that a given quantitative character is controlled by a series of independent genes which are cumulative in effect. Each gene is assumed to contribute a unit of quantity such as the units of height, weight, etc. In the wheat endosperm it was assumed to have three identical genes for colour, viz., R_1R_1 R_2R_2 R_3R_3 and white r_1r_1 r_2r_2 r_3r_3 and the $F_1 = R_1R_1r_1$ R_2r_2 R_3r_3. This theory was amply confirmed in maize by East in 1910.

Mendel himself crossed tall and short peas and showed that the difference in size was very simply inherited and caused by just one pair of alleles of a single gene. It is not precisely the quantitative nature of these variations which sets them apart from qualitative ones, but the fact that some variations are gradual or continuous so that clear cut classes can be distinguished only with difficulty or not at all.

Quantitative traits are often susceptible to environmental modification. The skin colour of one person can be lighter or darker depending upon the amount of exposure to sunlight. Animals and plants grow larger and heavier with abundant food and on good soil. Polygenes, the genes that bring about heritable variations in quantitative traits, are not a separate category of genes. They are simply genes the different alleles of which produce small phenotypic differences, of about the same order of magnitude as the differences caused by usual environmental fluctuations.

The hypothesis of multiple factors, proposed to explain the inheritance of quantitative characters, assumes that some character differences are determined by series of independent genes. The effects of these genes are cumulative or additive that is, each gene contributes a certain quantity of colour, or height, or weight, or fertility, and the phenotype that develops shows a simple summation of these quantities.

C.B. Davenport in 1913 reported results of studies regarding the inheritance of skin colour in negro and white populations in United States of America. In U.S.A. the populations derived from marriages between negro and white individuals are known as mulattoes. The offsprings from negro-white marriages give intermediate skin colour in the first generation. When such individuals inter marry among themselves, all shades of skin colour are obtained. If two loci A and B are responsible for the skin colour, negroes can be represented by the genotype AABB and whites as as aabb. Mulattoes will be AaBb with intermediate skin colour.

The difference in skin colour between negroes and whites sums to be due to more than two pairs of pigment genes, possibly to four or seven more pairs. These pigment genes are not necessarily equally potent; some may cause production of more pigment than others. But Davenport's hypothesis is essentially correct in that the heredity of skin pigmentation in man is due to the action of several colour genes with incomplete or with no dominance and with additive effects.

GENETICS
MENDEL'S LAWS

Gregor Johann Mendel (1822-1884), the Austrian Monk, carried a series of experiments on inheritance and laid the foundation of modern Genetics. His experiments were conducted on sweet pea (*pisum sativum*). The results of his experiments were published in 1866. Mendel's fundamental laws of inheritance are known after his death as Mendelism. Mendel's work was recognized only in 1900, when Mendel's laws were rediscovered by Hugo de Vries, Carl Correns and Erich von Tschermak.

It is customary to deal the Mendelism into two fundamental laws :

1. Mendel's first law – Law of segregation
2. Mendel's second law – Law of Independent assortment.

Mendel's first law

This law can be illustrated by the Monohybrid cross. The monohybrid cross is one which involves two parents differing in one pair of contrasting characters (allelomorphs or alleles).

Mendel crossed tall and dwarf varieties of garden peas and found that their offspring in the first filial generation were all tall. When all these hybrids were self fertilized, they gave rise to tall and dwarf in the ratio of 3 tall to 1 dwarf. The resulting dwarf plants, on being self fertilized gave rise to dwarf plants only (that is, it bred true). Of the three tall plants one of the tall plant on being self fertilized gave rise to tall plants. It contained two factors for tallness, (homozygous tall). The other two tall plants contained factor for tallness and dwarfness. When self fertilized, they gave rise to tall and dwarf plants, in the ratio of 3 : 1 as did their hybrid parent (heterozygous tall).

In the above example, two plants with a pair of contrasting characters were crossed. A pair of contrasting characters is known as allelomorph. The offspring (hybrid) of F_1 generation possessed one of the parental characters. The character which expresses itself in hybrid offspring is known as dominant and that which is hidden, is known as recessive. Here the factor for tallness is dominant and the factor for dwarfness is recessive. The important point is that the factors occur in double dose in the parents, whereas the factors occur in single dose in the gametes.

Monhybrid ratio – 3 : 1 (Phenotype); 1: 2: 1 (Genotype).

example :

Monohybrid in Guineapig

	Guineapig (Black)		X		Guneapig (White)	
		BB			bb	
Gametes	B		B	b		b
F_1		Bb			Bb – Black	
F_2	B		b	B		b
	BB	Bb		Bb	bb	
	Black	Black		Black	white	

Phenotypic ratio = 3 : 1

Genotypic ratio = 1 : 2 : 1

Explanation

In a cross between the pure (homozygous) black Guineapig and pure white Guineapig, all the F_1 individuals (First filial generation) are black. When the F_1 individuals are interbred the F_2 generations consist black and white Guineapig in the ratio of 3 : 1. The parents are pure and they are represented by double letters since their body cells contain diploid number of chromosomes. The gametes are represented by a single letter because of the reduction division during the maturation of gametes. The dominant character is represented by the capital letter of the initial letter of the character and the recessive character is represented by the corresponding small letter.

The contrasting characters of Mendel are now known as allelomorphs. The contrasting characters in the above cross are Black and White colour. In the F_1 generation the black character is expressed while the white is unexpressed. Mendel called the character which is expressed in F_1 hybrid as the dominant character and the other latent character is called by him as recessive character. This has been sometimes called "Law of dominance". The phenotype of the F_1 is black and its genotype is Bb. In this hybrid there are two genes containing two dissimilar characters and it is now called Heterozygote. In parents (P_1), the genes are similar (allelomorphic characters) and they are known as Homozygous.

The F_1 individual produces two types of gametes, half of the gamete will have the black character (B) while the other half will have the white character. Thus the gametes are pure and they may contain only one of the allelomorphs but not the both. This is called by Mendel as the purity of the gametes. During maturation division the homologous chromosomes separate or segregate into the gametes. Only one member of the homologous pair is present in the gamete but not both. When the gametes of the F_1 hybrid unite, we will get three black and one white (3 : 1 phenotypic ratio). The genotypic ration of the cross is 1 homozygous black : 2 heterozygous black : 1 homozygous white (1:2:1).

If the cross is continued for F_3 and F_4 generations the homozygous individuals breed true while the heterozygous individuals behave like F_1 individuals. This is the important point of segregation in Mendelism.

Mendel's Second Law – Law of Independent Assortment

This Law can be illustrated by dihybrid cross. The dihybrid cross is one which involves two parents differing in two pairs of contrasting characters. When two or more pairs of opposed characters and the factors controlling them are brought into a cross, the two factors of each pair segregate and behave independently of one another. As an example of dihybrid cross we take Guineapig experiments conducted by William E. Castle of Harvard University, as follows :–

P_1 Phenotype black (short haired female) X White (long haired male)

Genotype BBSS X bbss

Gametes BS BS bb ss

F_1 Phenotype Black short X Long black

Genotype BS bs BS bs

Gametes BS Bs bs bs BS Bs bs bs

F_2

	BS	Bs	bs	bs
BS	BBSS	BBSs	BbSs	BbSs
Bs	BBSs	BBss	Bbss	Bbss
bS	BbSS	BbSs	bbSs	bbSs
bs	BbSs	Bbss	bbss	bbss

Ratio 9 : 3 : 3 : 1

Fig. A Dihybrid cross illustrating the Law of Independent Assortment

Castle has taken a pure (homozygous) Guineapig having black fur and short hair (BBSS) and crossed with a pure Guineapig having white fur and long hair (bbss). The contrasting characters in this cross are (i) white and black colour, (2) short and long hair. The F_1 individuals of this cross are having black and short hair (BbSs). This indicates the black and short dominating over white and long. The F_1 individual as a dihybrid because it is hybrid for both the characters taken in the cross. The F_1 individual produces 4 types of gametes. Each gamete contains only one member of each allelomorphic pair. This is the Mendel's principle of purity of gametes. When the F_1 individuals are interbred, we will get 16 possible combinations in F_2 generations. Scientists have found out a formula $(3+1)^n$ for finding out the F_2 individuals in a cross $(3 + 1) = F_2$ individuals of a monohybrid cross and n = number of contrasting characters involved in a cross. In dihybrid cross we will get $(3+1)^n = 16$ possible combinations. Similarly in trihybrid cross we get $(3+1)^3 = 64$ combinations in F_2 generations. The F_2 individuals are represented by the Checker Board method or Punnet's square, suggested by R.C. Punnet. This indicates that there are 4 phenotypes – black short -9, black long -3, white short - 3 and white short -1, or 9 : 3 : 3 : 1 is known as dihybrid ratio.

Adding up all the blacks and white, we will get 12 blacks and 4 whites. This is same as 3 blacks : 1 white. Similarly we get 12 short and 4 long that is 3:1. Thus in two sex characters each sex segregates in 3:1 ratio in F_2 generations. When we consider both the characters at the same time we will get 9:3:3:1 in F_2 generations.

Mendel did not know anything about chromosomes. He assumed that the characters are inherited as units and unit characters are controlled by something or factors. Mendel's 'something' or factors are known as genes. If two pairs of contrasting characters are involved in a cross, each pair act independently so far as the transmission is concerned. When two pairs of homologous genes are considered, the separation of the two members of any pair at meiosis is independent of the other pair. Allelomorphs in different chromosomes assort independently at gametogenesis. This phenomenon is known as Law of Independent Assortment, and is often spoken as the Mendel's Second Law.

Back cross

The back cross is made by mating the F_1 hybrids to one or other of their parents and the progeny obtained constitute the back cross generation. Such a cross of F_1 individual with either of the two parents is known as a "backcross". In such backcrosses, when F_1 is backcrossed to the parent with dominant phenotype, no recessive individuals are obtained in the progeny. On the other hand, when it is crossed with recessive parent, both phenotypes appear in the progeny. While both these crosses are "backcrosses" only the cross with the recessive parent is known as a "test cross". It is called a test cross, because it is used to test whether an individual is homozygous (pure) or heterozygous (hybrid).

Test cross

In this cross the F_1 individuals is crossed with the homozygous recessive parents. In other words, it is a back cross with a recessive parent. Mendel used to test the results of his experiments by crossing the F_1 hybrid with the pure breeding recessive parent. The test cross is used to test the individuals showing a dominant character whether heterozygous or homozygous. If the given individual is homozygous, the test cross is as follows :–

Homozygous individual X Homozygous recessive
Black Guineapig White Guineapig

BB bb
(individual in question) (known recessive)

Gametes B B b b

F_1 – Bb (Black) Bb (Black)

If the given individual is heterozygous, the test cross is as follows :

Heterozygous black X Homozygous white
Guineapig Guineapig

Bb bb

Gametes B b b b

F_2 – Bb (Black) bb (White)

The above test cross experiment indicates, if the individual in question is homozygous its F_2 individuals will show the same dominant phenotype when it is crossed with the recessive individual. If the individual is heterozygous when it is crossed with the recessive individual the F_2 individual of this will show both the dominant and recessive character in 1:1 ratio. The genotypic and phenotypic ratio in F_2 generation is identical that is, 1:1. This is due to the production of 2 types of gametes by the heterozygous individual in question.

Reciprocal cross

In effecting cross between two types differing in characters, any one type may be used as male or female parent. Thus, if type A is crossed with type B, the cross B ′ A is termed reciprocal. Whichever way the cross is made, the character of F_1 and mode of segregation in F_2 will be the same. This is to be normally expected because, phenotype is the resultant of interaction between the genotype and environment. Whether A or B is the maternal parent, the genotype of the hybrid between A and B is the same.

Parents : Brown X Blackish purple

pp PP

F_1 : Blackish purple

Pp

Segregation in F_2 is the same. From the consideration of genotypes there are no differences in the reciprocal crosses between homozygous parents.

Dominance and recessiveness

These two terms were coined by Mendel. The idea of dominance and recessive in a pair of contrasting character is the fundamental point in Mendel's experiment which is sometimes known as "Law of dominance". When two parents differing in a pair of contrasting characters are crossed, one character of the parent appears in the F_1 while the other character of the parent does not express in the F_1, but the F_1 is a hybrid consisting of both the characters. The character which is expressed in the F_1 is called dominant character while the other which is not expressed is known as recessive character. When the F_1 individuals are intercrossed, the parental characters appear in 3:1 ratio in the F_2 generation. The appearance of the parental character in the F_2 is due to the segregation of dominant and recessive characters in the gametes of the F_1 hybrid.

The dominant character is represented by the capital letter while the recessive by the small letter. These characters are now known to be carried on chromosomes as genes. They occupy some locus on homologous chromosomes. The gene which suppresses the expression of another gene is known as recessive gene. When a given locus is occupied by the dominant gene, the individual is said to be pure dominant, if it is occupied by the recessive gene it is said to be pure recessive. If they differ it is known as heterozygote. The dominant and recessive character cannot be determined directly but by making only a cross and observing the offspring produced.

Incomplete dominance

The dominant and recessive relation is not a rule in a pair of contrasting characters. Sometimes a blending of 2 characters may occur. In other words, full dominance does not take place in some cases and hybrids are intermediate type between the two parents. This is known as incomplete dominance or blending inheritance. The classical example of incomplete dominance is the inheritance of the plumage colour in Andalusian fowl.

In a cross between the black and white (homozygous) Andalusian fowl, the F_1 hybrid consists of both black and white markings and it is intermediate between the two parents. In this cross one character is not fully dominant over the other. Both the allelic genes are equal in strength so that one gene does not completely suppress the action of other gene. This phenomenon is known as Incomplete dominance or partial dominance. When the F_1 individuals are intercrossed the F_2 generation consists of parental types and intermediate types : one black, 2 intermediate and one white. The Mendelian monohybrid ration 3:1 (phenotypic) is modified into 1:2:1 in the above cross due to incomplete dominance. The black and white F_2 individuals are homozygous while the intermediate types are heterozygous.

The 4 O'clock plant (*Mirabilis jalapa*) affords another example of incomplete dominance. A cross between its two varieties, pure of red (RR) and white flowers (rr), results in a third variety having pink flowers (Rr) in the F_2 generation. These pink hybrids on self fertilization produce offsprings in the ratio of 1 red : 2 pink : 1 white.

10

CHROMOSOMES AND SEX DETERMINATION

Sex Chromosomes

In species where the two sexes are distinct, certain chromosomes (usually one or two) in a diploid cell differ from the rest in staining reaction as well as behaviour during cell division. These chromosomes are concerned with the determination of sex of the individual. They are thus called sex-chromosomes, while the rest of the chromosomes are referred to as autosomes. The sex chromosomes differ in size and behaviour from ordinary chromosomes. The sex chromosome may be smaller than the autosome and often appears hookshaped. In species of hemipteran insect (Lygeus) the immature germ cells have 12 autosomes (or AA composed by six pairs of homologous chromosomes) and in addition one pair made up of one X-chromosome and one Y-chromosome.

Sex Determination

The process whereby offsprings are caused to be either male or female is known as sex-determination; the chromosomes afford the machinery or mechanism of sex determination.

We can classify the possible types of sex-determination as follows : (1) Epigamic – the sex is determined after the zygote is formed; (2) Syngamic – it is determined at the time of fertilization; (3) Progamic – it is determined before the egg is fertilized.

1. Epigamic sex determination

Before chromosomal mechanism of sex determination was discovered there were a number of non genetic theories based upon epigamic supposition.

(i) Freshness and staleness of the egg

Some people believe that an egg fertilized shortly after ovulation tends to develop into a female, while that delayed in fertilization tends to develop into a male.

(ii) Vigour of the parents

Some people believe that the sex of the child depends upon the relative vigour of the parents. The stronger parent impresses his or her sex to the offspring.

(iii) Nutrition theory

Some people are of opinion that the sex of the offspring depends upon the nutrition of the embryo.

(iv) Male and female producing egg

Some people believe that the right ovary produces male producing eggs. This theory fails in birds where there is only left ovary.

2. Syngamic sex determination

The modern theory indicates that sex is determined syngamically or at the time of fertilization.

(i) Theory of heterogamesis

Correns (1906) advanced this theory and he was the first to demonstrate the sex according to the law of segregation. The female is homozygous and recessive, the male is heterozygous and dominant. The cross is as follows :

P_1	Male	Female
	M f	f f
Gametes	M f	f f
	M f (male)	f f (female)

Chromosomal mechanism of sex determination

Today Biologists believe that the sex is determined at the time of fertilization by the type of gametes. The difference in sex is due to the difference in their chromosomes. In 1901 Mc Clung first reported that in the testes of certain Grasshoppers there was an odd-shaped apparently unpaired chromosome which he thought, was a sex determiner. The odd chromosome is now called the sex chromosome. The sex determination was first worked out by E.B. Wilson and one of his students, Miss N.M. Stevens. Stevens in 1907 and 1908 studied the meiosis in Drosophila and found the importance of sex chromosome in sex determination. The chromosomes which determine the sex of the organism are known as sex chromosomes while all other chromosomes are called autosomes. Since the sex chromosomes of a male differ in size and shape from the female, they are also called heterosomes.

The chromosomal mechanism of sex determination can be studied under two heads:

(A) Role of sex chromosomes in sex determination;

(B) Role of autosomes in sex determination.

A. Role of sex chromosomes in sex determination

In animals the following two types of sex chromosomal mechanism exist for the determination of sex:

(i) XX and XY types types of sex determination

(XY type) (A = autosomes)

Parents 2A + XY 2A + XX

A + X A + Y A + X A + Y

Offspring – A + X A + Y

A + X 2A + XX2A + X

Female Female

A + Y 2A + XY 2A + XY

Male Male

50 : 50

In most animals, the male is heterogametic while the female is homogametic. The female is composed of identical pair of chromosomes called X chromosome. The male, however, possesses only one X chromosome whose partner is the Y chromosome. The male carries unlike sex chromosomes (XY). Hence it is said to be heterogametic, and produces two types of gametes. The female carries similar sex chromosomes (XX) and hence said to be homogametic sex, and produces one type of gamete. The female consists of diploid set of autosomes and 2X chromosomes (2A + XX). It produces only one kind of X, all of which contain haploid set of autosomes and one X chromosome (A + X). The male consists of diploid set of chromosomes and an unequal pair of XY chromosomes (2A + XY). The male produces two types of sperms in equal proportion. Male determining sperm consists of haploid set of chromosomes with Y chromosome (X+Y), the other female determining consisting of haploid set of autosomes with one X chromosome (A+X). The egg fertilized by the sperm containing and X will produce female with diploid set of chromosomes and XX, and egg fertilized by the sperm containing Y will produce a male with diploid set of autosomes and XY. Male and female will be produced in equal number, 50 : 50. Sex is determined by the type of the sperm entering the ovum.

In Birds and Lepidoptera (Moths and Butterflies) the female is heterogametic XY or XO and the male is homogametic XX. The sex determining mechanism in this case is reversed so that birds lay two kinds of X, one producing male and the other producing female.

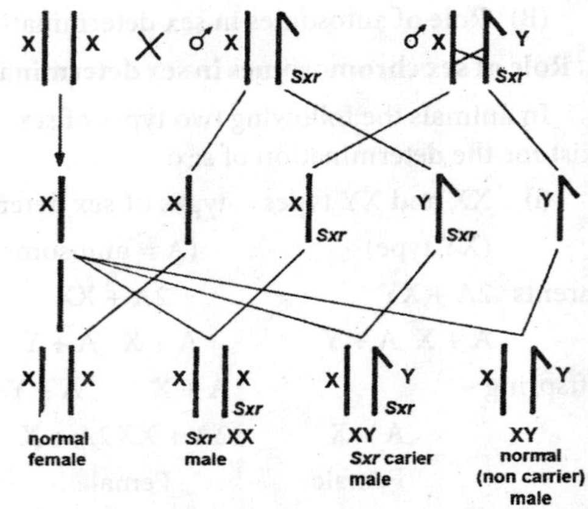

The inheritance of sex reversal gene *Sxr* carried by Y chromosome (note its transfer to X chromosome due to crossingover)

XO and XY type of sex determination : In this type the female is usually XX and the male is XO. The O indicates the absence of the Y chromosome in male. Both sexes will have the same number of autosome for example, in Pyrrhocoris (Bug) the male has 22 autosomes and IX chromosome and the female has 22 autosomes and 2X chromosomes.

As in the above type, female is homogametic and male is heterogametic. All the eggs produced by the female contain haploid set of autosome and an X chromosome. The male produces two types of sperms. Half of them contain haploid set of autosome and X chromosome and another half contain haploid set of autosome and lack the X chromosome. In this case also the sex is determined by the type of the sperm entering the egg. The determination of sex is quantitative and not qualitative. The sex is determined not by the Y chromosome but by the doses of X. If the zygote has IX chromosome it will develop into a male. If it has 2X chromosomes it will develop into a female.

The role of X chromosome in sex determination is proved by the following experimental genetics.

Experiments in Genetics : (i) Non disjunction of X chromosome; (ii) Gyunandromorphs and (iii) Polyembryony.

1. Non -disjunction of X chromosome

Bridges in 1916 clarified the role of X chromosome in sex determination by the phenomena of non-disjunction of X chromosome in Drosophila.

Occasionally it has been found that during the reduction division of the egg the X chromosome fails to separate (disjoin) and therefore passes to the same pole. As a result of this two types of eggs are formed; one type containing XX and the other type without X chromosome. This phenomenon of non separation of X chromosome during meiosis is referred to as non disjunction of X chromosome.

The non-disjunctional egg (XX) when fertilized by X sperm gives super females (3X), most of which fail to survive and with Y sperm gives normal female. Similarly the egg lacking an X chromosome (O-egg) gives with X-sperm exceptional male and Y sperm lethal zygotes which fail to develop. The exceptional male without X chromosomes are sterile.

When the exceptional female is crossed with a normal male it produces both exceptional male and female. The exceptional female gets its 2X chromosomes from her mother and exceptional male receives its X chromosome from his father. It is also proved that Y chromosome has no role in sex determination. But it is necessary for male fertility. Bridge's discovery of exceptional male and female by non-disjunction gives a striking proof to the doses of X chromosome in sex determination – one dose of X produces a male and two doses of X produce a female.

Non-disjunction of X chromosome is also noticed in human beings. This causes some abnormalities relating to sex and expression. In human beings one X without Y is an undeveloped female with no ovaries. In Drosophila one X is a male. In human beings XXY is a male and the Y chromosome in man is not inert and is capable of giving male phenotype while in Drosophila XXY is a female.

The non-disjunction occurs not only in X chromosome but also in autosomes. This phenomenon can occur in many animals including man. It has recently been found in some human beings 47 chromosomes instead of normal 46 chromosome. This is due to the non-disjunction. This phenomenon generally occurs in the egg cells upon fertilization, the zygote will get 47 chromosomes. This additional chromosome causes Mongolism, a serious neurological disorder.

2. Gynandromorphs

The role of X chromosome in sex determination was further confirmed by Gynandromorphs. Morgan and Bridges (1919) discovered this phenomenon in Drosophila. Gynandromorphs or mixed sex, having some parts of the body genetically and structurally like a female. This phenomenon is well known in insects, birds and mammals. The Drosophila noticed by Morgan and Bridges had the left half of the body like a female with the XX chromosome and the right half like a male with an X chromosome. Such animals are known as gynandrous or gynandromorphs. These animals are entirely different from intersex. The intersex is an abnormal individual which is intermediate between the male and female in characteristic and all their body cells are identical in genetical composition.

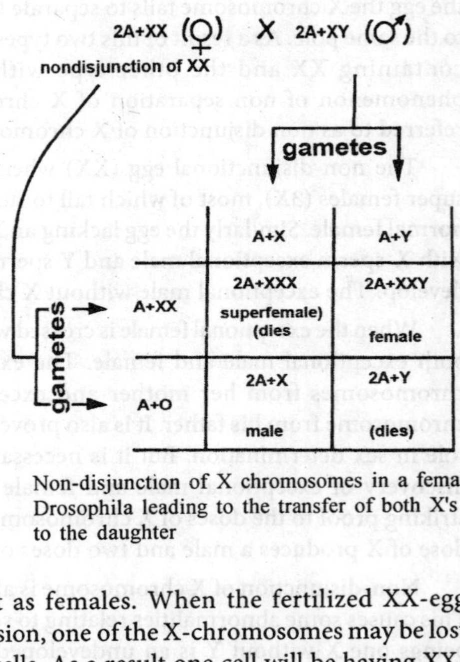

Non-disjunction of X chromosomes in a female Drosophila leading to the transfer of both X's to the daughter

Gynandromorphs start as females. When the fertilized XX-egg divides, often at the first division, one of the X-chromosomes may be lost in one of the two daughter cells. As a result one cell will be having XX-chromosomes and the other one X-chromosome. The cell having XX-chromosomes will develop into the female half of the body while the other cell with one X-chromosome will develop into the male half of the body.

The Drosophila noticed by Morgan and Bridges was heterozygous for white eye, a sex-linked character. In the Gynandromorph the female half of the body had red eyes, while in the male half of the body, white eye.

Thus the Gynandromorphs greatly strengthened the concept that the sex of every cell of the body is determined independently by its own number of chromosomes.

3. Polyembryony

The role of sex chromosomes in sex determination was further confirmed by polyembryony. Generally, only one individual is developed from a zygote. But sometimes more than one individual are developed from a single zygote. This phenomenon is known as Polyembryony. Such individuals are all of the same sex. The development more individuals from a single zygote is due to fission at some early stage of development.

Human identical twins derived from a single zygote are always of the same sex (monozygotic twins). Monozygotic twins in human beings is the simplest case of Polyembryony. Armadillo, the American mammal is the best example of Polyembryony. And always it has identical quads (four) from a single zygote. The more striking case of Polyembryony is found in parasitic Hymenoptera (insects) where upto 200 embryos may arise from one zygote.

Role of autosomes in sex determination (Genic Balance theory of sex determination)

Sex depends upon a large number of genes and these are distributed throughout all the autosomes and sex chromosomes. But the sex genes in the X are of such a nature that one dose of them in conjugation with the autosomes causes one sex to develop two doses, again in conjugation with the autosomes – the opposite sex. This was pointed out by E.B. Wilson (1909).

It is believed that both the autosomes and X-chromosomes have a hand in the determination of the sex. The X-chromosomes carry the genes for femaleness and the autosomes for maleness. In other words, the determination of sex is a matter of genic balance. This theory was propounded by Bridges in 1921, and is known as Genic Balance theory of sex determination. The Y-chromosome contains a few genes and is not concerned in sex determination.

Sex is determined by the number of X-chromosomes in relation to the numbers of haploid set of autosomes. The female has two haploid set of autosomes and 2X chromosomes (2A+XX). The male has two haploid set of autosomes and none X-chromosome (2A+XY). This indicates that an X-chromosome has a female determining strength of 1.5 and a haploid set of autosomes (A) has a male determining strength of one. 2A+XY is a male because the male determining strength is 2 and the female determining strength in one X-chromosome is 1.5. In this the single X is not strong enough to overcome the male tendency located in the autosomes, hence 2A+XY is a male. 2A+XX is a female because the male determining strength in the two sets of autosomes is 1+1=2 and total female determining strength in 2X chromosomes is 1.5+1.5=3. In this case the double dose of the female tendency is strong enough to overcome the male tendency of autosomes, hence 2A+XX is a female.

The genic balance theory of sex determination was experimentally proved by Bridges from his work with triploid Drosophila. The triploid female is represented as 3A+3X. It is produced by the union of normal X autosome sperm and an egg which through some accident in cell division came to have 2X chromosomes and two sets of autosomes instead of one each.

The triploid female produces various types of eggs. Some of them have one X and two sets of autosomes (2A +X). When this egg is fertilized by the normal X containing sperm (A+X) it gives rise to 3A + XX which is sexually intermediate between the normal male and female. Such individual is known as Intersex. The intersexes are sterile. In Drosophila

Table: Different doses of X-chromosomes and autosome sets and their effect on sex determination in Drosophila.

Ploidy level	Number of X chromo-somes	Sets of auto-somes (A)	X/A ratio	Sex
Diploid	3	2	1.50	Superfemale
Triploid	4	3	1.33	
Haploid	1	1	1.00	Female
Diploid	2	2		
Triploid	3	3		
Tetraploid	4	4		
Triploid	2	3	0.67	Intersex
Tetraploid	3	4	0.75	
Diploid	1	2	0.50	Male
Tetraploid	2	4	0.50	
Tetraploid	1	3	0.33	Supermale

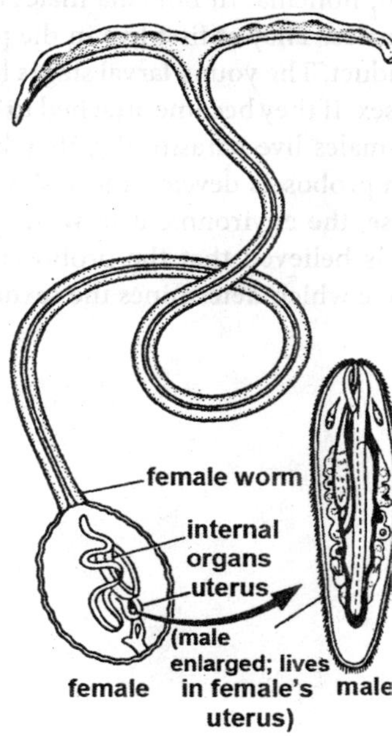

A female and a male insect *Bone.lia,* showing that the male lives in the uterus of the female

3A+2X is not a female. It is intersex. The intersex differs from the normal female (2A+XX) only in the presence of an extra set of autosomes, which, therefore, must carry the male factors which cause the intersexuality.

2A+XXY is a female even though the Y chromosome is present. This also indicates that they Y-chromosome does not take part in sex determination as is described by Bridges as 'neutral'.

The work of Goldschmidt on the gypsy moth made a valuable addition to our information on the chromosomal mechanism of sex determination. This intersect shows remarkable dimorphism. Goldschmidt found that the offsprings of matings between males and females from any geographic locality consist of males and females only. But if strains of European origin are crossed with those of Japan, the progenis contain some intersexes. To account for these results he supposes that the sex in the gypsy moth is determined by the interaction of factors for maleness carried in the X-chromosome and factors for femaleness carried in the cytoplasm. These factors vary in strength. In any one race the strengths of these factors are so adjusted by prolonged natural selection. That two doses of maleness carried in 2X-chromosomes dominate the femaleness, and gives rise to a normal female. However the sex factors are relatively weak in European and strong in Japanese strains so that XY individuals that should become females turn into intersexes.

Environments rather than chromosomes may also determine sex in a worm, Bonellia. In Bonellia males are very small in comparision with the females. They at first live in the proboscis of the female and later in her oviduct. The young larval stages have the capacity of developing into either sex. If they become attached to the proboscis of an adult female, on which males live parasitically, they become males. Those which fail to reach a proboscis develop more slowly and usually become females. In this case, the environment in which the larvae develop determines the sex. It is believed that the proboscis of the female contains a sort of hormone which determines the sexual traits of the larvae.

11

GENE

Johnasen (1909) derived the term gene from Darwin's word 'pan-gene' by dropping the first syllable. It was used to express the Mendelian unit 'factor', 'determiner', element or allelomorph which "grow", reproduce themselves auto catalytically and undergo non- contaminative segregation and are distributed to individuals of the next generation through the chromosomes which 'synapse' 'cross over' and assort into germ cells.

Gene (Gk, genos = race) is actually the basic concept of Genetics like the atom, proton and electron of the physical sciences. The gene of most of the authors and the 'pan-alles' of Dawson and Whitehouse(1952) have never been observed directly. Their existence is concluded from their expression. We can believe in the material and physical basis of the existence of gems, for breeding experiments have shown them to be the "causative factors" for their various characters present in an adult. They have been regarded by most of the geneticists of today as the unit of function related all to the morphogenetic process of embryo and hence to the characters of adult. Many regard them as the material basis of inheritance.

The study of the integrated dynamics of life - the morphogenetic and phylogenetic concepts about various organisms, the developmental and evolutionary trends of their ontogeny and both the classical and modern considerations of all the major aspects of Genetics such as mutations, sex-determination. Mendelian inheritance, Heterosis, etc., all revolve round the vital problem of the nature of the gene and gene action.

There are several genes in each chromosome. It has been estimated that there are about 40,000 genes in a human cell which contains 23 pairs of chromosomes. This is possible because these hereditary structures are very minute. Gene has been estimated to occupy about a millionth of a millimeter distance on a chromosome. Gene in the same chromosome are said to be linked.

Position of the Genes

The position of a gene in the chromosome is known as its locus. The basic assumption is that gene has a real existence. Goldschmidth (1940) while discussing the theory of gene considers gene not to be a corpuscle but a relational condition in a major structure. However most of the authors including Wright (1945), Whitehouse and Darwin in (1952) and Sayar (1953) believe in the existence of genes as real organic particles. Nearly all consider that they are lodged on the 'backbone' of the chromosome known as chromonema embedded in their own chromatin material (the chromomere). These chromomeres are arranged in a linear fashion. The linear arrangement of genes has been shown by crossing over experiments, and on this basis Wright (1945) has defined the Mendelian gene as a block of self duplicating chromosomal material which is not divided during the process of crossing over or chromosome breakage and rearrangement. Thus genes are considered as units in crossing over, which occur between them and through them.

The earlier workers considered gene as an organized complex of ultramicroscopic organic molecules occupying specific places. It is to be noted that more than one gene may be present at one locus. They have been called as multiple genes or 'multigenes' by Sayar (1953). There were groups of genes arranged in sets, only one member of the set being ordinarily on the linear file. All other genes, it seems are held together by some form of bond or attachment. A single gene may occur in several different forms or states called alleles. Many genes have only two alleles, each of which controls and alternative expression of the same trait. For instance, blue and brown eyes in human beings are alternative expressions of the same trait. The two alleles of a gene may frequently be related to each other as dominant and recessive. Frequently, a gene may show a sudden change in state is called mutation and the new allele consequently formed is known as a mutant. A mutant gene causing death is known as lethal gene. Genes on one chromosome may be transferred to another. This may be a result of crossing over during meiosis or due to translocation.

Duplication of each chromosome during mitosis is preceded by self-duplication of genes of that chromosome. Self-duplication of genes is called replication. Thus, segregation of chromosomes is preceded by replication of genes.

Chemical Nature of Genes

According to Koltzoff genes are of protein nature. Most of the genochemists consider them to be lipo-proteins. Ii is very unlikely that genes are formed of basic proteins, because these substances, are not sufficiently complex to give the possibilities of high specific characteristic of the genes. The genes may be provisionally accepted as being a protein molecule, consisting fundamentally polypeptide chains. It is admitted that Deoxyribose Nucleic acid (DNA) which has been shown by many to enter into genetic control may form the chemical base of the gene.

It is possible to find out the number of nucleotides in a gene if the molecule weight of the gene is known, since each base pair has a molecular weight of about 600. Thus in the bacteriophage T4. which has over a 100 genes and a chromosomal molecular weight of 120 million, each gene has an average MW of 1.2 million.

Duplication of Genes

Since genes are segments of the DNA molecule, it follows that the gens will undergo duplication when the DNA molecule replicates. This occurs during the interphase preceding mitosis. The two strands of the DNA double helix separate from each other. In sexually reproducing forms all the cells in the body have been ultimately derived from the zygote, and therefore normally have identical gene sets.

When regarded analytically, the gene multiplication is not some sort of swelling or division but consist of an actual, building up of a new gene by the side of the old and in the damage of the old gene itself. Some picturise gene as a crystalline body, whose autocalytic growth is by surface condensation of constituent simpler materials from the surrounding medium. The reproduction of gene is pictured as a simple split of this fibrous crystal when its growth has exceeded the size limits. Wright (1945) in agreement with other workers has opined that genes somehow act as a model on which a daughter gene is formed as a whole. Nucleic acid regeneration has beer, thought to be connected with this in some way or the other.

Importance of Gene Reproduction

The sporophytic organisms arises from zygote which has in itself the chromosomes - the latter possessing two representatives of each cone locus. During the course of development each cell gets the replica of each gene complement. Thus it has to reproduce many times. Muller (1938) considers gene as the basis of life not merely because it can reduplicate itself exactly, but just as much because it undergoes mutation without losing the power of reduplication.

Gene Action

Genes act by controlling the structure and rate of production of specific protein, (enzymes). The DNA of each gene forms a complementary mRNA strand, which attaches to the ribosome. Here it serves for arranging tRNA molecules in a specific sequence. Each tRNA molecule brings with it a specific aminoacid. Thus the sequence of aminoacids is determined by the sequence of nucleotides in mRNA. This in turn is determined by the sequence of nucleotides in DNA (gene). Since the structure of the enzymes is controlled by the genes it follows that genes determine traits.

Gene Regulation

Jacob and Monod (1961) proposed the operon model to explain the control of gene activity. It was assumed that there are three kinds of gens, structural genes, operator genes and regulator genes. Structural genes produce mRNA. Operator genes control structural gens by acting as switches in controlling mRNA synthesis by the latter. Regulator genes produce substance which block the operator genes. These different types of genes together constitute the operon.

Gene Mutations

Gene mutations have been considered of great value, and mutation is considered sudden and discrete change in gene, not the loss of it. It has been found that different genes have different rates of mutation. It may occur at any point in life history of an organism but usually during or before maturation of germ cells. The mutated gene being recessive effect is most common. Only by virtue of selection the rare advantageous one gets established and helps in evolution. To account for gene mutations various authors have given various speculations about genes.

Muller and others, who have worked on X-ray induced mutations, concluded that gene is a very stable molecule that is, combination of atoms with definite positions and electronic configurations in which an influx of energy from outside or oscillations within produce change of equilibrium of atoms of a molecule.

On the contrary there is the hypothesis of Anderson and Eyster who regard genes as composed of constant number of genomeres or genic elements which may or may not be identical. Thomspon hypothesised that gene consists of a main particle anchored in chromosomes, the protusomes to which a number of one or more particles, the episomes are attached and mutation is regarded as loss or addition of one or more episomes. Goldschmidt opined that are not free molecules and he alluded the possibility that quantity of gene might turn out to be the number of links in chain molecules.

Mutations may be intragenic or point mutation or intergenic. Point mutations include alternations in the structure of the DNA molecule within a gene. Intergenic mutation, of which chromosomal changes in structure are examples, involve long regions of DNA, that is many genes. Mutations occur much more frequently in certain regions of the gene than in others. Mutations involving single nucleotide can revert to normal gene structure. Mutations which occur under natural conditions are called spontaneous mutations.

Gene Control

Genes Control nearly all the characters of an organism either directly or indirectly. They have been shown to control the orientation of the planes of cell division of various algae. Genes may control one character such as shape or colour of an organ (known as substance genes) or may control the biological pattern (pattern gens).

Goldschmidt (1938) argued in favour of quantitative control that is, different allelomorphs producing differing amounts of an enzyme which catalyze the same reaction to different degrees of catalyze different reactions. Sinnott and Dunn (1936) and Whaley (1942) have shown that shape of fruits and leaves are under the control of genes.

A gene is related to a character through a chain of processes to which behaviour at each level determines structure at the next while this gives a secure basis for behaviour at higher level. In fact each character is always affected by many genes as well as by environmental factors and each gene in general has multiple factors. Beadle and his coworkers and Jervis (1947) stated that a gene may be specific for one reaction and there is one to one correspondence between genes and enzymes. Bridges (1938) points out to the importance of linkage studies that is, the manner in which various genes are linked together. He thinks that these studies will throw light on the interaction of adjacent and neighboring genes in producing joint effects, on the different of phenotypic characters, affected by adjacent genes, and on the general distribution of the genes affecting a given character.

Supplementary Genes

The supplementary genes are two separate dominant genes located in different homolgous chromosomes and they interact together to produce a new phenotype. This interaction of genes was discovered by Bateson and Pinnet in Fowls.

Complementary Genes

Two or more dominant genes, neither of which can produce its effect unless the other is present. These gens complement each other and work as a team to produce a specific character. Such collaborative genes are known as complementary gens. These individually have similar effect but when together cause a different effect.

Duplication Genes

When two pairs of genes produce the same phenotype, they are known as duplicate genes. 1n this case the effect of one gene cannot be distinguished one from the ether.

Triplicate Genes

Triplicate genes are three dominant genes, any one of which can produce the same phenotypic effect.

Cumulative Genes

Cumulative genes are two pairs of genes that affect the degree of expression of the character. Cumulative genes are similar to duplicate genes. However, the difference between the two is that the duplicate genes produce the same phenotypic effect, while cumulative genes are two pairs of genes that bring about different degrees of phenotypic expression according to the number of vanes that are present. Thus cumulative genes are quantitative in expression rather than qualitative.

Lethal Genes

A gene which causes the early death of its carrier is called lethal gene and the mutation which produces lethal is a mutation. The time of action of the lethal action of the lethal gene may be at any time in the life from gamete to the adult. A gene which cause death to the gamete is said to be gametic lethal. A gene which prevents the development of the zygote is known as zygotic lethal. The lethal genes may also be autosomal lethal genes and sex linked lethal genes.

Genes Controlling Sex

Genes have explained the problem of the occurrence in many species of two different types of individuals - males and females. It is known that whole chromosome having large number of genes rather than single gene controls the sex. However, there are other instances where individual single genes were found to be responsible for the determination or expression of sex. In Drosophila a transformer gene has been identified, which if present in homozygous conditions converts a female into a sterile male, but does not act upon normal male individuals.

Genes and Evolution

Evolution has been considered as change in the nature of the gene or rearrangement of genes. Evolution may be any of the following methods :

1. Through gene-mutation - the natural selection of adaptive mutations or the beneficial mutations. This may be an accidental drift even getting itself established in the population.
2. Through position-effects.
3. Through "block- changes". This may be through either of the following:
   (i) Changes in whole chromosome that is, polyploidy or heteroploidy by which quantity of genes is increased or decreased.
   ii) Change within portions of chromosomes such as translocations, duplications, etc. Due to these changes the genetic composition of the gamete is changed eventually leading to evolution - the microevolution as Goldschmidth prefers to call it.

When the gametic pattern or the gene atmosphere known as 'genotypic meliu' is changed the mode of action of all the genes is changed. This gene atmosphere, as we may call it, may be changed by other factors and it may be considered as of great importance in evolutionary studies. Thus the whole drama of life and evolution is a resultant of the conflicting, play of forces that has arisen out of genes peculiarly opposite properties of multiplying itself unchanged and of mutation.

GENE INTERACTIONS

Two or more different pairs of genes interacting to produce the same trait are called multiple genes or polygenes. Many characters among animals and plants are controlled by such genes. Bateson and Punnett (1900) performed experiments on poultry and concluded that "genes were not separate elements producing distinct individual effects, but they could interact with each other to give rise to altogether new types of phenotypes". According to them the monohybrid and dihybrid ratios (3:1 and 9:3:3:1) are true only when there is full dominance and independent assortment. If the dominance and independent assortment is incomplete the Mendelian ratio will change.

All the biochemical reactions taking place in the cell are subject to intermediate metabolism. The intermediate metabolism convert a precursor substance into end product through a biosynthetic path way which can be represented as follows:

$$\begin{array}{ccc} + & + & + \\ g_1 & g_2 & g_1 \end{array}$$

P (Precursor $\rightarrow$ Enzyme e_1 $\rightarrow$ A $\rightarrow$ Enzyme e2 B $\rightarrow$ Enzyme e3 $\rightarrow$ C $\rightarrow$ and product) In this case if g1 is a mutant gene, the B $\rightarrow$ C will not change. Therefore an organism which has mutation in g1 will have a specific requirement for C.

According to this concept the following genes have been recognized which interact with each other.

1. Complementary genes, (2) Supplementary genes, (3) Epistatic genes (4) Duplicate genes, (5) Modifying genes, (6) Pleiotropic genes, (7) Cumulative genes, and (8) Lethal genes.

1. *Complementary genes* : When two genes independently remain unexpressed but are effective when they interact with each other, are called complementary genes. In this case one gene completes the action of other gene. Interaction of such genes alter the dihybrid ratio to 9:7 in the F2 generation.

2. *Supplementary genes*: When tow or more pairs of genes effect in a combined manner then they are called supplementary gens. It does not act as a determiner but modifies a character determined by a basic gene. The ratio being 9:3:4. The variety of comb-forms found in fowl illustrates the action of supplementary genes. A dominant gen R (having a recessive allele r) controls the formation of rose comb, while another dominant gene p (having a recessive allele p) is responsible for it pea comb. Both these types of combs are dominant over single comb which, therefore, always has the genotype rrpp.
3. *Epistatic genes*: An epistatic gene is one which influences the expression of other gene. Thus any gene or gene pair that masks the expression of another is epistatic to that gene while the gene which is masked is called as hypostatic gene. The ratio being 13:3.
4. *Duplicate genes*: When two pairs of genes, situated on the same loci in different chromosomes are present and either of them is sufficient to produce a single character, such genes are called its duplicate genes. The ration being 15:1. Some duplicate genes act in a similar way, they are thought to have a common origin, perhaps, in the course of evolution. They arose as duplications of original genes and then became slightly different in function result of mutation.
5. *Modifying genes*: A gene which is incapable of producing an effect but can alter the effect of other gene is called as modifying genes. A modifying gene is called suppressor of it suppresses and enhancer if it enhances the visible effect of another gene.
6. *Pleiotropic genes*: When one gene influences more than one character, such genes are called a pleiotropic gene.
7. *Cumulative genes*: When a number of gens collectively influence the characters of other genes then the genes are called as cumulative genes. Cumulative genes are quantitative in expression and act as multiple genes. According to Davenport, skin colour is determined by cumulative alleles. There are many traits in man which involve more than two pairs of cumulative genes. More the number of genes involved in a trait, the greater the variety of its quantitative expression.
8. *Lethal genes*: Some mutant gens create lethal effects that is, the organism is not able to survive. Such genes are called as lethal genes. If a gene becomes dominant, it creates immediate effect is, death of the organisms but some lethal genes have delayed effect and the organism takes time to die.

Epistasis

Owing to dominance, the presence of the recessive allele in a heterozygote may be obscured or hidden. It sometimes happens that what two different genes, which are not alleles, both affect the same par or trait of the organism, the expression of one covers up or hides the expression of the other. A gene that thus masks or prevents the expression of another is said to be epistatic to it, and the gene that is hidden is said to be hypostatic. Epistasis can be of follwing types -

(i) *due to recessive allele* : A hides the effect of B.

(ii) *due to dominant allele* : A hides of effect of B or vice versa. In other case, it can in both the directions also, which means that both genes are mutually expistatic to each other.

In mice, the wild body colour of known as agouti, characterized by bonding of individual hairs. The agouti colour is controlled by a gene, say A, which is hypostatic to recessive allele C. The dominant allele C in the absence of A gives coloured mice. Moreover, in the presence of dominant allele C, A gives rise to agouti, Therefore, CCaa will be coloured mice (CCaa) are crossed with albino (ccAA), agouti mice (CcAa) appear in F1. cc hides the effect of AA and is therefore epistatic.

The complications introduced by epistasis are comparable to those produce by dominance; that is, tow or more genotypes are indistinguishable in appearance. In cases of epistasis, however, there are always two or more genes involved, each of which affects the same part of the organism. This same condition occurred in fowls, but in fowls both genes are expressed, producing a new or different condition of the part. In epistasis, on the contrary, the competition of two genes for expression in one part results in the apparent triumph of one and the suppression of the other, so that the original traits are recovered but in modified ratios.

Position Effect

The chromosomal rearrangement due to duplication, translocation, inversion or deletion cause sometimes phenotypic changes. The changes produced as a result of chromosomal aberration forms "position effects", or in other words, the gene exerts a different effect in its new position which constitute "position effect". The production of bar-eye in Drosophila can be cited as an example of position effect.

According to Lewis the position effect has been classified as of two types :-

(i) Variegated type
(ii) Somatically stable type.

(i) Variegated Type

Muller (1930-41), Gowen and Gay (1934), Schultz (1936), Demerec and Slizynska (1937), Dubinin, Tiniakov (1935), Griffen and Stone (1940), etc. studied position effect on Drosophila. They considered mostly eye colour and bristles. According to them the chromosomal aberration may involve heterochromatin or euchromatin and heterochromatinzation produces variegated position effect. These effects result in somatic instability.

(ii) Somatically Stable Type

The chromosomal aberrations sometimes cause somatically stable position effect which includes barred eye, hairy wings etc. In bar character eyes, the eyes become narrow and number of facet is reduced. This character arise due to duplication of genes.

The following two theories tend to explain the mechanism of position effect :

(i) *Kinetic Hypothesis*: According to this hypothesis "the local interaction, between the gene products of adjacent loci" produces position effect. This means that a single gene call not produce position effect instead the action is influenced by neighbouring genes which produce position effect.

(ii) *Structural Hypothesis*: It assumes that a short of physical change is produced in the gene locus at the time of breaking which causes position effect.

Lethal Genes

A lethal gene is that which produces an effect which departs so sharply from the normal condition that its possessor is unable to survive. Most lethal genes being recessive cause death only when homozygous. Although the victims of lethal genes do not live to reproduce. such genes are being constantly propagated through heterozygous individuals. Different lethal genes differ in the time at which they bring about their lethal effect the time depends upon the development and functioning of the structures, the abnormalities of which cause death. But lethal genes, which cause defects of digestive organs, lungs or kidneys, do not cause death before birth as these structures do not function during embryonic stages. Lethal genes are of wide occurrence among animal and plant species

Lethal genes in Mice: In the house mouse, yellow coat colour is due to a gene Y which is dominant to all genes for other coat colours. It is further known that all yellow individuals are, in fact, heterozygous (YY). When two such individuals are bred together, they always produce offsprings in the ratio of 2 heterozygous yellow : 1 non-yellow, whereas the expected ratio is l pure yellow : 2 heterozygous yellow : 1 non-yellow. The actual ration (2:1), which is of course an unusual ratio, is due to the fact that the homozygous yellow individuals (YY) die in the embryonic stages. The gene Y, in. mouse, is thus lethal, causing death in the homozygous state.

Lethal gene in corn: In plants, the gene for albinism is lethal. Among plants, pigments (chlorophyll) are vital for life processes. Albinism which is known to occur in corn causes early death of the plant. A corn plant, heterozygous for this gene, lives a normal lifespan and propagates this lethal gene; when two such plants are bred together, the offsprings frequently show the albino character. Among animals albinism is not lethal as the pigments do not perform any vital function.

Sex-linked lethal genes: A lethal gene present in a sex chromosome (X) is called a sex-linked lethal gene. The XX females, heterozygous for a lethal gene, pass it on to 50% of their male offsprings, which consequently die as they lack a dominant allele to prevent its lethal effect. Those XX females also pass it on to 50% of their female offsprings, but since the latter have a dominant allele in the other X chromosome (received from the male parent), they survive. In this way, the sex-linked lethal genes disturb the 1:1 sex ratio. Conversely, 2 females : 1 male sex ratio is an indication of the presence of a sex-linked lethal gene.

Intermediate lethal genes: In some cases, the lethal gene is not completely recessive, but intermediate, showing a partial effect in the heterozygous condition. Their effect is, thus, the intermediate genes far flower colour in four o'clock plant.

In domestic fowl, an intermediate lethal gene, when heterozygotous, gives rise to a peculiar condition, called creeper. The "creeper chickens" have short and crooked legs; they are unable to move normally and creep about without lifting their bodies off the ground. The same lethal gene, when homozygous, causes death during the embryonic stages.

In man, several intermediate lethal genes are known. One such gene, when heterozygous, causes a condition; called brachyphalangy. In this condition, the middle bone of each finger is highly reduced and fused with one of the remaining two; the fingers thus appear to have two joints instead of three and are greatly shortened.

Multiple alleles

Most genes occur in two alternative forms or states, both influencing the same trait alternatively and occupying the same locus in homologous chromosomes. Such different forms of the same gene are referred to as "alleles" and are said to be allelic to each other. Some genes, however, may occur in more than two allelic forms. In such cases the various allelic forms are collectively referred to as multiple alleles. A set of multiple alleles may contain three, four, and even upto twenty or more members. All the members essentially occupy the same locus in homologous chromosomes. All the members of a set of multiple alleles are in fact the mutant forms of the same gene.

In a set of multiple alleles, one member is always dominant to all others and one is always recessive to all others, the former as usual, is denoted by a capital letter while the latter is denoted by the corresponding small letter. All the other alleles are also denoted by the corresponding small letter. All the members are written in a series or sequence which is such that each member is dominant to all those which are written after it, and recessive to all those written before it.

Multiple alleles for eye-colour in Drosophila

The gene for eye colour in Drosophila affords a good example of multiple alleles. This gene has a many as fourteen alleles situated in the same locus of the X-chromosome. Of these the gene W for red-eyes is dominant to all others while w for white-eyes is recessive to all others. The other alleles are responsible for intermediate shades between red and white. Same of these alleles arose as mutants from the gene W, while others arose as mutation from other alleles which in turn mutated from W. The entire series of alleles, grading gradually from red (dominant to all) to white (recessive to ail) can be represented as W (red), ww (wine), wco (coral), wt (tinged), wh (honey), Wee (ecru), wp (pearl), wi (ivory) and w (white). These alleles, in various combinations, show intermediate effects for example, a fly with genotype wcoW (heterozygous for "coral" and "white") has eye-colour similar to "apricot".

Multiple alleles for ABO Blood groups in Man

Several genes in man produce multiple allelic series which affect an important physiological characteristic of the human red blood cells. The red blood cells have special properties (antigens) by which they respond to certain specific components (antibodies) of the blood serum.

Landsteiner discovered in 1900 that when the red blood cells of one person are placed in the blood serum of certain other persons, the cells may become clumped or agglutinated. If blood transfusions were made between persons of two such incompatible blood groups, the transfused cells were likely to clump and occlude the capillaries in the recipient, sometimes resulting in death. However such reactions occurred only when the cells of certain individuals were placed in serum from certain other persons. It was found that in respect to blood cells there are two antigens, A and B, and two scrum antibodies that agglutinate them. If A type antigen is present, the blood group is termed A; if B type antigen is present, the blood group is called B; if both the antigens are present, the blood group is called Ab, and if neither is present, the blood group is termed O. The blood group character is controlled by a set of three alleles.

Multiple alleles for Rh factor in Man

Landsteiner, Wiener, Mourant, Levine and others discovered another proteinous substance in the red blood cells of Rhesus monkey. Later, they discovered that the same substance is present in about 85% human beings also. They called this substance as Rh factor after the Rhesus monkey. People having this factor are called Rh positive and those whose blood is devoid of it are Rh negative. The transfusion of Rh positive and Rh negative blood has fatal consequences. Rh negative condition in a woman proves fatal for its second Rh positive child. The first Rh positive child is born normal but during the pregnancy period the mother develops in her blood antibodies against the proteinous substance, the presence of which is referred to as Rh positive condition. When the second child is also Rh positive these antibodies enter the blood stream of the foetus and cause its death. This condition is known as erythroblastosis foetalis.

The Rh factor is determined by a series of four pairs of multiple alleles, which can be designated as R^1, R^2, R^o, R^z, r', r'', r^y, r. The alleles denoted by capital letter give rise to Rh positive condition while the others to Rh negative condition.

GENETIC CODE

In the long molecule of the DNA with numerous pairings of specific bases many permutations of the bases are possible and the precise sequence of bases is the genetic code. Proteins have 20 different kinds of essential aminoacids, nucleic acid has only for different kinds of bases. The 20 aminoacids are the alphabets of the language of proteins. In the same way the four bases are the alphabets of the language of nucleic acids. It is through mRNA that the genetic information is passed on to proteins. Since one is four alphabet language and the other with 20 alphabets, it is not possible that one alphabet (single base) of RNA may be equivalent to a single alphabet (aminoacid) of protein. In that case the alphabets of RNA will be enough far just four aminoacids. If a sequence of two bases of RNA is used for an aminoacid, only 16 (4 Í 4) doublets are possible. Since there are 20 aminoacids to be coded, the doublet code would not be enough, and a minimum of triple code would be required.

singlet code
A
G
C
T

doublet code			
AA	AG	AC	AT
GA	GG	GC	GT
CA	CG	CC	CT
TA	TG	TC	TT

triplet code			
AAA	GAA	CAA	TAA
AAG	GAG	CAG	TAG
AAC	GAC	CAC	TAC
AAT	GAT	CAT	TAT
AGA	GGA	CGA	TGA
AGG	GGG	CGG	TGG
AGC	GGC	CGC	TGC
AGT	GGT	CGT	TGT
ACA	GCA	CCA	TCA
ACG	GCG	CCG	TCG
ACC	GCC	CCC	TCC
ACT	GCT	CCT	TCT
ATA	GTA	CTA	TTA
ATG	GTG	CTG	TTG
ATC	GTC	CTC	TTC
ATT	GTT	CTT	TTT

A singlet code, a double code and a triplet code

Crich (1961) revealed the triplet nature of the code, that is the sequence of 3 bases out of the 4 bases determines the type of protein to be synthesized. According to this triplet system, the 4 bases can be coded in 64 patterns, each directing the synthesis of a specific protein.

The genetic code has the following properties :-

(i) the code is triplet, (ii) the code is degenerate, (iii) the code is overlapping, (iv) the code is commaless, (v) the code is non-ambiguous, and (vi) the cede is universal.

(i) *The code is triplet* : - Singlet and doublet codes are not enough to code for 20 aminoacids, triplet code is the minimum required. In a triplet code of 64 codons, there is an excess of 44 codons, and so, more than one codon are present for the same aminoacid. In a quadruplet code there will be 4×4×4×4 = 256 possible words.

(ii) *The code is degenerate* :- As stated earlier, there are 64 possible codons in a triplet code of which 61 have been shown to code aminoacids. Since only 20 aminoacids take part in protein synthesis it is obvious that there are many more codons than aminoacid type. Except for tryptophan and methionine, which have a single codon each, all other aminoacids involved in protein synthesis have more than one codon. A non-degenerate code would be one where there is one to one relationship between aminoacid and the codon, so that 64, 44 codans will be useless codons.

(iii) *The code is non-overlapping* :- As the DNA molecule is a long chain of nucleotides, it could be read either in an overlapping or non-overlapping manner. The genetic rode could thus be overlapping or non-overlapping. In the non-overlapping code each letter is read only once white in the overlapping code, it would read three times, each time as a part of a different word.

(iv) *The code is commaless* : - It means that no punctuations are needed between any two words. In other words, after one aminoacid is coded, the second aminoacid will be automatically coded by the next three letters and that no letters are wasted for telling that one aminoacid has been coded and that now second be coded.

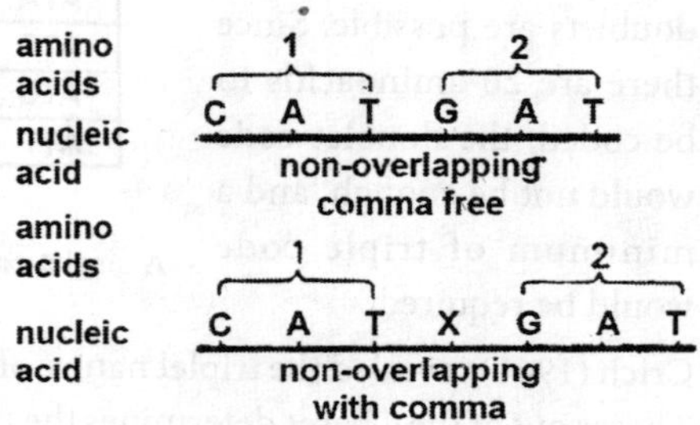

Genetic code, without comma and with comma

(v) *The code is non-ambiguous* :- It means that there is an ambiguity about a particular code, whenever it is found, a particular codon will always code for the same aminoacid. In an ambiguous code, the same codon could have different meanings or in other words the same codon could code two or more than two different aminoacids.

(vi) *The code is universal* :- The genetic code is valid for all organisms ranging from bacteria to man. It is essentially the same for all organisms and is therefore said to be universal. The universality of the code was demonstrated by Marshall, Caskey and Nirenberg (1967), who found that *E. coli* (bacterium), xenopus laevis (amphibian) and guineapig (mammal) amino acyl tRNAs use almost the same code. This showed that the code is essentially universal.

STRUCTURAL ALTERATION (CHANGES) IN CHROMOSOMES

The structural changes in chromosomes are sometimes, loosely referred to as mutation. These changes may or may not involve modifications of chromosome morphology but they alter the hereditary characters of the organism and sometimes raise it to the level of new species or races.

In an organism structural changes may be suspected by evidence from mitotic chromosomes when (i) there is a change in size of the chromosomes, (ii) related changes in size of two chromosomes, (iii) changes in the position of the centromere and (iv) change in the number of chromosomes attributable to fragmentation or due to secondary changes. The changes in the structure of a chromosome may take place bath at mitotic and meiotic phases. During the resting phase of the nucleus, the chromosomes lie inside the nucleus tike a tangle of threads. During prophase, chromosomes are long and slowly disentangle, and arrange themselves for the second stage of cell division. In doing so, sometimes the chromosomes may break and the broken ends of chromosomes reunite giving rise to chromosomes with different gene arrangements. A normal chromosome must have one centromere and two ends. The chromosomes exhibit the peculiar property of uniting at the broken end only and not at chromosome ends. If for any reason, chromosomes break and reunite differently at the broken ends, they cause new arrangement of genes and this in turn may be reflected in the breeding behaviour of the organisms.

Breakage of results in parts of chromosomes becoming separated out of the main one. These are known as fragments. Any fragment that lacks a centromere is incapable of orientation and spontaneous movement on the spindle. They lag and are soon last, being left out of the daughter nuclei. Such fragments lacking or centromere are known as acentric. By misdivision of a centromere, a telocentric chromosome may arise; this is frequently lost in meiosis. By an internal division such a chromosome may acquire two arms and an isochromosome results. An isochromosome has two identical arms.

The centromere is an important entity in the chromosome. When chromosomes break and reunite, the possibilities are : (a) a fragment with centromere may unite with another fragment without centromere, (b) a fragment with centromere may unite with another centric fragment, (c) two-non centric fragments may unite.

Breakage as well as breakage and reunion of chromosomes may involved any of the following types of structural changes, viz., deletion, duplication, simple translocation, Reciprocal transtocation, and inversion.

Small structural changes may not alter the chromosome morphology but large changes maybe detected even in mitotic division of the cell by the following peculiarities : (i) change in the size of chromosome consequent on loss or addition of a segment; (ii) change in the position of centromere; (iii) change in the number of chromosomes.

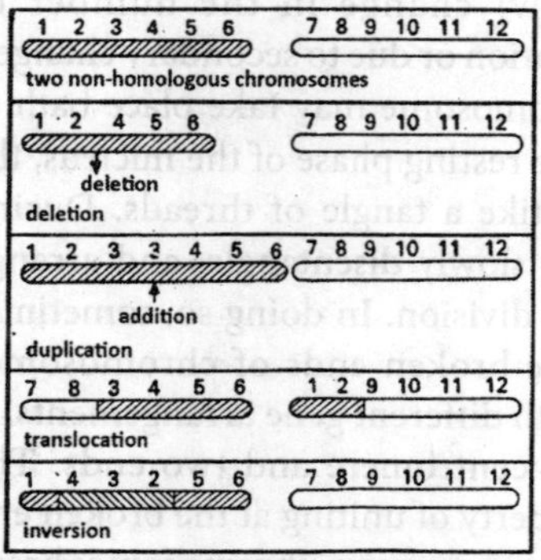

Different kinds of changes in chromosome structure

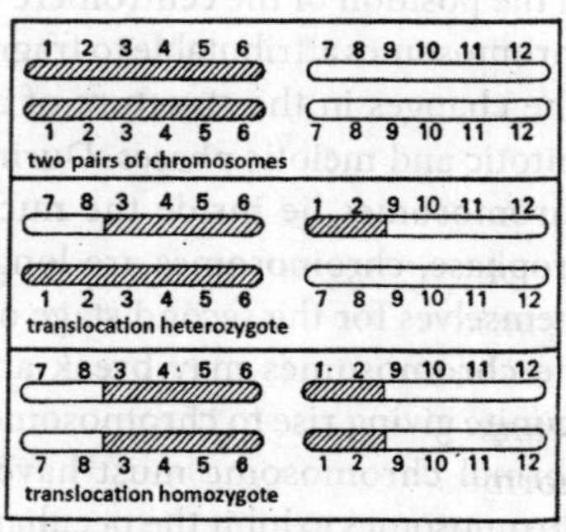

Chromosome constitution of a translocation heterozygote and translocation homoxygote

Any structural change in a chromosome brings about a disturbance in the existing genetic balance.

Deletion

The toss of a terminal segment of a chromosome dividing it into a monocentric and acentric fragment is deficiency. This. is the simplest structural difference since it can affect only one chromosome. Deletion is the loss of an intercalary segment of a chromosome. This requires that the two breaks shall be in the same arm of a chromosome. These two terms are often used as synonyms. These changes are lethal or semilethal and have very little significance in evolution. In this type of structural change, the total gene content of the organism is affected. If ABCDEFG are the genes in a chromosome, then ABCDE is deficiency and ABFG is deletion. When deletion is small, the chromosome may not reveal reduction in size under cytological, observations. Generally, deficiency or deletion survives only when heterozygous. Homozygous deletion proves lethal. In Drosophila, many of the lethal mutations proved to be deletions. Lethal effect of a deficiency or deletion in the haploid or in homozygous diploid proves the importance of even a few genes in the normal development of an organism.

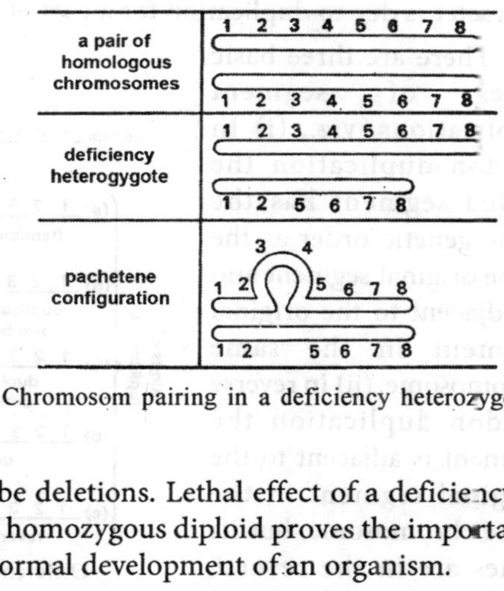

Chromosom pairing in a deficiency heterozygote

Duplication

In a diploid organism, any section of a chromosome is repeated twice. If in addition to this normal condition, a segment is further repeated, it is called duplication. The duplicated segment may be attached to another chromosome. Though duplication leads to increase in the total gene content of the organism, it may sometimes lead to lethal effect. There may be two types of duplications. One type of duplication results from the addition of a segment of a chromosome to a chromosome. Another type results from the addition of a small centric piece of chromosome to a genome. Duplication by the addition of a segment to a chromosome depends upon the breakage in the chromosome since a new chromosome segment cannot fuse with a normal chromosome end.

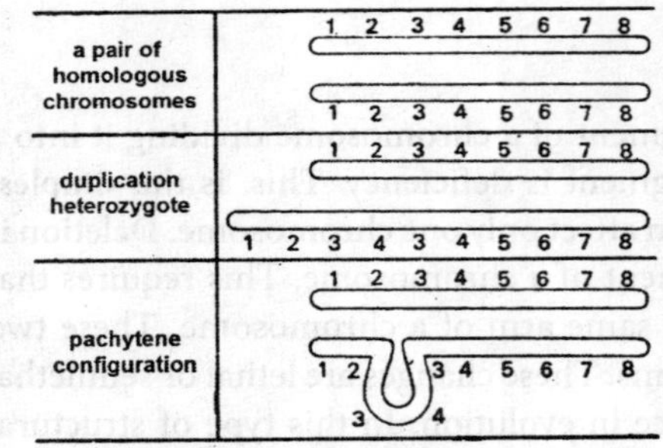

Chromosome pairing in a duplication heterozygote

One of the classical examples of duplication in Drosophila is that of bar eye. Bar eye is a character where the eyes are narrower character is due to duplication for a part of a chromosome.

There are three basic types of segment duplications, viz., (i) In tandon duplication the added segment has the same genetic order as the same original segment and is adjacent to the original segment in the same chromosome. (ii) In reverse tandon duplication the segment is adjacent to the original segment in the same chromosome, but its genes are in the reverse order. (iii) In displaced duplications, 3 segment is inserted into a different chromosome.

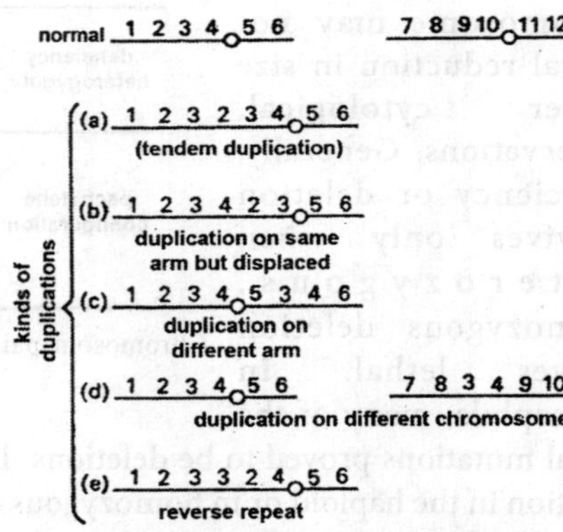

Different kinds of duplications in chromosomes

The effects of duplications on viability are generally less deleterious than those of deficiencies, so that relatively long duplications survive.. The individuals carrying duplications show various abnormalities in bodily characters and when these abnormalities are known they may be used to identify the carriers of the corresponding duplications.

Studies in the salivary gland chromosomes show that in a number of places there are repetitions of sections of genes and these are termed 'repeats'. Duplication leads to the formation of 'repeats'. Dobzhansky and Metz have emphasised the importance of the 'repeats' as the only method other than polyploidy by which the number of genes in a germ plasm may be increased. Duplications also suffer cellular elimination either immediate or delayed.

Inversion

If there is reversal of the linear arrangement of genes in a segment without change in the total gene content, it is termed inversion. In a chromosome ABCDEFG inversion of the segment BCDE will change the chromosome to AEDCBFG. In such inverted segment the centromere may also be included or not. A second inversion may take place inside the first inversion and it is then termed included inversion. The genetic consequence of inversion is suppression of crossing over.

In Diptera inversion can be directly observed in the banding of salivary gland chromosome. In heterozygotes, far inversion, the inverted segment forms a loop to bring the homologous parts opposite to each other for pairing.

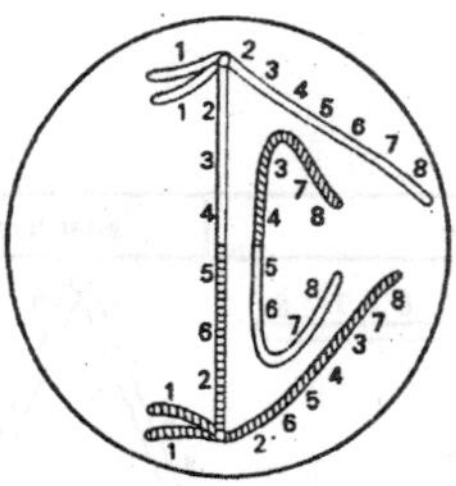

Dicentric bridge and an accentric fragment at ansphase I

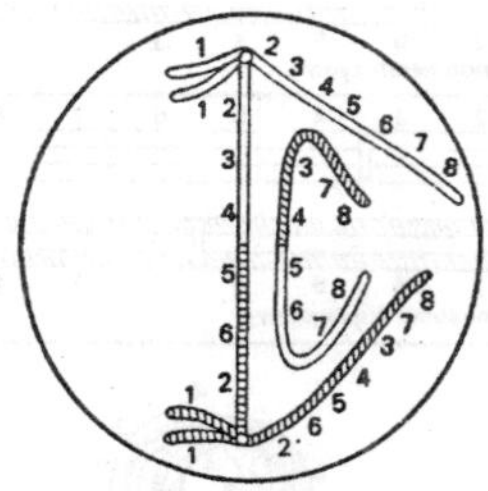

Dicentric bridge and an acentric fragment at anaphase I

The inversion may be paracentric, if the inverted segment does not include the centromere. The inversion may be pericentric. if it includes the centromere.

A simple cross-over within the loops will lead to the formation of four types of chromatids, two resembling the parental ones, one with two centromeres (dicentric) and one without a centromere (acentric). The acentric chromosome has no power of movement during cell division and

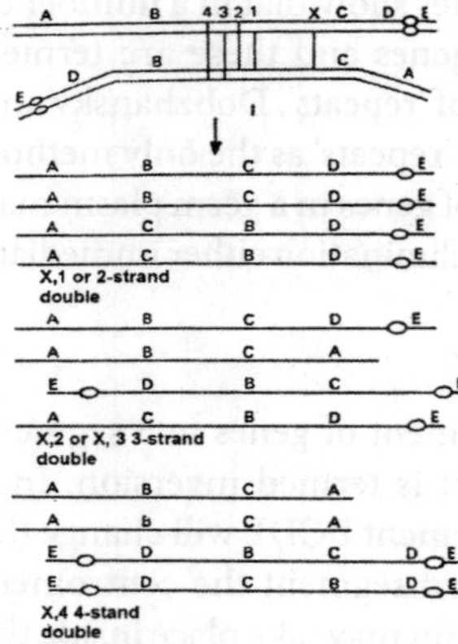

Consequences of 2-strands, 3-strands and 4-stands double crossovers within a paracentric inversion

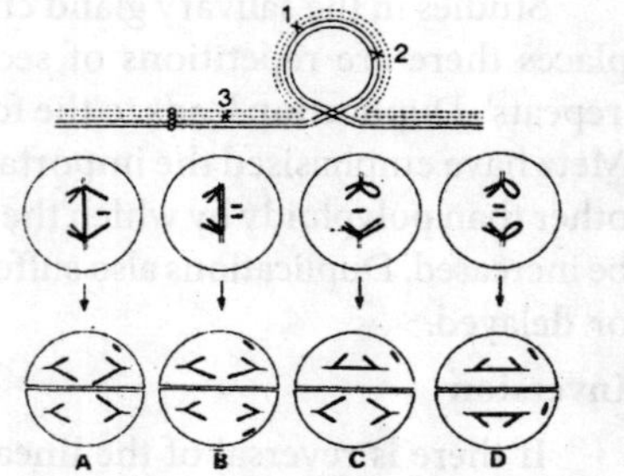

On the top is shown inversion loop in an inversion heterozygote. Below are shown anaphase I (AI) and anaphase II (AII) configurations (A-D) resulting from four different combinations of crossovers within and outside the inversion loop. A. Single crosover at positions 1 or 2; B. 4-strand double crossovers at positions 1 and 2; C. 3-strand double crosovers, with one crosover at position 1 or 2 within inversion loop and the other crossover outside the loop at positions 3; D. 4-strand triple crosover at position 1,2 and 3 (redrawn from McClintock, 1938)

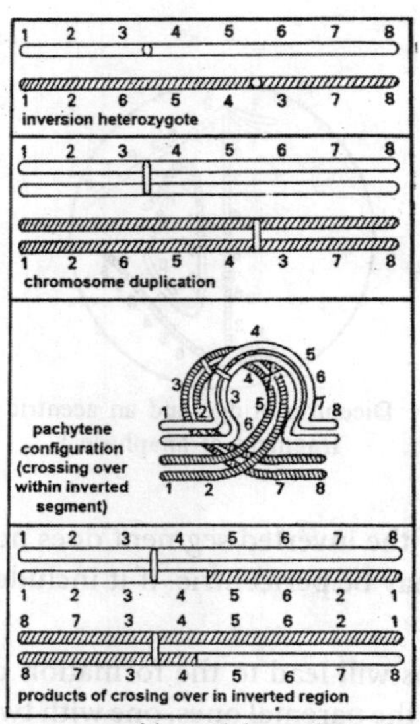

Chromosome pairing and the products of crossing over in a pericentric inversion heterozygote

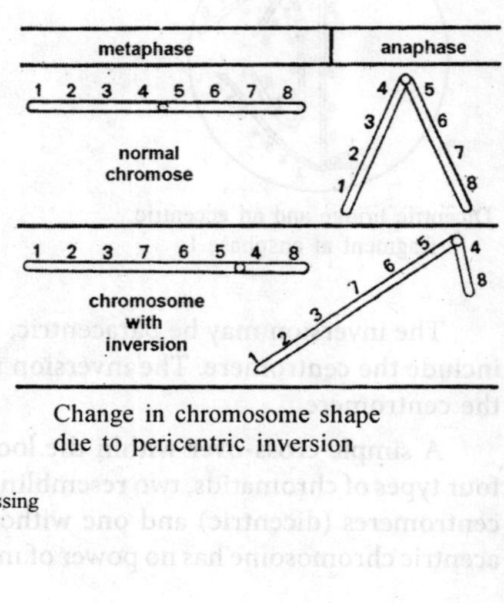

Change in chromosome shape due to pericentric inversion

hence lays as a fragment in the centre of the cell. The dicentric chromatid has two centromeres which pull the chromatids in opposite directions and the whole chromatin is stretched between the two poles forming a chromatin bridge.

Inversion like translocation provided instrument in establishing the species relationship in Drosophila. It has a great evolutionary significance. The major effect of inversions may be to restrict the recombination of gene loci by crossing over to maintain in the population of a specific segment of a chromosome.

Inversions occur in plants as well as in animals and probably appear most often in natural populations.

Translocation

Bridges (1923) first discovered translocation in Drosophila melanogaster. Translocation occurs usually in the chromosome. It results from the transfer of a segment of a chromosome to different part of the same chromosome or to a different chromosome. In the latter case the transfer may take place between homologous chromosomes or between non homologous chromosomes. If, however, this exchange of segment occurs between the non-homologous chromosomes, this translocation is termed as reciprocal and the subsequent meiotic behaviour of the chromosome become altered for a potential genetic effect. When a chromosome breaks due to external or

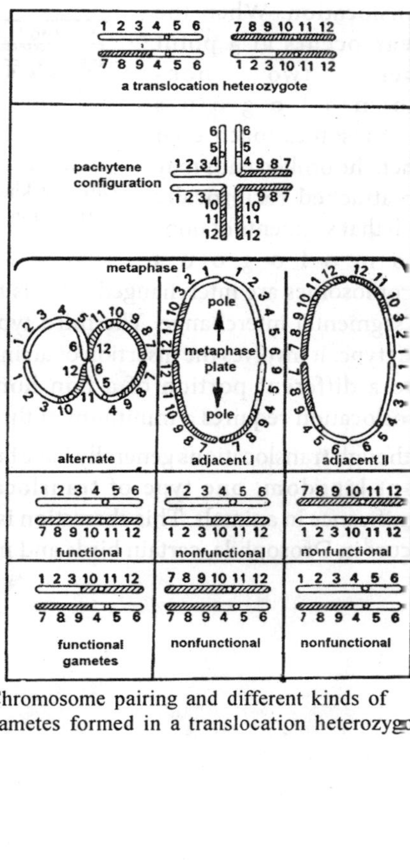

Chromosome pairing and different kinds of gametes formed in a translocation heterozygote

internal stress, the broken segment may get attached to the nearest chromosome which may not be its homologue. This is termed simple translocation. If ABCEFG and TUVWXYZ are two non-homologous chromosomes, the segment FG may be translocated to the other chromosome causing the following simple translocation. When the break occurs at a point where two non-homologous chromosomes touch each other, the broken ends may get attached reciprocally such that segments of non-homologous chromosomes are interchanged. This is termed reciprocal translocation or segmental interchange: The third type of translocation is known as shift type. It involves the insertion of an interstitial piece of a chromosome into a different portion of a non homologous chromosome. Shift translocation requires a minimum of three breaks in the chromosome.

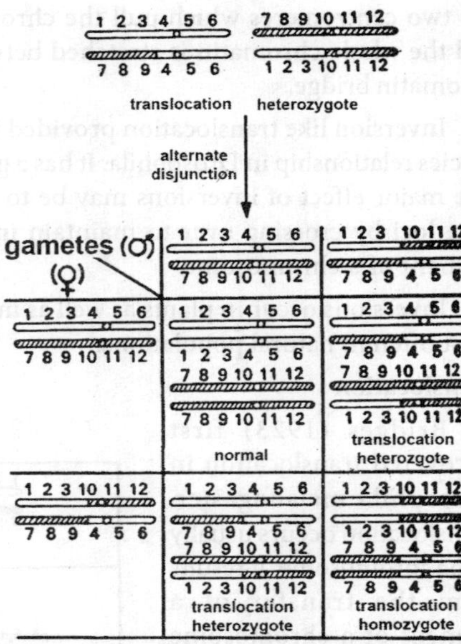

Different kinds of progenies obtained due to self fertilization in a translocation heterozygote

Although translocations generally have been of greater importance in the plant kingdom, one type of translocation has some evolutionary significance in animals. This aberration is described as a centric fusion. It occurs in Drosophila, certain birds and mammals.

UNIT – V
EVOLUTION

12
HISTORY OF EVOLUTION

Present day biologists accept evolution as an explanation of the variety of living forms – plants and animals. The word "evolution" is a Latin one and literally means gradual "unrolling" or "unfolding". Herbert Spencer first used the name evolution to give an explanation of all that was going on in the Universe from the movements of stars to the development of animals and plants from simpler forms. Strictly speaking, evolution has to do with change. And change is almost a law in nature. Evidences show that everything within our comprehension is always undergoing changes at its own accord in every possible direction. Hence evolution may take place in different fields. The origin of the stars and other solar systems of the universe is cosmic evolution ; the gradual change of land masses and climates taking place on earth is geologic evolution ; the transformation from a primitive state of society to a well organized society is a sort of social evolution ; origin of the physical world is inorganic evolution.

Evolution in reference to plants and animals is organic evolution. We are to deal with organic evolution.

Organic evolution may be defined as the gradual development of complex highly organized animals or plants from simple pre-existing animals or plants since the dawn of life on the habitable planet. Perhaps the most concise definition of evolution is found in the expression of Charles Darwin himself : "descent with modification". The primitive and the ancient forms of organisms have undergone gradual modifications or changes to best adapt to the environments as desired by Nature and have evolved or unfolded into more complex living organisms. The change from simple to complex forms is not sudden and accidental but it occurs through a series of slow and steady changes during different ages.

Path of Organic Evolution

When the earth was solidified and sufficiently cooled down, the first speck of living substance – in the nature of complex protein, originated in the sea water about one billion years ago. Gradually by the chemical combination of water and certain organic compounds already present on the earth an organic substance called *Protoplasm* was formed. This protoplasm exhibited the properties of life and marked the beginning of living things on the earth. Through ages protoplasm became differentiated into the units of life known as the "cells". Evidently the first forms of life were very small and unicellular which later differentiated into multicellular forms. As the environmental conditions also changed from time to time these effected the setup of the organisms. There ought to have been many other causes of these changes in the individual, but those were handed over to the offspring and more and more diversified and specialized forms of individuals came into being. Thus out of simple beginnings by a slow but steady and orderly change through centuries the present day forms of animals and plants have been attained. This we call organic evolution. So long there will be life present, evolution will go on and it is still continuing. But this process of evolution is so slow that very little of its sure presence can be seen within the short span of man's life.

Organic evolution is more a law than a theory and is supported by a good number of facts. With the progressive advancement of our biological knowledge it becomes evident that evolution is intermingled with the whole fabric of biological science and without it Biology becomes reduced to a descriptive catalogue of the various animals and plants, an enormous mass of details with no principle to make them into one.

I. Evidence from comparative morphology or anatomy

This can be studied under the following sections:

(1) Classification – its principles: The classification is a sort of scheme for grouping plants and animals according to the actual relationship existing between them and is done on the principle of evolution. There are however, many possible ways of classification of plants and animals. We may classify animals according to their habitats or their diet, without taking into account of their structure. But this method of classification cannot bring out the relationship between the animals, and hence this is untrustworthy and said to be artificial. On the other hand, natural classification seeks to show the blood relationship of animals, to group together those whose similarities are shown by their being like one another in structure or architecture. Similarity in form of structure reflects common ancestral kinship. More related the organisms are, closer become the similarities in form or structure. So, the degree of this similarity in form existing between organisms will also be a measure of the degree of their remoteness from or closeness to common parental stock. In this way the natural classification which depends on the structural resemblance of organs brings out obviously how the different kinds of animals can be derived from ancestral types by their organs being modified in divergent lines, like the branches of a tree.

Now on the principle of classification it is possible to arrange different phyla of the animal kingdom in a series of progressive complexity beginning with Protozoa (unicellular), passing through the Coelenterata (multicellular and diploblastic), Platyhelminthes (triploblastic acoelomates) and Annelida (triploblastic coelomates) and then gradually passing to the Chordates. The Chordates themselves show certain common features at least in the presence of notochord. Again, the Chordates include the Vertebrates. Fishes, Amphibians, Reptiles, Birds and Mammals are the distinctive vertebrates as they all possess a common vertebral column. Although all these grades of vertebrates can be placed in certain definite classes, each class shows many agreement with one or the other of the remaining classes, for example, Amphibia with Fishes, Reptiles with Amphibia, Birds and Mammals with Reptiles. These similarities amongst all the members and classes of the chordates clearly indicate that they are descendants of common ancestor.

Hence a review of the principle of classification will lead us to conclude that the different groups of animals indicate a common ancestral kinship and also a step wise series of gradual changes.

(2) Homologous and Analogous organs : In considering comparative anatomy of plants and animals it would be worthwhile, first of

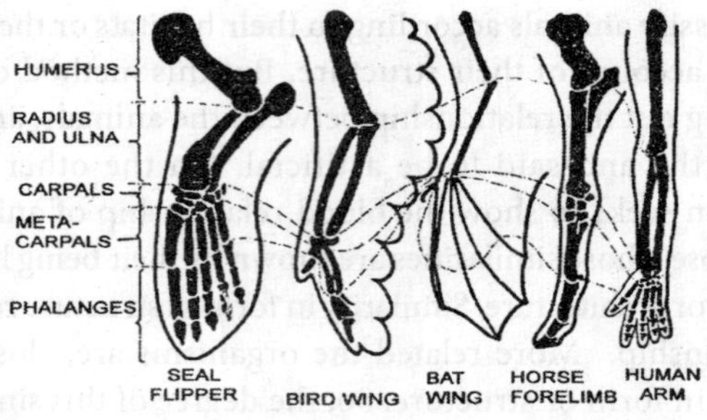

Homology in the forelimbs of seal, bird, bat, horse and man. (apparently different but constructed on the same basic pattern)

all, to distinguish between homologous structures and analogous structures. Homologous structures (Homologos = agreeing) are those which are similar in anatomical structure and embryonic origin though not in their function. Analogous structures (Gr. Analogia = ratio) are those which are functionally similar and, despite superficial resemblance in form, are actually unlike in anatomical structure and embryonic origin. Organs which are similar both in origin and function are spoken of as homo-analogous organs, for example, the wings of birds and bats.

Homologous organs provide strong evidence in support of organic evolution. In this connection some examples of homologous organs can be cited.

(i) Among the invertebrates, the mouth parts of various insects may have diversity in shape, sizes and detail structures due to the varied functions they are to perform. Some may be modified for chewing as in the mouth parts of cockroaches, some may be modified for piercing and sucking as in female mosquitoes, and so on. However, all these mouth parts are homologous structures as they are constructed on a general plan and have the labrum, labium, maxillae, hypopharynx, etc. in common. This necessity of a general plan can only be explained by accepting that all of them inherited their main structural characters from a common ancestral group, but all have undergone different sorts of adaptive modifications.

(ii) Among vertebrates, the fore-limbs of various species show a wide range in adaptive modifications in response to varied functions. In this connection we may assume for a while a prototype or generalized fore-limb from which each of the various vertebrate types of fore-limb has evolved by modification or adaptation to a distinctive mode of life. This prototype fore-limb would be constructed on the pentadactyle (five-toed) plan and would consist of a single bone, the humerus, in the upper arm ; two parallel bones, the radius and ulna, in the lower arm ; eight small bones, the carpals, in the wrist ; five parallel bones, the metacarpals, in the palm ; the three phallanges in each of the digits or the fingers. Let us now keep in the mind this prototype or generalized fore-limb, and start examining the fore-limbs of the toad or salamander, the crocodile, the bird, the bat, the whale, the mole and the man. It will be seen that each fore-limb has the common foundation and that each is at the same time modified or adapted towards the accomplishment of a tentative function in its environment or mode of living. From this it is inferred that the greater the structural similarity, the closer the kinship. In other words, these vertebrates must have had evolved from a common ancestral type (having pentadactyle limbs).

(iii) In the middle ear of mammals there are three ear ossicles known as the malleus, incus and stapes. These pieces of bones are found to be homologous with the articular, quadrate and hyomandibular structures of the lower vertebrates.

(iv) The heart of the toad, lizard, bird and guinea-pig are built on the same general plan in every case. In adaptation to different modes of living the vertebrate hearts have undergone modifications from the normal type. Thus the heart is two-chambered in fishes and is admirably adapted to its aquatic environment. Two-chambered heart of the fish has been modified into the three chambered heart in the toads or frogs (amphibia) but still it is not sufficient to check the admixture of pure and impure blood. In the lizard (reptile) the heart becomes incompletely four-chambered (ventral being incompletely divided). In bird (aves) and guinea-pig (mammal) the heart becomes completely four-chambered with two auricles and two ventricles. And this type of heart is perfectly adapted to separate and direct distinctly the

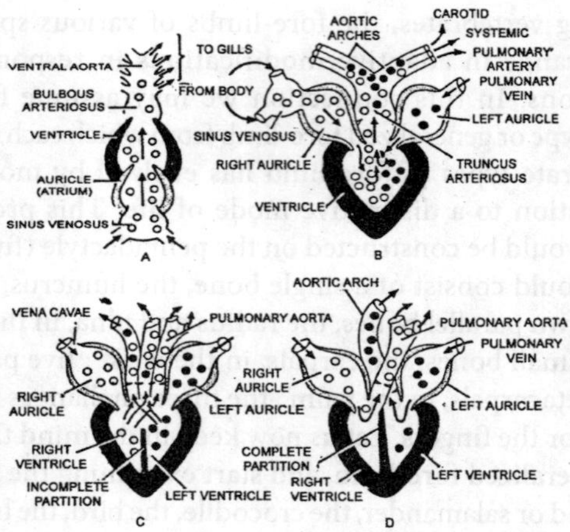

Heart and blood vessels arising from it in the vertebrate series showing homolgy in structure and distribution . A-in fish; B-in amphibian; C-in reptile; D-in mammal.

pure and impure blood to their respective destination. This progressive modification in the structure of the heart in the vertebrate series is a paraphrase of the principle of organic evolution.

(v) The fate of aortic arches in the vertebrate series also furnishes good evidence of organic evolution. Although in course of evolution some aortic arches of vertebrates have disappeared and some have undergone changes, all of them are derivable from a common *hypothetical ancestral type* of aortic arch.

Illustrations of Analogous Structures

Comparative anatomy of the vertebrates, such as the shark (a fish), the ichthyosaur (an extinct reptile) and the porpoise (a mammal) reveals that all of these aquatic vertebrates are superficially alike in having fusiform body and paired and unpaired fins. But again it is seen that these structures, are not similar in their origin. Hence they are analogous organs. Although analogous structures do not imply closeness of ancestral relationship, they however, indicate modification along diversified lines of descent.

(3) Vestigial organs : These are certain structures which were once well developed and useful to the possessor but now, due to the change of

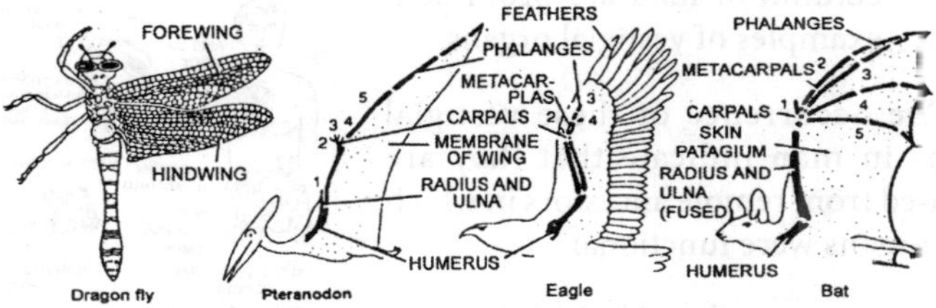

Analogy in the wings of insect, pterodactyle, bird and bat (Apparently similar but constructed on different patterns).

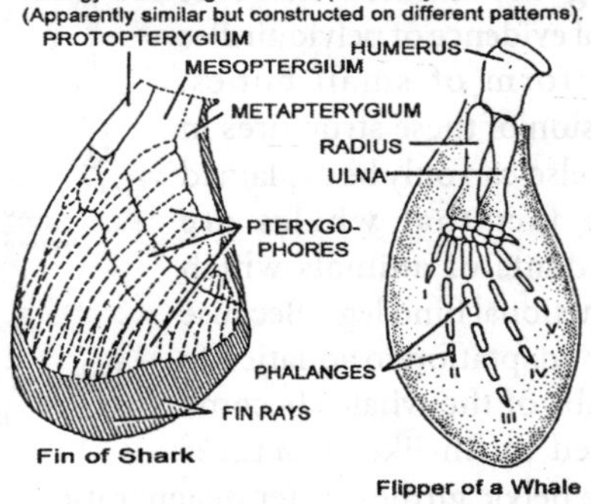

Analogy in the paired fins of shark and flipper of a whale.

environmental conditions, they became functionless and are in the way of degeneration. Vestigial structures are however, homologous with the functional structures in other closely related species.

(i) In man himself there are about 180 vestigial structures, according to Wiedersheim. The muscles concerned with the movement of the pinna are very small, rudimentary and useless in man. But in related lower forms such as cow, dog, guinea-pig, etc., they are well developed, functional and are used to move the ear for catching sound waves.

(ii) The vermiform appendix in connection with the caecum of man is useless vestigial organ, but is homologous to the well developed functional appendix of rabbit.

(iii) In the same way, the gill-slits or visceral clefts in the foetus of man, the nictitating membrane or the third eyelid, the coccyx at the lower end of the vertebral column of man are prominent examples of vestigial organs.

The occurrence of these vestigial organs in man indicate that they are inherited from remote ancestors in which those organs were functional.

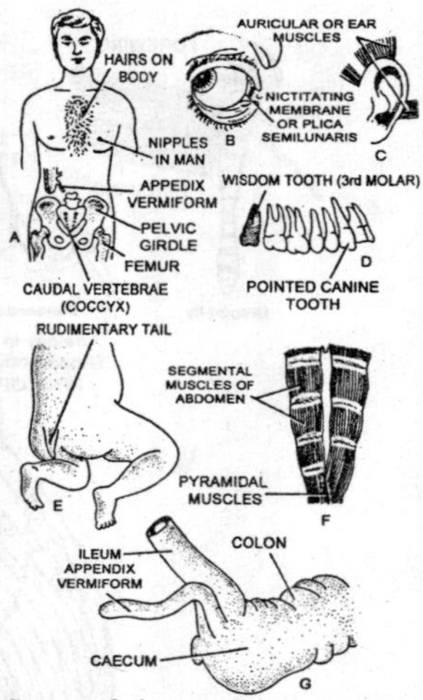

Some of the vestigial structures in human body.

(iv) Among the whales there is vestigial evidence of pelvic girdles in the form of small bones. Possession of these structures in whales also can only be explained by the fact that whales are descendants of animals which had functional hind legs. Because of their adaptation to aquatic life the limbs of the whales become modified to fin-like structures and the pelvic girdles suffer degeneration.

(v) Rudimentary hind limbs occur in the pythons of India and Africa bringing out the fact that pythons are descendants of animals which had these structures useful in their life.

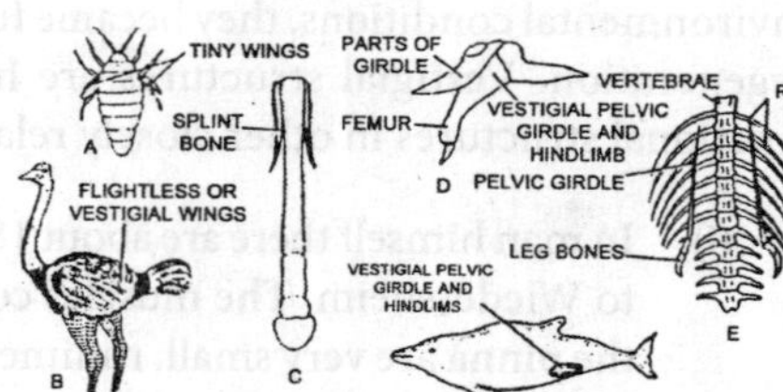

Vestigial organs in different animals

(vi) The ostrich of Africa and Arabia and kiwi of New Zealand are non-flying birds having greatly reduced wings – all justifying the principle of evolution.

(vii) The crayfish of the caves are sightless, the vestigial eye stalks are without eyes. Obviously vestigial evidence of eyes can rationally be explained only on the basis of descent from those ancestral forms having functional eyes.

(viii) In the common garden slug the mantle is reduced and the shell is vestigial. This also gives clear evidence of its derivation from snail ancestral forms.

Atavism

The term atavism denotes reversion to a ancestral type. In some cases, a character not present in the immediate ancestors but exhibited by some great grand parents of remote past may suddenly reappear after its absence in a few recent generation.

Under atavism have been included three very different things which are as follows :

1. *Family atavism* : It includes the transmission, within a family of individual characters in latent condition for several generations and their sudden reappearance after a lapse of time. The example of this is found in red hairs of a child, which the immediate parents or grand parents do not show, but which was in evidence several generations back.
2. *Race atavism* : In this are included, the case where there is a more or less regular reappearance in a race of characters another race, from which the first may have been derived. Such, for example, are the instances of the profuse development of hairs on the face and body which occasionally occurs in man, as in Russian "dog man".
3. *Atavism of teratology* : The appearance in a race of abnormal character which, however, are normal in other supposedly ancestral races. Examples of this are the external hind limbs of which is single recorded instance occurred in a humpback whale taken off Vancouver. The ancestral terrestrial atavus of the whales had their structures which were gradually lost among other adaptations to aquatic life, Fistulae or permanent abnormal openings of the neck, which sometimes occur among human beings; this has been considered as relics of the ancient gill-clefts of our piscine ancestry.

The cause of atavism may be explained by assuming that the atavistic characters though present in all the successive generations but are transmitted in the latent or recessive stage and may suddenly appear as potent or dominant.

In conclusion, it may be said that less marked cases set down to atavism may be instances merely of normal regression. Many cases of more abnormal structure, which are realty due to abnormal embryonic or post-embryonic development, are set down to atavism. It is also used to imply the reversion that takes place when domestic varieties are set free and when species or varieties are crossed.

(4) Connecting links or missing links: Animals which stand in an intermediate way between two big divisions of the animal kingdom are preferably called connecting links or missing links. Such forms ought to be present if each individual is to evolve out of a pre-existing lower ones. Moreover one always finds connecting links while arranging a number of existing organisms in progressive series in evolutionary lines. There are connecting links not only between animals related to one another but occasionally in large groups of animals too. In these animals we see possession of combined characters peculiar to both the groups, thereby pointing out possible relationship and common ancestry of these groups.

(i) Thus the *Monotremes,* the primitive mammals possess both reptilian and mammalian features. Reptilian features of Monotremes include laying of eggs, possession of a cloaca in which the urinogenital ducts open, possession of T-shaped interclavicle in its pectoral girdle. Mammalian features of Monotremes include possession of hairs, and suckling the young ones after hatching. The existence of Monotremes till to day indicates the fact that either this animal is a stage in the making of mammals from reptiles or reptiles and mammals have been diverted in different lines from a common ancestor like Monotremes ; of which the first case is more acceptable.

(ii) The class amphibia also furnishes an intermediate position between the aquatic fishes and the terrestrial reptiles. This is because amphibia possess fish-like characters on one hand and reptilian characters on the other. The chief fish-like characters of amphibia include (i) gill respiration, (ii) caudal fin (at least while the amphibia are young), etc. Amphibia also resemble the reptiles in their acquisition of lung for terrestrial respiration, etc.

(iii) The Lung-fishes (Dipnoi) occupy more or less an intermediate position between the typical fishes and the amphibia in their organization.

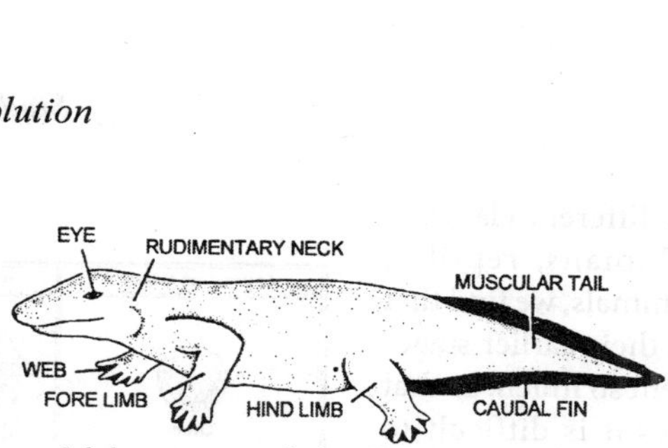

Ichthyostega, a missing link between fishes and amphibians

(iv) The Peripatus is a peculiar worm-like animal having both annelidan and arthropodan characters and serving as a sort of connecting link in the chain of organic evolution. Peripatus is a rare creature, distributed in the forests of Africa, Australia, Asia, South and central America, West Indies, etc.

Its annelidan characters include the following: (i) striped jaw muscles ; (ii) modification of some of the appendages as mouth parts ; (iii) with chitinous cuticle ; (iv) tracheae as respiratory organs ; (v) presence of salivary glands ; (vi) with haemocoelic cavity ; (vii) with closed excretory organs ; (viii) with tubular gonads round the gut.

Peripatus resembles the annelids in having – (i) thin flexible cuticle; (ii) stump – like hollow legs ; (iii) simple eyes ; (iv) segmentally arranged excretory organs ; (v) unstriped muscle ; (vi) no true head.

II Embryological evidences

Embryological studies of plants and animals provide strong evidence of the existence of evolutionary processes. With the exception of certain specialized types of reproduction, every multicellular plant or animal starts its life from a simple *unicellular* oosperm or zygote. The zygote of each species is unique in that it is capable of producing an individual of that species, but there are many features of embryonic development common to any large group of animals.

Thus in all the cases of multicellular animals, the zygote divides and redivides into many cells which, by foldings and other alterations pass through series of common stages – blastula, gastrula in which the definitive structures are laid down and reach the embryo. Finally by gradual differentiation and growth the embryo changes into the characteristic adult. If we trace the embryological development of series of vertebrates belonging to different classes – fishes, amphibians, reptiles, birds and mammals, we find that they agree in their earlier stages of development so much, so that in many cases it is difficult to distinguish between them, but in the later stages gradually they show marked differences.

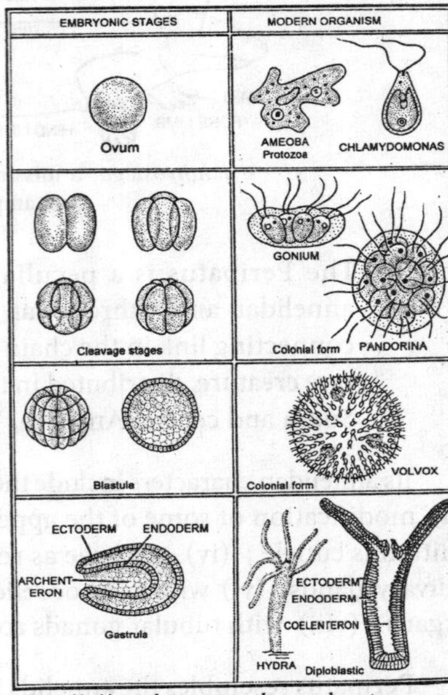

Parallelism between the early stages of embrybonic development at various levels of organisation

It has also been observed that during the development of an individual (*ontogeny*) there are certain stages which only repeat the history of the race to which the individual belongs (*phylogeny*). This is in a sense, a parallelism existing between the development of the individual and development of the race. This is explained by supposing that a highly evolved individual in the course of its development passes through a number of structural stages which are quite unlike the adult form but resemble other lowly evolved adult animals. This sort of embryonic repetition was described by Haeckel (German – 1804-1919) as the Law of Biogenesis or the Theory of Recapitulation. In other words, Haeckel's theory states that the "ontogeny repeats phylogeny" or, the development of the individual (ontogeny) repeats the evolution of the race (phylogeny) in a condensed form. According to this, the zygote was started to represent the protozoan stage, the gastrula the coelenterate stage and so on. If we accept the Recapitulation Theory, we have to agree the point that amphibians have evolved from fish-like ancestors, reptiles from amphibian ancestors ; birds and mammals from reptilian ancestors. In this connection a classical example can be cited. The tadpole larva of a toad or a frog resembles its fish-like ancestors. The tadpole swims and breathes like a fish in water by the development of fins and gills. In short, the tadpole bears no resemblance to an adult toad or frog into which it develops by metamorphosis. To all intents and purposes, the tadpole larva of toad or frog repeats the structures of the ancestor (fish) from which it originated. Therefore, the only significance of having this tadpole stage in the development of toad or frog would be that it represents the descent of amphibians from the fish.

In the same way, the presence of gills, gill-slits and multiple aortic arches in embryos of reptiles, birds, and mammals are considered to be the relics of the respiratory apparatus of their remote fish-like ancestors. Available fossil record also indicates that gill-breathing aquatic vertebrates preceded the air-breathing land animals. In point of time the sequence of their appearance was cartilagenous fishes – bony fishes – amphibians – reptiles – birds and mammals.

In the entire field of comparative embryology, the story of bee embryonic development of almost any organ in the vertebrate presents a similar pattern : there is similarity in the way in which organs begin to develop ; but later on as differentiation begins the dissimilarities become more clear as the similarities recede more and more to the smaller and ultimately to the smallest taxonomic grouping. Let us take the case of the heart. In the very early embryonic stage of all vertebrates, the heart begins its existence as a muscularized tube. This subsequently becomes compartmentalized and progressively more modified in each group of vertebrates. Evidently, during development the hearts of birds and mammals pass through fish and amphibian heart stages. This is a case of "recapitulation" as well as common descent with modification. In the same manner, developmental history of other organs of the vertebrate body, such as the aortic arches, the brain and the kidney, also demonstrate their evolutionary history.

Lastly, groupings of animals in their proper systematic positions have been possible with the help of embryology. Relationship of adult animals is established through embryos. We can take the example of sacculina which is a parasitic Crustacea found attached to the abdoment of the crab in the form of a tumor. The sacculina has undergone such a degeneracy as an adaptation to parasitic life that its actual identity as an arthropodan animal could only be recognized through its larva. The other is the case of Ascidia whose position in the chordates was recognized by its tadpole larva. "Were it not for the assumption that the life history of the individual broadly tends to summarise the evolutionary history of the race and that earlier stages in ontogeny may repeat those of phylogeny, the taxonomic classification of these parasites (sacculina) and sendentary animals (ascidia) would virtually be impossible and the systematic zoology would probably be load with errors".

III. Paleontological or Geological evidences

Paleontology (Gr. *Palaios*, ancient) or the science of fossils presents the best evidence of evolution in the organic world. Any geologic remains or impressions of organic life may be termed a fossil. Sir Charles Lyell, the eminent geologist, defines fossil as "any body or traces of body, animal or vegetable, burried and preserved by natural causes." Literally the term fossil means something that is dug up (Lat. *fodio*, dig). It was Leonardo da Venci (Italian, 1452-1519) who first recognized that fossils were evidences of animal life in the past geological time. Fossils may be produced in a variety of ways.

Kinds of fossils: On the manner of their formation, fossils are distinguished as follows –

Those furnishing direct evidence –

(i) Actual remains: These are the actual dead bodies or parts of organisms with the original tissues in tact preserved in ice or some chemicals; e.g., the huge mammoths and the rhinoceros found buried in the ice of arctic region, and many insects found enclosed in tact in amber, the resin of trees.

(ii) Petrified fossils (Minute replacements): These are found embedded in rocks and are formed by the replacement particle by particle of the original organic matter of the animals by minerals as calcite, quartz, etc., resulting in petrification. Only the parts of the animals such as the bones, shells and teeth are preserved in this manner.

(iii) Coarse replacements: In this case only the moulds or casts of animals are preserved as fossils. These give the exact form of the original animal thus decayed.

(iv) Prints : Foot prints of some ancient animals are found preserved in rocks. Such prints give a clue to the proportions of the entire animal. Such as the case of reptilian foot prints abundant in rocks of prehistoric time.

Those furnishing indirect evidence –

(i) Coprolites i.e. solidified excreta, or casts of same provide signified information about the food and feeding habits of extinct animals.

(ii) Artifacts – such as flints of prehistoric times used by Neanderthal men, etc.

Taking all kinds of fossils together, a vast amount of evidences have been accumulated with respect to the kinds of animals and plants which have existed on the earth since the dawn of life.

Fossils are found to have been deposited in the various layers of the earth's crusts. Our earth consists of layers or strata of rocks. These layers have been formed owing to sedimentation on the surface through thousands of years since the very existence of earth. Organisms died during one age have been buried in the sediment of that age. Another layer of sediment with its fossil characteristics was deposited above the last layer and this process was taken over and over again. Consequently, the different layers or strata of the earth indicate different ages (geological times), and any fossil found in these strata can be approximately identified to that particular age. We can divide the age of the earth into five large groups each of which represents an immense duration of time called an era. In the succession of geological time the eras are the Archeozoic, the Proterozoic, the Paleozoic, the Mesozoic and the Caenozoic. These eras are divided into 'periods', which may be further sub-divided into 'epochs'. The accompanying table

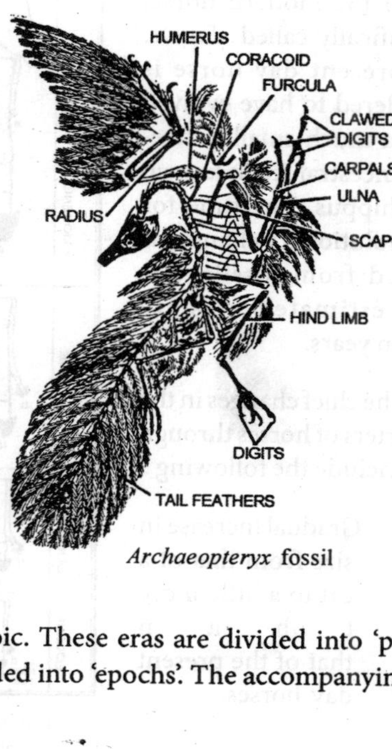

Archaeopteryx fossil

indicates the subsequent layers of the fossil-bearing rocks with their estimated ages thus identified. It is to be understood that fossils of organisms buried in the lower (deeper) strata are older than those embedded in the strata above them. By examining such fossils one can reproduce the past history of organisms on the earth. But the records of the organisms which we call fossil records or geological records are incomplete at best owing to several causes. Nevertheless, there can be found in one part or other of the geological record, successions of beings or of events in life history which are consistent with an evolution from simple to complex, accomplished during a long period of time.

An instance is a fossil bird, called Archaeopteryx which existed in the Jurassic time (155 million years old). Archaeopteryx possessed characters common to both reptiles and birds. Evidently it serves as a connecting link between reptiles and birds.

Another example is that of the modern horse, scientifically called *Equus.* The present day horse is considered to have evolved from a much smaller, five-toed ancestral stock known as Eohippus. The time for this evolutionary change, as studied from fossils, has been estimated at sixty million years.

The chief changes in the characters of horses through time include the following :

1. Gradual increase in size from that of a cat to a little more than that of the present day horses.

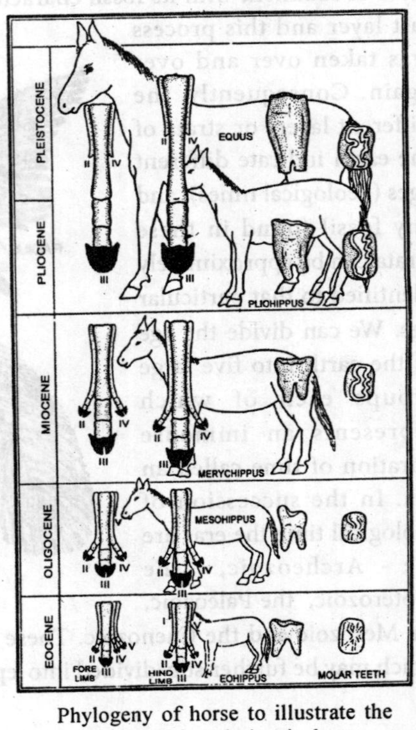

Phylogeny of horse to illustrate the process of evolution in horse

2. Increase in the length of the parts of the head.
3. Elongation and mobility of the neck.
4. Lengthening of the two pairs of limbs for quick running.
5. Fusion of some of the bones in each fore-limb to lend better hinge joint.
6. Gradual loss of toes from five to one on each foot.

Hiving undergone all these changes through a slow and steady process of evolution, the present day horse (Equus) has been attained.

IV. Evidence from Geographical distribution

The distribution of life over the earth's surface at various time is called geographic distribution ; evidences in support of the doctrine of evolution derived from these distribution are known as geographical evidences. The distribution of plant or animal life on the surface of the earth is far and wide. Some of them are equally distributed over the earth's surface and hence called cosmopolitan, but such examples are found to be rare. It is seen that plants and animals are by no means uniformly distributed upon the surface of the earth. Each country is represented with its characteristic flora (plants) and fauna (animals). The climatic conditions of two countries may be similar, but the distribution of flora and fauna in both the countries may not be alike. There are cases of *isolated distribution.* Great Britain and New Zealand are almost alike in climatic conditions but the living forms of the two countries are unlike. Likewise, Africa and Brazil have similar environmental conditions, but the elephants, antelopes and great apes (chimpanzee and gorilla) of Africa are not found in Brazil. This is also observed that Great Britain and Japan which are separated by thousands of miles have similar faunas, whereas, Bali and Lombok, two small islands in Malay Archipelago, separated only by 15 miles wide, have dissimilar faunas.

Again, there are certain forms of plants and animals which are only peculiar to a country and not distributed anywhere else. They may be recognized as endemic forms. The African giraffe may be cited as an illustration of endemic fauna. Similarly, otter shrews are found only within the equatorial forest belt of Africa. Pronghorns are restricted to the north western prairie land of America. Among the plant there is one gymnospermic plant which is endemic to China alone. Furthermore, some animals are found to be discontinuously distributed. The tapirs occur in Central and South America and again in the Malay Peninsula and Sumatra – thus affording a curious example of *discontinuous distribution.*

All these examples of geographical distribution reflect the principle of "descent with modifications". It is presumed that particular species of organism develops at a definite place and with the "rapid increase in number in geometrical ratio", the members migrate in all available directions. In this way, the farther they moved away from their place of origin the more they altered from the original. In such movement or migration limits are set by natural barriers : wide oceans, difference in salinity and temperature influence the dispersal of aquatic animals ; intensive heat and light prevent the migration of aerial forms like the birds; deserts, high mountains, difference in vegetation, etc., check the movement of terrestrial forms. Moreover, these barries do not remain constant in the geological time. The face of the earth has undergone continuous change in the past and is constantly changing. In some region of the world, the land is gradually sinking, whereas in other parts, it is gradually coming up. Land masses now totally separated by water were at one time linked up, facilitating intermigration of animals. For example, at one time when there were "land bridges" between India and Africa there existed species of elephants common to both the continents. But since the severance of the two continents each of them is now represented with its own characteristic species of elephants.

Thus, frequently it has happened that representatives of once widely distributed groups of animals have become isolated in new environment where 'competition' is not severe. In order to adapt themselves to the new environment they become modified. Hence the same variety of animals of the various isolated lands differ greatly in their acquired characters. The Kangaroos of South America and Australia though fundamentally alike, appear as distinct species. This is further understood by the fact that Kangaroos developed during the period when South America was connected with Australia. Later, Australia became disconnected with South America, carrying away its own share of Kangaroos. In the new environments thus encountered, Kangaroos underwent modifications and acquired characters so much so that they were transformed into new species. The Kangaroos of South America have affinities with those of Australia, indicating their descent from a common ancestor.

One of the strongest evidences from biogeographical data stems from the study of flora and fauna of the Oceanic islands (islands formed by some subterranean volcanic disturbance and far removed from the nearest continental shelf). One such example is the group of Galapoagos islands, situated on the equator 600 miles west of South America. Charles Darwin thoroughly studied the flora and fauna of these islands when he visited them during his voyage in the Beagle (1813-1836). Darwin discovered that while the plant life on earth of the Galapagos group of islands, presented a close kinship for each other, they were specifically different. Further, he found that all of the plant life on those islands evidenced a close degree of kinship to similar plants on the mainland of South America. The explanation was that species of plants on the various islands of the archipelago represented plants which migrated from the mainland and underwent subsequent modifications to suit the new environment.

Next, among the fauna which impressed Darwin very much were the birds, called finces. It was observed that there were finces of the same two genera spread over all the islands of the Galapagos group. But each island form was recognizably distinct from all others, although presenting relationship with each other. In other words, it was more or less true to say that each island had its own characteristic species. The explanation is that in some way or other long years gone by the ancestors of these finces had come from the mainland of South America. When finces colonized a new island, they would be in a slightly different environment from the one they had left. Further they could not readily migrate from island to island because of the prevailing barriers. Gradually in succeeding generation the finces most fitted to the new surrounding would survive and leave offspring, whilst the weakest would die off. Segregated from the parent stock, the colony of finces would evolve into a new species suited to the new island and recognizably different from the original.

These and many others led Darwin to formulate his theory of evolution by Natural Selection. To put precisely, geographical distribution reflects "descent with modification".

V. Physiological and Biochemical evidences

These are derived from the various functional aspects of the living bodies. All organisms are alike in being composed of protoplasm. The basic biochemical constitution and functions of protoplasm are the same in plant and animal cells. Again, all animals agree in the fundamental processes of metabolism, irritability and reproduction, which are actually the manifestations of the "living stuff", i.e., protoplasm. This universal occurrence of protoplasm in all the animals at least points to the kinship among different animals and this kinship is in exact parallel line which is supported by other evidences of evolution. It is true that protoplasm manifests minor variations from species to species, but out of these minor variations has sprung up the variety of organisms that we know them to day.

Another line of attack to explore the physiological evidences of evolution is upon the biochemical test of blood (Serology) and endocrine organs. Animal blood contains certain elements known as blood elements. These blood elements are characteristic to each species of animal and are stored in the serum – the watery fluid of the blood. In order to find out the blood relationship of man with any other mammal, we can follow the following method, employed by Nuttal and Grahm-Smith, as follows –

First of all human blood is drawn and allowed to coagulate. After coagulation the solid portion is slowly removed and only the watery fluid thus left behind is called serum. This serum contains the distinctive blood elements of man. By injecting intravenously small doses of the serum of man in another mammal, say a Guinea-pig, the antibody is formed. If this antibody is allowed to mix with the serum of a fresh human being, a heavy white precipitate is formed. If it is treated with the serum of Antrhopoid apes (example, Gorilla), the precipitation will be less formed. The precipitation occurs in direct proportion with

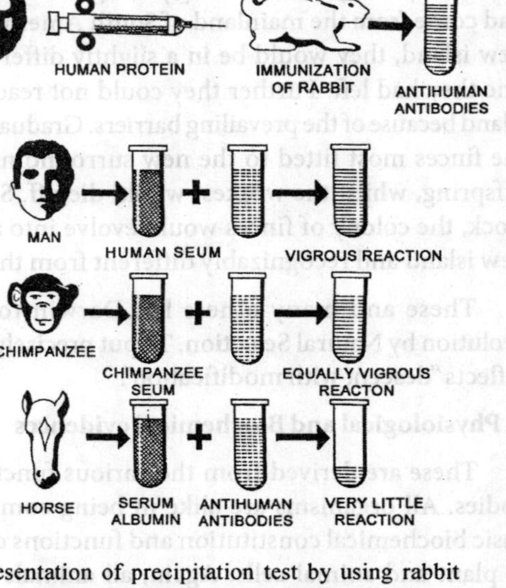

Representation of precipitation test by using rabbit containing antibodies against sheep serum

the degree of kinship. So, as we proceed downwards along the evolutionary scale, the precipitation becomes gradually less abundant. Closest the kinship heaviest is the precipitation; distant the kinship lesser is the precipitation. This is the essence of "descent with modification".

Chromosome chemistry

The chromosomes of all living organisms basically consist of nucleoproteins. The nucleic acid is essentially deoxyribonucleic acid (DNA) and proteins are essentially histones and protamines. Associated with chromosomes there are some other kinds of proteins like globulins and some amount of RNA are also found. Such a high degree of uniformity in the composition of chromosomes suggests a common origin.

Enzymes and hormones

There are identical enzymes and hormones in large groups of animals and plants. The metabolic pathways they follow are also similar. The existence of these fundamental similarities must be regarded as evidence for an underlying kinship among all living beings. Trypsin and amylase are found in a wide variety of animals, ranging from Protozoa to Mammalia, while amylase is found from sponges to Mammals.

There are a number of hormones which throw light on the organic evolution. For example, thyroid hormone is common in all vertebrates. If the hormone extracted from mammalian pituitary glands is supplied to amphibians it is as effective as the amphibian hormone itself. The hormone is also essential for the metamorphosis of frog. If frog's thyroid gland is removed surgically, the frog will not metamorphose. Yet feeding of mammalian thyroid tissue will correct the deficiency and permit metamorphosis.

Thus within the array of biochemical and physiological similarities and differences is to be found considerable evidence for evolution and for the solution of specific phylogenetic problems.

VI. Evidence from artificial selection

By experimental breeding of animals it has often been possible to raise new varieties of plants and animals apart from the originals. For example, various forms of domestic pigeon today have been derived from the rock or wild pigeon, by artificial selection.

VII. Genetical evidences

Genetics is the science of heredity and variation. Heredity is "resemblance based on descent", or transmission of parental characters to the offspring. Differences among individuals of a species are known as variations. Evidences in support of the principle of evolution obtained from the study of heredity and variation are known as genetical evidences. It has been observed that in certain organisms evolutionary changes suddenly appear to mark them off from among the normal. These large variations are called mutations (postulated by Hugo de Vries). Once a mutation appears for some cause, it is sure to be transmitted to the coming generation. Organisms with mutations are isolated by some means and mutant type is intebred, so that the mutation becomes permanent. When these mutations are inherited to the offspring, new characters become apparent as a result of which fresh mutations and ultimately new species are produced.

13

ZOOGEOGRAPHICAL REGIONS OF THE WORLD WITH CHARACTERISTIC FAUNA

On the basis of distribution of land mammals, the world's surface is divided into six primary regions, called the zoogeographical realms, and each realm has its characteristic fauna. The six realms are –

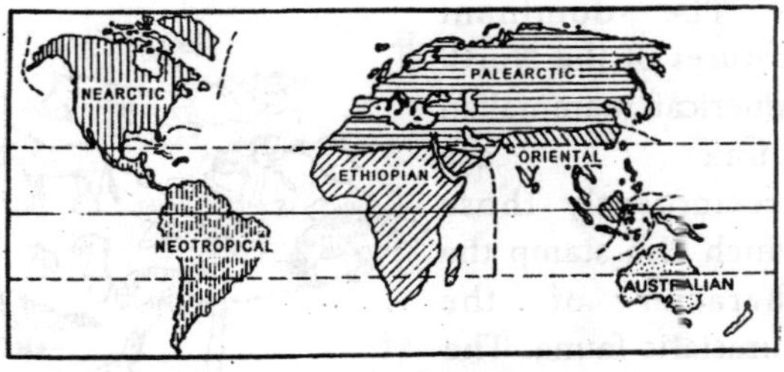

Different zoogeographical regions of world

1. Palearctic region
2. Ethiopian region
3. Oriental region
4. Australian region
5. Neotropical region
6. Nearctic region.

1. Palearctic region

The Palearctic region includes the whole of Europe, the part of Africa north of tropic of cancer and whole of Asia excepting India, Siam, South east China and Japan. The Sahara and Himalayas are the effective barriers. Palearctic region is divided into four sub-regions viz., European, Mediterranean, Siberian and Manchurian.

The Palearctic region is very wide and it shows great variations of temperature, rainfall and great diversity in its surface features. The fauna of this region is very much similar to that of Nearctic region. So Heilprin proposed the union of the two into one great region calling it the Holarctic realm and dividing it into two portions, an old world or Eurasiatic division and a North American or Nearctic division.

The Palearctic region has about 135 families of terrestrial vertebrates. Out of this, 33 are the families of mammals, 68 are of birds, 24 are of reptiles and 10 are fishes and amphibians. Among the Mammals, the family Caprinae and the family Bovidae containing sheep and goats are represented in plenty. The family Cervidae containing the deer is also well represented. Among the monkeys, the common type is the Barbary monkey (*Macacus innus*). The carnivora constitute an important feature in the Eurasiatic fauna. The badge (Mele) is found throughout the northern Europe and Asia, in Japan, China, etc.

Geographic limits and chracteristic fauna of Palaearctic Region

The dominant features of the North American mammalian fauna are preeminently those which also stamp the character of the Eurasiatic fauna. The common animals are the deer, mouse or elk, reindeer, bison, cats, lynxes, weasels, bears, wolves, foxes, beavers, hares, squirrels and marmots. One species of implacental mammals – the virginian opposoum (*Didelphis virginianus*) penetrates as far north as the Canadian frontier. Among the birds the common families are – Turdidae (thrushes) with the true warblers Sylvia, redstart, robin and nightingale; Sittidae (nut hatches); Paridae (tits), Laniidae (shrikes), Corvidae (Crows), Hirundinidae (swallows), Sturnidae (starlings), Alaudidae (larks).

Among the reptiles of Palearctic region, there are 25 species of snakes, 5 species of chelonians and 32 species of lizards. Among the snakes the common types are the vipers and the water snakes. Among the lizards, the species *Lacerta vivipara* and *Lacerta agilis* are common.

Among the amphibians, the tailed forms like the Newts, Salamanders, etc., are found. The tree frogs like Hyla and the toads like Discoglossus, Bufo, etc., are also represented.

The fish fauna of the Palearctic region is characterised by the special development among fresh water forms, of the carps (Cyprinidae), salmon (Salmonidae), pikes (Esocidae), Perches (Percidae), stickle backs (Gasterosteidae), sturgeons (Acipenceridae) and lampreys (Petromyzon).

2. Ethiopian region

This region consists of whole of Africa and Arabia, south of the tropic of cancer, together with Madagascar and the small adjacent islands. It is divided into four sub regions, viz., East African, West African, South African and Malagasy. The life in this region is more or less uniform as it lies between the tropics. In the north of the region is the great Sahara. South of this, there is a great luxuriant tropical forest with an abundant and very distinct fauna.

In the Ethiopian region, the common mammalian fauna include Carnivores and Ungulates. Of the Ungulata there are two families which are solely restricted to the region. Hippopotamidae : Cameleopardidae or the Giraffes. The Hippopotamidae includes two species which are found in the large rivers from the Cape to the Sahara, and the Cameleoparidae comprises only one species which is cosmopolitan throughout Africa. In this region there are two horned Rhinocerotidae. The antelopes are plenty.

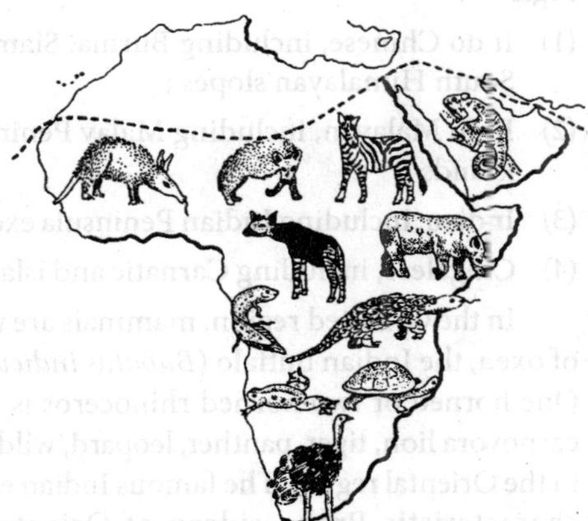

Geographical limits and characteristic fauna of Ethiopian region

Among the Carnivora, there are the lion, leopard, panther, hyena, jackal and the aard wolf (Proteles). Of the primates, the family Simidae is represented by Chimpanzees and Gorillas. In the island of Madagascar, only Lemuridae is found.

Among the birds the common are vultures, eagles, secretary birds, ostriches and parrots. Among the reptiles some of the deadliest poisonous snake like Puff-adder are found in the Ethiopean region in addition to the common vipers. Among the fishes, Polypterus and Protopterus are found in this region.

3. Oriental region

This region includes India, Burma, Ceylon, Formosa, Sumatra, Philippines, Java, Borneo. This region is characterised by the most luxuriant forest growth which extends even to an elevation of from 8-10 thousand feet along the slopes of the Himalayas. It is divided into four sub regions :

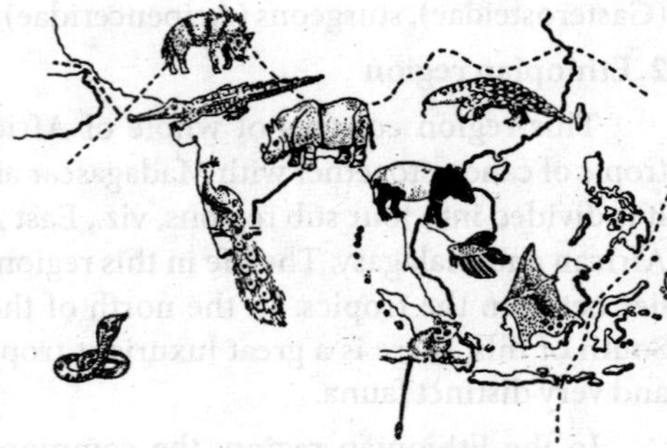

Geographical limits and chracteristic fauna of Oriental region

(1) Indo Chinese, including Burma, Siam, Assam, Southern China and South Himalayan slopes ;

(2) Indo Malayan, including Malay Peninsula, with the Indo Malaysian islands ;

(3) Indian, including Indian Peninsula exclusive of Carnatic ;

(4) Cingalese, including Carnatic and island of Ceylon.

In the Oriented region, mammals are well developed. Different types of oxen, the Indian buffalo (*Bubalus indicus*) are the common mammals. One horned or two horned rhinoceros is present in Assam. Among the carnovora lion, tiger, panther, leopard, wild dogs, fox and hyena are found in the Oriental region. The famous Indian elephant (*Elephas indicus*) is the characteristic Proboscidean of Oriental region. Mice, squirrel are distributed throughout the region. The bats are also found.

The most important of the Oriental primates are the macaques (macacus), for example, Bornean nose-monkey. The Orangutan is confined to Borneo, and Sumatra and the long armed Gibbon (Hylobates) extends from Java to Assam and China. Of the family Tarsidae, only one species, Tarsius spectrum is found in Sumatra, Borneo. Galeopithecus or flying lemurs are found in Malay Archipelago and the Phillipinus.

Among the birds, the laughing thrushes (Timalidae), Hill titi, Green bulbuls, Warblers, the tailor bird, Sacred minah (Eulabis), the sun birds, the jungle fowl (Gallus) and peacock are commonly noticed in Oriented region.

The reptilian fauna includes among other snakes, the giant python, coral snakes, pit vipers, varanus, geckoes, iguanas, flying lizards (Draco), the crocodiles and gavialis. Most of the common fishes which are edible are found in the Oriented region.

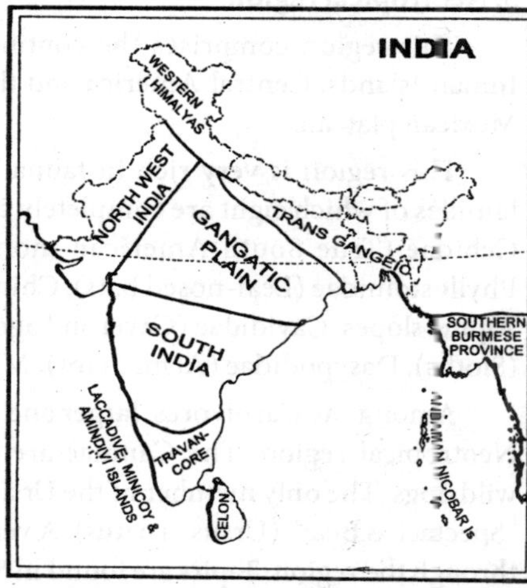

Zoogeographical subdivisions of Indian subregion

4. Australian region

This region includes the whole of Australia, New Zealand, New Guinea, the Moluccas and neighbouring islands. The Australian region is divided into four sub-regions, viz., Austro-malayan, Australian, Polynesian and New Zealand.

Australia is characterised by a peculiar climate with a remarkable fauna.

The fauna of Australian region is interesting because many primitive types are found here. The monotremes and marsupials are found in the Australian region. Among the birds the common varieties are the Australian Ostrich (Emu), Cassowary, Cockatoos, Parakeets, Parrots, Black Swan, Kooka burra, and the laughing jackess.

The reptilian fauna consists of snakes and lizards. Poisonous snakes are more than the non-poisonous snakes. There is only one species of crocodile in Australian region. Among the Amphibian, tree frogs are represented in plenty. Toads are represented by a limited number of species. Among the fishes, two species of lung fishes belonging to the genus Ceratodus are found in Australian region.

5. Neotropical region

This region comprises the continent of South America, the West Indian Islands, Central America and the low lands on either side of the Mexican plateau.

This region is very rich in fauna. There are about 30 mammalian families of which eight are completely confined to this region. They are – Cebidae (True South American monkeys), Hapalidae (Marmosets), Phyllostomidae (Leaf-nosed bats), Chinchillidae (Chinchilla, confined to Alpine slopes, Caviddidae (Cavia and agouty from Mexico), Bradypodidae (Sloths), Dasypodidae (Armadillos), Myrmecophagidae (Ant-eaters).

Among the Carnivores, larger and smaller cats are distributed in the Neotropical region. The Canidae are represented by various forms of wild dogs. The only member of the Ursidae found in South America is the "Spectacled Bear" (Ursus ornatus). A very few species of deer are scattered through the region. Tapirs are found in South and Central America, Malay Peninsula, Sumatra and Borneo.

The bird fauna of the Neotropical region comprises about 700 genera of land birds. Humming birds (Trochilidae) include about 120 genera and 400 species. The Macaws comprises about 80 species. Other characteristic families of South American birds include Rhamphastidae, Tinamidae (Tinamus), Struthionidae (Ostriches).

The reptilian fauna of this region includes the giant boa and Anacondas, alligators, crocodiles and iguanas. Among the amphibians, the toads and frogs (especially the true frogs) are plenty. The fish fauna includes catfishes, Electric eel, lung fish or dipnoi.

6. Nearctic region

This region includes Greenland and North America. The peculiar faunas are opposums, rattle snakes (reptiles), Axolotl (amphibia), Lepidosteus (pisces).

BARRIERS

Barrier is a natural factor which obstructs the wandering of animals from one region to another. Barriers may be topographic barriers and climatic barriers. A physical obstruction such as a mountain range which prevents the animal from crossing is an example of topographic barrier. Himalayan mountain range is an effective topographic barrier which prevents the distribution of animals between Indian and Eurasia. The Sahara Desert stands against dispersal of animals from the Palearctic to the Ethiopian. A climatic factor such as temperature, rainfall, humidity, vegetation, etc., which varies from place to place prevents animal distribution.

Degree of heat is very important in limiting animal distribution. However, the distribution of tiger and elephant shows that this does not very much alter their distribution. For example, tiger has its normal home in the hot districts of India and the Indian archipelago but is also found in colder climates such as in the elevated regions of the Caucasus and the Altai chain and in the Himalayas and also in the cold plains of Manchuria. The influence of temperature is much more marked in the cold-blooded animals. Thus the amphibians and reptiles are tropical and temperate in their distribution, rapidly diminishing in numbers towards the poles. Lack of moisture also controls the distribution and the effect is more marked in the extreme cases where it produces the desert conditions where only forms adapted to withstand drought can survive, for others it forms insuperable barrier. The increase of moisture may produce swampy conditions which may make the area impassable for creatures not adapted to them. Increased humidity also has marked effect on the vegetation and also in the spread of insect life.

Vegetative barriers

The influence of vegetation on barrier is both direct and indirect. The forest living, arboreal animals cannot live or cross the regions where forestation does not occur, while huge and thick jungles form barriers to large terrestrial animals who are incapable of penetrating it. The vegetation also effects the distribution indirectly as it forms the important source of food. The primates live in tropical forests as they feed on fruits, nuts and blossoms as well as insects and birds of these forests.

Large bodies of water

Extensive bodies of water, when not frozen, form very important barriers especially to terrestrial vertebrates like the amphibians, reptiles and mammals. Fresh water fishes are also prevented from crossing large bodies of salt water. To the modern amphibians salt water constitutes a most effective barrier as the common salt is poisonous to them, even one percent solution preventing the development of their larvae. Amphibia are, therefore, almost completely absent from oceanic islands. Moreover, the tailed amphibians such as sirens, newts, salamanders, etc., are restricted to northern hemisphere, for the southern land masses, Australia, Africa and South America are isolated by oceans are incapable of crossing through small migratory routes. For some reptiles, notably the crocodiles and marine turtles, the seas afford no obstacles. The serpents, though many of which are good swimmers, but are incapable of passing large bodies of salt water with the exception of some snakes. Adult lizards are also incapable of passing an oceanic barrier, though the eggs in some cases could be transported to the islands. With the birds, it is only the flightless forms such as the ostrich, rhea, apteryx, etc., which are incapable of oceanic migration for even small birds are carried far on favouring winds. Among mammals, except for whales and seals, bodies of water of a greater expanse than 20 to 50 miles are impassable when not frozen.

Marine environment presents few barriers for the animals inhabiting it. The land masses which project into the ocean often form an effective barrier. Depth acts as a barrier to the animals inhabiting the littoral zone. The entry of fresh-water into the sea acts as a barrier to the spread of littoral forms in shallow waters.

The land mass is the major barrier which affects the dispersal of fresh water animals from one fresh water environment to the other. In the lotic environment, currents are the major barriers. Currents are deterimental to small suspended animals. Similarly waterfalls form an effective barrier to many freshwater animals. The impurity and lack of salinity of sea water afford an effective barrier to the dispersal of certain marine animals like bracheopods, echinoids, crinoids, starfishes, squids and foramina.

QUESTIONS AND ANSWERS

Q.1. What do you mean by zoogeographical realms ? How many zoogeographical realms are there in the world ? Write briefly the characteristics and the important fauna of any one.

Ans. Zoogeographical realms are concerned with the distribution of animals over the world. On the basis of distribution of land mammals, the world's surface is divided into six primary regions, called the zoogeographical realms, and each realm has its characteristic fauna. The six realms are –

1. Palaeartic region
2. Ethiopian region
3. Oriental region
4. Australian region
5. Neotropical region
6. Nearctic region

Palaeartic region is the largest of the six regions and it covers an area of 140,00,000 sq. miles. It more or less embraces the whole of the Eurosian continent except South of Himalayas, Persia, Afghanistan, Africa, North of Sahara, British Isles and Japan. Wide range of temperature, greater fluctuation in the amount of rainfall, greater diversity of surface features are the characteristics of the Palaeartic region.

There is considerable similarity between the fauna of Palaeartic and Nearctic region. This similarity led Heilprin to propose the union of the two regions into one great region namely Holarctic Region or Realm.

The Palaeartic Region possesses representatives of 135 families of terrestrial vertebrates composed of 33 families of mammals, 63 of birds, 24 of reptiles, and 10 of amphibians and 13 of fresh water fishes. The mammals include Talpidae (Moles), Beavers; Birds – Gold crests, Divers and Grouse ; Amphibians – Proteus, Salamanders; Fishes – Perches, Sticklebacks, Pikes, Sturgeon; Reptiles – Turtles, Shinks, Lacertids, Anguidae, Colubrids, True vipers and Pit vipers, etc.

Q.2. Describe the Australian region stating dominant fauna.

Ans. Australian region includes the whole of Australia, New Zealand, New Guinea, the Moluccas and neighbouring islands. The Australian region is divided into four sub-regions, viz., Austro-malayan, Australian, Polynesian and New Zealand.

Australia is characterised by a peculiar climate with a remarkable fauna.

The fauna of Australian region is interesting because many primitive types are found here. The Monotremes and Marsupials are found in the Australian region. Among the birds, the common varieties are the Australian Ostrich (Emu), Cassowary, Cockatoos, Parakeets, Parrots, Black swan, Kooka burra, and the loughing jackals.

The reptilian fauna consists of snakes and lizards. Poisonous snakes are more than the non-poisonous snakes. There is only one species of crocodile in Australian region. Among the Amphibian, true frogs are represented in plenty. Toads are represented by a limited number of species. Among the fishes, two species of lung fishes belonging to the genus Ceratodus are found in Australian region.

Q.3. What are the important faunas of the Ethiopian region ?

Ans. In the Ethiopian region, the common Mammalian fauna include carnivores and ungulates. Of the Ungulata there are two families which are solely restricted to the region. Hippopotamidae, Cameleopardidae or the Giraffes. The Hippopotamidae includes two species which are found in the large rivers from the Cape to the Sahara, and Cameleopardidae comprises only one species which is cosmopolitan throughout Africa. In this region there are two horned Rhinocerotidae. The antelopes are plenty. Lion, leopard, panther, hyena, jackal, chimpanzees and gorillas are prominent. Other important mammals of the Ethiopian region are – Chyromyidae (Aye-Aye), Chrysochloridae (Golden Moles), Protelidae (Earth wolf), Bathyergidae (African Mole Rats), Lophiomyidae (Crested Rats), Pedetidae (African jumping Hares), Flying Squirrels, Aard-Varks, etc. The birds include – Secretary Birds, Guinea Fowls, Helmet Birds, Plantain Eaters. Reptiles include – Girdled Lizards, and Amphibians include – Clawed Toad. Among the fishes, Polypterus and Protopterus are found in this region.

Q.4. What is the importance of the study of zoogeography ?

Ans. The study of zoogeography helps to understand evolution of animals and land masses.

Q.5. Emus and Casowarries are found in one of the following regions :

(A) Australian region (B) Neotropical region

(C) Nearctic region (D) Continental islands. **Ans.** (A)

Q.6. The largest zoogeographical realm is –

(A) Ethiopean (B) Palaeartic

(C) Oriental (D) Nearctic **Ans.** (B)

Q.7. Which zoogeographical realm characterised by the presence of Sphenodon and Monotremes ? **Ans.** Australian region.

Q.8. Name the zoogeographical sub-regions where the following animals are found :

(A) Musk deer (B) Sangai

Ans. (A) Musk deer is found in Indian sub-region.

(B) Sangai – found in Indian sub-region (Manipur).

Q.9. Describe the Australian region stating dominant fauna.

Ans. Australian region includes the whole of Australia, New Zealand, New Guinea, the Moluccas and neighbouring islands. The Australian region is divided into four sub-regions viz., Austro-Malayan, Australian, Polynesian and New Zealand.

Australia is characterised by a peculiar climate with a remarkable fauna.

The fauna of Australian region is interesting because many primitive types are found here. The monotremes and marsupials are found in the Australian region. Among the birds the common varieties are the Australian Ostrich (Emu), Cassowary, Parrots, Cockatoos, parakeets, Black swan, Kooka burra, and the loughing jackess.

The reptilian fauna consists of snakes and lizards. Poisonous snakes are more than the non-poisonous snakes. There is only one species of crocodile in Australian region. Among the Amphibian, true frogs are represented in plenty. Toads are represented by a limited number of species. Among the fishes, two species of lung fishes belonging to the genus Ceratodus are found in Australian region.

On the whole, the Australian region has 134 families of terrestrial vertebrates of which 30 are quite peculiar composed of 8 of mammals 17 of birds, 3 of reptiles and 2 of amphibians.

The Austro-Malayan sub-region is characterised by the presence of 130 families of terrestrial vertebrates. In the Australian sub-region Wombats, Marsupial Mole, Duck Bills, Emus are confined. In the Polynesian sub-region tooth-billed pigeons are present. In the New Zealand sub-region 34 families of terrestrial vertebrates are found. *Sphenodon punctatum* is found in the New Zealand.

14

ADAPTIVE RADIATION AND CONVERGENCE

Creatures of same or closely related stock are often found to go several ways in search of food and safety giving rise to varied adaptations reaching the several extremes of evolutionary lines. This idea of segregation from the normal stem form was recognized by Lamarck as "embranchement", Darwin called it "divergence" whereas finally Osborn stated it in the form of a Law, which he called "Adaptive radiation". Adaption to environment is one of the most remarkable qualities of living organisms. In a large isolated country varying in its topography, vegetation and climate, with slender chance of migration, animals of a group, like the Marsupials in Australia, assume forms adapted to burrowing (fossorial), running (cursorial), climbing (scansorial) and flying (volant). If, however, animals of different groups come to share a common habitat, they give rise to adaptive convergence.

Law of Adaptive Radiation

As stated by Osborn, the law states that each isolated region if large and sufficiently varied in its topography, soil, climate and vegetation would give rise to a diversified fauna. The larger the region, more diverse the condition, the greater would be the variation in animal forms. From a primitive stem form, radii go out in four diverse directions, adaptation being mainly of limbs and feet also of teeth, directions being arboreal, subterranian, cursorial and aquatic.

Adaptive radiation

Arboreal (living chiefly or wholly in trees) → **Aerial or Volant** (Flying animals)

Rectigrade (Gigantic, heavy-bodied, limbs adapted to sustain great weight)

Semi-Arboreal (good climbers but living largely on the ground)

Aquatic (Living chiefly or wholly in the water) ← **Amphibious** (Good swimmers but living largely on the land) ← **Terrestrial** (Ground living, plantigrade, five-toed and clawed) → **Cursorial** (Digitigrade Good runners on finger and toe pads) → **Cursorial** (Uniguligrade Swift runners on tips of toes)

↓

Fossorial (Good diggers but living largely on the surface of the ground)

↓

Sub terranean (Living chiefly or wholly underground)

Osborn applied the Law mainly to mammals but it is shown to be equally true for other animals by Matthew, such as amphibians, reptiles and birds. The central or focal type was conceived by Osborn as a short-limbed, ambulatory form, with five clawed digits upon the approximately equally developed feet. It was small and generalized in its feeding habits, insectivorous or omnivorous and therefore with simple – short-crowned teeth.

Four type of radiation depending on feeding habits :–

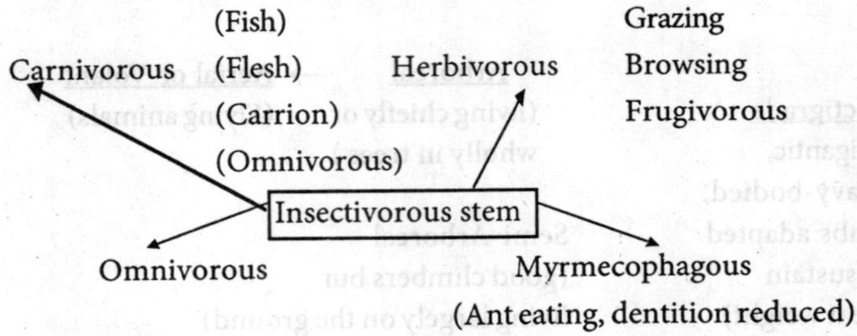

Causes of Radiation

The impelling causes of adaptive radiation are taken to be the need of food and safety.

Though there are many minor roads along which evolution was possible in general, the animals diverge in four major directions as stated above. Out of these four directions, the aquatic and fossorial are the most specialised so that they find it difficult to turn to be generalized reaching their stem form and can be called one way trails through which many go but none return. Whereas birds and cursorial ones recturn though not in the same way as they went.

Primary and Secondary Adaptation

Adaptive radiations may be direct or primary if they lie in the original line of radiation as from terrestrial through scansorial to volant, or may be reversed or secondary when the return direction is indicated. Thus there is often seemingly a reversal in the direction of evolution as there are many instances of flightless birds, which have reverted to their original environment. But this does not actually contradict the law of irreversability of evolution, which says that organs lost can never be regained and that a specialised form can never turn to be generalized. Thus in the above example, the flightlessness which is a degenerative process have impelled those animals to the land and is not a case of reversal.

Local radiation

The term adaptive radiation is only suitable when all the vertebrate classes as a whole are considered, inhabiting a vast area, while the differences arising within a group of closely related forms of a particular locality should be described as the local adaptive radiation as they obviously not always follow a straight course but branches, turning and changing direction. Example can be drawn from African Rhinoceros and Miocene Horses. Both of them distinctly divide into two groups, one grazing and the other browsing with associated distinction in teeth structure.

Contemporaneous radiation

It is often found that the fauna of two or more completely isolated continents with different focal types proceed through different stages of radiation with a very remarkable parallelism all along the course, which are otherwise called as contemporaneous radiation.

During the Tertiary time contemporaneous radiation took place in three great zoogeographical realms, Arctogea, Notogea and Neogea. The first including the whole of Northern Hemisphere and Africa, the second, South America and the third Australia.

In Arctogea the central or focal type is an advanced one, represented in a general way by Malayan insectivore, Gymnura.

In Notogea it is represented by the Opossum which Osborn says at least from the preservation of dental prototype of pro-mammals, are closest to the insectivore among placentals.

In Arctogea the cursorial adaptations is manifested by dogs, whereas amongst the Notogean Marsupials, Tasmanian wolf, which is very dog-like in contour, occupies the same position.

The herbivorous Ungulates of Arctogea are represented by the herbivorous bandicoots and kangaroos of Notogea.

Arboreal squirrel of Arctogea are represented by the marsupial "Sugar Squirrel" of Notogea.

Though no truly volant forms comparable to the bats of Arctogea exist in the Australian fauna, placental bats form a good substitute for the same.

This coincidence of contemporary evolution and radiation is termed to be contemporary radiation.

Successive radiation

Osborn recognises some important landmarks in radiation which can clearly be followed in succession from the Mesozoic to the day by which primitive insectivore type gave rise to the diversified mammalian fauna, which he termed successive radiation.

Conclusion

The living beings are wonderfully plastic, which in their efforts to find food and effect safety become adapted in course of time to all possible conditions of life, earth, air and water. Yet a highly adapted or specialised form become as it were stereotyped and incapable of a radial change.

DESERT ADAPTATION

Introduction

The role of evolution is unanimoresly accepted today as the Living Laws of Nature behind the problem of species forming and the run of life. This evolution, it is further supported, is governed by the laws of natural selection. Organisms are selected not on the basis of conformity to an ideal life and plan, not in relation to complete functional efficiency but on the basis of survival. The forms that exist are those, that have managed to survive and survival may be and often is achieved by a curiously making device, adaptation.

Desert adaptation

Adaptation to a desert life is otherwise known as desert adaptation. Desert is a level sketch of drifting sand where scarcity of water is extreme, characterised by rainless or nearly rainless climate. The drought may be said to be almost continuous, there being no regular occurrence of rainy season. In some years there may be torrential rainfall for a few days only. During other years practically no rain may fall.

In the tropical countries desert conditions prevail if the average rainfall is under 15 inches a year and in temperate under 10 inches. Consequently a desert may be defined as an area where evaporation of water is in excess of precipitation. The total of such areas have been estimated at one fifth of the entire land area of the globe.

Life in desert

The struggle for existence is exceedingly severe there and three primary needs of organisms stand out in prominence, viz., food, safety and reproduction.

Indeed moisture getting, moisture conservation and defense against physical and biotic environments are of prime importance in adaptation of animals in the desert.

Moisture getting

Plants secure moisture by sending down tap roots which penetrate deep into the soil and find out the subsoil water or some river stream. There are also superficial lateral system of roots which absorb water during the scanty rainfall. The date palm flourishes only where its roots have access to water. Along the banks of the Nile where the eroding action of the river has bared the roots of the palms, they may be seen going to a very great depth until they reach the water bearing strata.

The desert contains poisonous spiders, lizards and venomous snakes. The ostrich is the outstanding desert bird, and the gazelle the wild ass and the camel are great desert travellers. The desert lizard (*Moloch horridus*) carries spines over its body, and the spinescence and hard body surface prevent evaporation of water from the body. The desert lizard sips the dews that fall at night and that is the only drink they can have. Willey records that Moloch horridus while alive absorbs water like blotting paper when put into it.

Moisture conservation

Plants conserve moisture by having under ground reservoirs of water store as in wild gourd. In this plant the water reservoir is enormous in size corresponding to the circumference of a man's body, and consists of a tap root which contains water in its pulpy mass for months at a time.

In cacti the stem contains a large mass water in its pulp which is renewed during each humid season. The barrel cactus thus affords a source of drinkable water for thirsty.

A greatly thickened bark may also contain water as in Jatropha – loss by evaporation being prevented by a varnished and glazed surface.

Water storage in animals is also exhibited by camels. These animals have developed water cells in the wall of their rumen (1st division of the stomach). The water cells are cavities with narrow mouth protected by sphincter muscles acting like the draw string of a bag. When the animal drinks, the water not only reaches its stomach where it is absorbed and utilised but the water is also stored in these cells and later doled out by the relaxation of the sphincter muscles at the time of need. Hence the camel can travel from oasis to oasis for even 5-6 days without water but in such cases the animal needs rest.

Avoidance of evaporation

Plants avoid evaporation of water by the modifications of the leaves.

Desert shrubs have very small leaves or the leaves may be absent as in Cacti. If leaves are present, they either fall off at once with the coming of drought or fold themselves so as to present the smallest possible surface for evaporation. The hairiness and varnished surface already mentioned, also serves for the conservation of water.

Animals on the other hand conserve water by being non-perspiring because the physiological value of perspiration (excretion and heat regulation) are offset by the ill effects of the loss of the precious moisture. Practically non-perspiring mammals are a response to aerial adaptation.

Defence : I against nature, II Against other animals.

I. Against Nature

(a) *Extremes of temperature :* The temperature in desert in daytime is very high, on the other hand, during night it is very low, cold and chilly. Desert animals protect themselves from the extremes of temperature either by finding a great rock or they must burrow to escape the extremes of temperature.

(b) *Against ubiquitous sand :* Sand assails the three important organs of animals economy, viz., eyes, nostrils and ears. Eyes are protected by overhanging head shields, as in Typhlops, a burrowing snake. The margin of the lid is broadened into plates which are furnished with scales as in Agama, Phrynocephalus (lizard). In Teratoscincus, the upper lid is enlarged. In Mabecia the lower lid is enlarged, with a transparent window in it, so that the eye can be closed without impeding sight. In extreme cases, as in Ablepharus, the lower eyelid is transformed into a transparent cover, which is fused with the rim of the reduced upper lid. As an adaptation to desert condition, the camel has also large eyes which are guarded by long, abundant eyelashes. This is a response to the reflected heat of the blistering sand and rocks.

(c) Nostrils in digging animals are held upwards. In moist snakes they are protected by complicated valves or reduced to pinholes. In camels the nostrils are capable of being closed. In Saiga antelope of Australia, the animal has a much peculiarly inflated nose.

(d) The ear openings may be protected by scales. They may be small or totally absent as in lizard. In camels ears are protected by hairs.

II. Against other animals

Colouration of the body is the most conspicuous of the adaptations to desert life. Colouration furnishes protection against other animals. Desert creatures have no green colouration of the body, but they are generally sympathetically tinted – grey, brown, or red, harmonizing with rocky or sandy desert or may show double colour adaptation to suit the local conditions, for example, Gazelle found in sand is whitish; or those found near volcanic beds are dark grey. The desert lizard (Moloch horridus) carries spines over its body, and the spinescence and the hard body surface prevent evaporation of water from the body.

Conspicuously marked venomous spiders and wasps are found as a desert attribute. All the desert reptiles are poisonous, rattle snakes heading the list. The bite of a little trap-door spider is sufficient to take the life of its competitor. Tarantula is another overgrown spider. It has a ferocious bite and it makes an ugly wound. The scorpion and the many legged centipede are also poisonous.

Speed is necessary to an extreme degree for the preservation of life in the desert, for the animal has to travel far and wide for food getting, to pursue or to evade the pursuit as the case may be. Many of the lizards are so swift that the eye loses sight of them as they dart from rock to rock. The gazelle, the wild ass and the camel are great desert travellers. Speed is a characteristic of the dwellers of the desert. This speed shows itself in the slender form, long limbs, and often in the sand adapted feet of the desert wayfarer. Those of the camel, with the broad, yielding pad and secondary retrogression from unguligrade to digitigrade, are splendidly fitted to the yielding sands. Eremias has very large crural (shank) shields. In scapteria, the digits are broadened out into shovels.

Senses of hearing, sight and smell are highly developed in desert animals. In them, intelligence increases in relation to the developed hard conditions of life.

In the case of plants the first defensive need is anchorage against the almost continually flowing winds. This is excellently afforded by the deeply penetrating root system already referred to.

Development of spines as organ of defense in desert plants is universal, also another function naturally water conservation may be attributed to them. The spines are various shapes and size, and are arranged in peculiar patterns which worry the intruder and leaves him bleeding, but yet the jack rabbit, deer and other desert cattle will partake of the plant fruit, stem and trunk avoiding the spines as far as possible.

Chemical Characters : Desert plants have disagreeable odour and taste which also subserve as defensive mechanism against being eaten up. The sage brush of American desert has such a disagreeable odour that no mammal except the jack rabbit will eat them and the flesh of the rabbit is so much impregnated with the odour that no human being will eat either of them if any other food is available. The gazelle, one of the most admirably adapted of desert animals, is confined to tufts of wiry grass and a few dwarf and strongly scented aromatic herbs for food.

A conception about the origin of aromatic odour and other chemical properties in desert plants is that it is merely a response to aridity. Geologists have brought forward ample proof of the presence of salt lakes in bygone times near the present day desert. Probably these chemicals are absorbed with the water by the searching roots of the plants and later elaborated as such in the plant body.

Origin of desert life

Forms of desert animals vary to such an extent that these ranges are far greater than the desert limitations. A few of them undergo a perfect adaptation to live in desert, example, camel, ostrich.

Others are nearly temporary migrants desertwards and return to more humid regions during the period of fertility. The temporary dwellers are very large in number, and they make an exodus as soon as the water dries up and the vegetations begin to wither.

Conclusion

Adaptation and evolution can do miracles. The widespread desert and semidesert lands which have occurred from time to time in the geologic past have been of the prime importance as in evolutionary stimulus and has given rise to some of the momentous changes in the organic life, like the origin and evolution of horse.

CAVE ADAPTATION

Cave is a natural hollow, under the surface of the earth or in a mountain or hill usually in rock formation with an opening. The majority of caves have been formed by the dissolution of lime stone and they are most frequently found in regions where massive lime stones of considerable thickness are found near the surface of the ground.

The most famous cave area in the world is probably that which lies in the Calcareous Alps of Central and Southern Europe extending through France to Austria and Yugoslavia. The world's longest surveyed cave (37.6 miles) is in Switzerland. Dry caves are found in the rock of Gibralter, Malta and Lebanon. In the United States of America the most famous cave areas are the Kentucky (mammoth cave) Missouri and New Mexico. Well known caves are present in the Himalayas, Malaysia, Indonesia, South Africa and Australia.

Like the deep sea, the cave environment provides stable conditions for animals to live in. The conditions are more or less similar in the different caves, hence it results in the production of a number of parallel or convergent adaptations.

The cave environment is characterised by uniform darkness, relatively high humidity, feeble fluctuations of temperature, absence of air currents, etc. Absence of light has a telling effect on its inhabitants.

The cave animals may be (i) permanent cave dwellers such as turbellarians, chaetopod worms, leeches entomostracans, amphibods, isopods, decapods mites and true spiders, fishes and salamanders. (ii) occasional cave dwellers such as bats and owls. (iii) accidental cave dwellers or stragglers.

Cave adaptations

Among the permanent cave dwellers many morphological adaptations to suit the cave environment are met with. Cave animals are either colourless or pale white in colour. This is due to the absence of light. For example, Dina absoloni (leech), many Crustaceans, cave snails. If coloured, they are generally paler than the epigean relatives, for example, cave beetles. Proteus develops a dark brown or jet black colour when exposed to light.

Many cave arthropods are characterised by weak exoskeleton. The cave snails have thin shells. Among the fishes and collembola, the scales are lost altogether. The skin of the cave insects is much thinner than their corresponding surface dwellers.

In many cave animals, eyes undergo varying degrees of degeneration and are completely absent in the freshwater cave fishes, for example, Stygicola and Leucifuga from Cuba and Amblyopsis inhabiting the mammoth caves of America. In Typhlomolge and Typhlotriton (Salamanders) the eyes are completely absent. The absence of eyes is an instance of convergent regression. Consequent to the loss of visual organs, the sense organs well developed. Cave insects, myriapods and arachnids are characterised by the presence of long legs and antennae often provided with tactile hairs. Chaemoreceptors are well developed in cave animals. The cave isopod Asellus has larger sense bulbs than the land Asellus. Elongation and slender body is another trait among cave animals particularly in Crustacea.

In cave urodela, retrogression of endocrine system is noticed. The thyroid gland of Proteus is said to produce a hormone to which the tissues are quite unresponsive. Since the cave animals are shielded from the rigors of the struggle for existence it has become the refuge of many relics. The closest terrestrial relatives of such cave relics seem to have been wiped out by the natural selection. The snails of the genus Lartetia, Bathynella (a primitive Crustacean) Proteus (Salamander), Troglochaetus (annelid) are the notable relics.

Remarkable neotenic animals found in the caves are Urodele Proteus and the polychaete. Many cave dwelling forms have become taxonomically unclassifiable owing to the accumulation of archaic characters, for example, Bathynella. Some of the archaic features that are noticed are the metameric extensions of the lateral line system on the head of Caecobarbus; the ossification of the branchial and hyoidal arches in Proteus; absence of lung-books in cave spider and the degeneration of trachael system in Coleoptera. Life in caves is an antithesis of the feverish activity of the surface dwellers.

DEEP SEA LIFE (ADAPTATION)

Adaptation is the reciprocal fitness of the organism and environment. Organism lives under diverse conditions of life, and accordingly they are so modified and so moulded so as to fit the environment. We thus find that the inhabitants of the deep sea also manifest a profound impression of their habitat upon their structure.

Deep sea : The deep sea begins at the edge of the continental shelf at a depth of about 200 metres. In the greatest "deep", the depth is 35,400 ft.

Conditions of deep sea

(1) *Perfect stillness:* The currents are sluggish and may be practically non-existent.

(2) *Extreme cold:* At 1000 metres depth the temperature is about 50°F while below it, the water may be near freezing. It is due to the ocean currents from the polar regions ever sinking down.

(3) *Absolute darkness:* Sunlight falling on the surface and penetrating the water is quickly absorbed, red rays first and the blue end rays last. Such light as exists in the deep sea is due to the luminescence of the organisms.

(4) *Intense pressure:* Increasing at the rate of one ton per 1000 fathoms depth.

(5) *Food supply :* The source of food lies in the upper layers of the water wherefrom it falls down as oozes. Many of the creatures live in the great pelagic zone where life-giving heat and light are prevalent and where green plants flourish. These algae form the food of the ooze animals. The ooze is in a state of suspension, probably a foot or more in depth, and to this come fishes with feeble masticatory organs to feed upon the ooze creatures, and in their turn form the food of the more aggressive, predaceous sort.

Deep sea fauna

The seemingly inhospitable depths of sea support a great diversity of animal life. Prominent among these are siliceous hexactinellid sponges, sea pens, echinoderms, molluscs, various fishes notably the macurides (related to the cod), the brotulid fishes of the order Heteromi and in the arctic region, the liparid fishes. None of these groups are products of local evolution but are all independent migrant from shallower seas – either from pelagic or littoral zone.

Modifications

1. *General form of the body:* The deep sea forms are usually small and their flesh, thin and flabby, but that is where they are relieved of the terrific pressure to which they are normally subjected.
2. *Skeletal structures:* The deep sea forms are frail and weak with the ossification or calcification of skeletal structures much reduced. The reduced calcification in the invertebrates is due to the freezing cold (which shows deposition of calcium carbonate) and intense pressure, which increases its solubility in water and renders it hard to precipitate as skeletal matrix. In fishes the scales are reduced or absent and the skeleton is somewhat rickety. The weak skeleton of fishes was suggested by Roule to be due to insufficient Vitamin D.

3. *Colour:* The extremely diverse colours of the light zone are wanting and simplified colour is the rule. They may be scarlet due probably to the colour of the blood showing through the thin skin or they may be black. The significance of jet black colour of many forms is doubtful. The fish, Macrurus filicauda reverses the standard faunal colouring of the sea fishes in that it has a black belly and is silvery on top. The enemy looking down on the fish from above sees only the silvery back which blends with luminous environment, while to a foe looking up from below, the black belly would blend with the overlying darkness and thus become practically invisible.
4. *Luminescent organs:* Luminescent organs or photophore occur on many forms. They are of various shapes and size and are variously distributed. Sometimes photophores of different parts of the body emit light of different colours (many fishes and one squid). The photophores usually consist of an aggregation of light producing cells with a lens associated with them. They are controlled by the nervous system. Definitely in vertebrates and probably in other forms also their function may well be alluring besides light emitting. The light giving function may be either diffused over the entire body or localised in highly modified organs. They may assume the form of round, shining, mother-of-pear coloured bodies, imbedded in the skin, or smaller round globular bodies arranged symmetrically in series along the side of the body and tail.

   This phosphorescence seems to have been acquired before the deep sea migration occurred, necessitated by the nocturnal pelagic habits. Such forms are diurnal vertical migrants, coming to the surface at night and sinking below the light zone during the day time. This habit might have aided in their adjustment to pressure changes and thus made easy their abyssal journey. Phosphorescence is absent in all fresh water fishes.
5. *Eyes:* Many forms are blind but others have the eye increased in sensitivity. Many have telescoped eyes (that is, eyes raised on stalks) but the value of this elevation is doubted. In fishes the sensitiveness of the eye is increased by (i) increase in the number of rods per unit retinal area ; (ii) the complete or almost complete absence of cones (which are concerned with the colour vision) ; (iii) lengthening of the cones; (iv) more cones supplying each nerve fibre so that their effect may be summated; (v) increase in the size of the pupil and lens.

Some have eye like concave mirror which absorbs the greatest possible light.

6. *Tactile organs:* There are many forms of long feelers and slender attenuation of the fins such as can be best used in deep waters.
7. *Air bladder:* Though present in many forms, they are probably unfunctional. In others they are absent, and in some cases its tissue becomes highly reticulate and charged with fat which gives buoyancy to their possessor.
8. *Power of mastication:* Those which feed on oozes have lost the power of mastication, while other larger forms which feed on the former have wide gape of the mouth and powerful mouth armaments.
9. *Reproductive modification:* In their dark environment means must be found for bringing together the two sexes for breeding purposes. According to Beebe, in lantern fishes the patterns of photophores differ in various species and between two sexes also so that they serve for intraspecific recognition and for bringing together the two sexes for breeding. In the angler fishes the much smaller male is permanently attached to the female by its head, its skin fuses with that of its partner and draws the nourishment from its blood supply so that it is a parasite upon its partner. Many have wonderful contrivances for the care of young and others produce young in large numbers.

Distribution of Fauna in the Deep Sea

Among the invertebrates, the sponges form an important element in the deep sea fauna, and the coelenterates such as corals, hydroids and their allies are also well represented. Of the annelid worms, while the majority are undoubtedly littoral, deep sea forms are also common (tube building worms). Of the mollusca, the polycypoda have a great vertical distribution, that of the mussel, Mytilus being from the shore to 3000 fathoms. The gastropods are also found in 2000 fathoms. Of the Arthropods, we have barnacles from 3000 fathoms. Ostracods from 2000 fathoms, decapods such as crabs, shrimps and lobsters ranging down to 2500 fathoms though true crabs are largely shallow water forms, few occurring below 400 fathoms. Of the elasmobranchs, the true sharks have been taken at depths of from 345 to 400 fathoms and the Rays down to 600 fathoms. The Holocephali or silver sharks are distinctly abyssal. Many teleosts are also deep sea forms.

One of the most striking features of the deep sea and of the cave as well is their changelessness. There is nothing to mark the flight of time, no day or night, no sequence of seasons, and the sameness of conditions year in and year out must have a marked influence on the inhabitants. The stream of individual life as well as of evolution is quickened by environmental changes and is lulled into repose where change is not. Thus, these forms, when once they are adapted to the peculiar conditions which, as incoming migrants, they have to meet, practically cease their evolution as they diminish their individual activity and consequent metabolism.

CURSORIAL ADAPTATION

In order to survive, the organisms modify themselves so as to fit the environmental conditions around themselves. This plasticity of living organisms of adapting themselves to their surroundings, constitute one of the most remarkable characteristics and in doing so, they become highly modified.

The adaptation undergone by animals for rapid progression on land constitutes the cursorial adaptation.

There are a large number of cursorial animals, for example, frilled lizard and other desert reptiles, running birds, kangaroos and bandicoots, dogs, cats, specially the cheetah, horses, camels, deers, antelopes, besides a host of extinct forms, including many dinosaurs. Following modifications are found in the animals adapted for speed.

1. Body contour

To reduce the resistance of the air, the body becomes streamlined, the curve line of the body quite even and without any break and the body spindle-shaped, at least when in action.

2. Change in foot posture

The primitive plantigrade gait of the mammals becomes digitigrade (all cursorial mammals except Ungulates) and even unguligrade (supported on the hoop surrounding the unguals or the terminal phalanges of the digits). Some of the speediest of animals – dinosaurs, birds, dogs, all mammals in fact but the ungulates – have merely perfected the digitigrade gait, developing special sole-pads for the absorption of the shock of impact. Ungulate animals show all gradations from the semi-plantigrade condition of the lower forms to the high, stilted hoofs of certain of the African antelope. Certain ungulates like the modern camels have become secondarily digitigrade in response to locomotion in yielding sand.

3. Loss of digits

Plantigrade animals are generally 5-toed, while the cursorial forms invariably show a tendency to reduction of digits. The five-toed becomes four-toed, three –, two –, or even one toed, two toes in the artiodactyles and one in the perissodactyls being the irreducible minimum. The kangaroos also have lost their hallux. The frilled lizard of Australia, Chlamydosaurus, is five-toed but the lateral toes are shorter than the median ones. When Chlamydosaurus runs on its hind feet, the outer and inner toes are raised off the ground and the animal makes a three-toed track.

4. Formation of cannon bone

Concurrent with the loss of digits, there is a compacting of the bones of the podial and metapodials, the latter may actually fuse to form a single cannon bone which adds to the strength of the digits.

5. Reduction of ulna and fibula

Without any exception there is a tendency for the reduction and subsequent disappearance of the ulna in the forearm and the fibula in the shin.

6. Loss of universal movement

All the joints of the limbs except that of the girdles become such that movement is possible only in anterior and posterior directions due to the formation of tongue and groove joints as in the elbow and knee joint of horse. The movement of the limbs is pendulum-like and confined in one plane, except the hip and shoulder.

7. Lengthening of the limbs

The change of the gait from the plantigrade to unguligrade, and ungulate in itself considerably elongates the limb by raising the manus and pes to raise above the ground. Besides it there is an actual elongation of the limb bones, specially of the distal ones. The proximal ones remain short in order to provide an appropriate fulcrum for the whole limb and hence an efficient movement of the limbs. The growth of the distal segments result in the increase of length and by the modifications of limb and girdle muscles the lengthened limbs have been and additional adaptation for speed.

8. Loss of general utility

In the quadrupedal forms, the fore limbs which primarily have a prehensile function, lose their general utility and become adapted for rapid locomotion but at definite slower space than the hind limbs, as is quite clearly shown by the phylogeny of horse and camel.

9. Bipedality

Another method of quick progression is through acquisition of the bipedality – when the forelimbs become only prehensile and reach the ground only during rest or may never reach the ground. Bipedality has been evolved specially in the frilled lizard, Chlamydosaurus, many extinct dinosaurs, birds, kangaroos and the rodents. The bipedal forms show the following special adaptations.

(a) Reduction of the forelimbs

A marked disparity soon arises between the size of the fore and hind limbs and the former becomes comparatively very small. The hind limbs, however, undergo the same general function as described above, viz., lengthening, loss of movement, etc.

(b) Counterpoise

Some sort of counterpoise is always necessary in a semi-erect biped and the tail usually assumes this function. In the kangaroo and in the dinosaurs it is a powerful organ and serves as a prop, like a third limb, when the creature rests without coming down on all fours. The tail may be comparatively short and heavy in larger forms or extremely long and slender in more lightly built creatures. Many dinosaurs and bipedal lizards have a long, attenuated tail. Among the birds which have no tail, the long, tail feathers subserve the function in pheasant, while in Ratitae the long neck and head suffice. The Ostriches raise their wings to support themselves.

(c) Shortening of neck

There is a remarkable cervical reduction along with a short head, thus cervical vertebrae may be shortened or fused. In Dipus (Jerboa) all the cervicals except the atlas are ossified.

Mental Precocity

Mental precocity becomes essential in cursoiral animals. Rodents and carnovores have very feeble young, but they are kept hidden until able to shift for themselves, while the ungulates have remarkably mentally precocious youngs. With all other forms which depend upon speed for safety, the young animal must be able to keep up with the herd almost at once.

Significance of Cursoiral adaptation

Both the birds and mammals have evolved from cursorial reptiles, the former from bipedal ones and the latter from the quadrupedal ones. Back of this lies the impelling cause of increasing aridity. Speed adaptation not only gives rise to some of nature's most beautiful and perfect machines, but it seems to have a much deeper meaning.

The following is the list of Vertebrates which shows Cursorial adaptation:

1. *Reptilia*: Lizards, snakes, especially frilled lizards, Carnovorous and amphibious dinosaurs, herbivorous beaked dinosaurs.
2. *Birds*: Cassowaris, Ostriches, Emus, Rheas, etc.
3. *Mammalia*: Kangaroos, Bandicoots, Hares, Rabbits, Jerboas, Dogs, Cats, Cheetah, Horses, Deer, Antelopes, Giraffe, Okapi, Camel, Tasmanian Wolf, South American Ungulates.

PELAGIC ADAPTATIONS

The pelagic animals are diverse and are specialised in many ways for pelagic mode of life. A common feature of all the pelagic forms is their ability to maintain themselves in the open waters without sinking to the bottom. Some of them are pelagic throughout their existence while others lead a pelagic existence only for a short period. The pelagic fauna is mostly composed of the larvae of many animals which live as adults in the benthic zone. Pelagic animals have evolved several ingenious methods for keeping afloat.

As the bodies of pelagic animals are heavier than water special devices are necessary to reduce the specific gravity. In most of the animals the shell or skeletal materials ae very much reduced. The weight of the foraminiferan shell is reduced by an increase in the size of the pores and by the enlargement of the opening of the shell. The pelagic Crustaceans have either weakly calcified or uncalcified exoskeleton. Among the pelagic gastropods there is a progressive reduction in the shell. The pteropods have very thin shells. The pelagic lamellibranch has an uncalcified shell. Among the cephalopods the pelagic Loligo and Oigopsidae have a delicate narrow uncalcified internal shells.

Reduction in the specific gravity has been attained in many pelagic animals by taking large amounts of water. The water is incorporated in their transparent jelly like tissues. The leptocephalus larva of eel, Cyrstallogobius and Aphla among planktonic fishes are watery and transparent. Radiolarians contain oil drops in their protoplasm. Siphonophores have found the most effective means of reducing the specific gravity by having air or gases in their pneumatophores. In Halistemma in addition to the apical float or pneumatophore, four or five pairs of swimming bells (nectocalyces) filled with air serve as organs of floatation and stability. The pelagic nudibranch has gas in the intestine which seems to play the same role as in siphonophore. Another method by which the pelagic animals avoid sinking from surface is by changing their body structure. The simplest method is by enlarging the ventral surface which results in the flattening of the body. Such flattened bodies are met with in hydromedusae, scyphomedusae. Copepods with their elongated appendages set with bristles are able to effectively maintain themselves at the surface.

Larger animals, keep themselves at the water surface by active swimming movements. A wide spread means of maintaining themselves at surface water is by jet propulsion that is, taking in water and ejecting it with force which enables the animals to propel either forwards or upwards. In the case of Tomopteris and Alciopa parapodia are used for this purpose. Among the pteropods the foot is modified to form paddle like or oar like structures. The phenomenon of surface tension also plays a large part in preventing the small pelagic animals from sinking.

AQUATIC ADAPTATION

Adaptation to environment is one of the most obvious and at the same time remarkable qualities of living organisms. In fact it sums up nearly the whole result of evolution. Adaptation to water medium is known as aquatic adaptation.

Aquatic animals

Among aquatic types of vertebrates – whether fish, mammal or reptile there is in general same fish, like body contour, with same sorts of locomotory structures, etc.

Mechanical problems of water habitat :

(a) To overcome buoyancy of water

(b) To overcome resistance of water

(c) Problem of propulsion of body

(i) By sinuous (undulating) motion of the body

(ii) Supplementary action of 4 lateral fins

(iii) Horizontal steering of body by median system of fins.

Aquatic adaptation may be of two types

(a) Primary and (b) Secondary.

(a) Primary aquatic adaptation : When the adaptations remain in the original direction, it is said to be primary and the subsequent changes remain more or less in the same direction from the very appearance of the animal. *Example* – Aquatic adaptation of fish.

(b) Secondary aquatic adaptation : When the adaptive changes divert from the original direction they are called secondary adaptation. The changes are directed along different lines due to change of the original home of the organisms and they subsequently adapt themselves to some new environment. *Example* – Aquatic adaptation of whales.

Modifications of the primarily aquatic vertebrates

Primarily aquatic animals are generally the gill-breathing vertebrates, which have never had a terrestrial ancestry, but have evolved from more primitive aquatic progenitors.

Body contour

The body is stream-lined with no protruberences which would retard the swift passage of the animal through the water. The head is sub-conical, the edges of the jaws and gill covers fit precisely, and even the eyes conform accurately to the curvature of the head.

Locomotion

This is effected by lateral undulations of the flexible body, aided by the fins. The fins are paired and unpaired fins. The unpaired fins may be more or less continuous from the head along the mid-line of the back, around the tail and forward along the underside as far as the vent. In some cases the continuous fin-fold is broken up as dorsal, caudal and ventral fins. They are stiffened by fin-rays of elastic bone or cartilage. The increase of resistant surface in the fish is obtained through all these median fins. The caudal fin acts as a propelling organ. The paired fins maintain the body in a horizontal position, the pectorals make the fish dive and the pelvics aid to rise to the surface.

Swim bladder

It is an outgrowth of the alimentary canal, filled with air or gas. It is the homologue of the lung of the terrestrial animal. Its function is largely hydrostatic but it also functions as a respiratory organ. When the creature is about to sink, the body is slightly compressed through muscular contraction and with it the swim bladder. When the muscles are relaxed, the compressed gas in the bladder expands and the specific gravity is decreased, and the creature rises.

Secondary aquatic adaptation

Lung breathers are the secondarily aquatic forms, which through stress of circumstances – inhospitable lands where food was scarce or competition severe – were forced to return once more to the primal home of their remote ancestors, and the following changes have taken place in them.

Advancement in organs

When the lung breathers turned back to the waters, they readopted only the externals of fish life, but kept in varying degrees the higher brain and the more efficient methods of aeration of the blood and of locomotion.

Body contour

Body becomes stream-lined, with shortened neck, cylindrical chest and enlarged tail. This assumption of the fish-like form is shown by Ischthyosaurs, Cetacea, Sirenia and Pinnipedia. In them, the brain-case becomes shortened and the facial portion of the skull tends to elongate with an elongated slender snout or rostrum. In the whales, the cervical vertebrae may be fused into a solid, compressed mass of bone. In ancient reptiles, the vertebrae retain their ancient simplicity. In the higher forms the vertebrae tend to simplify secondarily. This simplification includes the centra or bodies of the vertebrae and especially the zygapophyses. In the whale bone whales the articulation of the ribs and vertebrae is extremely loose.

The Galapagos lizards live on certain rocky islands of the Galapagos group. They possess a flattened swimming tail and a slightly compressed body as their aquatic adaptation.

In truly aquatic type the chest tends to become cylindrical. The chest is modified as to bring the internal cavity higher toward the back. This insures greater stability of floatation and increased lung capacity. In swimming forms the bones tend to become light and spongy.

The sea snake which is highly venomous has tail vertically compressed like a rudder. In amphibious crocodile of river, the feet are partly webbed and the tail is long and vertically compressed and by its lateral movement, the crocodile swims fast. The other adaptive features are shifting of nostrils at the tip of the snout which is kept above the surface of water while the body is kept concealed under water. The internal nostrils open far backward into the throat on account of cutting of air passage in the mouth cavity by fusion of palatine bones. Further adaptive mechanism, is the closure of ear pit by two scaly flaps which are operated by special muscles when the crocodile dives.

In aquatic mammals, the external ears are lost and the nostrils move toward the apex of head as in the whales, some reptiles. The eyes shift higher on face in amphibious types as Hippopotamus. In truly aquatic types, the eyes do not shift their position and the eyes become adapted to aquatic vision.

Limbs

In the sea going turtles the limbs are modified into oar-like paddles with shortening of proximal elements and lengthening of distal elements of limbs, and the exoskeletons are reduced, and the body is stream-lined and in most the head is non retractile and the tail disappeared.

Among birds the Penguin that sits erect on land on the tail, the legs being set forth back on the trunk, is wonderfully adapted to swimming and diving. The wings are flattened to form the powerful paddle or flipper. The legs are webbed and used as a rudder in swimming.

In water birds the feet are webbed and the feathers are water proofed as in Duck. The Jacanas which appear to walk on water are adapted for life on floating leaves with elongation of anterior digits on the hind limbs.

Among the mammals, the modern Cetacea which includes the whales and porpoises are characterised by adaptation of many of their morphological characters to special mode of life in the sea. The body is stream-lined and the tail is compressed into a horizontal fin. The hind limbs disappeared, the pelvics are rudimentary. The fore limbs are flattened into paddles, the proximal limb bones are shortened and the digits become elongated. Zygapophyses are absent. The sternum is reduced.

In aquatic carnivores (Seals and Walruses) the forelimbs are modified into paddles for swimming and the hind limbs being soldered to the tail become inefficient for walking on land.

Integument

In aquatic animals the skin undergoes modification in the line of reduction of armoring, of hair, of skin glands, muscles and nerves. The hair is lost in marine mammals. The Whales and Sirenians possess a few bristles around the mouth. As a compensation against the loss of hairs, the mammals have developed a layer of fat called blubber beneath the skin for conserving body heat, and the skin glands the secretion of which will be washed away by water, disappeared.

Mouth armament

In general, the jaws being no longer of any use for crushing food loose their power to a great extent. The teeth also suffer modification. In Globicephalus the teeth may be over one hundred ; whale has but a single tooth. In baleen whales, the teeth are entirely absent.

Precocity

In the gregarious aquatic animals mental precorcity is necessary. They exhibit ability to keepup with the mother.

Size and speed

Aquatic animals exceed all others in size and usually develop a high speed. For example Sulphur bottom Whale reaches a length of 87 feet.

VOLANT ADAPTATION

The role of evolution is unanimously accepted today as the Living Laws of Nature behind the problem of species forming and the run of life. This evolution is further supported, governed by Natural Selection. Organisms are selected not on the basis of conformity to an ideal life and plan not in relation to complete functional efficiency but on the basis of survival. The forms the exist are those, that have managed to survive and survival may be and often is achieved by a curiously making device, adaptation.

Adaptation to aerial life is otherwise known as volant adaptation. This is also the adaptation to flight. There are organisms successfully adapted for quick movement in the air. Air is a homogenous medium and the animals inhabiting it modify uniformly and beautifully to offer the least possible resistance to the attainment of speed. However, these animals cannot spend all their life time in air. They must come back to the trees or earth or sea when they wish to rest. Hence, their adaptation is always a "double one" and consequently, their body is suited to fly in air or take rest on trees or sea as the circumstance may arise.

The primary aim for the animals adapting the air is to achieve maximum amount of flight.

Flight is of two types: (i) Passive or gliding flight, and (ii) True flight.

1. **Passive flight:** This is a passive fight comparable to a gliding aeroplane without engine power. In this, the creature merely takes an initial leap from a height point and, held up by certain sustaining organs and impelled by gravity, glides to a lower level, sometimes covering a horizontal distance of many yards in the meanwhile. Gliding is usually associated with the development of skin along the creature's flanks, supported by extension of ribs beyond the body wall, but generally also between the forelimbs and the hind limbs.
2. **True flight:** True flight also implies a more or less profound modification of the forelimbs which become as a consequence unsuited to ordinary progression. True flight seems to be confined to the strictly air breathing vertebrates (wherein it has been developed thrice but once in each class). True fliers may move the wings with varying degrees of rapidity from the extreme speed of a humming bird's wing to the measured cadence of a winging crow.

Modifications of volant animals

Correlated with the power of flight, the aerial (volant) animals show primary and secondary modifications both in their external and internal organization, and the degree of modification is directly proportional to the power of flight.

1. Body contour

Body contour in volant animals is second only to that of the purely aquatic forms in its degree of perfection for the lessening of resistance. The body is moulded in such a way as to offer the least resistance when passing through air. The true flying forms are also often smaller in size.

2. Flying mechanism

Those flying fishes (e.g., Exocoetus) have their pectoral fins greatly elongated and enlarged for a "gliding movement in air". In higher forms special organs like the "patagium or wings" are developed, and these form the sustaining surface.

(a) Patagium

Patagium is a fold or series of folds of the skin supported by elongated ribs or by the fore limbs and their digits. However, most soaring mammals have their patagium supported between the fore and hind limbs, and sometimes the skin fold extends in front of the fore limb to the neck and again between the hind limbs and the tail. In the flying lemur, Galeopithecus the patagium extends from the sides of the neck to the tip of the tail, even including the digits, which are webbed as though for aquatic life.

If the patagium is supported mainly by the elongated fore limbs and their digits, the flight ensues as in Pterosaurs, wherein the enormously elongated outer finger sustains over half the membrane, and in the Bats, whose second, third fourth and fifth digits perform a like function, the first alone being free. In both groups, the membrane extends from the arm to the sides of the body and also to the front of the hind limb. An interfemoral membrane is also variably present in Bats.

In the "flying dragons", the body is depressed and the sides extend outward into a pair of large wing-like membranes, supported by 5-6 elongated ribs. The entire device can be folded like a fan.

(b) Feathers

These are diagnostic of birds. They consist of a quill or calamous and the reachis or shaft. On the rachis a double series of barbs are developed, carrying a similar double series of barbules, again giving rise to barbicels, which in the distal rows usually terminate in hooklets. These catch in the folded margins of the next proximal row, thus producing a firm surface. Each flight feather, therefore, forms a membrane like collectively sufficient to maintain the bird in the air even when a few at a time are lost as during the moulting season.

(c) Wings

The wings are mere modifications of the forelimbs in the flying forms. The bat wing as compared with the other wings is least modified. The following changes take place in the associated parts. The humerus becomes well developed, the radius long and curved, while ulna is vestigial. The pollex or thumb is always free and has claw.

In the smaller bats, Michrochiroptera, the second finger although distinct is not free from the third but is attached to it distally, the two combining to support the anterior margin of the wing. The 4th and 5th digits are well developed. In the Megachiroptera, the second digit is independent of the 3rd and bears a claw like the first.

In the Pterodactyl wing, the radius and ulna are more nearly equal.

The wing is flexed between metacarpel and proximal phalanx rather than at the wrist as in birds and bats.

The wings of the birds are highly specialised. The wing feathers greatly increase the striking surface of the wings without increasing the weight of the body. The reduction in the number of digits in the hand takes place. The bones of the arm and wrist fuse to maintain the rigidity in the wing and in co-ordinating the movement of the upper arm, forearm and hand.

(d) Wing muscles or Pectoral muscles

Wing muscles are well developed on the breast bone or keel of the sternum. These muscles are pectoralis major, minor and coraco-brachialis. These are responsible for the movements of the wings.

3. Skeleton in flying vertebrates

(a) Pneumatic bones

The weight of the body is decreased by the peculiar structure of bones which show a spongy internal structure. The central cavities of the bones are usually hollow, and many of the bones contain air sacs connected with the lungs.

(b) Sternum and shoulder girdle

Animals with true flight develop strong breast bones which are provided with keels for the origin of the pectoral muscles. The shoulder girdle becomes very rigid by the development of clavicles. In the flying birds (Carinatae) the scapula and coracoid are united by an articulation; in the flightless birds (Ratitae) they are firmly co-ossified. The sternum in Ratitae is raft-like and bears no keel.

4. Brain and sense organs

The brain and sense organs are well developed in direct ratio with the powers of flight. In birds and Pterosaurs, the brain has well developed hemispheres and much enlarged optic lobes. The eyes in birds and pterodactyle are large and also provided with sclerotic plates which would resist variable pressure and aid in rapid focussing. The bats have well developed tactile sense and remarkable ears.

5. In birds, air sacs are developed to reduce the specific gravity of the bird, and increase the efficiency of the lungs.

Examples of Flying Vertebrates

Flying fishes

There are several genera of flying fishes, each of which represents a separate volant adaptation.

1. **Exococtus :** This fish is allied to skipper and garfish and is found in tropical and sub-tropical seas. This is a trim-built creature having large and greatly elongated pectoral fins and much smaller pelvic fins. The pectoral fins are the main organs of flight. The lower lobe of the tail fin is invariably the longer and it aids in giving the final impetus to the fish as it leaves the water and also in accelerating its speed if in the course of its flight it comes near enough to the surface of the sea. The length of the flight is however variable, sometimes reaching to 300 yards.
2. **Dactylopterus :** It is found in Sargasso sea. Various species of this fish are known as "flying gurnets". Mosely states that the smaller species of Dactylopterus flies by rapidly moving its wings in the style of Grasshoppers.
3. **Pantodon :** It lives in the Congo and Nigeria rivers of Africa. The fish is 3-4 inches long. It can leap out of water and flutter through the air for some distance.
4. **Gastropelecus :** This is also a small flying fish, found in the rivers of British Guinea. This is also a small compressed fish with long and curved but not particularly large pectoral fins. It skims along the surface of water for 40 feet or even more beating the water with its pectoral fins. Then it leaves the water for a distance of 5 to 10 feet and when exhausted falls sideways into the water again.
5. **Pegasus volitans :** This is a little fish found along the coasts of Japan, China, India and Australia. It also skims a short distance above the surface of the water by means of its broad pectoral fins.
6. **Cypsilurus :** It is also a common flying fish with elongated pectoral fins for leaping long distance in the air.

Besides the above living forms of flying fish, several extinct forms of flying fishes have also been discovered, and some of the them are :–

(i) Dollopterus from the Middle Triassic of Jena, (ii) Thoracopterus and Gigantopterus from the Upper Triassic of Austria, (iii) Exocoetoides and (iv) Chirothrix of the Upper Cretaceous of Mt. Lebanon, Syria. Of all these extinct forms, Chirothrix is of particular interest on account of the huge size of pectoral fins, which seem to imply powers of flight fully equal to those of living Exocoetus and Dactylopterus.

Flying Amphibia

The tree frog Rhacophorus is the sole example of the volant adaptation among amphibia. Its feet are webbed and the digits are terminated in adhesive pads. There are rudiments of patagia in front of and behind the arms.

Flying Reptiles

1. **Chrysopelea :** It is a flying snake, found in Borneo. It glides down obliquely through the air. The body is rigid, and the ventral side is concave to sustain the animal in its fall.

2. **Ptychozoon :** It is a flying or fringed gecko of the Malay countries. It is provided with lateral expansions of the skin along the sides of the neck, body, tail and limbs and between the toes.

3. **Pterodactyls (flying dragon, extinct reptiles of Mesozoic period):**

   They were first discovered in the Upper Triassic period, and they ranged from Jurassic to Upper Cretaceous period and later died down. They were akin to birds, possessing true flight. The little finger wings were well developed. The legs and the tail were essentially avian. The body was short, the neck and head elongated. But the tail was curiously elongated with spoon-shaped terminal end. The wing was only a membrane (patagium).

Birds

They form an excellent example of the perfection of aerial adaptation among animals. The earliest known birds were the extinct Archaeopteryx and Archaeornis. Among the living birds, the Neognathae are capable of flight, while the Palaeognathae (Ratitae) are flightless birds.

Flying Mammals

1. **Bat:** It attains true flight. The forelimbs are modified into wings for flight. The wing is formed by continuous fold of skin (patagium) which begins from the shoulder and extends between the long fingers of the forearm to the hind legs and even to the tail. The thumb is short, the ulna is reduced, while the radius is long and curved in the forearm. The hind limbs and the pelvic girdle are poorly developed, while the pectoral girdle is strong, and sternum bears a keel.

2. **Petaurus:** It possesses a patagium extending between the fore- and hind limbs. The tail is very large and bushy.

   The genus Acrobates includes two species of flying phalangers which possess narrow patagia extending from the elbow to the knee along the flank. The long fringing hairs borne by the patagium, together with those on either side of the tail, aid in flight.

3. There are two families of rodents which contain flying forms. The families are Anomaluridae and Sciuridae, of which three genera viz., Pteromys, Sciuropterus and Eupetaurus are volant. Anomalurus of the family Alumaluridae, has a well developed patagium extending from wrist to ankle but narrowing in front of the leg from the knee down. Pteromys has a well developed patagium extending as far as the digits.

4. **Galeopithecus :** This is a flying lemur found in the forests of Sumatra and Borneo. In this animal the patagium reaches its highest development and extends as a continuous fold of the skin between the head and the entire length of the tail. Thus the soaring powers of the flying lemurs are very great.

5. **Propithecus :** It exhibits volant adaptation but in this mammal, the flight is limited. The patagium is greatly or completely reduced and the powerful hind limbs help in the soaring of the animal.

COLOURATION AND MIMICRY

Introduction

Nowhere else is the plasticity and adaptability of living organisms better demonstrated than in the phenomenon of colouration and mimicry, which make a fascinating subject to the student of natural science and has attracted a host of workers to work on it.

In nature colour is the outcome of some sort of interference with the beams of white light, either through the absorption of certain of the component rays, allowing others to be reflected to the eye, or by some arrangement of surface sculpturing orprismatic structure. In animal body, colour is due to deposition in the body of some pigments which are the products or by-products of metabolism or certain waste products or reserve products.

Colour discrimination

1. Wallace (1895) stated that the animals have probably passed through a progressive series of changes, at first possessing general sensitiveness to light, then developing an ability to discriminate between different wave lengths and finally acquiring some power to discriminate.

2. There has been considerable differences of opinion as to whether certain animals possess colour vision (Frisch, 1923) or do not (Hess, 1921).
3. Sparrow (1923) suggests that colours may often be adopted for eyes that see in a different way for those of man.

Colouration in animals is of universal occurrence. Every conceivable type of colour is found : red, yellow, blue, brown, white, or a mixture of colour patterns. Usually colouration is fixed or specific. However, in certain animals such as insects and mammals, the colouration varies during different stages of their life – time after moulting or at the sexual period.

Colour production

There are two factors through which the prevailing colours in nature are produced : the first is chemical, and the second is physical.

Chemical colouration is caused by the presence of pigments. These are the waste products or by-products of metabolism. They are found in nearly all portions of an animal's anatomy. The pigment containing cells are differentiated into plain pigment and chromatophores. The plain pigment is found on the surface of the body and gives an unchanging hue to the animal, that is, one incapable of rapid temporary alteration. The chromatophores are quickly changeable pigment containing cells. Each of these has the form of a small sac with thin and highly elastic walls, supplied with fine muscle fibres and nerve endings. When the muscle fibres are expanded, the sac is drawn up into a minute globe, and when contracted, the sac is flattened out into a disc. The granules of pigment deposited in each of the chromatophores may be either red, yellow, orange, or black, and other shades are produced by the combination of these primary colours. The initial stimulus to colour change is received partly through the action of the hormone (intermedin) of the pituitary gland, partly through another hormone of the adrenal glands and partly through nervous system.

In some animals, the colouration is merely due to the absorptive powers of the chemical substance of which tissues are composed, as for example, the haemoglobin gives the red colour to the blood of the vertebrates and certain worms, and so also the haemocyanin gives the blue colour to the blood of Octopus. Still in some cases colouration may be due entirely to the nature of food consumed. For instance, the pink colour in feathers of the flamingo is caused by eating food (shrimps) containing carotenoids. For the same reason the lobsters are blue in shell and red in antennae.

Physically, colouration is due to some arrangement of surface sculpturing which refracts a beam of light and breaks it up into its different coloured rays. For instance, the sculptured surface of a beetle's wing acts as a crystal prism in the production of colours. The tropical butterfly Morpho ranges from blue to a greenish hue, while the ruby-throated humming-bird or the neck of some pigeons changes from a brilliant metallic red to a lustrous green.

Classification of colouration in the animal kingdom

After R.S. Lull	After E.B. Poulton
I. Indifferent colours	
II. Valuable colours	
1. Sympathetic colours	Cryptic colours
(a) Protective	Procryptic colours
(b) Aggressive	Anticryptic colours
2. Alluring colours	Pseudo episematic pseudosematic
3. Mimetic colours	Pseudo aposematic pseudosematic
4. Warning colours	Sematic
5. Signalling colours	Aposematic Sematic
6. Recognition marks	Episematic Sematic
7. Confusing colours	
8. Sexual colours	Epigamic colours

I. **Indifferent (Non significant) colours :** These are considered to be hereditary colours and are important to certain ancestors of different environment, for example, brilliant scarlet colours of fin rays of certain deep sea fishes. Another example is that of the colours or markings such as the spots on the uniformly black fur of a melanic leopard, or those sometimes seen in the coat of a domestic horse.

II. **Valuable colours :** These colours are useful to the possessor in various ways. They have been classified as follows :

1. **Sympathetic, Cryptic or Concealing colouration :** This colouration makes animals blend with the environment in which they live and thereby helps them – (i) to escape from being detected by enemies, or (ii) to lie in wait for their preys. The first is called protective

colouration, for example, Arctic hares have camouflage to escape from the Arctic foxes; the second is known as aggressive colouration, for example, Arctic fox is aggressively coloured to enable it to approach its prey unnoticed.

The principles of protective and aggressive colourations find various modes of expression in different animals. For example, the South American toad, *Bufo typhonius* and *Bufo superciliaris* are strikingly similar to the leaf lying on the forest floor. The crabs living among the sea weeds clothe themselves with pieces of weed and thus escape from being discovered. On the other hand, the Sphingid caterpillar, *Leucorphampha triphtolemus* of Brazil inflates its anterior segments of the body so as to expose two large eye-like spots which make it resemble the head or hood of cobra, thus terrifying other species.

2. **Alluring colouration:** This is the colour worn by animals for advertisement. For instance, certain protectively coloured African lizard bears a brilliant patch of colour at the corner of the mouth which acts as a lure for the unwary. The angler fishes and star-gazers attract the prey by means of lures.
3. **Mimetic colours :** These may be concealing or warning resembling between the animal and other objects – animate or inanimate. For instance, in certain forests of Madagascar, the colouring of many lizards, beetles, bugs and other insects so closely resemble the lichenous that they are almost invisible.
4. **Warning or Revealing colouration:** This is characterised by conspicuous colours or markings that give notice to would be enemies. The poisonous and unpalatable animals in general possess conspicuous colours such as red, yellow, etc. For example, coral snake, gila monster, tiger, salamander and many caterpillars and butterflies. The need for advertisement of these species is that there is the need of avoiding or warning a predator to which it is no use of if such an animal is not eaten after it is killed. Warning colouration sometimes carries with it the assumption of an attitude which hightens the effect and may be designed to strike terror to the enemies, for example, hood of cobra. The deadly poisonous spiders are all conspicuously coloured. The dorsal fin of the Weever-fish is deep black in colour. Upon provocation this fin is erected and spread out in a conspicuous manner, suggesting that it is designed to strike terror to the enemy's heart.

5. **Signal marks :** These are common in gregarious animals. On noticing an imminent danger, any member of a herd of deer usually raises its tail and thus exposes the white signal on the underside of the tail. This acts as a warning to the others and in an instant the herd is in full retreat. The American antelope (Antilocapra) has conspicuous areas of white hair on either rump which can be flashed through a spreading of the hair, and forms a danger signal.
6. **Recognition marks :** These are meant for recognition by the members of the same species, such as the red and orange spots on the side of a brook trout, salvelinus fontinalis. Recognition marks are also many insects such as butterflies and moths. They are visible only when the animal is in motion. The sphingid moths and certain grasshoppers have bright red colour on the undersurface of wings and abdomen, and these are not exposed when the insects rest with wings folded. When the insect is in flight the colour is suddenly flashed to mislead the enemy.
7. **Confusing colours:** The recognition colouring of moths and butterflies are very conspicuous. However, after flight when the animal suddenly settles, the brilliant colour instantly disappears, since its exposed colouring now harmonizes with the support on which it rests. This sudden disappearance of the conspicuous colour is very confusing to a human observer.
8. **Sexual colours :** Sexual colours distinguish the sexes of the animals. The males of birds and other forms are often much more conspicuously coloured than their females. For example, the male peacock has bright colours, the male cardinal bird has gorgeously coloured plumage. The young males which have not yet reached sexual maturity are also protectively coloured.

Mimicry

The term 'mimicry' signifies the resemblances which organisms bear to other organisms or to inanimate objects in form, colour, attitude, and action. In mimicry, an animal also resembles a different species of animals and so departs in appearance from the group to which it belongs. The disguise deceives its enemy and the mimicry is concealing and protective. Mimicry may be classified as follows :

1. Protective mimicry
2. Warning mimicry

3. Aggressive or Alluring mimicry
4. Simulation of death.

1. **Protective mimicry:** In this the animal mimics an object as to protect itself from the enemy. The caterpillar of the geometrid moth, and the stick insect, appear like twigs or sticks of plants, the leaf insects by the green colouration and pattern of wings, appear like the leaves of plants, and the kallima butterfly resembles the dried leaves. These are examples of protective mimicry. The greatest enemies of insects are the lizards and birds, and the mimic mistaken, for a part of the plant is not attacked by its enemy. In the industrial area of England a species of moth is found that by mutation gives rise to coloured forms that when they settle on tree trunks blackened by soot become indistinguishable and escape destruction. This is another example of protective or cryptic or concealing mimicry. In the leaf insect, phyllium, the wings and flattened and expanded body and limbs are all green except for irregular small yellowish spots which simulate the fungus or rust growths upon a leaf so that the total resemblance is very precise. There are other butterflies which look like leaves, simulating not only the general hue of a dead or withered leaf but its peticle midrib, venation. One such butterfly is Caenophlebia from Bolivia, in which the upper outer angle of the fore wing forms the apparent stem or petiole of the leaf.

2. **Warning mimicry:** Often quite palatable and harmless forms are coloured or shaped like some other harmful, poisonous or inpalatable forms of a closely related or distantly related group. Some species of butterflies are palatable and these resemble those species of butterflies which are unpalatable and so these are avoided by birds. The Viceroy butterfly mimics the Monarch butterfly (Danaus).

   The butterfly, Prionereis resembles Delias in company of which it always flies and rests just like the latter on the red flower of Lantana. Among reptiles there are certain brilliantly coloured poisonous snakes belonging to the family Elapidae. When they possess a strong poison they are practically harmless to man because of the limited extent of the gape. Each of the several species of poisonous coral snakes is mimicked by other species of harmless snakes belonging to different genera. Among insects again there are a number of imitators, both active and passive. The butterfly Papilio polytes is polymorphic having females of different forms. Some females mimicking Papilio aristolochioe, a few mimicking P. hector, and the females simulating different species have better chance of survival from the attack of the enemy. A few species of butterflies resemble the wasp which for its offensive nature of stinging is just avoided by its enemy. The spider, Amyclea lineatopis mimics the common red ant. The spider resembles the ant in outer form of the body and in colouration. It moves with the file of ants, keeping a little side distance from the latter, and as soon an ant has strayed away from its marching column, the spider jumps upon it from the tree by hanging down a spider line, and escapes with the victim.

3. **Aggressive mimicry:** This is often found in carnivorous forms to attract or lure or to simply lie in wait for the prey. Thus spiders are found on golden-rod and other flowers. Their yellow bodies harmonize with the flowers upon which they rest as to render them invisible to the visiting insects which for the prey of the spider. The stinging wasp is yellow in colour. The yellow and the red signify danger and they warn other animals to leave them alone. However, sometimes the head of the aggressor is concealed by a colouration which is known as the directive mark, and the aggressor waits for the victim to come near the dangerous part of its body. There are also colours which allure prey to the aggressor's mouth. The angler fish carries on its head a line which sways, and the food fishes are allured to the mouth of the angler fish. There is another spider which resembles an orchid blossom more or less closely, both in colour and form. This resemblance is an alluring one and is advertising.
4. **Simulation of Death:** It is well known in the American oppossum, Didelphis virginiana, whose act of feigning death is too well known to be termed "playing possum". This is a sort of adaptation to save its life when attacked by an enemy that prefers to kill its prey. Many insects, such as beetles and plant bug fall to the ground when they scent danger, and lie inert on the ground.

Wallace's rules of mimicry –

The following conditions are necessary for success in protective mimicry.

1. Imitative species must occur in the same area and occupy the same station as the mimicked.
2. The imitators are always the more defenseless and the model is avoided by the enemy.

3. The imitators should always be less numerous than the model as otherwise experimental attack by the enemy will reveal the true nature of the mimic and the bluff will be exposed.
4. The imitator differs from those allied to it by phylogeny.
5. The imitation is only superficial, effecting only external visible characters.

Causes of mimicry

According to Weismann, natural selection is the main factor in the production of mimicry. To produce perfect mimicry, sharp sudden mutation and its preservation by natural selection together with persistence of the original form from which it originated, side by side with it, till the original disappeared has to be assumed.

According to recent views, the mimicry is caused due to the action of genes. Fisher suggested that disadvantageous genes have a tendency to become recessive while advantageous genes become dominant. Some think that mimicry arises as a result of a single gene mutations. The pattern thus evolved is then perfected by the action of modifying genes and natural selection.

QUESTIONS AND ANSWERS
COLOURATION AND MIMICRY

Q.1. What is mimicry?

Ans. Mimicry is a special form of adaptive colouration in animals serving as protective mechanism to ensure better survival of the species. The term mimicry signifies the resemblances which organism bear to other organisms or to inanimate objects in form, colour attitude and action.

Q.2. Distinguish between Batesian mimicry and Mullerian mimicry.

Ans. Two types of mimicry are recognized. In the first type the model is protected from predators by an unpleasant taste or odour or by the possession of stings or irritating hairs, while the mimic is not so protected but at the same time escapes from its predators by its accurate and deceivingly detailed resemblance to the model. This is called Batesian mimicry.

A second type of mimicry namely Mullerian mimicry was described by Fritz Muller after a detailed study of the mimetic species of butterflies found in South America. Mullerian mimicry involves a number of different species uniform in appearance and unpalatable. In Mullerian several abundant and well protected species combine together to have some warning colours. Education of predators to avoid the warningly coloured models is facilitated when a number of unrelated species resemble each other and all have protective adaptations. The yellow and the black bands exhibited by unrelated species of wasp is an example of Mullerian mimicry.

Q.3. Distinguish between protective mimicry and warning mimicry.

Ans. In protective mimicry the animal mimics an object as to protect itself from the enemy. The caterpillar of the Geometrid moth, and the stick insect appear like twigs or sticks of plants, the leaf insects by the green colouration and pattern of wings, appear like the leaves of plants, and the kallima butterfly resembles the dried leaves. These are examples of protective mimicry.

Warning mimicry includes all those cases of protective mimicry in which the non-poisonous and harmless organisms and the palatable forms resemble and advertise to be non-palatable. Some species of butterflies are palatable and these resemble those species of butterflies which are unpalatable and so these are avoided by birds.

Q.4. The sea dragon Phyllopteryx is very similar to sea weeds in appearance. What is the advantage in possessing that shape ?

Ans. The sea dragon Phyllopteryx resembles like fronds of sea weed due to the presence of cutaneous outgrowths over the body and showing concealing mimicry and thus protect themselves from their enemies.

Q.5. In some animals the colouration of the body enhances their chance of survival. Justify the statement by giving suitable examples.

Ans. Some animals change their colour to match the background and enhances their chances of survival.

Example – (i) A white crab Cryptolithodes mimics a white quartz pebble of the beach in having smooth rounded form and texture and white colour. So, it is difficult to recognize it. (ii) The pupae of the Swallow tail butterfly, look green when attached to plant stems and grey when attached to the tree trunk or stones.

Q.6. Give two differences of cryptic and warning colouration.

Ans. *Cryptic :* (1) Cryptic colouration makes animals blend with the environment in which they live and thereby helps them to escape from being detected by enemies, or to lie in wait for their preys.

(2) Cryptic colouration misdirected the predators and protect them from their enemies. The crabs living among the sea weeds clothe themselves with pieces of weed and thus escape from being discovered.

Warning: (1) Warning colouration is characterised by conspicuous colours or markings that give notice to would be enemies. The poisonous and unpalatable animals in general possess conspicuous colours such as red, yellow, etc.

(2) It is used for their defence because its mimic is able to delude and frighten the enemy. Warning colouration sometimes carries with it the assumption of an attitude which heightens the effect and may be designed to strike terror to the enemies.

BIOLOGICAL CHEMISTRY

Q.1. What is intermediary metabolism ?

Ans. The chemical reaction in a cell that transforms food into simple molecules required for the structure and growth of the cell is termed intermediary metabolism.

Q.2. What is oxidative phosphorylation ?

Ans. It is the process by which ATP is formed by the use of the energy liberated during the electron transport system.

Q.3. What is glycogenolysis ? Describe its pathway in liver.

Ans. When the level of blood sugar (glucose) is lowered, glycogen from the body is converted into glucose inside the liver. This process is called glycogenolysis.

The breakdown of glycogen in muscle and liver is initiated by the enzyme phosphorylase. Cyclic AMP stimulates the activity of the phosphorylase. The debranching enzyme amylo 1, 6 glucosidase causes the hydrolytic splitting of 1, 6 linkage and the combined action of these enzymes converts glycogen to glucose 1-phosphate. The action of phosphoglucomutase is reversible and glucose -6-phosphate is formed from glucose -1-phosphate. A specific enzyme glucose -6-phosphatase exists in liver and kidney. This enzyme removes phosphate glucose -6-phosphate and free glucose to diffuse from cell into blood. To activate cyclic AMP in liver and muscle, hormone glucagon and epinephrine are required.

Q.4. Where does the glycogen occur in significant amount in the body ? In which group of carbohydrate is it included ? Write any two properties of glycogen.

Ans. Glycogen is tored in significant amount in the lever. It is included in polysaccharide.

Properties: (i) Glycogen is a non reducing sugar with iodine it gives red colour. (ii) It is precipitated from aqueous solutions by addition of ethyl alcohol and is fairly suitable to hot alkali.

Q.5. How does a conjugated protein differ from a simple protein? Give two examples of each of scleroprotein and chromoprotein.

Ans. Conjugated proteins are those in which the protein molecule is united with a type of molecule other than a protein. The chemical group thus united is called a "prosthetic group". Simple proteins are those proteins which on hydrolysis yield only amino acids or their derivatives.

Scleroprotein, example : Keratin, Collagen

Chromoprotein, example : Haemoglobin, Haemocyanin, Cytochrome.

Q.6. Describe briefly fibrous proteins and globular proteins.

Ans. Fibrous proteins are insoluble in water, dilute acids, alkalies, dilute salt solution and organic solvents. Globular proteins are soluble in one or more solvents.

Q.7. Distinguish between endoenzymes and exoenzymes.

Ans. Endoenzymes are those which act only within the cells. They are metabolic enzymes. Example, Cytochrome oxidase. Living cells liberate certain enzymes and they catalyze vital reaction in the cell's environment. These enzymes are known as exoenzymes. Example, Amylase, Lipase, Proteases, etc. (Digestive enzymes).

Q.8. What type of reaction is catalyzed by isomerases ?

Ans. Isomerases catalyze the inter conversion of a compound to one of its isomeres. For example, in the anaerobic breakdown of carbohydrate to lactic acid, trios phosphate isomerase converts 3-phosphoglyceraldehyde to dehydroyacetone phosphate.

Q.9. Write the properties of enzymes.

Ans. The enzymes are colloidal in nature. The enzymes promote chemical reactions. The activity of the enzymes is increased when the temperature is raised as in any chemical reaction. There are certain enzymes which continue to act on the substrate even at high temperature. The activity of certain enzymes can be greatly increased by the presence of certain simple substances in small quantities such as calcium and magnesium ions. The gastric glands secrete inactive pepsinogen and this is converted into active pepsin after the addition of an acid. The pancreas secretes an inactive zymogen namely trypsinogen which is converted into active trypsin by the action of enterokinase present in the intestinal juice. Reversability of actions is seen in certain enzymes. They are of great help in metabolism. For instance, in the liver the glucose is converted into glycogen by glycogenase. This happens when there is an excess of glucose in the blood stream. When there is a deficiency of glucose in the blood, the same enzyme is capable of reconverting the insoluble glycogen into soluble glucose which then enters the general blood stream.

Enzymatic activity is greatly influenced by acidity or alkalinity. Enzymatic activity takes place satisfactorily only at a particular optimum pH that is, hydrogen-ion concentration. For example, the gastric enzyme called pepsin reacts only in an acidic medium while an intestinal enzyme called trypsin can act only in an alkaline medium (pH about 8.2). The same enzyme acting on different substrates may require different optimum pH. All the digestive enzymes are hydrolases that is, they catalyse hydrolytic processes.

Q.10. Classify the enzymes according to their reaction specificity.

Ans. (1) Transferases, (2) Oxidoreductases, (3) Lyases, (4) Hydrolases, (5) Isomerases (Mutases), (6) Ligases (Synthetases).

Q.11. What is gastric juice ? Name important gastric juice composition for protein digestion.

Ans. Gastric juice is the fluid secreted by gastric glands or the cells present in the stomach namely, parietal cells, mucus cells and chief cells. Pepsin and rennin are the gastric juice composition for protein digestion.

Q.12. What will happen to the food if the stomach of a person does not secrete any gastric juice ?

Ans. If the stomach of a person does not secrete any gastric juice, digestion of food is not possible.

Q.13. Describe briefly how the lipids are absorbed in the intestine.

Ans. As a result of digestion, lipids (fats) are hydrolysed to form fatty acids and glycerol. The fatty acids and glycerol are absorbed by the lacteal vessels present in the intestinal villi. From the lacteals they find their way into the lymph vessels and hence to the thoracic duct, ultimately reaching the blood stream. Frazer (1940) stated that fats could be absorbed only in the form of finely emulsified fat droplets. According to the Solution theories, fats are said to be absorbed in the form of soaps. The unbroken fats, long chain fatty acids and glycerides are absorbed through the crypts between the microvilli of the intestinal absorptive cells.

Q.14. Name the different carbohydrate digesting enzymes and glands found in the digestive system of mammals.

Ans.

Name of the digestive enzyme	Glands
1. Salivary amylase	Salivary gland
2. Pancreatic amylase	Pancreas
3. Intestinal amylase	Intestine
4. a-glucoside	Intestine
5. a-galactosidase	Intestine
6. Invertase	Intestine

Q.15. If there is no secretion of bile in the digestive system, what will happen to the process of digestion ? Write three points.

Ans. If there is no secretion of bile in the digestive system, the following points may occur.

1. The creation of alkaline medium in the intestine may be disturbed.
2. Dissolving of fatty acids may not take place.
3. Emulsification of fats will not take place.

Q.16. Do you find any analogue in pepsin and trypsin ? Pepsin is active of pH_2, while trypsin at pH_8. Why is it so ?

Ans. No. Pepsin is active in acid medium in the stomach whereas trypsin can act only in alkaline medium in the intestine.

Q.17. Name the three pairs of salivary glands in Man.

Ans. 1. Parotid glands, lying just in front of the ears.

2. Submaxillary glands, located beneath the angles of the lower jaw.

3. Sublingual glands, lying beneath the tongue.

Q.18. State the functions of hydrochloric acid in the process of digestion of food in mammals.

Ans. 1. The living material is dissolved between the cells by the hydrochloric acid so as to make them readily available for the action of the enzyme.

2. It provides a good medium in which the enzymes of gastric juice can carry out their work quickly.

3. The bacteria which have been taken in along with food are destroyed by the hydrochloric acid.

Q.19. What is digestion ? Write the process of chemical digestion of carbohydrates in mammals. What happens to carbohydrate reaching the liver ?

Ans. Digestion is characteristic of animals where most of the food consists of complex organic substances which are chemically inert and often insoluble. These food substances cannot be directly used for the metabolism of the body, and must be broken down first into soluble and diffusible substances before they can be absorbed by the cells. Such a process is called digestion. Digestion involves mechanical factors such as mastication and deglutition.

Carbohydrates are hydrolysed into their respective monosaccharides step by step by the carbohydrases. The following varieties of enzymes are involved in the digestion of carbohydrates : ptyalin, amylase, glucogenase, sucrase, lactase, maltase, cellulose, etc. Starch digestion is effected by the following enzymes : ptyalin, amylase, maltase, sucrase, and lactase. The chief monosaccharides found in common food stuffs are glucose, fructose and galactose. These require no digestion and hence absorbed as such. There are three common disaccharides which require digestion namely, maltose, lactose and sucrose. Digestion of these three takes place in the small intestine since the intestinal juice contains maltase, lactase and sucrase or invertase respectively. Uncooked starch is indigestible while cooked starch breaks up into natural grains rendering digestion easy. Salivary amylase from saliva and pancreatic amylase from pancreatic juice are concerned with starch digestion. As a result of the action of these amylases starch is converted into maltose. The maltose is later acted upon by the intestinal maltase yielding glucose, the end product of carbohydrate digestion which along with other monosaccharides is absorbed from the small intestine.

Q.20. Explain how proteins are digested in the different regions of the alimentary canal of a mammal.

Ans. Enzymes that act on proteins are known as proteolytic enzymes or proteases. During digestion the proteins are broken down to their component amino-acids step by step by the action of different proteolytic enzymes. Protein digestion is essentially a series of hydrolyses of peptide linkages. Bergman and Bledwin divided the proteases into two groups : Endopeptidases and Exopeptidases. Endopeptidases attack the central peptide bond and are also capable of acting on simple proteins namely peptones, for example, pepsin, trypsin, cathepsin, erepsin and chymotrypsin. Exopeptidases attack the terminal peptide links and act largely on the products of proteinase action particularly polypeptides. The exopeptidases are divided into three types : Carboxypeptidases, Aminopeptidases and Dipeptidases. Carboxypeptidases are secreted in the pancreatic juice. Aminopeptidases and Dipeptidases are present in the intestinal juice. Carboxypeptidases and Aminopeptidases act on polypeptides converting them into dipeptides and amino-acids. Dipeptidases act on dipeptides converting them into amino-acids. Renin is an enzyme which acts on milk proteins namely cascinogen and convert them into casein.

The proteins are first broken down into simpler substances by the proteinases and the final stroke of peptide digestion is effected by peptidases. Pepsin acts strongly only in an acid medium. It is secreted by the gastric glands in an inactive form called pepsinogen which is activated by the hydrochloric acid present in the stomach. By the action of pepsin proteins are converted into proteoses or peptones. Trypsin acts in an alkaline medium. It is secreted by the pancreas in the form of trypsinogen. By the action of trypsin peptones are converted into polypeptides. Erepsin is a powerful proteolytic enzyme which converts polypeptides into amino-acids which are the end products of protein digestion. Erepsin is secreted by the intestinal glands. Chymotrypsin is also a pancreatic enzyme. It acts on the alkaline medium and has a strong milk clotting action. Cathepsin acts in a neutral or in a slightly acidic medium. It is activated by reducing agents cysteine and glutathione. It is found in mammalian liver and spleen.

ADAPTATION

Q.1. What do you mean by adaptation ? Explain briefly the adaptation shown by the animals in desert environment.

Ans. Adaptation to a desert life is otherwise known as desert adaptation. Desert is a level sketch of drifting sand where scarcity of water is extreme, characterised by rainless or nearly rainless climate. The struggle for existence is exceedingly severe there and three primary needs of organisms stand out in prominence, viz., food, safety and reproduction. Indeed moisture getting, moisture conservation and defense against physical and biotic environment are of prime importance in adaptation of animals in the desert.

The desert contains poisonous spiders, lizards and venomous snakes. The Ostrich is the outstanding desert bird, and the gazelle the wild ass and the camel are great desert travellers. The desert lizard (*Moloch horridus*) carries spines over its body, and the spinescence and hard body surface prevent evaporation of water from the body. The desert prevent evaporation of water from the body. The desert lizard sips the dews that fall at night and that is the only drink they can have. Water storage in animals is also exhibited by camels. These animals have developed water cells in the wall of their rumen (1st division of the stomach). When the animal drinks, the water not only reaches its stomach where it is absorbed and utilized but the water is also stored in these cells and later doled out by the relaxation of the sphincter muscles at the time of need. Hence the camel can travel from oasis to oasis for even 5-6 days without water but in such cases the animal needs rest.

Animals conserve water by being non-perspiring because the physiological value of perspiration (excretion and heat regulation) are offset by the ill effects of the loss of the precious moisture. Practically non-perspiring mammals are a response to arid adaptation.

Defence : I Against nature, II Against other animals.

I. Against nature

(a) Extremes of temperature : The temperature in desert in day time is very high, on the other hand, during night it is very low, cold and chilly. Desert animals protect themselves from the extremes of temperature either by finding a great rock or they must burrow to escape the extremes of temperature.

(b) Against ubiquitous sand : Sand assails the three important organs of animals economy viz., eyes, nostrils, and ears. Eyes are protected by overhanging head shields, as in Typhlops. The margin of the lid is broadened into plates which are furnished with Scales as in Agama, Phrynocephalus (lizard). In Teratoscincus, the upper lid is enlarged. In Mabuia the lower lid is enlarged, with a transparent window in it, so that the eye can be closed without impeding sight. As an adaptation to desert condition, the camel has also large eyes which are guarded by long, abundant eyelashes. This is a response to the reflected heat of the blistering sand and rocks.

(c) Nostrils in digging animals are held upwards. In most snakes they are protected by complicated valves or reduced to pin holes. In camels the nostrils are capable of being closed. In Saiga antelope of Australia, the animal has a much peculiarly inflated nose.

(d) The ear openings may be protected by scales. They may be small or totally absent as in lizard. In camels ears are protected by hairs.

II. Against other animals

Colouration of the body is the most conspicuous of the adaptations to desert life. Colouration furnishes protection against other animals. Desert creatures are generally sympathetically tinted – grey, brown or red, harmonizing with rocky or sandy desert or may show double colour adaptation to suit the local conditions, for example, Gazelle found in sand is whitish ; or those found near volcanic beds are dark grey. The desert lizard (*Molch horridus*) carries spines over its body, and the spinescence and the hard body surface prevent evaporation of water from the body.

All the desert reptiles are poisonous, rattle snakes heading the iist. The scorpion and the many legged centipede are also poisonous.

Speed is necessary to an extreme degree for the preservation of life in the desert, for the animal has to travel far and wide for food getting, to pursue or to evade the pursuit as the case may be. Many of the lizards are so swift that the eye loses sight of them as they dart from rock to rock. Speed is a characteristic of the dwellers of the desert. This speed shows itself in the slender form, long limbs, and often in the sand-adapted feet of the desert way farer. Those of the camel, with the broad, yielding pad and secondary retrogression from unguligrade to digitigrade, are splendidly fitted to the yielding sands.

Senses of hearing, sight and smell are highly developed in desert animals. In them, intelligence increases in relation to the developed hard conditions of life.

Q.2. Define adaptive radiation.

Ans. Creatures of same or closely related stock are often found to go several ways in search of food and safety giving rise to varied adaptations reaching the several extremes of evolutionary lines. This idea of segregation from the normal stem form was recognized by Lamarck as "embranchement", Darwing called it "divergence", whereas finally Osborn stated it in the form of a Law, which he called "Adaptive radiation".

Q.3. In what way is convergent adaptation different from divergent one.

Ans. In some diverse forms similar adaptations occur concerned with locomotion, food getting and offence and defence. Such adaptations are referred to as convergent adaptation. If animals of different groups come to share a common habitat, they give rise to adaptive convergence. In divergent adaptation, same or closely related genera become adapted to different kinds of environment reaching the several extremes of evolutionary lines.

Q.4. Distinguish in one point between habitat and adaptation.

Ans. Habitat is a place of an organism where it lived, on the other hand adaptation is the fitness of an organism to its environment.

Q.5. Distinguish between aestivation and hibernation.

Ans. Aestivation is period of suspended activity (on the part of many tropical animals) or dormancy during summer to avoid the scorching heat of the sun. Aestivation is noticed in the snail (Ariophanta), lady bird beetles, lung fishes, etc. Hibernation is a sleeplike, inactive, torpid condition, marked by a lowering of metabolism and body temperature, found in certain animals during winter. Among mammals hibernation is met with among insectivores, bats and rodents.

Q. 6. Define cursorial adaptation.

Ans. The adaptation undergone by animals for rapid progression on land is known as cursorial adaptation.

Q.7. What is pelagic adaptation?

Ans. Adaptation undergone by the organisms of the plankton and necton which inhabit the open water of a sea or lake is called pelagic adaptation. A common feature of all the pelagic forms is their ability to maintain themselves in the open waters without sinking to the bottom.

Q.8. What is pelagic fauna?

Ans. The animals of pelagic region are called pelagic fauna.

Q.9. Define cave adaptation. Explain cave adaptation in animals by giving examples.

Ans. Morphological adaptations undergone by the permanent cave dwellers to suit the cave environment is known as cave adaptation.

Cave animals are either colourless or pale white in colour. This is due to the absence of light. For example, *Dina absoloni* (leech) , many crustaceans, cave snails, Amblyopsis (fish). If coloured, they are generally paler than the epigean relatives. The cave arthropods are characterised by weak exoskeleton. Among the fishes and collembola, the scales are lost altogether. The skin of the cave insects is much thinner than their corresponding surface dwellers. The loss of visual organs due to the absence of light is a wide spread feature seen in cave animals. Eyes undergo varying degrees of degeneration and are completely absent in the fresh water cave fishes. The absence of eyes is an instance of convergent regression.

Consequent to the loss of visual organs, the sense organs are well developed. Cave insects, myriapods and arachnids are characterised by the presence of long legs and antennae often provided with tactile hairs. Chaemoreceptors are well developed in cave animals.

In cave urodela, retrogression of endocrine system is noticed. The thyroid gland of proteus is said to produce a hormone to which the tissues are quite unresponsive. Since the cave animals are shielded from the rigors of the struggle for existence it has become the refuge of many relics. The snails of the genus Lartetia, Bathynella (a primitive Crustacean), proteus (Salamander), Troglochaetus (annelid) are the notable relics.

Remarkable neotenic animals found in the caves are the Urodel Proteus and the Polychaet. Life in cave is an antithesis of the feverish activity of the surface dwellers.

****

INDEX